Sun at Midnight

The serpent painted on a wall in the Goetheanum.

I approached the very gates of death
and set one foot on Proserpine's threshold,
yet was permitted to return,
rapt through all the elements.
At midnight I saw the sun shining as if it were noon;
I entered the presence of the gods of the under-world and the
gods of the upper-world,
stood near and worshipped them.

— Lucius Apuleius, *The Transformations of Lucius*[1]

1. Lucius Apuleius, *The Golden Ass,* tr. Robert Graves (London, Penguin, 1950), p. 241.

Sun at Midnight

The Rudolf Steiner Movement and Gnosis in the West

Geoffrey Ahern

ⓒ

James Clarke & Co

James Clarke & Co
P.O. Box 60
Cambridge
CB1 2NT
United Kingdom

www.jamesclarke.co.uk
publishing@jamesclarke.co.uk

ISBN: 978 0 227 17293 3

British Library Cataloguing in Publication Data
A record is available from the British Library

First Published, 1984
Revised and expanded edition, 2009

Contents

Foreword   9
Prologue   .   11

Part One: The Development of the Rudolf Steiner Movement

1. 'Must I Remain Silent?' A Life of Rudolf Steiner   16
   The first seven years (1861-1868)
   Seven to fourteen (1868-1875)
   Fourteen to twenty-one (1875-1882)
   Twenty-one to twenty-eight (1882-1889)
   Twenty-eight to thirty-five (1889-1896)
   Thirty-five to forty-two (1896-1903)
   The Anthroposophical Years (c. 1903-30 March 1925)

2. The Establishment of the Movement   41
   The phase of charismatic leadership
   The phase of schisms
   Establishment

3. How the Movement is Organised   60
   The School of Spiritual Science
   The National Anthroposophical Societies
   The Camphill communities
   The Christian Community
   The two Goetheanums

Part Two: Thought and Deed
in Anthroposophy

4. Meditations and Applications   86
The path of knowledge
Sciences
Arts and Education
The Threefold Commonwealth

5. Man Today, Karma and the Macrocosm   105
The nature of man today
Karma and repeated earth lives
The macrocosm
Language

6. The Evolution of the Macrocosm   122
Being
Saturn
Sun
Moon
Earth
Jupiter
Venus
Vulcan

Part Three: Gnosis in the West
or the Western 'Esoteric Tradition'

7. From Gnosticism to Rosicrucianism   141
Gnosticism
Hermeticism, Kabbalism, Alchemy and Rosicrucianism

8. Modernity and Gnosis   161
Gnosis containing modernity
Modernity containing gnosis
The influence of the East

Part Four: Different Perspectives

9. Interpretive Visions   182
     The gnostic reduction of the social to spirit
     Reduction of spirit to society in the social sciences
     Social evolutionism
     The spiritual, changes in collective consciousness
          and Western gnosticism

10. Western Orthodoxy, Mysticism and Gnosis   198
     Gnosticism, Catholic orthodoxy and Neoplatonism
     The Renaissance and Reformation
     Modernity, Gnosticism and Mysticism

Appendix: Some Ways In   214
     Eighteen convergencies towards Anthroposophy
     How did people become Anthroposophists?

Notes   224
Tables   242
Bibliography   247
Index   262

For Ivon

Foreword

This second edition has been extensively rewritten and updated. The world of 'Anthroposophy' – as the Rudolf Steiner movement is called – has moved on since the first edition in 1984.

My aim for this second edition has been to notice the major developments in Anthroposophy in the past two decades without altering the purpose of the original book. It was, and is, intended to describe the thought world of Anthroposophy and its social practices, and to relate these to their historical and contemporary contexts, especially gnosis in the West or, as it has been called more recently, 'the Western esoteric tradition'. In order to signpost the significance of the rich and fascinating historical heritage, the book has been re-titled for the second edition to emphasise gnosis. The first edition was called *Sun at Midnight: The Rudolf Steiner Movement and the Western Esoteric Tradition'*. 'Sun at Midnight' is inspired by Lucius Apuleius' description of his transformation experience in the mysteries: he describes (see the epigraph to this book) how at midnight he saw the sun shining as if it were noon.

I first encountered Anthroposophy through looking for an unresearched topic in spiritual religion for a PhD. From the hindsight made possible by twenty further years, my application then of the unrelenting perspectives of the sociology of religion and knowledge seems to have had something of a defensive quality about it. I was not convinced by Anthroposophy then, and I have not been since. Yet on revisiting the subject recently for this second edition I have, among other reactions, found much in it to admire. My (impossible) intention has been neither to collude nor unfairly to accuse where there is controversy, for example, over the state funding of Anthroposophical (or 'Waldorf') education. I am acutely aware that there is an inevitable trade-off between bringing in external perspectives credibly, and unwittingly misrepresenting the subject through the lack of an insider's total immersion. What follows is an external interpretation of a cosmology and way of life or, as it is sometimes called, a construct of the second degree. I am not aware of any other comprehensive account of Anthroposophy by an outsider aiming to look empathetically in.

There have been changes in the order of the first six chapters. A major alteration has been to reposition the account of how eighteen Anthroposophists found Anthroposophy. In the first edition this was chapter one, but it is included here as an appendix. The information now belongs to the past and in any event was not from a representative sample, so I have decided it should no longer be introductory. However, I include it, with a much-needed edit, because I believe it contains valuable information.

Many Anthroposophists have helped me in both editions. I am very appreciative of their spirit in doing so, the spirit that holds that inquiry about truth matters. Because I have promised anonymity – they have usually sought it – I am not in a position to identify them. Thus I am not able to thank by name most of the major contributors.

The doctoral research which, years ago, preceded this book benefited considerably from the advice of David Martin, to whom I owe much. I am also grateful for the support of the late Bryan Wilson. The research was funded by the SSRC as it was then called, now the ESRC (Economic and Social Research Council). Non-Anthroposophists who helped the first edition in different ways included Eileen Barker, Rita Bultemann, John Costello, David Docherty, David Levy, Gillian Mullins, Desa Ozim, Fiona Rowell, Nick Rowell, Andrew Skarbek, Edna Swayne, Adam Warcup and John Woodcock. There have been many non-Anthroposophical influencers since, far too many to single out.

This second edition would never have been produced were it not for a non-Anthroposophical backer, who suggested it out of the blue, invested in it financially, and thereupon was generous with time and energy. Again, by his own request I am not in a position to name him. The wisdom of my wife, the artist Ivon Oates, has both sustained and challenged me throughout. I owe much to Rondel Linder for her very thorough and unstinting work preparing the second edition. Adrian Brink and Ian Bignall of Lutterworth Press have given the book careful and expert attention, and I am grateful for this. Of course, what follows here is my responsibility.

Geoffrey Ahern

Prologue

Kathleen had questioned me closely, asking what I would like to do if life became calmer and more settled. I answered her that I would probably spend a month at Dornach, near Basel, at the Swiss Steiner Centre, the Goetheanum.[1]

– Saul Bellow, *Humboldt's Gift*

The spirit of the movement founded by the 'spiritual scientist' Rudolf Steiner is a modern expression of the so-called Western 'esoteric tradition' (sometimes the word 'occultism' is also used). This – in a broad sense – neo-gnosticism is a hidden thread within some of the most archetypal works of Shakespeare, Goethe and W.B. Yeats. It has profoundly influenced German and English-speaking imaginations, and also it seems to have been part of the matrix from which modern science emerged.

Relating Western gnosticism to the development of world religions, secularity and modernity is the concern of the last of the four parts of this book. The penultimate part is a brief outline of major historical and metaphysical features of the neo-gnostic or 'esoteric' tradition as it has been reconstituted in the West.

The first two parts attempt to portray what is almost certainly the most differentiated contemporary instance of Western neo-gnosticism, the Rudolf Steiner movement or, as it is known, 'Anthroposophy'. Any account of this is inevitably subjective and impressionistic. This book approaches the subject from an outside and also an English-speaking perspective. The topic is introduced in part one through the extraordinary life of Rudolf Steiner (1861-1925), the history of the movement from its origins in Germany through Nazi times and beyond, and a description of its organisation, membership and belonging in the internet age. Part two summarises the movement's spiritual 'science', including the many practical outlets, and its anthropology and cosmology. Then, in the further two parts of the book, the relationships between gnosticism and Anthroposophy are examined and placed in their Western cultural context past and present.

The Goetheanum, the centre of this modern mystery movement, is only a few kilometres outside Basle. Designed by Rudolf Steiner, it appears to many like a rock that is living inside. On approaching the huge concrete structure, facets, curves and angles emerge which not only convey a German organic feel but infuse extra dimensions into it. Surrounding buildings and houses are similar or have similar features. The Goetheanum and its complex are on an escarpment backed by a hill, a strangely transmuted contrast to the mundane Swiss suburbia nearby.

The reality within this sacred space is very different from the 'normality' outside. Large doors with bronze handles lead into long, hushed galleries. When I was there, plants – roots as well as tops – were exhibited on many of the walls. The atmosphere within is of German-speaking spirituality. The construction is named after the many-sided genius Goethe; indeed it is said to be the only place in the world where *Faust Part Two* is regularly enacted. It is the physical centre for the members of the movement, whose direct subscription has grown very considerably, to around 50,000. Far more people still are affected by the movement's activities. These days members are located all over the globe.

Visitors cross the huge concourses within to meditate on a large carving of three sinewy, striving forms, two 'opponents' without whom we cannot grow and 'the representative of humanity', who has the upper hand. One opponent, Lucifer, represents passion and fantasy (contrasted with imaginative truth); the other, given the Zoroastrian name of Ahriman, is perceived as a grimmer reality still, the force of hardening, especially when it takes the form of dried-up intellectualism. The sculpture, partly chiselled by Steiner himself, expresses the need to hold a balance between the two extremes. Allowing them to reveal their inadequacy is redemptive. An analogy is made Anthroposophically to the second part of *Faust*. Mephistopheles here is seen as consciously trying to upset evolution and as thereby serving it. From a non-Anthroposophical position there seems to be an implicit dualism between Ahriman's hardening and the spiritual position of the representative of humanity. Anthroposophists, however, state there is no dualism in their position against hardening because matter has a role in evolution, and because materialism properly seen is a spiritual reality.

Through improving their karmas in spiritual struggle, those committed believe they will be in a purer inner state when, as they suppose, they are reborn. Within the broader structure of the Anthroposophical Society, its School of Spiritual Science has the mission of developing the inner core. Members are immersed in the meaning of Steiner's complex revelation, given in the first two decades of the twentieth century. It tells of the origins of the cosmos, its future respiritualization and man's identity with it. He called this 'Anthroposophy'* or 'awareness of one's humanity'. Thus those committed to this vision of life are known as 'Anthroposophists'.

Outsiders who visit the Goetheanum may well be impressed by the strange environment. Approaching Anthroposophy from 'normality' as the result of a chance contact, nothing at first made sense to me. I was never converted[2] while carrying out my research. Had this been otherwise, the chance contact would have come to be my 'karma' and meanings which are Anthroposophical would have become the meanings of all life everywhere. Many outsiders, confronted with radically different thought systems, will reinforce their own 'normality' through outright rejection. A more interesting possibility is to explore in order to gain some kind of understanding.

On one of the pink walls there has been painted a light blue, almost turquoise, serpent, about three feet in diameter, which coils round in a complete circle, so that the thin tail-end is inside, but not touched by, the mouth. A formidable eye looks out from the head. This 'seal'– see the frontispiece of this book – can be taken as a 'cosmic script, expressing the task of man's repeated lives on earth: that the I recognises itself'.[3] The head and eye represent consciousness and awareness. In being turned back around the tail they signify transcendence through knowledge of one's spiritual origins. The distinctiveness of the Anthroposophical serpent, compared with serpents in other spiritual interpretations,[4] gives clues about the distinctiveness of Anthroposophy: the serpents' details – head, eye, teeth or gums, whether the tail is within or across the mouth, or touching or not – all differ. The watchful head surrounding and

* *Anthropos* (man) and *sophia* (wisdom) are essential elements of Syrian-Egyptian gnosis (see chapter 7). The terms were synthesized by Thomas Vaughan in his *Anthroposophia Theomagica (1650)*. The Swiss Ignaz Troxler (1780-1866), a disciple of Schelling, propounded an anthropology he called anthroposophy which had many resemblances to Steiner's Anthroposophy (see H. Ellenberger, *The Discovery of the Unconscious*, US, Basic Books, 1970, pp. 206-07). Steiner stated he derived the name from a work by Robert Zimmerman, who was Professor of Philosophy at the University of Vienna; he attended lectures by Zimmerman while a student at Vienna's Technical University. (Paul Allen, ed., *Rudolf Steiner. An Autobiography* (New York, Rudolf Steiner Publications, 1977), Note 361-A, p. 491.)

almost fused with the tail depicts in Anthroposophy the destiny of the conscious mind, which is to transcend self-centred individualism and materialism. Meanwhile the hardness of matter will transmute into the spiritual essences which are its rightful nature.

What does all this 'Anthroposophy' mean? Our story begins with the life and times of Rudolf Steiner.

Part One

The Development of the
Rudolf Steiner Movement

1. 'Must I Remain Silent?'
A Life of Rudolf Steiner

'I'm going South to-night to the magicians.'
'You had much better not, Rudolf', said someone. 'A few quiet
hours in Puritania with me would be better for you – much
better.'
– C.S. Lewis, The Pilgrim's Regress
('Rudolf Steiner' and 'Immanuel Kant')[1]

Rudolf Steiner's *Autobiography*[2] has been given only one heading, a cry from his heart: 'Must I remain silent?' From about the age of forty this Austrian, a trained scientist from peasant-turned-proletarian origins, began to reveal his spiritual vision to occult circles in Berlin. He was far from silent in the last part of his life, the first quarter of this century. He became a charismatic leader, casting a spell on many. His deep eyes were impressively large in a thin, sensitive face which became increasingly lined. He had a full head of dark hair and often dressed in an unusual way: frequently he would don a fully flowing cravat. Physically short, a primal power seemed to many to well up from within him. As a result, cultivated speakers of *Hochdeutsch* were not put off by his outlandish German, the dialect of eastern lower Austria. What had this man to be silent about?

He was convinced that he was directly in touch with the 'spirit-world'. This struck him as immediate reality. The sense realities that make up everyday life for most tended to pass him by. However, he did not undergo a dramatic, God-given revelation. He was a highly gifted intuitive, a riddle whose feet were on ground of his own. Steiner attempted to find certainty through a lifelong inner development of wrestling with philosophical and spiritual problems. This development is a model for Anthroposophists today and so is a vital part of their identity. It is also essential background to both the history and cosmology of the movement he founded.

Rudolf Steiner's spiritual experience was not one of usual prophecy. The prophet is struck by a terrible and holy ultimate he generally calls 'God'; typically, it appears to come from outside him. This numinous kind of experience, where it becomes the basis of a new religion or sect, is frequently different from a mystical or 'esoteric' outlook. Examples include orthodox Zoroastrianism, Judaism, Christianity, Islam, Sikhism (to a lesser extent), Mormonism and the Unification Church. These tend to have a strong social order and generally do not encourage contemplation; knowledge of God is typically deferred to after death and salvation is closely associated with prescriptive ethics. Though the prophet may come from most social backgrounds, any religion that develops around his experience tends to cater for the needs of the mass of people at a time of deep-seated change. Fundamentalist religion in our 'post-modern' period locates itself through looking back, often to a prophetic founder. Prophets generally challenge the contemporary status quo and in return are persecuted. No wonder many have tried to avoid the call to bear witness.

Thus Zoroaster wrote: 'To what land shall I go to flee, whither to flee? From nobles and my peers they sever me, nor are the people pleased with me, nor the Liar rulers of the land.'[3] The great Hebrew prophets endured tribulation: they emerged preaching from Jahweh cult centres, which were an alternative Jewish establishment to the typical Middle Eastern despotism of kings like Solomon. The historical Jesus suffered a terrible, isolated end. Muhammed, experiencing Allah, was terrified that he was going mad; later, virtually isolated, he was forced to withdraw from his native Mecca to Medina. Guru Nànak (1469-1539) does not seem to have suffered persecution, but his founding message was more synthetic (of Hinduism and Islam) and mystical than prophetic. The institutionalisation of contemporary Sikhism, which resembles prophetic religions, arose out of the trials and tribulations of the Sikhs in the Punjab since the time of Nànak, their first guru. Joseph Smith, who claimed that his *Book of Mormon* was derived from golden plates given to him by an angel, found it necessary to travel away from the 'Gentiles' of the East Coast of America to the wilds of Utah. The fabulously wealthy 'Reverend' Moon protected himself in his Korean stronghold, but the force of his conviction, the result of the energy of the revelation that assailed him, has led to thousands of people giving up conventional identifications.

Had Rudolf Steiner had usual prophetic experience, the cry from his heart would probably have been, 'How can I avoid speaking?' rather than, 'Must I remain silent?' God did not appear to him through a terrible burning bush or its equivalent. Instead it was Steiner who was burning to end the spiritual isolation to which the development of his intuition had led. Contemplatives generally seem to be much less persecuted than prophets. Rather than preach to the masses with a message that confronts the powers that be, and which is radically different itself, they usually have a more conservative appeal, recruiting those of relative education and wealth (however universal the intentions). Contemplatives find an oceanic truth within or through the self, generally in a gradual, tolerant way. They tend to describe the ultimate as ineffable, with a pantheistic feel, rather than define it as a specific creator God who is self-existent.

Steiner's revelation is contemplative, not theistic, using the senses of the words defined above. His essential cosmological idea is that the world hardened from spirit and that its destiny is to become spirit again. As microcosms with free will, human beings are central to the redemption of the cosmos from an over-hardness of matter. The head of the Goetheanum serpent described at the end of the Prologue is identified with original macrocosmic spirit. Anthroposophists strive to leave materialism and egocentric individualism behind and to develop larger spiritual identity instead. The pattern of the serpent can be interpreted as both underlying and existing within the meanings of Anthroposophical social life.

Steiner saw spiritual development as the meaning of the evolution of the world. The condensation of the cosmos into matter has, in the Anthroposophical view, enabled this development of consciousness to begin. But the result is currently some separation between increasingly significant consciousness and the macrocosm. Perhaps this is why the serpent in the Goetheanum has a very large eye and does not touch the tail it encloses in its mouth.

Contemplatives with approaches resembling Steiner's have been well regarded within the general social status quo during their lifetimes. Upanisadic contemplatives, the Hindu élite, have been highly respected in India for their secluded search for *brahman* or the Absolute. The Buddha attracted much goodwill from fellow nobles as well as others. It was the privileged mercantile class that seems to have provided most support for early Buddhism and Jainism, which was founded by Mahāvira who, like the Buddha, was the son of a chief. His asceticism was extreme given that he died through voluntary self-starvation (the rite of *sallekhana*), but he was not persecuted by others. The philosophical idealism of Plato was the thought of a socially well-insulated, authoritarian contemplative who rejected the demotic in his own Athens. Even Kabbalism,

Neoplatonism and Sufism – minority contemplative traditions within the commanding orthodoxies of Judaism, Christianity and Islam – have been precariously tolerated by these prophetic traditions.

Why then did Rudolf Steiner, who wanted to tell of his experience, feel constraints? If contemplatives, unlike the generality of prophets, are often tolerated by most of their contemporaries, why should he have written his heartfelt, 'Must I remain silent?' Part of the reason seems to have been that acclamation by a few people and an absence of active persecution are not the same thing as understanding and acceptance by the educated and cultivated. Steiner's charismatically expressed philosophical and spiritual position was close to, if not over the boundaries of, contemporarily perceived stigma. Were Steiner alive today, more of an immediate bridge of understanding might be found through the contemporary discovery of 'synesthesia', the unusual experiencing of one kind of sense impression alongside another.

Also, Steiner was impelled towards action. He did more than share his intuitions with a trusted few. He inspired, though the educational form of lectures, an active social organism with many applications, and centred this around a sacred building. It is no detraction from his benign achievement to point out that this energy, as with many other leaders, might have been linked to another characteristic which has often carried something of a self-perceived stigma: physical shortness. Indeed, from an Anthroposophical point of view, Steiner would before birth have chosen the most appropriate physical body for his mission.

Steiner was claiming far more than many mystics who attempt to convey or suggest the ineffable through feeling. He believed in carrying clear and defined ideas into the soul. From his intuition he gave answers to just about every question that can be asked. He wrote that this was not a cold process and that he experienced a flood of warmth as a seer. He is considered to be an occultist because he described things that are normally unknowable or hidden, and yet he claimed virtual inerrancy.

The social pressures for silence were also increased because he was alive during the development of our modern era, an age when dismissal or reduction of the spiritual has generally been the dominating moral and intellectual force. This, in an epistemological more than experiential sense, was frequently the attitude of the people he seems to have met most: intellectuals, writers and artists. In a time of philosophical materialism Steiner was not a mere vague mystic, but from a very spiritual point of view rejected Darwinian orthodoxy. He also offended the long inherited tradition of Western culture, given that Christian orthodoxy was based on the suppression of gnosticism and Manicheism. No wonder Steiner had difficulties in finding people who could understand.

Here was a man who earnestly needed to press his perceptions on others. Was he a fraud? The probity of many other occultists such as 'Madame' Blavatsky or Gurdjieff was much doubted by contemporaries. However, there seems to have been no significant suggestion that Steiner was consciously dishonest. Admittedly, his Anthroposophy is structurally similar to Western gnosticism and doctrinally often closely resembles contemporary systems of thought, notably Theosophy; yet Rudolf Steiner stated that everything Anthroposophical derives from his own, original spiritual research. But by itself this does not make his revelation necessarily mistaken, let alone dishonest. Cultural relativism has been a modern pointer to nihilism and seers such as Steiner have fought against it.

The firm sense perception that normally consolidates during childhood and youth only seems to have developed for him when he was thirty-five. As will be seen, this correlates with the Anthroposophically significant age of thirty-five, when the fifth seven-year period of development starts, and also with the cosmological middle period in Anthroposophy when spirit solidifies. His inner world seems to have included spiritual intimations which most people leave behind in childhood or even infancy: as an adult he had direct access to spiritual experience with his scientifically trained and philosophically knowledgeable mind. He would probably have had no difficulty with the present consensus among psychologists that we perceive the world indirectly through physiological mechanisms, so that what we see 'out there' is really a sort of predictive description. Steiner's distinctiveness comes rather in his belief that he had demonstrated the falsity of the assertion that concepts (as contrasted with percepts) are subjective. He held the spiritual activity of thinking to be absolute. He took it as much for reality as naive realists do the sense world. It was thus that he concluded 'spiritual science' was possible.

Steiner would sometimes refer to himself impersonally to emphasize his belief in the objectivity of his spiritual research. He believed that his spiritual path was entirely independent of his emotional life, which he kept private. He did not agree with psychologism, the view that intuitions deriving from introspection are only subjective, consciousness of these being located entirely within the skin and not at all in the world. For him, the spiritual activity of thinking, or living consciously within thoughts, is both within the skin and out in the world. Unlike many modern intellectuals, Steiner did not give out a sense of experiencing himself as essentially set apart from his environment. It was of his cosmic consciousness that he so needed to speak.

His *Autobiography* was written in instalments while he was on his deathbed. Perhaps this is why its initial clarity seems to become more defensive and rambling. Other autobiographical sources date from after the time he broke his silence. Descriptions of his early life by others are rare or unidentified. The sketch here, which very largely focuses on his formative experiences, is necessarily based on his later descriptions of his earlier development. Even taking this scarcity of early information into account, it can be said that the life of this unusual man certainly had a strongly heroic aspect. However, it has tended to be uncritically transformed into legend or myth by adoring followers. His many attractive personal qualities, such as geniality and humour, are often idealized to the point that the Anthroposophical biographies have been hagiographies.[4]

What is *not* stated is highly informative. Steiner scarcely mentions the erotic, nor in a psychological vein does he scrutinise his microcosmic self for the darkness he attributes to his macrocosmic demons, Ahriman and Lucifer. Bringing in issues such as these is not the only way that the interpretation here, which from an Anthroposophical point of view comes from an undeveloped consciousness, differs from hagiography. This book mentions thoughts which insiders have not widely publicised: for example, Rudolf Steiner seems to have believed that he was the reincarnation of Eabani, the consort of the hero of the Assyrio-Egyptians.[5] Also, though Steiner believed in seven-year growth periods[6] in which the individual human being recapitulates the evolution of the macrocosm, this framework does not seem to have been adopted by biographers writing about Steiner's own growth. Anthroposophists do not consider it legitimate to attempt to do so, apparently because he himself did not link his own biographical experience to his revelation.

The eminent psychiatrist Anthony Storr in a work on gurus, *Feet of Clay*, suggested the presence of narcissism in that 'even ostensibly humble gurus like Rudolf Steiner retain grandiose beliefs in their own powers of perception and their own cosmogonies'. He also wrote that Steiner, though neither suffering from paranoid schizophrenia 'nor being psychotic in the sense of being socially disabled' shares 'certain characteristics with patients whom psychiatrists would designate as paranoid'. In the DSMIV 'this diagnosis would now be Delusional Disorder: Grandiose Type'. But otherwise he described

Steiner as a mild, gentle, good, kindly man of high ideals and high intelligence who inspired other people and who certainly did far more good than harm.[7] The modern medical model disqualifies vision which is unevidenced by sense perception, and, as described, qualifies from a sense-based (or positivist) perspective the traditional saying attributed to Jesus: 'by their fruits shall ye know them'. 'Pure' vision, even of a contemplative kind, is perceived by many to be pathological unless and until it becomes culturally controlled and licensed. For those who consider the psychological outlook described above to be reductionism and who yet wish to retain and develop contemporary psychological diagnostics, Steiner might be interpreted as having characteristics in common with a positive form of schizotypal personality.

The First Seven Years (1861-1868)

Rudolf Steiner's *Autobiography* is interesting because his mother is not described, except for a dutiful reference to her loving care for her children. There is not even a passing mention of (for example) her finely drawn features or her oval, sensitive face. Was mother earth lacking from the beginning? Perhaps this had something to do with why, as will be seen, older maternal women were to figure prominently in Steiner's adult life.

There is a sense of dislocation. Like many leaders, his origins were culturally marginal. His translated writings state that his birthplace, Kraljevec, which is now in Croatia and near Hungary, was 'far distant from the corner of the earth to which I rightly belong'.[8] He was surely affected by his feeling that his family should be elsewhere:

> Both my mother and father were true children of the glorious Lower Austrian forest district north of the Danube. . . . My parents loved the memories of their native region. When they spoke about it one felt that although destiny caused them to spend the better part of their lives far from that district, their hearts were still there.

Their roots were in the peasantry. His father (1829-1910) and paternal grandfather had been gamekeepers for a Count von Hoyos-Sprinzenstein. His mother (1834-1918),[9] who came from a family long settled locally in the Horn area, had been a servant in the count's household. The still-feudal count forbade marriage between the pair, whereupon they eloped. Steiner's father was just in his thirties when he suddenly broke out into a newly industrialised world. He was employed for very low pay as a telegraphist, then as a stationmaster, on the new Austrian Southern Railway, the latest technology in the Hapsburg Empire.

Rudolf Steiner was born just after this 'emancipation' from the land. The probable effect on him was considerable. In the deepest sense he identified with the rhythmic nature associated with his peasant forbears; but the railway, telegraph and machines seem to have aroused his talent for science and conceptual thought. This contrast was brought home by his parents' sense of dislocation. The great influence of the early years of life is more widely believed in today than it was when Steiner wrote his *Autobiography*, and as a responsible eldest child, Steiner had an earlier and sole exposure to the stress of their change. His sister Leopoldine and brother Gustav were three and five years younger respectively. During his first three or four years the child Rudolf, for whom contact with the sense world outside was to be so little preferred, moved twice with his parents. They were transferred from Kraljevec to another station for a short while and then yet again were moved to the station at Pottschah, an Austrian village near the Styrian Alps, where they remained for five years. It was on the mountainous, beautiful Semmering line, a contemporary technological marvel; the stationmaster's house, though, was makeshift rather than designed for settled living. It was also cut off from the traditional village community.

Rudolf Steiner was to become convinced that he had chosen his parents and their dislocated situation while he was in the spirit world waiting to be born. His karma, so he came to believe, was to act as a spiritual guide to the modern age, to lead sceptical modern man to a true perception of the spiritual within and beyond him. In thus reflecting, Steiner did not allow space for a psychological interpretation of his youth, but instead interpreted it cosmically, in terms of destiny and reincarnation.

In later life, though he was aware of the early works of Freud and Jung, he never psychologised his sense of cosmic mission. From a general psychodynamic (Freudian and Jungian) perspective he could be interpreted as never having lost his sense of infantile omnipotence, as never having gained a Kleinian depressive position of realistic acceptance. The potential opposition between psychological and spiritual interpretations is manifest. It is, however, the aim here to draw attention to the psychological perspective without thereby being dismissive of the spiritual. Though from a psychological perspective Steiner may have had inner 'splits' partly related to an original feeling of helpless disconnection, his extraordinary spiritual energies were surely also in keeping with his innate temperament. He fought courageously and with humanity for what was most essential to him, the paramountcy of spirit, against the ascendancy of what his near contemporary, the poet Yeats, called 'this filthy modern tide'.

Steiner describes in his Autobiography his much-mentioned, much-loved father, with whom he greatly identified; sympathetically, humorously and with sadness. He felt him to be working out of a sense of duty only, so that life became monotonous, punctuated only by outbursts of temper and essentially absurd political arguments. The railway had contracted him in both senses of the word: it had become a life-denying force. However, it was from this background that his son was to develop a life-affirming spiritual science of the organic. Around him the linearity of the rails and telegraph wires were linked to the cycle of the seasons on the Styrian mountains, such as the Schneeberg, which rose gently out of a green landscape. As a child Steiner accepted technology only so long as it seemed to have that inner reality from which his father had become alienated.[10] In this sense, he as the eldest of the Steiner children was living through and attempting to resolve his father's problem. Thus he was happy with a local mill where he was made welcome, but antagonised by a nearby textile factory, whose manager cast a veil of mystery over what was hidden within its walls. Later, this outlook became philosophical: he was strongly to oppose Kant's assumption that the 'thing-in-itself' cannot be known.

His *Autobiography* is overwhelmingly concerned with the gradual development and deepening of his spiritual life. In his childhood he had an awareness, analogous to the animism of primitive peoples, of 'Beings' within mountains and trees. He felt he lived clairvoyantly with the 'spirits of nature' after an important childhood experience (which he did not date). A relative seemed to enter the waiting-room, saying, 'Try now and in later life to help me as much as you can'.[11] Then he learned that the relation had killed herself at the same time that he had 'seen' her. This, as much else, may or may not have been a screen memory: that is, an apparent memory which was really created by his mind at a later date (in this case, 1913). Revealingly, he also stated that he was silent about what he saw because he feared ridicule from his family. The boy was not in a social reality where he could break through the separation between his inner life and the world (as represented by his family) by talking about his spiritual experiences. A double life was developing. It was only much later that his pent-up spiritual energies burst upon the world.

Seven to Fourteen (1868-1875)

This highly intelligent and perhaps lonely and unhappy boy found a route to development when he discovered the abstract purity of geometry.

> That one can work out forms which are seen purely inwardly, independent of the outer senses, gave me a feeling of deep contentment. I found consolation for the loneliness caused by the many unanswered questions. To be able to grasp something purely spiritual brought me an inner joy. I know that through geometry I first experienced happiness.
>
> In this early relation to geometry I recognize the first beginning of the view of the world and of life that gradually took shape within me. In childhood it lived in me more or less unconsciously; by my twentieth year it had assumed a definite, fully conscious form.[12]

Geometric shapes and forms enabled Rudolf Steiner's extraordinarily gifted spirit to rise above subjectivity. By the time he was a youth he began to identify with literary equivalents of geometry, Lessing, Goethe and Schiller, who were introduced to him by a doctor who frequently travelled on the railway. This may have influenced Steiner's later decision, in early middle age, to leave his native Austria to work in the Goethe Archives at Weimar.

His background had some similarities to being a son of the manse because he was an outsider, yet had contact with all kinds of people. Indeed, it was growing up in such close proximity to the station and its travellers that enabled Steiner to encounter the doctor-passenger who opened his mind to German literature. Perhaps the doctor was even a model for some of Steiner's more unusual characteristics: the doctor once had a railway employee stand on the platform with his tongue out so that he could have a look while travelling past on a non-stop train, and telegraphed a diagnosis from further up the line. Steiner was from the start of his life aware of distant destinations making all types of people converge on the station. At Pottschah, it had even rivalled the church as a centre, as country folk and local worthies such as the school master, the priest, the accountant from the estate, and often the burgomaster came to greet that modern wonder, the steam engine, on the few occasions that it stopped.

The marginal nature of Steiner's younger years was not limited to the distinctiveness of his station homes. He also started living on the edge of one of the bitter nationalist divisions in the disintegrating Austria-

Hungary in which he grew up. When he was seven the family moved to a small village called Neudorfl, just outside Austria, in Hungary, after his father was appointed stationmaster there. This meant that the young Rudolf Steiner, at a time when his social awareness was beginning to form, became highly conscious of the tensions between Austrians and Hungarians. The energetic pro-Magyar patriotism of a local priest was to remain in his mind throughout his life. Steiner was filled with aversion by the flatness of Hungary stretching away to the East, and was sad that his beloved Styrian Alps were now in the distance.

Steiner's *Autobiography* displays a stoical humour (perhaps a psychological defence or denial), and because of this his pain at being rejected by the village children, as when they barred him as a newcomer from a traditional nut collection game, can only be guessed at. Furthermore, the stationmaster's house, his home, was set above the village proper, being separated from it by some land and the local church. Left to his own devices, he had many chats with the adult villagers, whom he describes as basically children themselves. He does not identify friends of his own age until his university years, though he writes that he had many companions at school as an adolescent. His sister and brother, who were probably too young and different to have interested him, are also hardly mentioned. The main stated influences on his childhood and youth were adult and male.

His father, whom he greatly imitated in his early life, was a freethinker. Perhaps this was why the son was little affected by priestly instruction, though he found meaning in Catholic ritual and music. As has not been uncommon in Catholic cultures he was generally unimpressed by the local clergy, especially with a nearby monk who had fathered children.

Schoolmasters were to influence him more and more (later, his spiritual science was to be organised around 'lessons' and 'classes'). Steiner had decided that he wanted to become a teacher himself. Uniquely for his village, at the age of eleven he won a place at the technical *Realschule* in the neighbouring town of Wiener-Neustadt, now an industrial centre. Education was making him a different kind of person from the remainder of his poor, newly proletarian family. It seems even to have cut him off from his intelligent father, who had decided that his son's future lay with the railway. The gap between the village school and the *Realschule* was great, but by the age of fourteen Steiner had striven so much that he was listed as a pupil of excellence.

Fourteen to Twenty-one (1875-1882)

During these years, Steiner later stated, the essential question was 'To what extent is it possible to prove that what is active in human thinking is really spirit?'[13] 'A "subject matter" that remains outside thinking as something one can only "reflect upon" was to me an unbearable idea. I was convinced that the actual *reality of things* must enter into one's thoughts.'[14] Mathematics was a foundation for this.

This questioning was separate from his schoolwork, even though he performed very well and identified with many of the masters. When he was only fifteen, he read Kant surreptitiously in a boring history class whose teacher, nevertheless, awarded him the grade 'excellent'. He also studied the philosopher in the little spare time he had. Steiner commented later that he had not noticed how much their convictions conflicted. From his school he absorbed strict scientific method and a mechanistic model of nature. But this, and even geometrical drawing, about which he was very enthusiastic, seem not to have affected him as much as the education he provided for himself. He was an unusual pupil because of his deep-seated predicament, the division between his paramount intuitive reality and the sense world. With his increasingly philosophical cast of mind he understood this as a conflict between spirit and the scientific materialism then in its heyday. When he was about eighteen he let go of the claims of the latter.

It happened when he rewrote Fichte's *Science of Knowledge* in order to clarify his own ideas.

> Formerly I had been at pains to find concepts, applicable to the phenomena of nature, from which one could derive a concept of the 'I'. Now my goal was the opposite: starting from the 'I' I wanted to penetrate to the creative processes in nature. Spirit and nature stood before my soul in all their contrast. I experienced a world of spiritual beings. That the 'I', itself spirit, lives in a world of spirits, was a matter of direct perception for me. But I could not reconcile the physical world with the spiritual world I experienced.[15]

He did not rebel against the tough external conditions of his life but worked dutifully and very hard. There was the vegetable garden to cultivate. This was no irrelevance: supper during his childhood consisted simply of a piece of bread and butter or cheese. Travelling to and from school took up to three hours a day. According to his sister Leopoldine he would be in fear of gypsies and often up to his knees in snow struggling with heavy books. No doubt, despite the absence of a 'youth culture', many of the other pupils at the *Realschule* tasted whatever illicit delights there were in Wiener-Neustadt. There is no suggestion of anything of the sort in Steiner's *Autobiography*, though he states that he was always of a sociable disposition. For him the best the town seemingly had to offer was a visit to the doctor who was introducing him to German thought. He was also engaged tutoring contemporaries at the *Realschule* so that he could contribute money to his hard-up parents.

The railway company eventually transferred father and family to Inzersdorf, a suburb of Vienna, expressly so that Rudolf Steiner could commute to and from the city's *Technische Hochschule* (Technical College). He won a scholarship to study mathematics, natural history and chemistry. His *Autobiography*, which describes his childhood only perfunctorily, now starts to mention warm friendships. It states that his student companions generally followed 'the ideal', which they could not reconcile with actuality, and often had tragic endings. Steiner was elected chairman of the students' German Reading Room. Of great importance was his friendship from his first year with a lecturer in literature, Karl Schroer, whose dedication to Goethe influenced him enormously.

During his commuting Steiner made friends with a simple, mystical countryman, Felix Kogutski, who sold herbs in the city. Steiner saw him as special, as a healer who used 'atavistic' (i.e. unconscious) clairvoyance. 'Gradually it seemed to me as if I were in the company of a soul from bygone ages who, untouched by civilization, science and modern views, brought me an instinctive knowledge of the past.'[16] He was the model for 'Felix Balde', a character in the mystery plays Steiner wrote much later. In 1958, villagers who were questioned recalled 'Felix', as he is known to Anthroposophists, much more banally: they did not consider him to be special.[17]

Steiner informed[18] the French occultist Edouard Schuré that at about this time in his life he had been 'initiated' by the 'M'. Anthroposophists say they do not know who 'M' was. The impersonality and the letter are reminiscent of the Tibetan 'Masters' who supposedly communicated with the Theosophical Society founder Helena ('Madame') Blavatsky. (Later in his life, as we will see, Steiner's 'Anthroposophy' was to break away from the recently created Theosophical Society). 'M', like Felix, was anti-clerical, but unlike him taught a conscious clairvoyance. Strong, masculine and using the terminology of Fichte, he advocated 'slipping into the skin of the dragon', the spirit of the materialistic modern age, in order to understand it and so overcome it. As Steiner later wrote that he had not found inner truthfulness in Viennese Theosophy, 'M' perhaps was not a follower of this spiritual movement. 'M' – if he was of flesh and blood – may have followed a more Western path, particularly a revived Rosicrucianism, as the movement named after Christian Rosenkreuz is termed (the history of these spiritual identities is outlined in part three). The term 'M' is also reminiscent of the mythical 'Book M' of Christian Rosenkreuz over two centuries earlier, and indeed, Steiner saw Anthroposophy as a spiritually complete Rosicrucianism.

Twenty-one to Twenty-eight (1882-1889)

At this time an 'esoteric' revival was beginning to sweep North America and much of Europe. Steiner probably first encountered Theosophy through a book in 1884;[19] as he states that he deplored this book, he presumably read it. His *Autobiography* perhaps protests too much in denying the influence of Theosophy on him during his Vienna years: an influence can be effective without being consciously accepted.

About twenty years later Steiner's 'independent spiritual research' would come up with findings that were strikingly similar to Theosophy's. The idea of karma is one example. He believed he could perceive reincarnation spiritually before he met Theosophy, a perception which had been stimulated by his adolescent reading of Lessing. The previous 'epochs' of the earth, such as 'Lemuria' and 'Atlantis', are other similar findings (for these, see chapter six). He was probably much more conscious of what he rejected in Theosophy, especially towards the end of his life, once his Anthroposophy had severed all connection with Blavatsky's movement.

Theosophy and especially Western 'esotericisms' such as Rosicrucianism and Kabbalism have cosmologies whose structures have resemblances to the pattern of the Goetheanum serpent which was described towards the end of the Prologue. The circling serpent corresponds to a circling cosmology in which matter has fallen from spirit, but will, at least to some extent, be restored to its former state in a new way. This circling structure is generally not analyzed and so made explicit; rather, it lives as the poetical, mythic cohesion for the particular doctrines of the esoteric synthesis in question. For example, the 'Hyperborean' and 'Lemurian' epochs are explicit Anthroposophical teachings, but the hardening or falling of the latter from the state of the former is part of the more implicit, serpent-like structure. It was probably during his Vienna years that Rudolf Steiner, perhaps at an implicit level, thoroughly absorbed this circling pattern.

However, it seems to have been in his early Anthroposophical years that he consciously worked out, or 'spiritually researched', his fully spiritual, descending, cosmic evolution in which man is macrocosmic (this is the subject of chapters five and six).

This evolutionary pattern corresponds closely to his personal dilemma. He saw with his intuition how the minds of people like his father had become more and more materialistic and cut off from life and meaning. Against modern tendencies, Steiner was opposed to the development of individualism and complexity where connection is severed from thought: that is, in Steiner's meaning, severed from direct experience of the spiritual world. In an English literary setting this loss of connection is analogous to Wordsworth's lines: 'Shades of the prison house begin to close upon the growing boy'. Steiner, in combating this (in esoteric terms) 'microcosmic' process, could hardly have failed to connect it with the macrocosmic fall into the world symbolized by the serpent. The redemption of or from the world, the circling-back pattern of the serpent towards its tail implicit within Western esoteric systems, surely was a model for action.

His immediate concern in Vienna was to 'slip into the skin of the dragon'. This involved understanding contemporary science. He was wrestling with current evolutionary theory, especially that of Haeckel, the materialist enthusiast for Darwin, and exploring ways of reconciling it with his spiritual perception. He became an expert on Goethe's imaginative, holistic science, which he saw as a bridge between the spiritual and material worlds. His aim was to show how matter is, when perceived truly, an offshoot of spirit. Thus he was engaging with the dualism of his perception, the disconnection between his intuition and his sense-awareness. He felt he could hint of this to others, but not speak fully. It was only much later that the hermetically sealed retort in which his thoughts were bubbling came apart. Rudolf Steiner had learned how to keep his own counsel after he had written to a former teacher stating he could follow a former classmate who had died into the spiritual world. He was much shaken by the lack of any reply.

At the early age of twenty-two he was entrusted with editing Goethe's writings on natural science as part of an edition of *Deutschen Nationalliteratur* ('German National Literature').[20] The furthest he decided he could openly go in opposing the materialist thinking of his time was to advocate the contrasting philosophy of objective idealism. This, inwardly, he saw as the cloak of spiritual knowledge. He would openly say that man would be pitiable if he could not find fulfilment within an independent world of ideals, but needed help from external nature instead. This thinking developed into his seminal book *The Philosophy of Freedom.*

Steiner's problematic adjustment to the world was not just sensory, it was also social. Edouard Schuré later observed that Steiner had an extreme, empathetic and feminine sensibility.[21] Anecdotes of his younger years are also telling, as when Friedrich Eckstein, a factory-owning Theosophist, described how the young man used the informal *du* inappropriately and generally 'did not know a thing'. This is can be explained in part by his 'upwardly mobile' emergence into the middle-class Vienna of the 1880s. Steiner may well not have noticed his merely social *faux pas.*

There is a similar unearthliness about Steiner's love life. He recounts an early 'beautiful friendship' with a girl who 'had something of the archetypal German maiden about her'.[22] His erotic feelings are never mentioned, in relation to this encounter or elsewhere, but he does state that the image of her was frequently to stir within him. The shy soulfulness of this encounter was in contrast to the contemporary medical world's naming of sex as a diagnostic cause, a background for the psychoanalysis to come. (Indeed, Ellenberger, writing in relation to continental European medical contexts, stated that by the 1880s 'Victorian hypocrisy' was mostly a thing of the past).[23]

The youthful 'beautiful friendship' seems to have been succeeded by an attraction to maternal figures. While living with his parents and family Steiner was made welcome by Herminie, the maternally natured wife of his literature lecturer, Karl Schroer, at their home. On the latter's recommendation he became a resident tutor, thus leaving his own family. From 1884 he taught the four sons of Ladislaus Specht, a Jewish businessman who lived in Vienna. Steiner grew close to Pauline Specht, their mother. Later in his life, in Weimar, he was to lodge with Frau Anna Eunicke, a widow eight years his senior who had also had a large family. After this, he lived in Berlin, for a short while in utter misery in lodgings, and then moved in under Anna Eunicke's roof and married her. It seems likely that she moved first to Berlin and he followed.[24]These older, maternal women played a major part in Steiner's life until around the time he spoke publicly about his Anthroposophy.

Until he was about thirty, tutoring was Steiner's livelihood. Much of his twenties was spent tutoring the Specht children. He was now perhaps able to enjoy the childhood play he had missed. Steiner was moved by a spirit of altruism to give extraordinary understanding and arduous care to the 'sleeping soul' of one of the children, who had water on the brain. The effort was enormously worthwhile: the boy became a doctor of medicine. From this and other tutoring experiences

germinated Anthroposophical education, including the curative, and
Steiner's thinking on the nature of man. Had Steiner compromised with
materialism and 'come' to his senses in a psychiatrically approvable
way, Anthroposophy, including the high quality of its caring, could
hardly have come into being. Perhaps his early death might also have
been prevented, for in part he was to become a totem sacrificed to the
needs of his devotees. In contemporary Western culture, permeated
as it is by psychotherapy and counselling, someone now placed as
Steiner was then might come to understand themselves as personally
'split' and needing to integrate the elements of their experience.

Steiner presumably felt it would be inappropriate to speak about his
spiritual awareness to Dr Breuer, Freud's collaborator, on the occasions
when the former discussed medical subjects with Frau Specht. Nor did
he go as far as he could have done at the 'almost magical'[25] Saturday
evenings held by the pessimist poetess Marie delle Grazie. The
discussions, which were held under a red-shaded ceiling lamp, were
on cruel, senseless, overpowering nature. Steiner said it was no sunny
illumination but always sombre moonlight, with threatening, overcast
skies. Still, he greatly enjoyed these encounters with his despairing
anti-Goethean opposites. In other groups, where people were more in
accord with him, or in famous Viennese coffee-houses, such as the
Griensteidl-kaffee, he found gaiety and illumination, as well as the
usual warmth and friendliness. But even in this company he did not
confide his inner state, that taking shape within him was what has been
translated as 'a spiritual vision of the world of living truth'.[26]

Through a leading Theosophist, Maria Lang, Steiner became
friendly with the harmonious and well-known author-to-be Rosa
Mayreder, who has been described as expressing all that was best
in the woman-steeped aestheticism of Vienna.[27] She thought Steiner
did not pay enough attention to the physical world. Through her he
met architects whose ideas probably influenced his later designs,
including those for the two main Anthroposophical sacred buildings,
the 'Goetheanums' (the first one was burned down in 1922).

Vienna developed Steiner's cordial and sociable traits. Through
living in the capital of the Austro-Hungarian Empire he became
involved in its twilight, though not as a partisan Austrian nationalist.
In 1888 he tried to bring a more spiritual impulse even into journalism
and politics through briefly editing a weekly, *Die Deutsche
Wochenschrift*. It is very likely that Steiner would have had more
readers if, instead of his spiritual perspective, he had one-sidedly
identified either with the interests of the ruling class or with the social
utopianism of Marxism.[28]

Twenty-eight to Thirty-five (1889-1896)

Through the influence of Karl Schroer, Steiner, now an expert in the recondite area of Goethean science, was invited to Weimar, the 'Goethe-city', to edit nearly all the morphological part of Goethe's natural scientific writings for the Weimar Sophia edition. Rudolf Steiner left Vienna for Weimar when he was twenty-nine and never lived in his native Austria again. In the *Autobiography*, which describes his life in Weimar at great length, he called this transition the end of the first chapter of his life.

He maintained in Weimar the difficult silence about the spiritual beings he saw, the breaking of which he believed was the end of the second chapter of his life. Meanwhile, sense-perception continued to give him problems:

> I had to observe natural objects repeatedly in order to be able to identify them. . . . The external world really appeared to me somewhat shadow-like or picture-like. It moved past me like pictures whereas my relationship with the spiritual always had the character of concrete reality. . . . My inner world was really separated from the outer world as if by a thin wall. . . . It was as if I had to cross a threshold when I wanted to have intercourse with the outer world.[29]

During these years, spiritualist séances were much more prevalent than they are now. Steiner seems not to have been involved in séances, but nevertheless mentions how on two occasions he had had experiences of second sight in connection with women with whom he was or was to be emotionally involved. He thought he was in contact with the spirit of the man who, when alive, had been most important to them. The first was the recluse father of the 'archetypal German maiden' he loved. Even though the two had never met, Steiner (while he was living in Vienna) gave his funeral address. He thought that, again in a non-spiritualistic way,[30] he was close to the spirit of the also-reclusive late husband of his Weimar landlady and wife to be, Anna Eunicke. Again, Steiner had never met him.

Outwardly, life was relatively easy. Steiner entered into the minds of numerous interesting people with great warmth and insight. As already stated, he was lodging with Frau Anna Eunicke and her family. In 1891 he found a Platonist professor (at Rostock University) who accepted his doctoral thesis.[31] There is much in the *Autobiography* about the ferment of ideas in the high culture of Weimar which, through the amiable patronage of Grand Duke Karl Alexander, was dedicated to the memory of Goethe and Schiller. The Goethe Archives where he worked were a point of intersection for scientific, artistic and courtly circles. Though Steiner was not in accord with the dry philologists there, he also knew people who wanted to live in the present, the 'Liszt-era'. He mixed with a Nietzschean circle[32] and had interesting discussions with the feminist writer Gabrielle Reuter.

Despite the cultural atmosphere of the Goethe Archives, in spirit Steiner seems to have felt acutely alone. Trying to understand his predicament in universal terms, he spent much energy empathizing with and distinguishing himself from well-known contemporary thinkers. He was chilled by a meeting with the famous philosopher Edouard von Hartman, whom he felt did not inwardly listen but instead maintained that mental pictures by their very definition contain no reality. A meeting sought by Haeckel led to a comment in Steiner's *Autobiography* much later, that Haeckel's materialist ideas were possessed somewhat fanatically by an interest pursued in a former life on earth, in particular by a strong desire which had been related to Church politics. Seeing Nietzsche prostrate during his illness, Steiner felt profound empathy, believing that such a fine soul's acceptance of scientific materialism had inevitably led to tragedy (syphilis as a specific cause was not mentioned). The *Autobiography* states: 'In inner perception I saw Nietzche's soul as if hovering over his head, infinitely beautiful in its spirit light, surrendered to the spirit worlds it had longed for so much but had been unable to find before illness had clouded his mind.'[33]

Thirty-five to Forty-two (1896-1903)

When Steiner was thirty-six he left Weimar for Berlin. It seems that Anna Eunicke was already there. Fending for himself during his last year at Weimar, he found his sense perception was improving.

> I was aware that I was experiencing an inner transformation of soul-life which normally occurs at a much earlier age. . . .
> I found that the reason that people grasp neither the physical nor the spiritual world in their purity is because at an early age a transition takes place in the soul's existence: from being bound up with spiritual life it comes to experience the physical. Henceforth the physical sense-impressions are unconsciously mingled with the inner impressions of the world of spirit used in forming mental pictures.[34]

Steiner could perhaps have accepted and attempted to increase the mingling between his spiritual and recently improved sense perceptions, but he remained true to the unusual self he knew, his spiritual self. Though his awareness of matter had improved, it remained separate. Analogously his cosmology, which was quite soon to be revealed by him, was to reject hard physicality as gross or 'abnormal' and to perceive dense matter as a temporary aberration.

Given that the development of sense perception in childhood is generally an involuntary process, its development in Rudolf Steiner at mid-life put him in a most unusual situation. It perhaps gave him more need to communicate because the sense-world became more real. 'Must I remain silent? . . . At every turn I met the problem: how can I find the way to express in terms understandable to my contemporaries what I inwardly perceive directly as the truth?'[35] Keeping his own counsel still, in that he was not expressing his intuitions, he linked up with Anna Eunicke in Berlin.

Here, in the sophisticated metropolis of the Germany recently united by Bismarck, he moved in Bohemian circles. This change from the salons of Weimar reflected his inner state: in 1898 he was undergoing a dark crisis. The hard matter he had put aside was tempting him in the form of philosophical materialism while around him was a nightmare experience of an unreal city, a vision of the modern metropolis anticipating T.S. Eliot's *The Wasteland* and the dark vision of modernity in W.B. Yeats' *The Second Coming.* Steiner preserved himself from this abyss by accepting a spiritual foundation, a highly esotericised Christianity, which became the axis of his spiritual thought.[36] Recovering in 1899, he no longer lived alone in the capital, for he and Anna Eunicke became husband and wife.

Soon after his wedding to Anna Eunicke he began to break his silence. This proved to be a very challenging issue. Probably the secularised sophisticates found him comical and the aesthetes felt him to be a puzzle. Steiner perceived that the metropolitan literary minds he encountered were unaware that their destinies and his were karmically linked. Was Frank Wedekind, the famous dramatist, aware of how Rudolf Steiner regarded his hands? '*Such* hands! In a previous earthlife they must have accomplished things possible only for someone capable of letting the power of his spirit stream into the finest ramifications of his fingers'.[37]

Steiner once gave a spiritual address before an experimental production of a play (*L'intruse*) by the idealist writer, Maeterlinck, but the aesthetic listeners seem to have remained mere dabblers in the spirit. The readers of a literary journal, the *Magazin fur Literatur*, which Steiner edited were unenthusiastic about his spiritual glimmerings (anything more explicit their editor knew he could not include). He had more success teaching history for the Workers' Educational Association, but his contract was not renewed when the management realised quite how un-Marxist he really was. There was, however, a tribute to his rhetorical and, presumably, charismatic powers when in 1900 he was entrusted with an address to 7,000 typesetters.

Thus Steiner explored far and wide in frustrating attempts to bring others to a preliminary cognition of the spiritual. Sooner or later, though, it was likely he would encounter the potential following that existed, those who indeed were avid for a spiritual leader with his sense of mission. In August 1900, he had accepted an invitation from Count and Countess Brockdorff to speak on Nietzsche to an audience that included Berlin Theosophists. Invited again, this time he gave a fully 'esoteric' lecture on Goethe's well-known *Fairy Tale*.[38] In this company he was highly valued: his social dramatisation arising out of his need to communicate and perhaps justify his spiritual perception was here representative, whereas in more conventional circles it was stigmatised as exaggerated. Steiner discovered that the only way he could break his silence was to return to the kind of Theosophical milieu that he had encountered years ago in Vienna. The spiritual energy that he had for so long restrained began to well up from within. In 1902 he became the effective leader of German Theosophists. As most came to depend on him as a charismatic seer, his spiritual identity was increasingly confirmed and reinforced.

Through lecturing to Theosophists, Rudolf Steiner met Marie von Sievers, his esoteric partner and second wife-to-be, a year after marrying Anna Eunicke. Not only was Marie von Sievers six years younger than he, she was also esoteric and formidable. She came from a noble German-Baltic background and had been brought up in Warsaw, Riga and St Petersburg. She owned the Theosophical headquarters in Berlin, and at some point she and Steiner lived together in her apartment in this house. She looked up to Steiner, who had quite suddenly transformed into a charismatic leader, as the ultimate spiritual authority. From the end of 1903 Steiner and von Sievers were inseparably together at the centre of Berlin Theosophy, and in 1914, three years after the death of Anna Eunicke, Steiner and von Sievers would marry. His silence was utterly finished and there was nothing now to check his destined end.

The Anthroposophical Years (c. 1903-30 March 1925)

Though this chapter is concerned with the life of Rudolf Steiner, the information here also introduces the history of the movement as a whole.

Steiner's need to bring others into his esoteric world was much tempered by his liberalism and ethic of individuality. His social blueprint of the Threefold Commonwealth could, however, be considered spiritual Napoleonism. Steiner's face, the dark eyes becoming increasingly contrasted with lines and hollows, became quite well known in Wilhelminian Germany. Silence transformed into magnetic monologue. In all, he gave 5,965 lectures, the great majority in his Anthroposophical years.

The foundation of his spiritual movement was, in a sense, a triumphant vindication that in itself has brought immortality. In the first decade of the last century Steiner was mainly concerned with developing his own 'esoteric' synthesis.[39] Before and during the First World War he established Anthroposophy as a separate organisation, breaking away from Theosophy.[40] He also gave 'indications' for the development of artistic activities. From about 1913 he was designing and building the (first) Goetheanum, the central sacred building of Anthroposophy, in Switzerland. It was at this watershed time that he married Marie von Sievers. After the First World War he was largely concerned with the social applications of Anthroposophy. Apart from the time of armed conflict, he travelled widely in Europe, unflaggingly speaking evening after evening.

His influence was at its peak in the despair of post-First World War Middle Europe. Indeed, he presented Emperor Charles and other doomed hereditary rulers of his native Austria-Hungary and Germany with a social utopia, the Threefold Commonwealth (see chapter four). Though his childhood supper had consisted only of a slice of bread and butter, Rudolf Steiner's blueprint had no Marxist tinge. It and he were well publicised. An appeal based on it attracted many non-Anthroposophical signatures, including those of numerous professors, Gabrielle Reuter and Hermann Hesse. However, the Threefold Commonwealth had no influence on the political structures which followed the war.

Later, disaster struck. On New Year's Eve, 1922, the Goetheanum was set on fire. Throughout that terrible night Steiner was a model of fortitude. Then, after a display of spiritual disillusionment with his followers, he dedicated himself to the renewal of the Anthroposophical movement, laying the foundation stone for a new

Goetheanum. This '1924 Foundation event' was of great importance to the society because it was only at this stage that Steiner formally joined it. Anthroposophically, it is perceived as Steiner connecting his personal destiny to members, his recognition that the teacher should get entangled in worldly things, and a model for how development continues to the end, even when it comes to a seer's incarnation. In terms of sociological theory about charismatic leadership, it is, as will be seen, an example of the 'routinisation' (i.e. social embedding) of charisma. In terms of a biography of the human being it could also be understood as a step forwards in Steiner's attempts to integrate himself with the problematic sense world.

Once Steiner had broken his silence to Berlin Theosophists, he was a public man. He was desperately needed for revelations, for charismatic leadership. His thoughts about the nature of man and the ascending evolution of the cosmos towards the heights of spiritual realisation were elaborated in the first decade of the new century. As described, he believed his 'findings' (arrived at by spiritual research) were uninfluenced by similar ideas he was aware of through his conventional knowledge of Theosophy and contemporary thinking generally. These beliefs in the inerrancy of his intuition, like his earlier adoption of Christianity, perhaps enabled him to shut out from his spiritual self the forces he identified as the spirit's great opponents – materialism, or Ahriman, and chaotic, passionate fancy, or Lucifer.

Steiner appears to have become more and more insulated from the outside world as he acted upon his sense of heroic mission. Though he seems to have retained a few old friends, the generality of the intellectuals, writers and artists he had known were in a different world. Within Anthroposophy he had little private life: even his relationship with Marie von Sievers was in part at least a kind of externalized alchemical marriage for followers, in that it was a public, spiritualised relationship. Sexuality exercised a covert influence in his later career, through the perceptions of others. In 1906, he and Marie von Sievers led an esoteric society associated with sexual magic. Furthermore, he has been depicted as spiritually polygamous because he told a woman follower, Dr Ita Wegman, that a very ancient karma existed between them. Though this revelation might have been made for the sake of Anthroposophical cohesion, it was to have the opposite organisational effect through triggering later conflict between Dr Wegman and his widow.

His followers needed to idealize him. Steiner became omnipotently convinced that he was not only inspired by the Rosicrucian esoteric tradition but also by intangible 'Nordic', 'Hibernian' and 'Celtic' streams. As Anthroposophy grew around him, his social environment increasingly reflected back to him the uniqueness of his spiritual identity. Steiner seems in part to have been the prisoner of the expectations he satisfied. The more he developed the movement, the more the needs of members, exacerbated by his self-punishing sense of duty hemmed him in, day in, day out. His dilemma about remaining silent continued in the sense that he still felt unable to speak about what they could not understand. He also felt constrained by followers to talk about some themes, such as the Gospels and the Bible, more than he intended. Despite or perhaps in part because of his use of exhortation and strong criticism, his personal life, including his marriage, seems to have been swallowed up by the followers who devoted themselves to him. His charisma in large part, though certainly not entirely, seems to have been conferred by the mass of his followers, their empty, hungry inner 'splitness' and consequent need to project and idealize. As will be discussed more fully in considering the growth of Anthroposophy as a social movement (chapter two), in terms of contemporary leadership theory Steiner's charismatic leadership can in part be understood through psychodynamic psychology. His charismatic, authoritative leadership was symbiotic with his followers' dependence and their projection of infantile, or early, needs and fantasies which, though individual and perhaps different for each person, tended to have the common characteristic of being accompanied with awe. Steiner's need to speak authoritatively and his followers' idealizing of him as one entitled to speak with authority seem to have fed into each other in a quickening spiral.

Herman Keyserling, another spiritual leader, accused Rudolf Steiner of having a 'tremendous lust for power',[41] but this does not seem to have been a common complaint. His power, and perhaps need for power as charismatic leader, were bounded by his own Anthroposophical ethics. The – perhaps relatively few – really unscrupulous leaders of cults attempt to increase their hold through making arbitrary and, especially, contradictory decrees. In this way followers are prised away from conventional restraint and depend more and more on the cult hero. Steiner, even if his need for power was strong, remained consistent in his spiritual science and behaviour.

Steiner died of an excruciating illness at the age of sixty-three on 30 March 1925. No conventional diagnosis was made generally available, though one was promised,[42] explaining why he suffered anew after each meal. By the time Marie Steiner had answered a call to his bedside next to the burned out Goetheanum he was dead. It may be that he never thought that his illness, which started in the summer of 1923, would be terminal.

Steiner explained his illness by stating that in his spiritual life he had somehow lost connection with his physical body, though not with the physical world. He even said that it was precisely because in the spiritual and even in the physical world everything went on without the slightest error that the opposing powers were attacking his physical body (Perhaps because this was the only other route available).[43] For Steiner the way to handle Ahriman, the force of materialism, and Lucifer, the force of passionate fantasy, was explicitly to hold the middle ground. However, within the microcosm of Steiner himself, somehow the centre did not hold.

2. The Establishment of the Movement

It is a common feature of religious history that religions that attempt to fulfil and bring together the adherents of great religions hitherto in opposition end by becoming distinct faiths on their own account.[1]

— Ninian Smart, The Religious Experience of Mankind

The great changes associated with industrialisation and urbanisation have been generally linked in Europe with the decline of traditional institutional religion. This is apart from a few countries, such as Poland, when under the yoke of imposed atheistic materialism. In English-speaking, Protestant societies especially there have arisen liberal-democratic secular states and the cultural prescription that the individual should think for himself (and, more recently, herself) about ultimate questions.

Experimental contact with 'spirits of the dead' through a medium, filled a void felt by many in the changing conditions of the second half of the nineteenth century. Spiritualism[2] became extremely popular after Kate and Margaret Fox, of Hydesville, NY, claimed fraudulently that they had heard 'spirit rappings'. Throughout the USA and northern Europe it added mystery to the formalized Christian observances. In the UK, socially segregated séances were attended by bishops, detached scientists and 'irreligious' workers. The widowed Queen Victoria herself was interested in the possibility of communicating with a survival of the human personality after death. Mary Baker Eddy was a devotee before renouncing spiritualism and founding Christian Science; so was Helena Petrovna Blavatsky.

Known to her adherents as 'H.P.B.', Blavatsky founded the Theosophical Society in New York in 1875. This extraordinary Russian emigrée claimed to be inspired by spiritual 'Masters' in Tibet, though her highly synthesised esoteric revelation was also influenced by Hinduism, Buddhism, maybe Syrian-Egyptian gnosticism, and other non-Tibetan sources. She claimed that her esoteric synthesis is universally valid, a 'spiritual science' that expresses the 'true religion' from which the forms of world religions have been created. This appealed to many relatively educated people who were spiritually minded but perplexed by the growing trend towards cultural relativism. At this time there was a challenge to traditional Christianity from the new Darwinism, from the secular legitimacy of scientific materialism (the 'billiard ball' understanding of matter that pre-dated the new physics), and from the non-Christian religions that research and popular editions were making available. 'Theosophy' as Blavatsky's system was called – an old word, but now capitalized to reflect its use as a proper noun in specifically referencing her particular spiritual system – spread rapidly in the English-speaking world, attracting relatively few of the best intellects but some of the finest creative spirits of the time; examples of the latter included W.B. Yeats and Kandinsky. The mobility of forms and thought in the 'esoteric' movements of the time appealed to many of those, such as artists and poets, who were primarily engaged with the imagination. Conversely, 'esotericism' often appeared jumbled and ridiculous to those, such as scholars and intellectuals, in more conventional roles.

After Blavatsky's death in 1891, the organisational and moral flair of Annie Besant was the leading force behind Theosophy's second stage. The revelation was made more conceptual and the movement acquired a radical social conscience. It was particularly important for the part it played in the revival of Hinduism in India and Buddhism in Sri Lanka, and the spread of liberal democratic ideas in both nations.[3] By 1899 the society had 356 'Lodges', 187 in India, sixty-eight in America and fifty-eight in Europe. But Theosophy had made little headway in newly united Germany.

Its relatively late, though rapid, industrialisation appears to be an important reason why, in Germany, 'esotericism' spread in the early twentieth century rather than in the late nineteenth. Dr Huebbe-Schleiden, the leader of the German Theosophists, was a factory owner, and many of the other prominent German Theosophists seem also to have been occupationally involved with industrialisation. Also, the middle-class secularism associated with urbanisation seems not to have developed in the *Kulturkampf* of Bismarck's age; indeed, in the 1870s, voting according to Protestant/Catholic allegiance reached its highest point.[4] Theosophy itself was in many ways ill-suited for German speakers. Much of its style was Anglo-Saxon; most of its exoticism was derived from British colonies or British spheres of global influence. Furthermore, it made no reference to German Romanticism, the obvious rich, preliminary source for German esotericists.

Despite some visits by Blavatsky to Germany it was only in 1894 that a Berlin Lodge was given an official charter by the Theosophical headquarters (which was then located in Adyar, India). As Dr Huebbe-Schleiden lived in Hannover, Count and Countess Brockdorff took on most of the work. Rudolf Steiner was asked to lecture on Nietzsche at the turn of the century, a time late enough in the rapidly industrialising Germany to be propitious for the emergence of a seer. What follows in this chapter is an account of Anthroposophy which focuses on its phases of development as an organization and social movement.

The Phase of Charismatic Leadership

German-English-speaking differences

Besant felt little rapport with Rudolf Steiner but expected much from his leadership of the German Section of the Theosophical Society. He built up a sizeable new following in the growing industrial and urbanised life of Wilhelminian Germany. From 1902, when Steiner became General Secretary of the German Section, to 1913, membership expanded from a few individuals to sixty-nine Lodges. Fifty-five of these – about 2,500 people – seceded with him at that time to form the new Anthroposophical Society.[5] The others remained in the Theosophical Society and were led by Dr Huebbe-Schleiden. This divisive split between, broadly, Germanic and English-speaking esotericism parallels and was presumably influenced by the growing rivalry between Wilhelminian Germany and Edwardian Great Britain. The main Anthroposophical centres were Berlin, Munich, Stuttgart, Hamburg, Cologne and Leipzig, with Vienna and Prague also probably having had members.

'The people who came to Anthroposophy had usually failed to find in the scientific world conception and in the traditional religious teachings the spiritual content for which they longed,'[6] Steiner wrote. In general he saw Anthroposophists as homeless souls, while Marie Steiner later described the movement as a nursing home.[7] They both tried to counteract sentimentality. He was also aware of cultural differences within Anthroposophy (these have greatly multiplied since, see chapter three). Steiner perceived the Berlin followers as rationalistic and uniform, tending to take Anthroposophy as their sole guide. He thought the Munich members were much more artistic and individual. Gradually a relatively central German group formed around Countess Pauline von Kalckreuth and Fraulein Sophie Stinde.

As Steiner came more and more to teach his own revelation, emerging as the hero/leader of German-style theosophy, he faced increasingly strained relations with Besant, who became President of the Theosophical Society in 1907. He admitted that she was tolerant of his different direction until about 1905 or 1906, defending its right to exist even though she did not understand it. Up to this time he was using Theosophical terminology much more than was the case later and once even legitimised himself by saying, 'Mme Blavatsky intended to express this in her theory'.[8] From about this time, however, the divergence could not be ignored, because he was lecturing on the core of his Anthroposophy, soon to be published as *Occult Science*. Despite basic similarities, it was also obviously different in content and style from Blavatsky's *Secret Doctrine*. This new German 'Theosophy' was apparent to everyone at the International Congress at Munich in May 1907. Busts of Fichte, Schelling and Hegel were placed on pedestals in front of the speaker's desk, occult seals and columns designed by Steiner hung in the hall and Marie von Sievers presented drama and declamation which not only seemed to revive the ancient mysteries but also to express the true German spirit.

Steiner had joined the 'E.S.', or Theosophical Esoteric Section. In his *Autobiography* he wrote that this was for 'the sole purpose of informing (himself) of what took place'[9] and that he was uninfluenced by it. He then founded his own esoteric circle as an offshoot. In 1907 its connection with the 'E.S.' was severed by mutual consent. He stated that Blavatsky, through being inspired by her 'Mahatmas', or Tibetan masters, had recreated the mysteries atavistically (i.e. unconsciously, as contrasted with conscious 'scientific' access). For similar reasons he disapproved of Besant's espousal of Raja yoga.

Steiner's esoteric teachings followed the highly conscious trad-itions of German Idealism. Analogously, he used his holistic, Goethean science to refute Huebbe-Schleiden, who was trying to produce scientific proof of the physical, etheric and astral atoms of Theosophy's occult chemistry. Steiner publicized his separate system through a successful journal, *Lucifer-Gnosis,* but was forced to give up this activity because of the pressure of his lecturing commitments. In 1908 he spoke in as many as seven European countries.

Nevertheless, Steiner may still have been experimenting with social vehicles to convey his distinctive revelation. In 1906 Theodor Reuss, the leader of the Yarker Masonic Lodges in Germany and England, had empowered Steiner to lead a Lodge within the Ordo Templi Orientis. He was much criticised for accepting. Franz Hartman, a Theosophist from whom Steiner, in his *Autobiography,* had been at pains to dissociate himself, had founded a German Rosicrucian order which had fused with the Ordo Templi Orientis in 1888. Steiner thereby, at this point, associated himself with a seemingly ceremonious, ritualistic, hierarchical esotericism which is said to have practised sexual magic. It closed at the outbreak of war because it was taken for a secret society. Its reputation was very different from that of Anthroposophy, or of the Christian Community, for which Steiner near the end of his life in 1922 was requested by Dr Rittelmeyer and other Lutheran pastors to provide a spiritual basis.

The cultural gulf between Steiner and Theosophy, augmented by the military contest between the Germans and British, made a breach at some stage before the end of the 1914-1918 war unsurprising. The occasion for it was both unsavoury and ludicrous. Rumours surrounded a leading English Theosophist, the Rev'd Charles Leadbeater, who is said once to have written to Besant that one of his last incarnations had been in ancient Greece where pederastic propensities had been regarded quite differently. On an occasion that was to have far-reaching consequences, she was met by him at Madras station. An eager, large-eyed boy who was unknown to her shyly placed a garland around her neck and Leadbeater introduced him as 'our Krishna'.[10]

The Indian child, the son of an impoverished brahman clerk, was soon believed by Besant and many other Theosophists to be the 'World Teacher'. He was to become known as 'Krishnamurti'. The cult of Krishnamurti was given form in 1911 by the founding of the Order of the Star in the East. In 1912 there were 540 members, probably mostly Theosophists. They presumably did not foresee that later the culturally transplanted young man, despite the support of Lady Emily Lutyens, would not match the entrance requirements for Oxford University, would become fond of golf, and would decide he was not the 'World Teacher' but an ordinary guru.

The Order of the Star in the East was anathema to Steiner and most German Theosophists, who considered themselves Western and saw the descent of Christ as the redeeming cosmic event. Of the Theosophists who had not joined the separate Order, few if any seem to have severed links with the Society. Steiner and his Anthroposophical group, however, declared that no one who joined the new Order could remain a member of the German Theosophical Society. By the end of 1912 Besant had ensured that the charter of the German Section was revoked by the General Council of the Theosophical Society. A new one was issued for the fourteen Lodges that remained loyal. The newly independent Anthroposophy was, numerically, a relatively insignificant offshoot from Theosophy.

Besant complained that Rudolf Steiner's Executive Council sent her a telegram demanding her resignation 'couched in insulting language for the benefit of the public – as people of a certain type write on post-cards'.[11] Steiner attacked the 'Besant system', and someone else accused her of having 'descended to a very cruel and subtle slander'[12] against him.

The Anthroposophical Society and the building of the Goetheanum

In February 1913, against the background of rising tension that with hindsight led up to the First World War, Steiner and his 2,500 or so followers formed the Anthroposophical Society. They seem to have been overwhelmingly German or German speakers. To some extent chauvinism mingled with esotericism: for example, the Anthroposophical *Mitteilungen* of December 1912 stated, 'It is a notorious fact that King Edward was really the disturber of the peace'.[13] There were only a handful of English Anthroposophists. Led by H. Collison, they formed an anonymous club during the 1914-1918 war between Great Britain and Germany. The first eight had seceded from The Hermetic Order of the Golden Dawn, an occult organisation that was more Western in its outlook than Theosophy. There also seem to have been some founding members in the Netherlands and other European countries.

Steiner was accused of having had pro-German bias during the First World War. His close personal link with the Chief of Staff, General von Moltke, was generally noted. But however much Anthroposophy functioned as a German-speaking esotericism, in the eyes of its leader (and hence of its enchanted followers) it was valid because of its universality. There is no reason to doubt the genuineness of this belief. The choosing of Switzerland for the site of the Goetheanum does not suggest a narrow nationalism. The land, apparently, was offered on very favourable terms. Steiner rejected a possible site at Weimar because, he felt, it already had too many cultural (and personal?) associations. When, after the 'Festival of the Roofing of the Dome' in 1914, the faint sound of gunfire could be heard, Steiner became charismatically associated with one of the most visibly hopeful enterprises in Europe and, by now a pan-European figure, was not over-closely associated with the cause of what was to be the losing side in the war.

The building of the first Goetheanum together with the beginning of Anthroposophy's activities gave the nascent movement a social embeddedness which was largely lacking in Theosophy. This was centred on the commanding founder himself. Members continually looked up to him for 'indications' about what to do next. He also helped with personal problems and, through his authority as a sensitive, a custom arose whereby he would find the 'right' names for members' infants. Albert Steffen, the succeeding President of the Anthroposophical Society, wrote that Steiner's study was full throughout the day.[14] Steiner's words were transformational, including the requirement of thinking for oneself (ethical individualism), but the organisational reality – the 'glue' of the nascent movement – seems to have been a growing creative distance between Steiner and his followers. The implicit 'deal' (the 'psychological contract', in Schein's phrase) seems often to have been a relatively transactional one to do with latent emotional security needs: many of the followers seem to have needed a hero to idealise; and Steiner may have needed to feel legitimised through having followers. At the level of the organisation, a symbiosis appears to have formed between Steiner's life-long pattern of self-seclusion, and followers' needs for a certainty that lay beyond everyday human relationships. This is not to deny that Steiner in many situations also had a powerfully transforming effect on a great many individuals.[15]

The future emotional needs of two women in his life seem not to have been foreseen by Steiner's spiritual science, founded as it was on the primacy of thinking. These needs were inseparable from the organizational structures. Marie von Sievers, who had trained in Paris under Mme Favast, was of special assistance to her consort in the founding of eurythmy and speech formation. She was also, however, to play a major role in dissensions in the movement following her husband's death. Steiner, as will be described, sowed the seeds of future strife by bequeathing the copyright of his Anthroposophical publications to her. Many were to feel that the publications properly belonged to the movement. Further conflict was to arise after his death because, as has been described, in 1907 he had informed Ita Wegman, the Dutch doctor, that a very ancient karma existed between them. In 1923 it seems he told her that in a previous life she had been Gilgamesh and that he had been inseparably with her as Eabani. The withdrawal through death of Steiner's personal magnetism, which contained the many Anthroposophical tensions while he was alive, made it much more possible for problems to arise.

In the ashes of defeat the Austrian Kaiser, his cabinet chief, and the German foreign minister were all apparently aware of the salvation offered to Middle Europe through the Threefold Commonwealth,

Steiner's blueprint for societal rebuilding. Rudolf Steiner became a highly controversial figure in post-war Germany. Over fifty years afterwards Anthroposophists still seemed to be slightly disappointed that this attention died down together with the apocalyptic sense of chaos.

Perhaps partly because of the publicity surrounding Steiner's Threefold Commonwealth, the movement recruited well at the end of the war, even in England. The high society patina of pre-war UK Theosophy was probably lacking, though recruits were highly respectable. One member was a retired English admiral, another, a certain Miss Ross who raised funds through organising a sale of 'Rosswoollies'. Times had changed post-war, particularly in Germany. When Collison, the old guard English Anthroposophist, asked Steiner what a Junker (a Prussian aristocrat) was, he replied teasingly that this old guard Englishman was one himself. Later, in similar vein, Albert Steffen, the succeeding President, referred in the new Germany of 1942 to a Marquess who had 'raised the aristocratic habits in which he had grown up to a higher level'.[16]

Furthermore, the severe shock on New Year's Eve, 1922, when the original wooden Goetheanum burned down, did not result in a net loss of membership. It did, however, test Steiner's charisma to the limit. Whatever the personal cost, he did not fail his creation. In blaming the disaster on his followers' spiritual imperfections, he could be interpreted masochistically at a personal level, thereby preserving the potential redeeming spirituality of his revelation as a transcendent whole. The alternative, an admission that the karma of the Goetheanum, the symbol of the movement, was a tragic mistake, would surely have destroyed Anthroposophy. There are precedents where religions which need affirmation as a sign experience calamity instead. The Jews had preserved their cultural identity during the first destruction of the temple and exile by persuading themselves that these things had occurred because they had failed Jahweh. To this strategy Steiner added courage, calm and a commitment to rebuild which saved the situation.

The Laying of the Foundation Stone

A year later, at the Christmas Foundation Meeting of 1923, Steiner laid the 'Foundation Stone' for the new, concrete Goetheanum. From 1902 to 1923 was twenty-one years, or three of the seven-year periods significant in Anthroposophy, making this representation of the reconstruction of the whole society also a coming of age. In terms of the sociology of Max Weber, it represents the 'routinisation' or social embedding of Steiner's personal charisma. In 1923 the Anthroposophical Society became the General Anthroposophical Society with affiliated national societies. From within, the School of Spiritual Science was a new focus for 'esoteric' commitment and authority. Steiner thus committed himself organisationally to the newly reformed movement. The new concrete building (though it would only open, still incomplete, on Michaelmas Day 1928), represented a physical embodiment of the organisational foundation which served as substitute for Steiner in the years when he was no longer incarnated. Set up thus by the revered founder, these organisational arrangements, when accompanied by liberal democratic political conditions, have so far proven unassailable, and have been very significant in the healing of splits after Steiner's death.

By this time Rudolf Steiner seems almost to have become transhuman, a mythic object to be loved or hated. His, and von Sievers', marginal cultural origins may have helped stimulate these feelings in their adopted homeland, as in the case of other European leaders before and since, But this cannot apply to the many non-German members recruited through Steiner's constant post-war travels in Europe (though never to America). One follower was oppressed by 'a hideously evil picture' of his face which she never really believed in but could not wholly reject. But, for the most part, powerfully positive emotions were projected onto him.

Young doctors would bring questions to Steiner, 'this Everest of a man', to whose lectures it was an 'unforgettable liberation to listen'. He was a 'great initiate to whom we were privileged to speak'. 'Only he could guide me'. Vera Compton-Burnett stated that memories of him 'do not dim with passing years, but continue to shed their light upon the whole of life'. Her sister, Julie, recollected that 'the impression was not only of immeasurable goodness and greatness, it was as if the spiritual world revealed itself through his physical presence'. Another English member said he seemed taller than he really was and that his words were able 'to transform my whole life'. A Dutch member had the strange feeling that never before had he seen a 'Man'.

Organisationally, this charisma needs to be understood in terms of the relationship between Steiner and his followers. From the point of view of the psychological mechanism of projection, followers like those above did much to create Steiner's charisma and the atmosphere of awe which surrounded him (for an analysis of biographical factors in some members' choice of Anthroposophy see the appendix 'Some

Ways In'). The likely symbiotic psychological contract between
Steiner as guru and members as neophytes may have stood in the
way of developing a culture in which such followers could develop
a sense of their inspiration as internal to them (as contrasted with
projecting it onto Steiner). However, without this symbiosis between
leader and led, Anthroposophy as an organisation may have had
insufficient social 'glue' to form.

From a social psychological point of view on leadership in general,
Steiner's behaviour can, in part, be seen as matching that of prototypical
leaders held in followers' memories. The prototypical leader has been
defined as an abstraction of features common to leaders which has
been developed through experience, involving perceptual processes
such as selective attention, everyday storage, retention and retrieval. In
part also – in terms of social psychological theorising about charisma
in particular – Steiner's behaviour can be understood as matching
characteristics which were socially stigmatised and which pushed
him out to the edge of society, yet through his dominance enabled
him, through social dramatisation, to make a compatible group doubt
the validity of what was elsewhere assumed to be normal. These two
social psychological perspectives, on leadership in general and on
charisma in particular can, when combined, further understanding
about Steiner's ascent to charismatic leadership.[17]

In some ways, Steiner's leadership style seems to have had points
in common with narcissism. Maccoby states that some larger than life
leaders closely resemble Freud's narcissistic type. They are emotionally
isolated, and achievements can feed feelings of grandiosity. Because of
their extreme independence and self-protectiveness, it is very difficult
to get near them psychologically. They run a risk of isolating themselves
at the moment of success, and want to leave behind a legacy. They see
things that never were and ask 'why not?' Typically uncomfortable with
their own emotions, they dominate meetings with subordinates and are
often skilful orators. They need affirmation and, preferably, adulation,
and are acutely aware of whether people are with them wholeheartedly,
and sometimes show signs of paranoia. However, much of what
Maccoby writes cannot be made to fit. Narcissists lack empathy for
others, can be brutally exploitive, can rage at perceived threats, are
not troubled by a punishing superego, can turn unproductive when,
lacking self-knowledge and restraining anchors, they become dreamers
(Steiner was highly productive). Maccoby concludes that, despite the
drawbacks, narcissists can be extraordinarily useful, even necessary.
Indeed, in so far as Steiner's leadership style was narcissistic, much of
this distance and difference may have been essential to push through

the massive transformation that is Anthroposophy.[18]

Steiner's geniality, humour and sociability combined with his ethical, constant character, gave his charisma both an endearing personal touch and also a strong sense of service to others. His supremacy, and the strong criticisms he could make were perceived to be tempered with patience and reverence: for example, it was a matter of remark that he once waited a long time for a poor cobbler before beginning a lecture. No everyday impression could be made of him. He might declare that your dead father 'is of great help to us in the spiritual world'[19] or remark that radioactivity has only been present in the world since the time of Golgotha. His charisma was often reinforced sartorially with long cravats and through other effects, such as peering at you through a lorgnette while wearing snowboots. He had a way with children, had vegetarian tendencies, did not drink alcohol[20] and took snuff.

He was excellent at what has subsequently been described as servant leadership. In his pre-consumerist age an ethic of public service was far more prevalent in Europe. Thus through laying the Foundation Stone and thereby the organisational structures of the General Anthroposophical Society, a leader of undisputed charisma set up the stability of Anthroposophy to come, once a long period of dissensions had been survived. However, as already suggested, the distance between Steiner and his followers posed a dilemma for organisational development. On the one hand, if Steiner had better enabled his followers (or attracted more followers who had the potential to become spiritual peers or close lieutenants), organisationally he would have risked sharing charisma and resulting schisms. On the other hand, by increasing his charismatic authority he risked having an organisation which lived in his shadow, and which after his death would not have an embedded impetus of spiritual development to take it far up the spiritual path he revealed. The latter, a sense of relative disempowerment, has accompanied the organisational stability achieved after his death.

The distance still very much perceived between Steiner and everyone else may partly explain why the movement has been stable rather than highly dynamic. An additional cause may have been that, unlike other great spiritual edifices, the founding architecture of Anthroposophy's revelation and social structures was comprehensively complex, leaving relatively little scope for interpretive struggle. However, there are also external cultural reasons which explain why Anthroposophy has grown stably but not explosively (these are explored in chapter ten).

A further factor in the creditable but not exciting organisational growth of future Anthroposophy may tend to be generic to new cultic entities. Neither Steiner nor most of his followers had extensive prior experience of organisations, and of how it is very difficult to make them work well. The requirements for being a seer are not the same as the competencies required to be effective at the more sense-based aspects of organisational implementation. In Jungian terms – as expressed in the MBTI psychometric – it seems almost tautologous to suggest that seers are introverted intuitives. Admittedly, research has not led to general agreement about the traits required to be an effective leader, but rather has identified many different ones with, at the best, weak clusters.[21] However, this research has focused largely on business, military and other such organisations which do not have the revealed and total character of spiritual movements. Spiritual movements as a whole may tend to have implementation gaps. Though Steiner gave 'indications' about what might be developed he perhaps did not immediately appreciate quite how much task and relationship follow-up was required given the developmental distance between himself and his followers.[22]

Steiner's unassailable authority was and is preserved even in the loss of control apparently represented by his death. Both Blavatsky[23] and Steiner apparently stated that it would have been tantamount to black magic to use their occult powers to heal themselves of their very serious illnesses. Perhaps the reason why no diagnosis of Steiner's premature and shattering terminal illness has been publicized is that he saw illness as the symptom of a lack of spiritual harmony. As with the burning of the Goetheanum, the members were once again blamed (for putting him under strain). Otherwise it would have been all too possible to explore Steiner's spiritual deficiencies in the light of Anthroposophical medicine, or of his spiritual condition. Thus the idealisation of Steiner as a visionary continued to provide a focal point for the movement as a whole. Indeed, an initiate as great as he, some members seem to think, remains conscious as he goes into the spirit world after death.

The Phase of Schisms

Anthroposophy does not seem to flourish in authoritarian, intolerant societies. Through siting the Goetheanum in Switzerland, Steiner made it visible as a centre of peace and international freedom during the 1914-1918 war. It is doubtful whether it could have been built in Germany during these years. The liberal Weimar Republic seems to have coincided with a rise in membership, but the increasing totalitarianism of the 1930s led in the end to active persecution by the Nazis in the last years of the Second World War. This can be seen as the suppression of one occultism by another, that underlying much Nazi ideology.[24] Hitler, through his occultist espousal of ruthlessness of means (whether or not he personally believed his ends were good), can be interpreted in terms of black rather than white magic. Recovery and growth followed in the liberal democracy of post-war West Germany.

The conflict experienced in the Nazi years was accompanied by internal splits. As has been seen in relation to Theosophy in Wilhelminian Germany and Edwardian England, divisions within spiritual movements can have analogies with the situation outside. After the end of the Weimar Republic existing tensions led to a formal split within Anthroposophy: most of the German-speaking members separated from the others, even though the former were not Nazi. The unifying magnetism of Steiner had long been absent because of his early and unexpected demise. This exposed the cultural fault-line between the German-speaking and the increasing numbers of non-German-speaking members.

The slow growth of Anthroposophy since the First World War took place in an overall context, until the 1960s, of little if any growth for similar movements. The intellectual climate of the mid-twentieth century was relatively unfavourable to optimistic, spiritually evolutionist movements such as Theosophy. This had been easily the largest 'esoteric' system, with very many more members than Anthroposophy. Theosophy declined from the 1920s. This was speeded by Krishnamurti's (its reluctant World Teacher's) attitude of, 'Why did they ever pick on me?'[25]

Theosophy, until the emergence of Rudolf Steiner, had made little impact in the unique conditions of Germany, whose occultism and esotericism were not Anglo-Saxon. Yet Anthroposophy later spread in the English- and Dutch-speaking worlds when Theosophy declined. Theosophy lacked Anthroposophy's social embeddedness, as well as its intellectuality, apparent Christocentricity, applications and sense of community. By the 1930s the Dutch, English and other non-German-speaking memberships were no longer relatively insignificant. It was at this stage, despite the ordering of Anthroposophical social institutions which had been signified by the laying of the Foundation Stone, that the formal schisms occurred.

As has been suggested, the schisms, which took place between 1933 and 1935, were in many ways a reverse replay of the original Anthroposophical secession from Theosophy. Cultural legitimacy was with the loyalist German-speaking majority. Thus the first

English *Anthroposophic News Sheet* declared (at Michaelmas, 1933): 'Any translation can only imperfectly render Rudolf Steiner's words. May its imperfections induce readers to penetrate more and more into the German original'. The minorities, in breach of Steiner's constitutional ordinances, but following the Dutch and English Protestant traditions, set up 'United Free' Anthroposophical societies. In 1935 the great majority of Dutch and English members were expelled from the General Anthroposophical Society, by 1691 to 76 votes with 53 abstentions. Postal voting would have made no decisive subtraction from the German-speaking majority at this time. Meanwhile the European arena was building up to the 1939-1945 war.

The new President, the German-speaking poet Albert Steffen, presided over this period of internal conflict. After the shock of Steiner's death, his conservative-minded widow, who spoke no English, became the rallying point for the loyalist German speakers. Ita Wegman, the Dutch putative reincarnation of Gilgamesh, whose English was fluent, became a focus of dissent. She ran a clinic only a kilometre or so away from the Goetheanum at Arlesheim, but in another Anthroposophical world. Steffen was leading a movement which, with the death of Steiner, had passed beyond the stage of unifying charismatic leadership, and into one of bereavement, infighting over inheritance, and difficult self-definition. Steiner himself had once questioned 'the use of telling people over and over again that we are not a sect when we behave as though we were a sect'.[26]

The splits, which extended into the School of Spiritual Science, created a complex situation through leaving small minorities in each country affected. A very small but qualitatively important German-speaking group joined the dissidents. Less than a third of the Dutch membership remained loyal to the Goetheanum. This group was to grow more slowly than the dissident Dutch society. The English leader, Collison, remained loyal to the primary Anthroposophical body, together with a small minority of members who called themselves the 'English Section'. Collison himself saw the British Empire as the great stepping stone to a higher world consciousness. The roots of many of the 'English Section' seem to have been in the relatively conservative and imperially-minded Hermetic Order of the Golden Dawn. The other British Anthroposophists included pacifists and ex-Quakers.

The dissident Dutch included Ita Wegman and their General Secretary, Dr Zeylmans van Emmichoven. They appear to have increased their numbers considerably. At the end of the Second World War van Emmichoven took the initiative in trying to seek reconciliation with the primary Anthroposophical body through discussions with Steffen.

The dissident English Anthroposophists, led by the young Cecil Harwood, formed the carefully named 'Anthroposophical Society in Great Britain'. In 1930 total UK membership had been nearly 600. The movement appears to have become more communitarian and less metropolitan. It was comprehensible to Gandhi, who had himself been much influenced by Theosophy. On visiting a Rudolf Steiner children's home in 1935 he commented, 'no explanations are necessary'.[27] The Second World War was not a severe setback for English Anthroposophy because the movement, which in Germany was being increasingly put in the shadows by the Nazis, was not perceived as Nazi. The London headquarters was used as a canteen for H.M. Forces, whose numbers included members themselves.

There have been recent allegations that Anthroposophy in Germany was tainted by Nazism and racism. The claims, probably not from disinterested sources, state that Steiner's racial theories involve a small minority evolving, and that they link in with Hitler's. They suggest that, according to Anthroposophy, aboriginal peoples are descended from the already degenerate remnants of the third root race, the Lemurians, and are devolving into apes. It is further alleged that in 1922 Steiner said that the negro race does not belong in Europe, and that Anthroposophists today handle this not by outright denial that Steiner said this, nor by condemnation of him for saying it, but by explaining that Steiner was a product of his times In another, related controversy, it has been said that in 1937 Guenther Wachsmuth, a prominent Anthroposophist, expressed sympathy and admiration for National Socialism[28]. Furthermore, Weleda has been accused of having had state contracts throughout the war, and even of supplying naturopathic materials for experiments on prisoners at Dachau.

More generally, the allegations of racism are dealt with not only through mitigating admissions that Steiner reflected the mentality of his times. These other methods include denial[29] and the isolating of specific admissions through the claim that they are untypical. Indeed, given the Zeitgeist and the cultural proximity of German Anthroposophy to the often occult Nazi 'ecology' movement of blood and soil, it would be surprising if there were no compromising statements to quote. National Socialism and Anthroposophy, despite their fundamental differences, have in common an aversion to positivistic intellectualism. This reputedly was the basis for initial Nazi support for Waldorf (i.e. Anthroposophical) education. It is a good question how widespread

the Nazi mentality was among German Anthroposophists, and difficult
to assess how far Anthroposophy was less or more besmirched than
the general population in Germany, or than large sections of non-
German Europe and America where racist and anti-Semitic sentiments
were rife. Steiner, it seems, publicly rejected anti-Semitism. It is very
difficult to imagine Steiner agreeing, had he lived long enough, with
the abhorrent practical policies of the Nazis.

In 1930 the Anthroposophical President spoke of the need to purify
the ego 'of all that clings to it of a racial nature'.[30] Later, Jewish and
other members were emigrating, and the German Anthroposophical
Society itself was dissolved in 1935 on Himmler's orders, it seems
because it was international and individualistic. After 1936, the Swiss
Anthroposophists had to bear the brunt of financing the Goetheanum
because German contributions were blocked by the rigid Nazi
exchange controls. Rudolf Hess was apparently an Anthroposophist,
as was his wife.[31] But in 1941, when Hess was succeeded by Martin
Bormann following the former's journey to the UK, the many Steiner
schools were closed and Anthroposophical books were confiscated.
Himmler apparently viewed Anthroposophy as competition to his
own esoteric paganism.[32]

At this devastating time there was a further schism in the General
Anthroposophical Society at the Goetheanum. In 1942 its President
and Guenther Wachsmuth broke with Marie Steiner, accusing her of
using the copyright of Steiner's books too restrictively. The widow
was widely perceived to be using a subtle form of confiscation,
though she reconciled herself at about this time with Ita Wegman,
who died in 1943. On her death in 1948 Marie Steiner bequeathed
the copyright to Anthroposophical friends (the '*Nachlass* faction')
who were not members of the *Vorstand* (i.e. the overall Executive
Committee). The General Society tried to assert control over the
publication of Steiner's works but in 1950, after legal proceedings,
paid – without prejudice to its claims – 180,000 Swiss francs to the
legatees. The latter then rubbed salt in the wound by circulating a
pamphlet on the struggle.

Establishment

As already described, the 'Foundation Stone' laid by Steiner
at Christmas 1923 sanctified Anthroposophy's constitutional
arrangements. From these the 'United Free' schismatics had broken
loose. Because of their trust in Steiner they could not generally
justify their separate states. After the Second World War there

appears to have been considerable pressure from members in Dutch and British dissident societies to reunify according to the 1923 constitution.

The external conditions were more favourable than hitherto. With the restoration of liberal-democracy to West Germany, and to much of Europe west of the Iron Curtain, there came a steady expansion of membership. Also, the post-war economic boom seems to have stimulated the movement. Easy communications (latterly the internet), mass travel and European integration have resolved Europe's post-Charlemagne problem of political splits and economic tariffs. Anthroposophical members from different Western cultures have been enabled to identify with each other much more, and to develop specific applications, such as spiritual dance ('eurythmy'), the retail of special agricultural ('bio-dynamic') products and the making of 'Weleda' medications. The successful materialism of the consumer societies of the West produced sufficient public money for some of it to be used to subsidise Anthroposophical alternatives to the welfare state: for example, its 'Camphill' communities. At the same time, Anthroposophy benefited from the reaction against its paymaster, materialism, and against hedonism.

The Goetheanum itself is an example of this development of Anthroposophical infrastructure. In 1957 the Great Hall was at last completed. In 1963 donations and legacies to the General Society amounted to as much as 1,069,420 Swiss francs (though this was said to be exceptional). A Press Office opened there in 1965 and by 1970 there were two hundred salaried employees.

The post-war increase in Anthroposophical complexity seems to have made the German-speaking majority less comfortable in its assumptions. Mass education resulted in many new members, and these coincided with a post-war generation gap that made national differences less significant. The growth in American and other English-speaking memberships, particularly in the Camphill movement, together with the large Dutch and increasing Scandinavian following, placed Anthroposophy in a much more pluralistic environment.

The dissident Dutch, led by van Emmichoven for some years after the war, reconciled themselves to the primary Anthroposophical body and thereby the German-speaking majority without conditions. Eventually, in 1964-1965, Harwood, Chairman of the Anthroposophical Society in Great Britain, reluctantly also recognised the authority of the Goetheanum School of Spiritual Science. Konig, the leader/founder of the Anthroposophical Camphill movement, was reconciled through integrating the Camphill School of Spiritual

Science with the Schools of national societies whose allegiance was to the Goetheanum. The 1923 constitution was largely restored, though the *Nachlass* contention remained unresolved. Though Steiner's copyright expired in 1975, fifty years after his death, translation copyrights still continued, so the '*Nachlass* faction' (i.e. Marie Steiner's legatees) continued to exercise influence. However, by the mid-1980s bridges had been built and though some of the old animosities may still have lingered there was said to have been a strong will to be reconciled.

This new-found stability, as well as reflecting the outlook of individual decision-makers, probably has depended on the continuation of liberal-democracy in the wider cultures within which the movement is contained. It is unlikely to develop into the kind of tight millennialist organisation typical of many Protestant sects, such as the Jehovah's Witnesses, which separate humanity into the 'saved' (inside) and the 'damned'(outside). Instead, there is an ideal that spiritual consensus can permeate an inclusive social organism.

With the end of the cold war the pluralism within Anthroposophy continued to expand. In a sense, as with the emergence of email, the internet and multinational corporations, this is part of global pluralism. There are centrifugal forces of expansion far flung from the Anthroposophical centre in German-speaking Europe. English, the nearest to a common language, is second to most members' given language. Anthroposophical centres now exist throughout the world. In Asia and elsewhere they do not have implicit layers of Christianity as a common basis. The activities have also developed considerably as centres in their own right: indeed, they have often become contracted-out educational and other agencies for various governmental bodies. Also there are many influenced by Steiner's spirituality and the Anthroposophical way of life who do not join as explicit members.

The centripetal reaction has been to assert the legitimacy of the Christmas Foundation meeting and of the General Anthroposophical Society as ordained by Steiner. This is to counteract 'Anthroposophical' social forms whose Anthroposophy is diluted. Many members focus more on participating in externally sourced opportunities which if not embraced may become threats. For example, there have been powerful global movements, based on evidence-based practice research, requiring the registration of therapies such as those operating from an Anthroposophical basis. There are many opportunities to gain state funding for Waldorf and curative education.

A credible globalism has been developing, with a long-term

moving average of sustainable growth. Some of the less tangible aspirations in rapidly expanding world economies have been met by Anthroposophy.

Anthroposophy appears to have overtaken Theosophy to become a more numerous and significant contemporary Western 'esotericism'. Though total Theosophical membership in 1981 was officially estimated to be as high as 34,421 (compared to about 35,800 in 1980 for Anthroposophy), it had less community and its followers were then probably relatively elderly. Except for New Zealand, there was a marked decline since 1925 in Theosophical English-speaking and Northern European membership.[33] In 1981 over 10,000 Theosophists lived in India, an increase since 1925 of approaching 60 per cent. In 1925 there had been nearly 42,000 Theosophical members from forty-one national societies; by about the end of the 1920s the membership had shrunk to around 33,000. At one point there had been six Theosophical members of the House of Commons.[34] In the UK Theosophical membership figures intersected with Anthroposophy's in the early 1980s (at about 2,300-2,400). There were many small UK Theosophical units, or 'Lodges'. As a result, there was little of the larger scale to retain younger recruits, though quite a number were initially interested. In England in the early 1980s about half of Theosophists were over sixty years old and nearly all the remainder seemed to be above thirty. About a third lived in London. There were signs of renewal amidst Theosophy at this time, accompanied by a move to go back beyond Besant to Blavatsky. It appears unlikely, however, that any revived Theosophy could develop the applications and community that, as we shall see next, Anthroposophy has achieved.

3. How the Movement is Organised

A starlit or a moonlit dome disdains
All that man is,
All mere complexities,
The fury and the mire of human veins.[1]
    – W.B. Yeats, *'Byzantium'*

This chapter focuses on how the recent movement is organised. In the course of doing so it provides layered snapshots of membership, especially one taken in the early 2000s and another in the early 1980s.

The School of Spiritual Science and the 'First Class'

Not all Anthroposophists are visionaries but probably all acknowledge the legitimacy of vision. They generally aspire to become aware of 'etheric', 'astral' and other spiritual essences that, according to Steiner, transcend and in part at least infuse the world. The collective aspect of this striving tends to be concentrated in the School of Spiritual Science: it, more than any other social organ, is designed to be at the centre of the movement, the connecting corolla for its petals.

Steiner gave specific directions for spiritual research. The School of Spiritual Science has 'sections' for research to advance Anthroposophical education, natural science, mathematics and astronomy, medicine, social science, the appreciation of beauty, the appreciation of the plastic and visual arts and architecture, speaking, drama, eurythmy and music, painting and modelling, and the understanding of young people. The school has also been related to professional philosophy, psychiatry and psychology.[2] Steiner made provision for three Classes. Only one – the 'First Class' – is known to be in operation. There are no special conditions demanded for membership of the General Anthroposophical Society, which is exoteric and concerned with the external governance and arrangements of the movement. But the door of the First Class is not opened to everyone, and not all members wish to belong to it. Probably 10 to 30 per cent of recent General Society members have belonged to this inner society which, to outsiders, appears mysterious.

At least two years' affiliation to the General Society is a pre-condition for joining. Also, 'inner responsibility' for Anthroposophy has to be accepted. Rudolf Steiner, who was distressed at the state of the movement, founded the First Class in 1923 as an organ of regeneration. Anthroposophists stress the individual taking responsibility, in contrast to the old mysteries where the neophyte was deemed ready by the hierophant and taken through a process controlled by others. In Anthroposophy you have to know for yourself when you are ready to start. The regenerating source is believed not to be accessed through a priest, temple, guru or Rudolf Steiner, but through yourself.

The First Class adapts Steiner's meditative path for individuals. The latter is generally available in publications such as *Occult Science* and *Knowledge of the Higher Worlds*.[3] However, only the place and times of meetings of local branches of the School of Spiritual Science are published, together with the number of the 'Lesson' concerned (there is a cycle of 19). Members of this elite are pledged to secrecy, a vow which is usually strictly observed. I had no success when I asked for information about the mantras of the First Class: I was told that they 'belong to the School'. The nineteen Lessons of the First Class contain mantras from Steiner and his own commentaries on them. When as an outsider I asked questions about them (or the commentaries on them), this was one of the few acts that would, almost predictably, incur annoyance. Recently, however, and without authorisation, the 'Stunden' or Lessons of the 'erste Klasse' or First Class have been released in German on the internet, accompanied by arguments about the need for openness. They can also be purchased, though this is for a considerable sum of money (about £200 GBP).

Insiders have not perceived the First Class as secretive. Its authority is implicit; it is seen in terms of colleagueship, spontaneity and openness. The classes in the late 1970s, adjusting to the spirit of the times, were said to be intended as 'happenings' and Steiner was emphatic that his mantras, which are understood as 'given by the spirit of our time', should move from mouth to ear as 'living speech'. Recently there has been a practice of 'free holding' or free presentation out of one's individual work with the verses to encourage greater participation and thus esoteric deepening. Anthroposophists do not generally think in terms of the School's hierarchical power but see it as striving – and sometimes as stumbling – in the search for understanding and truth.

The dilemma is as old as that of religious renewal: what from the outside is seen as cultural elitism tends both to keep inspiration 'pure' and to inhibit it. Preserving a social boundary helps avoid trivialisation, but the price paid is the exclusion of outside creativity and thought. The power of the Lessons as agents of spiritual rebirth seems not so much intrinsic in the printed material, which appears unexceptional, as dependent on having a contained, spiritual context for study, sacred boundaries and engaged personal preparation building up to it.

To illustrate this let us take what purports to be an example. This is available in English translation. It starts almost immediately with a mantra. The first four lines:

> O man, know thou thyself!
> Thus sounds the cosmic word.
> Thou hearest it strong-in-soul,
> Thou feelest it mighty-in-spirit.

These and further mantras are contained within a lecture (Lesson 17) given by Steiner. The general content appears to have a great deal in common with the meditative path already generally available to the non-Anthroposophical public. Thus the lecture later refers frequently to the Spiritual Hierarchies and the Guardian of the Threshold, and contains comments such as matter is empty nothingness, spirit shines in matter and that the Being of Christ in the death of matter wakens spirit-birth.

Around the turn of the century Steiner himself was accused of betraying 'esoteric' secrets. He replied that the age required that they should be made public to those who had reached the stage of higher education. It was later, when he established his own inner circle, that he enjoined secrecy. The closed system means that no effective defence can be made against damaging allegations. Thus a serious Scandinavian researcher told me authoritatively that Tantric sex yoga is practised. Anthroposophists refute charges that Steiner himself experimented with sexual magic. Later strong denials to me by members of the School may necessarily have lacked evidence in support, but there is no reason to suppose that leading Anthroposophists are dishonest about such a matter. As has been seen, those apparent Lessons which have found their way out give no support to the sexual magic hypothesis.

The closed system also perpetuates the dominance of Steiner as 'the' seer. It is not open to outside scrutiny and thereby forced to adapt to criticism. Members of the school are, no doubt, already committed to Anthroposophy as objective truth. Anthroposophy is understood inclusively, as in the following insider's definition: Anthroposophy is the experience that the human being, motivated by love for truth, can know himself/herself and the world through the application of thinking and self-reflection. Yet the 'undogmatic' spiritual research which is the School's explicit aim seems at some level to be latently modeled on Steiner's clairvoyance. This could include the recent practice of 'free holding', or free rendering of the texts, though it might also lead to schism. An implicit inhibition on deviant thought – or, at least, its external expression – may encourage emotional dependence on the founder.

An advantage of this apparent absence of epistemological individualism is the tendency for the School, however much criticised, to be the authoritative and cohesive force of the movement. Centred on the sacred Goetheanum, it seems to be the main focus of direction-making and decision-taking. It has a hierarchical structure, the local branches being headed by 'readers', who have their own 'circle'. Emotional identification is helped through the use of sympathetic educational terminology: the 'School' of Spiritual Science, the 'First Class', 'Lessons'. I was told it was analogous to a 'university' and that its aim was 'development and research'.

It takes almost two years to go through the entire cycle of Lessons when there is a lesson each month. Because the Class members may not feel the continuity between the Lessons, and because attendance may have to be irregular for external reasons, in 2005 an intensive conference was held at the Goetheanum, taking only a week. All nineteen lessons were covered. The event was for First Class members only and there was no fee for the conference itself, as contrasted with food and lodging (the principle is that the substance cannot be bought). Members needed to bring a 'blue Class certificate' with them. The flier stated synaesthetically:

> Each morning, after a short transition pause, we will see silent eurythmy compositions inspired from the Class Lesson. Through the eurythmy something of the substance of the mantra is shown in movement-pictures. You can perceive the mantric verse as it were behind the sequence of movements that are shown. The composition in movement unfolds in clearly differentiated zones, following the form of the verses in the respective zones of the etheric, the soul and the spirit. The inner process is brought out in the various colours, in the differentiated forms in space; and in the gestures of the sounds and the soul-gestures.

Before dying unexpectedly in 1925 Steiner is said to have intended to found a 'Second' and 'Third' Class. There was a rumour – which was also denied – that a Second Class was being established. No such classes, however, apparently exist. As part of their striving, Anthroposophists try to understand what a Second and Third Class might have been like. There seem to be no indications from Steiner on this.

The General and National Anthroposophical Societies

While the most exclusive institution is the School of Spiritual Science, the most inclusive is the General Anthroposophical Society.[4] Members of national societies also have to belong to the General Society. Its constitution specifically bars discrimination on the grounds of nationality, social standing, or religious, scientific or artistic convictions.[5]

General Society members numbered approximately 49,300 members in early 2006, and are said to have numbered 50,942 in 2004 and 52,000 in 2001, a level which was more or less constant over the preceding five years. The figure was about 47,000 in 1990, about 35,800 in 1980, and in Rudolf Steiner's day seems to have been about 12,000. Recent overall General Society membership figures seem to combine a recent settling down in numbers in Europe with expansion in Asia and much of the third world. The General Society's financial turnover in 2005 seems to have been about 30 million Swiss francs, which was then convertible to nearly 23 million US dollars or about 13.75 million UK pounds. In financial terms this is roughly comparable to a small to medium sized corporation.

The President and executive council (the *Vorstand*) are proposed and appointed as a group, members having the right to vote against nominations. The *Vorstand* are usually prominent in the First Class. There is provision for the taking of major decisions, other than those affecting the School of Spiritual Science, on the basis of one member, one vote (the rules have implied that physical presence is a requirement). Thus some liberal-democratic procedures are formally observed in the external governance of the movement. Underlying this there is belief in the need for spiritual solidarity. For several decades, the national societies (after the healing of schisms) have recognized the supremacy of the School of Spiritual Science at the Goetheanum.

The national societies usually model themselves on the General Anthroposophical Society. The largest German speaking societies have been those of West Germany and Switzerland. Those of the UK and USA have been the most numerous in the English speaking world. The Dutch society has also been relatively large. The total membership figures for the General Society are not immediately available to non-members. National societies such as the West German have also been reticent about membership numbers. This may be partly because the time predicted by Steiner 'when Anthroposophists are reckoned by millions and not by thousands'[6] has not arrived yet. Still, though it is now over 80 years since he died, some consolation for disconsolate Anthroposophists may be found in patterns of the early growth of religions such as Christianity, which are not necessarily discouraging in the long term despite such a high volume prediction. It is also worth remembering that the number of people whose lives are based on Steiner's revelation is much greater than the membership figures. Not only are there members of the Steiner schools, the Camphill movement and the Christian Community (to be explained later in this chapter) who are not in addition members of their national societies, but there are also many people, sometimes including the most committed, who do not wish to join formally, often because they see any organisation as tarnished. A further significant point, which will be explored towards the end of this book, is that 'religious' (using this term very broadly) identities which are perceived as transcendent or dualistic contemporarily have a lower volume of recruits than those which are perceived as monistic. The latter are often mysticisms which adjust easily to consumerism, materialism, mass media manipulation and other dominant features of the spirit of the times.

Rudolf Steiner, a native Austrian, largely addressed himself in German dialect to Germans. Schisms after Steiner's death broadly followed a pattern of cultural and national divide between, on the one hand, German speakers and, on the other, those who spoke English or Dutch. Over the past century, especially with the development of the Camphill movement and US Anthroposophy, English-speaking members came to exert increasing influence, though the largest membership group was still native German speaking. Increasingly there were many people working at the Goetheanum trying to bridge cultural gaps. One particular issue has been the lack of provision for a postal or proxy vote (the lack of immediate presence being considered unspiritual). Members' physical presence at the Goetheanum for the annual meeting is and has been necessary if they wish to cast General Society votes. This historically has favoured the Swiss and West German members at the expense of the Dutch and English speakers, and has been an increasingly difficult issue given the post-War expansion of Anthroposophy in North America and globally.

The potential for disharmony through cultural differences may have increased along with global membership. This was the case even within a North Atlantic frame. A much-traveled German Anthroposophist told me that for German members it is very important to come to a clarity of ideas: 'You can't have supper unless you've solved it'. In the English movement, I was told, 'sympathy', 'antipathy' and 'getting on with people' matter, while all American Anthroposophists are interested in 'is whether the idea works; they don't mind if they get on with people'. Similar differences also appear in contemporary multinational businesses.

A further difference is generational. The generation that knew Steiner is dead, and it is said that contemporary Anthroposophical teachers are not looked up to as much as the generation of teachers that experienced him had been. 20-30 year olds do not have the same language as Steiner. They may be totally accepting of a spiritual perspective, with reincarnation a firsthand experience, but often have a radical or anarchistic attitude to form.

Worldwide, many people have been deeply influenced by Steiner through the many activities or through books yet are not formally members of the General Anthroposophical Society. Indeed, a great many third and fourth generation followers seem to be reaching out more towards like-minded non-Anthroposophists and to be making bridges with the outside world. Given this context, Sergei Prokofieff, a controversial Russian now on the *Vorstand*, has uncompromisingly stressed the importance of the '1923-24 Christmas Foundation Conference' (Anthroposophically shortened to the '1924 Foundation event'). This was the moment when Steiner personally joined the society and so is the central expression of its 'incarnation'. Prokofieff places strong emphasis on the need for explicit joining. This is a reaction to the centrifugal forces diversifying Anthroposophical activities, to spiritual globalisation which involves expansion outside Europe and a sense of confusion within it (similar to these areas' recent economies), and to diffuse allegiance in a pluralistic world.

A related issue is language. Though German speakers still constitute by far the largest national memberships, they are not a numerical majority. English, not German, is the unifying language; but for most it is a second tongue. Underlying linguistic differences are likely to be considerably more problematic for a spiritual movement than they are for organisations with more tangible purposes, such as those where success is measured principally by financial outputs.

Valid numerical perspectives on Anthroposophy have not been easy to piece together. Published information often did not state the context. My letters in the early 1980s to national societies (other than the Canadian and American) were generally unanswered. Informed sources disagreed on emphasis and, sometimes, facts. The information that follows, contemporary and past, may contain considerable inaccuracies.[7]

German-speaking Anthroposophy

The *Anthroposophische Gesellschaft in Deutschland* or Anthroposophical Society in Germany – an entity that was not amended to take account of the political post-war partition of Germany – had 19,280 members in 2001, a more or less static figure over the preceding five years, but a large increase from what seems to have been about 9,000 members in the early 1980s. The movement in Germany has tended to be regionalized around Hamburg, Munich, Stuttgart and Baden-Württemberg generally.

In Baden-Württemberg, the largest Anthroposophical concentration, there were probably over 2,000 members by the early 1980s. These included about fifty doctors of medicine (both Anthroposophically and conventionally qualified, it seems) and several clinics. 'Waldorf' education, named after the benefactor who enabled it to be founded in 1919, the owner of the Waldorf-Astoria cigarette factory in Stuttgart, has been especially strong here. It seems to have been some of these followers of Rudolf Steiner who some time ago disparagingly informed other esotericists, who like Anthroposophists claimed to be Rosicrucian, that they were *pseudo*-Rosicrucians.[8] The latter were building a Rosicrucian temple at neighbouring Calw in memory of J.V. Andreae (see chapter seven), one of the leading spirits of the Rosy Cross movement in the seventeenth century.

A further glimpse into the historical context of German Anthroposophy is given by the following story.[9] On the Western front during the First World War one soldier carried a copy of Goethe's *Faust* in his field-bag until, on his final wounding in 1918, it was destroyed. In his letters home he mentioned his loss. One day, while still in military hospital, he received (by the army post) literature about the *Wandervogel*, the German youth movement, and some material written by Rudolf Steiner. They became personal friends. 'Rudolf Steiner's personality was incredibly strong, he was so modest, so simple, so clear', this man said in 1982, just before his death. He had spent his life as an Anthroposophical 'bio-dynamic' farmer, an act of restoration influenced by the use of poison gas on the land while he was a soldier.

Many outsiders erroneously suppose that Steiner was an 'educationalist', rather like Froebel, without realising that the core of the movement is his spiritual science. 'Waldorf' education is the most visible application of Anthroposophy, especially in West Germany, where by the early 1980s there were about 110 kindergartens and over 70 schools. (The Netherlands, the next most numerous country, then had over 40 schools.) In 1975 Waldorf education accounted for as much as 6.4 per cent of the total population of West German independent schools. The demand was said to exceed supply by a factor of three to five times. Three or more Waldorf schools were for mentally handicapped children, and others offered special classes for them. As far as possible, fees have been charged according to capacity to pay. Teachers have sometimes renounced part of their salaries: thus the Free Waldorf School in Kassel once saved DM 420,000 during a school year.

Waldorf education was prohibited by the Nazis but spread remarkably since 1945. In 1956 there were 12,432 West German pupils; in 1965, 13,147; in 1975, 20,797 (including 600 handicapped pupils); and there were as many as 32,250 in 1981. In 1978 Baden-Württemberg had well over 8,000 pupils, Northrhine-Westphalia just over 5,000 and Lower Saxony, Hesse and Bavaria about 2,000 each. Hamburg had 1,340 pupils.[10] Thus the outreach of Anthroposophy is far larger than its membership figures suggest.

In West Germany, and probably elsewhere, the children are apparently secluded as far as possible from the disrupting influences of modern society. 'It is the intention of Waldorf pedagogues to let their children grow up in the unspotted faith of a good world without being disturbed.'[11] The love and communal warmth do not foster critical ability or a competitive cast of mind in pupils. 'The trainers in small as well as big companies have no idea what to do with them.'[12] Yet even in West Germany, where most if not all the teachers seem to be Anthroposophists, Steiner's revelation is not taught directly.

The movement is well-known throughout West Germany. Christian Morgenstern, Bruno Walter and Joseph Beuys have been stated to be supporters. From its stronghold in Baden-Württemberg, which was relatively undevastated by the Second World War, West German Anthroposophy expanded considerably during the West German 'economic miracle'. Nevertheless, there has seemed to be some defensiveness and fear of hostility despite its well established niche.[13]

The Swiss society has in many ways seemed to be identified with the West German. It had 5,201 members in 2001, a decline of about nine per cent over the previous five years, but many more than the probable 2,500-3,000 members in the early 1980s. The Swiss figures do not include the Anthroposophists in the Goetheanum, which is located in Switzerland. By the 1980s there were over twenty Swiss schools, with three in Basle and two in Zurich. All but four had local kindergartens. In addition, there has been the small dissident group, the '*Nachlass*' faction, who were the inheritors of old strife (see chapter two). The national society is put in the shade by the sacred presence of the Goetheanum.

A seer, like a prophet, can be relatively without honour in his own country: Austria, which Steiner left for Germany when nearly thirty, had only about three schools (two with local kindergartens) and few members in the early 1980s. Its membership in the early 2000s is unclear.

English-speaking Anthroposophy

Everyone was hanging on the words of an aged Vera Compton-Burnett when she described how as a young girl she left Blavatsky's Theosophical Society after travelling to the Goetheanum and experiencing its 'very foreign atmosphere'. In some ways the Anthroposophical Society in Great Britain in the twentieth century appeared to be backwards looking. The North American, Dutch, German and Swiss societies seem to have had more in common with each other than they had with an insular British membership.

There were 2,995 members in 2001, a figure which was more or less constant over the previous five years, and an increase from membership of about 2,400 in the early 1980s and, there is some reason to believe, about 2000 in 1974/5. Nevertheless there are said to be relatively few 20-30 year olds as members. It is also believed that many UK members prefer to affiliate directly with the Anthroposophical Society at the Goetheanum, bypassing the Anthroposophical Society in GB. The main clusters have been at Forest Row, Sussex, and in Gloucestershire. Many members lived in suburban King's Langley and around or in Bristol, Sheffield and Manchester. By 1982 only 172 lived in London postal districts and only about four in central London. Those who belong to 'Camphill' communities (to be explained later in this chapter) have daytime occupations which are explicitly Anthroposophical.

The increase in membership may have some connection with the tendency towards greater community in British Anthroposophy. The rapid expansion of the Camphill movement has been the main example of this. In the early 1980s its twenty or so UK communities may have accounted for between 500 to 1,000 of the 2,400 members then (only anecdotal information has been available). On the other hand there were perhaps around a thousand members who had little if any contact with the organized movement.[14]

In the late 1970s there had been considerable differences between Anthroposophists at the age, about thirty, of the eighteen converts described in the appendix (about my age at the time), and those who were a generation older. The latter seemed more polarised in their responses, perhaps because I then came from the younger, 'counter-culture' generation. Some of them were unwelcoming to my research interest: closed, anxious and controlling, a few tried to convert me, divert me, or both. Others were open, generous and full of character. Pragmatism was often curiously mingled with unusual ideas.

I was told: 'Sound common sense, [Steiner] said, will confirm ... The real Rosicrucians still obey the rule to keep themselves anonymous ... I believe in a physical Grail south of the Pyrenees.' People would talk about 'mystery schools' in the same matter of fact tone in which they might discuss making onion soup. Often the personas associated with managerial or professional occupations would be pronounced. In terms of the secular mindset of roles, older generation wives did not seem to have found much liberation through Anthroposophy. One younger member told me, 'Some older members, especially women, have studied Rudolf Steiner but are not what I'd call thinkers.' Often the most creative of this generation were German expatriates who had escaped the Nazis. Many had adopted English names. This often had not extended to English ways of thinking and these members seemed generally more theoretical and metaphysical.

Anthroposophy in the UK has moved with the times. Unsurprisingly the generation that in the late 1970s was most aged appeared to reflect various cultural forms of the inter-war period. The late Chairman, Cecil Harwood, was associated with the Oxford 'Inklings', the writing and social circle comprising J.R.R. Tolkien, C.S. Lewis and Owen Barfield, who was also an Anthroposophist. Harwood, the 'doyen of Anthroposophists', offered me the use of his house for my research though he scarcely knew me. In the 1930s many members were ex-Quakers, radicals and pacifists with sandals and rucksacks. Earlier Anthroposophists had also included an officer from the Black Watch and numerous governess-educated ladies. The typical member born after the Second World War, an elderly Anthroposophist told me, was from the 'grammar school type of family, not necessarily paying' (comprehensive schools were not well established then).

This places them in the British educational system then as intelligent children, probably from a background valuing education, who in the competitive examination for eleven year old state school children performed successfully and as a consequence went to the prestigious state grammar schools. They tended to be ambivalent about the old-world aura of past leaders. They also appeared to feel that the dynamic Camphill movement leaders, together with many readers and other members of the School of Spiritual Science, had the most charisma and spiritual impulse. They were disillusioned with other influential Anthroposophical figures then (in the mid 1970s) in late middle age.

All assemblies take place in Rudolf Steiner House in London, where hardly any members live; and, as at the Goetheanum, voting had only been for those physically present at the meeting. Active Anthroposophists not yet in their sixties usually could not afford the time and money involved in travelling to London. Council members themselves had to journey to Rudolf Steiner House in Baker St, London, yet after having travelled they were then sometimes thought of as reflecting metropolitan attitudes.[15] The six or so Council members I met then appeared to me to be shrewder and more cautiously worldly-wise than most of their Anthroposophical critics, and yet also idealistic, like almost all members. None seemed to be individually independent of Steiner: the consensus was, 'I only disagree with Steiner in my incompetence'.

The post-war US presence has in several ways been more dynamic than the UK one. The USA had 4,184 members in 2001, an increase of nearly 16 per cent from 1996 (3,609 members), and a considerable increase from the 2,400 or so members in the early 1980s. Membership has expanded greatly since the Second World War, overtaking that of the UK. By 2003 about 100 members lived in Chicago, Saul Bellow reputedly among them. In 2005 there were said to be around 800 Anthroposophical initiatives, such as schools and farms, in the US and Canada. The schools numbered about 52 by the early 1980s. Either in the Association of Waldorf Schools or in those purporting to be Waldorf schools, they were in the front line of the advance. The UK, because of the adverse tax and grant structure, then had only about sixteen schools, many of them small (however, there has been a financial incentive to care for disabled children and adults). Through Ralph Waldo Emerson, the US has also provided the name of an important educational and spiritual training centre, Emerson College, which is in Forest Row, England. This was through the influence of its founder, Francis Edmunds.

Saul Bellow has given a vivid impression of Anthroposophy's meaning in the context of the US in his *Humboldt's Gift*, where it acts as an other-worldly contrast to the culture of materialism, manipulation and criminality from which the protagonist, Charles Citrine, is attempting to extricate himself. Anthroposophists are spread now throughout the US with, for example, clusters in Ann Arbor (Michigan), Sacramento (California), Spring Valley (New York State), Detroit (Michigan) and Chicago (Illinois). Around 1980 most members probably lived in the East Coast states. Spring Valley, bought with an inheritance after the Second World War, was said to be 'bubbling with energy': it had a full school, eurythmy, a 'fellowship' (or retirement home for old people), a press, and a centre for 'Weleda' (or Anthroposophical) medicines. Property in Harlemville, a village bordering on Massachusetts, was bought so that children in New York City could have a place in the country. There have been other activities in New York state and New Hampshire. These included, as an integral part of Anthroposophical living, an attempt to establish a local currency based on windmill energy. By the early 1980s there was also a considerable Anthroposophical presence in California (in San Francisco, Los Angeles, Fair Oaks, Carmichael and Sacramento). There were also Rudolf Steiner centres in Washington DC, Pennsylvania, Colorado, and Hawaii, and three or four biodynamic farms in Wisconsin.

Canada had 458 members in 2001, a 30 per cent increase from the 350 or so members in the early 1980s. By then there were at least five schools. These were in Toronto, where a centre for adult education was also being set up, Vancouver, Quebec (a French-speaking school), Ottawa and London (Ontario). Edmonton has also had a centre.

In 2001, Australia had 559 members, a decline of 28 per cent from the 783 members in 1996, but a considerable increase on the 200 to 300 members of the early 1980s. The first Australian Steiner school was established in Sydney in 1962. Since then a centre for adult drama and three homes for mentally disabled children have been added. In New Zealand, two rich ladies with a sheep farm started a school in Hastings, and schools in Auckland, Christchurch and Wellington developed. By 2005 it had about 21 schools.

South Africa in 2005 had 20 Waldorf schools, all of which are said to be racially integrated, though many are in black settlement areas and so have mainly black pupils. There are also two training centres including Novalis Ubuntu, eleven biodynamic farms and four Camphill communities. It seems that black South Africans are not interested in becoming Anthroposophists. It is said that part of the reason is because they feel they have never lost contact with the spiritual. As might be expected the three main centres in South Africa have been Johannesburg, Cape Town, and Durban. In the apartheid era there were only a handful of Afrikaans members. The largest group was English-speaking. Traditionally there was a strong German influence. There were then no black or, it seems, coloured (i.e. what the apartheid regime defined as mixed race) members. I was then told this was not because of conscious exclusion but because of the enormous culture gap. Only the schools in Cape Town had permission to take in coloured or black children; in one of the schools in the early 1980s they each made up about an eighth of the total pupil number, though elsewhere the proportion was much lower. The Camphill movement saw itself as helping to break down racial barriers in South Africa, because it made it possible for whites to work directly on the land. There appears to have been nothing in the General Anthroposophical Society's constitution (drawn up in the racist Europe of the early twentieth century) which is racially discriminatory or specifically non-discriminatory. It appeared that most members in the early 1980s outside South Africa felt that the movement's spirit was opposed to apartheid.

Other Anthroposophy

The Netherlands in 2001 had 4,370 members, down eleven percent from the 1996 figure of 4,915 but up significantly from its 3,500 or so members in the early 1980s. By this earliest date it had over forty schools, and a successful youth movement. The Dutch have been especially successful in bringing Steiner's utopian and visionary plan for the future reconstitution of Europe, his 'Threefold Commonwealth', down closer to earth. Dr Lievegoed, a child psychologist, adopted a piecemeal approach in founding the NPI (the Netherlands Pedagogical Institute) in 1954. His concern in the 1960s that the society had closed forms led to a youth movement initiative.

A higher proportion of Dutch members than of those in the USA and UK seem to have been connected with commerce and industry; also, there have probably been more academics. The movement here, as elsewhere, has been very largely middle class. The Dutch medical side has been strong. One of the leading Anthroposophical doctors, Ita Wegman, was a close associate of Rudolf Steiner's, and Dr Zeylmans van Emmichoven, General Secretary from 1923, was a pioneer in Anthroposophical care of the soul (psychology in an etymologically pure sense).

The greatest concentration of numbers has been at Zeyst and nearby Driebergen. The NPI with its twenty-five to thirty senior workers has been based here. There have also been various businesses, such as the export of bio-dynamic food under the name of 'Aquarius'. Some charities, churches and other non-Anthroposophical organizations apparently used the 'Triodos' bank, an Anthroposophical organization which works with sister Rudolf Steiner institutions in the UK and elsewhere.

French-speaking members had been described to me as factual, specific and not so touched by the spirit of Anthroposophy. Data about French membership have not been available and membership numbers seem to be relatively small. In the early 1980s there were only about seven schools. Its membership in 1987-1988 was said to have been around 1,300.

Sweden in 2001 had 1,150 members, down 15 per cent from the 1996 figure of 1,357, but very much up – possibly because it has merged with the Finnish Society – from the membership numbers (said to have been 350 to 400) of the early 1980s. Even then it was a significant following for the North European country that seemed to have been least affected by the upsurge of cults and sects in the preceding decades. There were then about ten schools and a thriving, beautiful and famous adult education centre, based on Scandinavian languages, at Yärna. It is now said to be in decline. Norway had 916 members in 2001, and as many as 1,049 in 1996. Denmark and Norway, both with about ten schools each, probably had 250 or more members each in the early 1980s. There were three schools in Finland by the early 1980s, and Anthroposophy is said to be rather conspicuous in this culture with its overwhelming Lutheran roots. Anthroposophy in Scandinavia has been reported to be relatively well known and less overtly esoteric than elsewhere.

Italy had 1,305 members in 2001, up 19 per cent from the 1996 figure of 1,095, and it seems greatly up from the early 1980s. Catholic cultures such as Spain and Italy seemed to have had only a very few members then, though the combination of Vatican II and political liberalisation appear to have been favourable for the development of Anthroposophy.

In 2001 the major European plus the English speaking societies' membership – Australia, Canada, Germany, Great Britain, Netherlands, Italy, Norway, Sweden, Switzerland, and the USA – totalled 40,418 members (in 1996 the figure was 41,447). This leaves 11,785 members unaccounted for (11,410 in 1996). There are now said to be over 70 national Anthroposophical societies. One of the features of the past thirty years seems to have been a considerable geographical expansion of Anthroposophy. The provision of schools, sometimes accompanied by controversy over state funding, is a major aspect of this expansion.

Anthroposophy appears to have grown, or at least emerged, strongly in the past two decades in many of the old Iron Curtain countries. Behind the Iron Curtain, in post-Christian states which were totalitarian and officially atheistic, membership was apparently tiny, atomised and clandestine. Andrei Tarkosky, the Russian film director, is believed to have been interested. In the past two decades the charismatic Russian Anthroposophist, Sergei Prokofieff, has emerged. He has been criticised on the grounds that Rudolf Steiner based his path on reverence for truth and knowledge, not on reverence for him personally. New mutations of Anthroposophy and also Theosophy are said to have grown in Russia in the 1990s. A small Estonian society kept going during the communist era. Poland was said in 2004 to have three Waldorf schools. Membership in Hungary has reputedly grown strongly since 1989, the schools expanding the most: in 2004 there were said to be 17 Waldorf schools and 40 kindergartens.

Anthroposophy has grown in South America since the early 1980s. There was then a society in Mexico. Argentina had two schools in Buenos Aires and about 100 members. There was a strong medical movement in Brazil and a following of about 200 to 250. The former German-speaking school in Sao Paulo spoke Brazilian by the early 1980s, and had been supplemented by another. Ecuador, Chile, Columbia and Uruguay had one school each.

A 'Schools in Asia-Pacific' regional conference was founded in 1994-1996 as part of the 'Asia-Pacific Round Table'. Representatives came from Taiwan, the Philippines, India, Malaysia, Hong Kong, Singapore, Japan, Thailand and Nepal. There has also been expansion in Africa: an East African Waldorf Conference held in 2004 or 2005 had about 130 attendees.[16] In Israel in 2004 there were ten second year students at the Jerusalem Eurythmy Academy.[17] Economic development appears to favour Anthroposophical growth in educational and other areas.

Since the 1920s Anthroposophy has gradually grown in India and neighbouring countries. The Theosophical Society, which has a close involvement with India, seems to have had a following there of over 10,000 in the early 1980s. Though the Rudolf Steiner movement sprang from Theosophy organisationally, it has had no strong connection with India. The few members there were described as more Hindu than Anthroposophical. Elsewhere in the Third World there seemed in the early 1980s to be virtually no genuine following.[18] Apparently there were a few members then in Lebanon, and also Japan, where cults and sects have proliferated since the Second World War. Clearly the situation has subsequently changed. Schools of Spiritual Science are active in Japan, the Philippines and Thailand. Waldorf education is being integrated into local culture: 'it helps that lofty beings like Christ or Michael are known by other names'.[19] In 2004 close to 70 representatives from Taiwan alone met in Taipei to build a bridge across the various fields of work.[20] The first Waldorf Chinese kindergarten opened in Chengdu in 2004.[21] Chinese Waldorf teachers are researching how to integrate Anthroposophical thinking with Chinese tradition, its prescriptive curriculum for schools, and its current materialism.

Thus Anthroposophical global growth has been considerable over the past decades, with a discernible but undramatic Western European, North American, South African and Australian numerical decline in the past five years. As has been stated, activities such as education seem to be at the heart of Anthroposophy's effective outreach. Yet as described earlier there is a sense of disappointment among Anthroposophists. This is because Steiner had expected the membership to grow more rapidly, apparently mentioning on one occasion the figure of seven million.[22]

The Camphill communities

The Camphill movement has provided village communities and some urban houses for people who need 'special care' (such as handicapped children and adults). It started as a home for mentally handicapped children in the UK at Camphill, on the east coast of Scotland, and was based on Rudolf Steiner's revelation by the charismatic founder, Dr Konig, who died in 1966. From the 1950s there was vigorous expansion. In 2005 there were 90 communities in 20 countries. 47 were in the UK and Republic of Ireland, 20 in Europe/Asia (about twelve in Germany), nine in North America.[23] By about 1980 there had been over 60 communities. In 1981 there were about eight Camphill organizations in Scotland, about nineteen in England and Wales, and two each in Northern Ireland and Eire; there were about five in the USA and four in South Africa, plus one in Botswana; also, the movement had spread significantly to German-speaking countries, with about eight communities in Germany, three in Switzerland and two in Austria. There were as many as five in

Norway, but only one in the Netherlands, where Anthroposophy was already very strong in its social applications.[24] In the early 1980s the total permanent adult membership (excluding those being cared for) probably was surprisingly small in number (less than 1,000), as is the case elsewhere in the Rudolf Steiner movement. These figures were not disclosed.

There were growing numbers of emotionally disturbed children looked after. The communities have also cared for children with other disabilities, and for adults with IQs of between 40 to 60. A 'social work' outlook is foreign to Camphill. One of the leaders told me: 'The moment you let in the therapeutic point of view they become patients.' Secularised, medical model ethics of role- and time-bound concern have been replaced by intuitions about the interlinkings of karmas, and Anthroposophical knowledge generally. This has not been explicitly specified so much as summed up in the brochures as 'Christian'. However, later in this section some relatively orthodox, non-gnostic Christian influences on the Camphill communities' founder, Dr Konig, are also outlined. Some parents have said that there would be greater transparency if more Anthroposophically specific references were included in the brochures of Steiner schools, replacing the vague generalisations.

What in professional social work terms is an unorthodox attachment to the 'patient' (i.e., the karmic bond) has probably been at the heart of Camphill's reputation for resounding success. Its ultimate 'therapy' is genuinely beyond therapy. The deficiency or malady is felt to be transcended for that which unites all concerned, thus making a community. J.S. Bach may be played to a disturbed child because the music is perceived as spirit from the cosmos. It is hoped the hospital administrator would agree that this is more cost effective than tranquillising drugs. Though this kind of healing is general to the Rudolf Steiner movement it is probably at its most ubiquitous in the Camphill communities.

It is typical also of the Anthroposophical disregard for this-worldly realities that it has been stated that 'the line dividing co-workers (i.e. Camphill non-disabled adults) from villagers (i.e. the disabled) is non-existent'.[25] During my three week working visit to the large and original British community at Botton, in Yorkshire, I indeed found plenty of external evidence for the practical presence of this unavoidable line. The need to have the terminological dichotomy of 'co-worker'/ 'villager' suggests in itself that the unity between them is not an immediate social one. The villagers were led by the co-workers in carrying out farmwork and in manufacturing products such as candles, soap and ashtrays. They thereby have a meaningful purpose which, together with state grants, has enabled the communities to finance themselves effectively.[26]

At a more profound level, however, both villagers and co-workers are expressions of the rhythm of community life. Time at Botton is known through an almost medieval sense of the seasons. The course of the sun through the sky is the arbiter of the pattern of the day. Christian saints' anniversaries and festivals are celebrated, as are some pagan ones such as May Day. Anthroposophy and its social life are scarcely separable: there is no distinction between the revelation (as modified by Dr Konig) and Camphill's custom, ceremony, hard work and warm personal greetings.

Konig grafted onto Steiner's revelation a further theology of community which had Christian roots. This was partly derived from Count Zinzendorf who, around 1730, inspired the Moravian brethren. Konig's wife came from a Moravian background. Comenius (see chapter seven) and Robert Owen, the early nineteenth-century philanthropist and factory owner, were also influences.

At a surface level many of Botton's meanings seemed to me to be indistinguishable from those of the UK's at large, though football was unimportant. It was a matter of satisfaction that patrons of Camphill include HRH the Duchess of Kent and that a leading member of the community had been awarded a decoration (an OBE). Beyond this level of British culture was the interest in community, and gossip about it, of many of the transient helpers. About half the co-workers seemed to be temporary and hardly aware of Steiner's teachings. Camphill has had many working visits by young people who want to become involved for several months with practical communities. At the core are the committed Anthroposophical co-workers.

Camphill has traditionally expected those committed to it to live and die in community. The sense of belonging has perhaps been heightened by the requirement that all potential members, both co-workers and villagers, should have spent at least two years in the outside world before joining. Once one is in a particular village, there is no call to leave it. The Steiner architectural features, which increasingly became incorporated as Camphill prospered, are symbols of the largely invisible 'normality' surrounding one. The outside world has not intruded – there has been a taboo on possessing televisions – and financial independence has not been the norm. There is provision for simple, wholesome needs, and wages are deemed to have been voluntarily renounced.

A prominent co-worker spoke to me of the necessity of authority because of 'the pressure of things to be done'. The leaders exercise considerable personal power. 'Camphill is an entity to be reckoned with, it's so big', one told me. They generally seemed not to be unaware of having earned the respect they are shown. 'Some Anthroposophists would not dream of coming near the handicapped ... too touched by it ... can't face up to it', a leader declared over two decades ago. It was among these elders that I met the single prominent Anthroposophist who was fully prepared to admit disagreement with Steiner on a major question.

The immersion in community at Botton seemed to produce considerable unconscious identity analogous to Levy-Bruhl's *participation mystique*, an approach which has not been much adopted by anthropologists but which is illuminative of much in Anthroposophy. It was as if the end of the tail of the Goetheanum serpent had become largely fused with the mouth itself and the separation between the two scarcely existed.

Very many of the permanent Camphill co-workers have belonged to the School of Spiritual Science. By the early 1980s there was a formal connection between Camphill and the Goetheanum. About half the communities were then in the UK. Many Camphill members have joined the Anthroposophical Society in Great Britain on an individual basis and there have been close institutional links.

This description would be incomplete without some participation in the spirit of the Camphill day. The impression that follows was almost entirely derived from participant observation during a visit I made to the Botton community.

Breakfast starts at seven-thirty and work at nine. There is a discussion, while transplanting seedlings, about the need to plant during the right phase of the moon.

A change of plan has been necessary. Two co-workers are finding it difficult to explain this to the villagers. I start talking to one of the latter, who says he would not call himself an Anthroposophist. I ask why. He replies that you need to study to become one.[27]

At the coffee bar some young co-workers, two of whom have qualified as teachers and live together, are discussing *The Crucible*, which they have been rehearsing; also, they consider staging a future performance of one of Steiner's mystery plays. Three who are non-British are swapping experiences of Earls Court, London.

A villager drifts by. He is said to suffer from total memory recall.

During the lunch break no one reads *The Guardian*, the only media contact with the outside world. I remember the recent warning by a leading co-worker that a dictator would arise to meet the threat of pollution, and that consequently we were lucky to belong to Camphill. The shrieking of a neighbouring hard-pressed wife at some troublesome villagers who live under her roof subsides as her husband comes in from the fields. At lunch I realise with a shock that a greying, distinguished looking man is in fact a villager and that it is not he but another, wild-looking man who completes the complement of co-workers.

After the necessary two-hour break we all work in the greenhouse as heavy rain has rolled in from the hills. A villager diagnosed as schizophrenic gazes intently at apparently nothing and occasionally exclaims. The two co-workers present treat him with great consideration, but other villagers are grumbling noisily at him.

During the tea break a fairly young co-worker who is not quite committed to Anthroposophy tells me of the strain of responsibility. It is difficult to get away because the Camphill cars have to be signed out. Taking time out seems to many people like a public admission of guilt, a lack of loyalty to the ideals of living together in community.

Supper is the social event of the day. Villagers and co-workers ask friends from other community houses and 'neighbourhoods'. Villagers are talking of their 'girl-' and 'boyfriends' or holding hands with them. I recall that only very rarely are they allowed to marry and that I was told that the 'Scandinavian' remedy of a regime of permissiveness after vasectomy is considered un-Anthroposophical. Living in a family atmosphere is said to prevent energies being diverted into sexual channels. There is talk about the eurythmists who visited a week or so ago.

Grace begins and ends the plain but well-cooked meal. Then all take part in a Bible reading. During this I think of the co-worker who tends to be a scapegoat and wonder how the need to be a 'good' Camphiller allows for recognition of the negative in the self. However, later in the community evening I can almost believe that the darkening trees have etheric natures, and that I am as Steiner describes me.

These impressions from participant observation perhaps give a taste of the immersing power of total Anthroposophical community.

The Christian Community

The Christian Community was founded in 1922 by a Lutheran pastor, Dr Rittelmeyer, as a congregational community. Steiner was always in the background. It is based on the Anthroposophical revelation but has particularly stressed its Christian elements, including 'the transforming power of love – the Christ Impulse'.[28] Its relationship with the remainder of Anthroposophy is recently perceived as having changed worldwide, with more give and take and fewer factions. Many people now, it may be, do not perceive much difference between the two. The Christian Community synod recently hosted by the Goetheanum is said to have been more integrated than the previous ones in the early 1980s and the early 1970s. Traditionally, however, the Christian Community has always been seen as being completely separate from the other Anthroposophical organizations. Indeed, in the early 1980s a message even reached me from its headquarters in Germany requesting me not to write on it in the same book in which I was describing Anthroposophy.

Organisationally, it is certainly separate. But as already stated, it is based on the spiritual realities revealed by Steiner and so, at a more fundamental level, is Anthroposophical, though it has the distinctive function of a church.

Its extensive rituals have an esoteric rather than conventionally Christian feel. For example, the powers of the spiritual heights and material depths are acknowledged through holding the right hand up and putting the left hand out. The priests' chasubles have figures of eight to represent the infinite. The colours, such as the prevalent violet, relate to Steiner's spiritual science, especially perhaps his revelations about the 'human aura' (see table 1). In the communion (called the 'Act of Consecration of Man') the priest is not deemed to have a monopoly of grace, nor is grace believed to operate by virtue of his or her office, unlike the position in Catholic orthodoxy. The six other sacraments, five of which broadly follow stages of life, are Baptism, Confirmation, Marriage, Sacramental Consultation (or counselling), Anointing (which includes preparing for death) and Ordination. Steiner said the words of the sacraments came through him directly from the spiritual world.

The Christian Community appears in many ways to be a product of post-Christian, secularized society. It was founded self-consciously as a church, which is very unusual. There is no discrimination against women becoming priests (by the early 1980s they constituted a third of the priesthood in the UK, the highest national Christian Community ratio). In other ways it has been traditional. There is a hierarchy, from priests to *Lenkers*, *Oberlenkers* and finally the *Erzoberlenker*, which is translated into English as 'head' but which others say should be 'centre' or 'heart'. Also the ordinand vows not to alter the sacraments on his or her own initiative and to abide by the regulations.

In 2005 there were approximately 350 Christian Community churches worldwide.[29] In 2004 over 250 priests of the Christian

Community met at the Goetheanum for their annual international synod.[30] Overall its priesthood does not seem to have grown numerically over the past two decades. In 2005 and also in the early 1980s there seem to have been about 350 priests in all. Germany in 2005 had about 200, a probable decline since the early 1980s once the re-unification of Germany is taken into account. West Germany then had up to 200, and East Germany around 25 to 30. The Netherlands seems now to have the next largest number of priests. It seems to have had more than more than 20 by the early 1980s. Switzerland is reputedly the next most numerous after the Netherlands. Britain in 2005 had about 20 priests and in the 1980s had about 30, the USA about 20 then and now. France, with its Catholic politics, is said to be difficult to work in as a Christian Community priest.

This overall pattern of decline of the priesthood, or at least stasis, in Western Europe and the US, has been accompanied by growth elsewhere (there are broad similarities with the patterns of membership in the national societies). However there has been expansion in Australia, where the Christian Community took root in about 1993. In 2005 it had five priests (and New Zealand about three). In the past decade there have been three Japanese priests in Tokyo and about three priests in South America. Priestly visits are made to India and Moscow. There is currently no connection with Thailand. In traditionally Catholic Europe there seems to have been some recent expansion, with three priests in Italy and some work starting in Spain. There are a few priests in Baltic countries. In what seems to be a radical step the training seminaries have increased this century from the sole one at Stuttgart to two more, one in Hamburg and the other in Chicago. There has been further decentralisation because of the prevalence of websites. The headquarters, mirroring German re-unification, has moved from Stuttgart to Berlin.

It was and is very difficult for an outside researcher to assess congregational strength. In West Germany in the early 1980s it was likely to number many thousands, but much less numerous congregations were to be found elsewhere. In Britain, which is currently said to be holding its own, it seemed there were no more than 600 adherents in the early 1980s and probably far fewer. Britain may be typical of many secularised countries in that congregation strength seems to be growing where there is already Anthroposophical community, but has long declined in industrial cities such as Leeds and Sheffield. With the increase in Britain of those with virtually no religious upbringing, it is harder to establish a presence in many localities. In the UK there are, however, a number of members who broke away from Catholic backgrounds. Secularisation is said sometimes to be helpful to the Christian Community in that those who drift away from the more established churches may find in it a more acceptable form of what they miss.

Most members of the General Anthroposophical Society have not also been members of the Christian Community. Western esotericism is in part a reaction against institutional religion. They have been aware of it, however, and many attend the occasional service for specific reasons such as marriage. This probably applies to Camphill as well. Proportionately more members of the Christian Community have probably been likely to be members of the General Society or Camphill than vice versa. In Britain in the early 1980s this Christian Community proportion could have been a third, though in Germany it may have been rather lower because church-going there has not generally been perceived as such a drastic step as joining an esoteric society. The priests provide services for Camphill communities and teach in many Waldorf schools. The Christian Community does not have its own School of Spiritual Science and at this powerful level of identification clearly has links with the rest of Anthroposophy, for I was authoritatively told that about two-thirds of the priests were members of the First Class.

The Two Goetheanums

Anthroposophists everywhere remember the Old Goetheanum with reverence. An unknown incendiarist burned the building down late on New Year's Eve, 1922. Steiner watched the labours of the previous ten or so years turn to ashes and then committed himself to renewal. As discussed in chapter two, he said that the disaster arose because members were not trying hard enough to protect the Goetheanum spiritually.

It has been experienced by followers of Steiner through photographs, paintings, models, descriptions and, so it is thought, directly through visions. I heard a British member, during a Christmas Holy Night meeting, a New Year's Eve remembrance of the old Goetheanum, bear witness to its direct spiritual appearance to him.

Its two interlocking domes, one of which is smaller than the other, particularly hold the Anthroposophical imagination. It seems to express the Anthroposophical union of opposites in living form, and its evolution of mankind towards spiritual awareness. Anthroposophically this is the end towards which geology, biology, history, society and science strive and the essence of which they really consist.

It is a part of the lore of the Rudolf Steiner movement that the artillery from the First World War trenches could be heard when the Old Goetheanum was being built. While the foundations of Europe were being devastated this unifying symbol was being constructed. Its meaning is uplifting compared to that of the underground, doom-laden domes of the Marabar caves that so disturbed liberal, civilized Mrs Moore in E.M. Forster's *A Passage to India*, for the dome deriving from Steiner's intuition is seen as the visible forerunner of the spiritual salvation of European civilization. Unlike Wagner's *Festspielhaus* in Bayreuth it was visibly extraordinary. Wagner is said not to have believed that architecture or staging could express anything that approached his *Ring*'s music, but, in contrast, for Steiner all the arts are, as manifestations of underlying spirituality, necessarily integrated.[31]

The Prologue of this book described the new Goetheanum, which was more or less completed in the 1950s on the site of the old. Though reflecting later building materials, it is still sacred enough to unite Anthroposophists in common devotion, whatever their other divisions. It is a new form of organic architecture based on Goethean archetypal science and metamorphosis, the form arising dynamically from the principle of growth through to the detail as a *Gesamtkunstwerk*. It is also a centre at a more immediate level for the meditations and applications which, in Anthroposophy, are different aspects of the same core reality.

Part Two

Thought and Deed in Anthroposophy

4. Meditations and Applications

The spirit comes to guide me in my need,
I write, 'In the beginning was the Deed'.[1]
— Goethe, Faust Part 1

'You are like a sculptor trying to work with a rainbow (not merely ice or sand on the shore, which can be formed if given no permanence), a material which *cannot* be used for the purpose you intend.' This was a response to me from an Anthroposophist, after I had communicated my intention to research Anthroposophy, telling me how it was impossible to capture the being of Anthroposophy and keep it alive as words on paper.

The last chapter defined the Rudolf Steiner movement largely through describing the extensiveness of its main social institutions. Now that these boundaries are outlined it is time to pass on to elusive — and, as members will say, more important — realities. What is it like to be Anthroposophical? How can social living be 'esoteric', infused with spirit?

The image of the rainbow, which comes down from the sky and contains all colours in itself, is a good one. There are no hard and fast distinctions in Anthroposophical life. The many applications (even if they are practical, as in the case of bio-dynamic farming) are also, if *fully carried out*, forms of meditation which lead to transcendence in a more spiritual individuality. Steiner was very strongly influenced by Goethe. Though he interpreted his many-sidedness from a highly spiritual point of view, Steiner agreed with Goethe's belief in the redeeming sanity of action. It is these meditative applications, or applied meditations, that constitute the everyday being of the movement. They are the Anthroposophical rainbow-like coherence-in-decentralisation. Since they are supported by the sections of the School of Spiritual Science, the School has an integrative function.

Nearly all the applications are based on Steiner's 'indications', though there has been considerable work done since his death. They are aspects of his general cosmology (see chapters 5 &

6). Unless, as with the theory of relativity, which he described as brilliant nonsense, Steiner completely rejected new developments, they tend to be integrated with the revelation. Depth psychology is seen as concerned with 'soul' (not with 'spirit'). 'Flying saucers' have subsequently been related to his warning that, if materialism were to triumph, people might not understand the first signs of new clairvoyant capacities.[2]

There is a great deal of detailed written material on the applications; this is available from the society. Here I am attempting to produce an overview that illustrates their functions in relation to the movement as a whole.[3]

The Path of Knowledge

Anthroposophical spiritual exercises are available to the general public. The occult path is not restricted to the First Class (which seems to concentrate on spiritual research for the collective applications) but is published for the illumination of individuals.

The aim is 'to wrest the soul free from sense-perception and rouse it to an activity for which the outer impressions of the physical senses are without significance'.[4] The soul itself is viewed as subjective, but spirit is viewed as objective reality. This is the 'activity' to which the soul is roused. Steiner, who had been trained as a conventional scientist, thought his path to be spiritual 'science' because, he claimed, it leads to objective truth. In his book *The Philosophy of Freedom*[5] he states that percept (the philosophical term for an object of perception) and concept are two aspects of an underlying unitary reality. The purpose of his meditative path is to realise the unity and thereby transcend the binary division imposed by our physical organisation.

The Philosophy of Freedom is perceived as Steiner's most difficult work, and often also as the most significant[6]. It is based on the primacy of thinking. For Steiner it is through thinking that spirit presents itself most immediately to man. For him, observation of thinking is an exceptional state: he believed that, unlike feeling, our thinking is usually unobserved by us. Thinking, he states, is related to perceiving in the way waking is related to sleeping. For Steiner, our thinking is universal: there is only one concept of a triangle though it will be grasped differently by different individuals. Steiner agreed with the philosophical position that the given world, including our feelings and our physical organisation, consists of subjective mental pictures, but excludes thinking from this. As will be seen, he rebutted the criticism that his position on thinking is naive realism.

Steiner stated that a mental picture is an intuition related to a particular percept. My concept of a lion is not formed out of my percepts of lions, but my mental picture of a lion is very definitely formed according to a percept. Thus the mental picture is an individualised concept:

> The full reality of a thing is given to us in the moment of observation through the fitting together of concept and percept. By means of a percept, the concept acquires an individualised form, a relation to this particular percept. In this individualised form . . . the concept lives on in us and constitutes the mental picture of the thing in question.[7]

For Steiner, thinking is the element through which we take part in the universal cosmic process. Thinking cancels all separation and shows it to be due to merely subjective factors. Steiner asserts that I, in so far as I am part of the world process, am the same as the things outside. The forces at work are the same. The percept of the tree belongs to the same whole as my I. Something arises from the midst of the percept of the self, produced by one's own activity, which in its inner significance transcends the self.

Steiner criticised as metaphysical realism those concepts, such as heredity, which are not sense-perceptible. This is because the form which the metaphysical realist gives to his things-in-themselves is obtained by inductive inferences. Steiner saw his philosophy as a monism of thought: 'for monism feeling is an incomplete reality which, in the form in which it first appears to us, does not yet contain its second factor, the concept or idea'.[8] Thus for Steiner mysticism is erroneous because it is based on subjective feeling and yet it wants to experience directly what it ought to gain through thinking.

Steiner's understanding of what 'thinking' is includes warmth and is connected with love.[9] The essence active in thinking replaces the activity of the human organisation. The free spirit is the purest expression of human nature and is the last stage of man's evolution. Each one of us has in him a free spirit. A free being is one who can want what he considers right: Steiner espouses ethical individualism, not Kantian universalism.

From the point of view of psychologism or psychological reductionism, Steiner could be seen as an intuitive thinker who projected his preferred way of encountering life onto the cosmos. Others, for example feeling types, or those who live in sensation, would have different preferences. From such a perspective there would be no reason to exalt any particular preference, for example thinking, to a cosmic principle and thereby to exempt it from the critique of naive realism. However, an Anthroposophical response to this critique is that thinking is involved when a feeling is replaced, for example, when pity takes over from anger. We may be aware only of a change of mood, but replacing a feeling is seen Anthroposophically to be a decision involving cognition and responsibility. Again, the issue arises of how far this Anthroposophical prioritisation of thinking applies to all humans irrespective of cultural differences. Also, Steiner's proposition may be relativised through positing that feeling is often involved when one thought is replaced by another. A further issue is that Steiner's thinking seems to be very closely involved with warmth and love (qualities he was described as having personally), and so the question arises of how *The Philosophy of Freedom's* thinking as an activity is to be distinguished from feeling.

Because of his certainty of objective spiritual truth Steiner was sometimes literal rather than metaphorical. Images are frequently seen as relatively true at an imaginative (or 'clairvoyant') level rather than treated as fantasies which have been formed by the human mind merely in idiosyncratic isolation. Analogously, a member told me that psychoanalysis approaches the lower instincts 'through the forces of the moon-sphere' (that is, it symbolises them intellectually) but that Steiner knows them directly through the forces of 'the Sun-sphere'. Steiner thought that spiritual research revealed a literal human aura (see table 1). He described this as, on average, about twice as tall and three times as wide as the physical self. It has three interpenetrating 'sheaths', each of which is composed of spiritual colours. Their meanings vary according to the sheath; the lowest reflects the influence of the body on the soul while the highest mirrors the spiritual in man. Hence 'muddy yellow to brown' in the lowest sheath is the 'lowest stage of egotism'; in the middle sheath (where the colours are more distinct) 'bright yellow' is 'clear thinking and intelligence'; in the highest one 'brilliant golden yellow' is 'thinking with lofty ideas comprehending the divine world order', which has been 'purified from all sensory conceptions'.

Steiner's general cosmology also tends to be literal. He believed it is revealed through undertaking his meditative path. The first stage, 'Imagination', said to be related to the head, brings awareness of one's subjectivity. The second, 'Inspiration', said to be related to the heart, apparently reveals what happens between death and rebirth (though the exercises to see one's previous incarnation are separate), as well as changes on earth from the time of 'Atlantis' and the planetary embodiments. 'Intuition', which is related to the limbs, apparently enables one to see the 'Spiritual Hierarchies' and 'karma'.

However, few Anthroposophists would summarise the meditations in a lucid and brief manner, for 'it's a point of honour' among his followers not to give 'a potted version'.[10] This preserves the integrity of the experience. One by-product, however, is that the validity of the rainbow-like system cannot be easily questioned.

Imagination

> The truth of the matter is that, having to concentrate upon one symbolic or other thought picture, the soul is obliged to summon up from its depths much stronger forces than it is accustomed to employ in ordinary life or for the ordinary process of cognition. Its inner activity is enhanced thereby. The soul liberates itself from the body, even as it does in sleep. Only, instead of going over into unconsciousness, it now has a living experience of a world it did not know before.[11]

These words by Steiner are expressed pictorially in the symbol of the Goetheanum serpent described in the Prologue. At the centre of its enclosed circular space is an unobtrusive ring. 'One can identify oneself with it by feeling the smallness and within-oneself-secluded day-reality of self.'[12] Moving with one's eyes from the ring to the macrocosmic serpent seems to be a visual equivalent of what Steiner means when he states 'the soul liberates itself from the body' and 'has a living experience of a world it did not know before'.

Steiner mentions by way of example the building up of a symbolic thought composition which does not reflect nature, for example a black cross with – where the beams meet – seven resplendent bright red roses in a circle. He states that it is important that feeling accompanies the thought in the all-important process of constructing the image. His suggestion is that the roses could be felt to be passions and impulses which have been purified.

Thought pictures are not the only means of 'initiation'. Sentences, formulae or single words may be objects of meditation. Study of *The Philosophy of Freedom* is another route to 'sense-free thinking'. Occasionally, initiation may be spontaneous. This is said only to occur where the person concerned was exceptionally developed in his previous incarnation.

Concentrated meditation is said to perceive spiritual facts and spiritual beings which cannot be known by the senses. These have already been revealed by Steiner so the neophyte knows possible categories through which his or her experiences can be interpreted. Indeed, Steiner identified gnomes, salamanders, sylphs and elemental beings generally. One member told me he would have a 'direct glimpse of a being with bright eyes', that 'it would be dynamic' and might 'take a momentary form in consciousness'. He was replying after I asked how he could be sure that what he would see was a 'gnome'. Gnomes are not to be understood anachronistically as similar to mass-produced contemporary gnomes for the garden, but as an elemental equivalent of one of the angelic hierarchies.

When thinking 'reaches upwards' from the head towards Imagination it is said to purify the feelings and will of the 'astral body' and thereby transform it into a higher, more spiritual body (which is known as 'spirit-self'). As a result the human aura is said to become purified and more differentiated. 'Lotus-flowers' apparently 'revolve' when a pupil meditates and clairvoyant perception begins.

Inspiration

With Inspiration (also known as the 'Reading of the Hidden Script') the sense world of personal, soulful subjectivity is, it is said, known to have been left behind. The objective spirit world appears and with it some awareness of the archetypal – yet individual – 'I'.

The exercises involve a process of wiping out the Imaginative thought pictures and feeling what the soul was doing to produce them. Thus the black cross and red roses of the meditation already mentioned are encouraged to disappear. The result, Steiner stated, is the finding of bearings after the restless transformations of the Imaginative world (which may have analogies with Coleridge's 'fancy'). Through Inspiration the 'etheric body' is penetrated and, it is said, evolves to a higher spiritual body (known as 'life-spirit').

Few if any Anthroposophists around 1980 seemed to be considered to be consistently at this meditative stage. Those that are, it was said, would certainly not draw attention to their attainment. This is not to say that many do not have unusual experiences. For example, one young member told me: 'As one frees thinking from concepts, the centre of consciousness descends from the head to the throat.' But few interpreted their unusual experiences as exalted achievements in terms of Steiner's path of knowledge.

Intuition

No one beyond Steiner himself seemed to be credited with achieving the depth and strength of Intuition. On the way to it, Lucifer and Ahriman, appearing as the 'Lesser Guardians of the Threshold', are transcended through recognition of the sublime mystery of Christ, the 'Greater Guardian of the Threshold'. The successful conclusion, however, is viewed as leading to a conscious union with spirit within and beyond the body. Steiner stated that when an inwardly developed person says, 'I go through the door', his actual concept is, 'I carry my body through the door'. Conscious individual spirituality transcends and informs the physical body.

Intuition is attained through letting go of even the meditation on the soul-activity that led from Imagination to Inspiration. The physical body itself is said to be transformed spiritually into a body which is a higher evolutionary form (known as 'spirit-man'). This leads on to a state in which man is aware of himself as being at one with the macrocosm, yet also as a fully developed individual.

Sciences

'Science' for Anthroposophists is not what is usually meant by this English word in the Twentieth Century. German usefully has two words where English has one: *Naturwissenschaften* for strict (or null hypothesis-type) natural science, and *Geisteswissenschaft* for systematically making sense in the humanities. Steiner sought to 'free' the scientific method and spirit of research, which conventionally holds fast to the sequence and relationship of sense-perceptible events, from this 'restricted' application.[13]

Living Thinking, a path for the philosophically and mathematically inclined, and *Goethean Science,* which is based on observation, are generally held to be equivalent to the first stage of Imagination. Steiner was deeply influenced by Goethe's holistic scientific method, which he spiritualised as he adopted it into his burgeoning Anthroposophy. Goethean science's search amidst the multitude of plant forms for the archetypal plant (or *Urpflanze)* is considered a first step towards spiritual knowledge.[14]

There has been considerable Anthroposophical investigation of 'etheric' forces. They are identified with the 'four elements', the archetypal activities of earth, water, air and fire, which were once dynamic qualities in the medieval cosmos and are now Anthroposophical ('fire' is linked to 'warmth'). There is also a belief, consonant with traditional astrology, that minerals on earth are permeated by etheric streams from different planets; for example, lead is said to be affected by such influences from Saturn, tin from Jupiter, and copper from Mars.

Anthroposophical science is used to integrate conventional scientific discoveries made since Steiner's time. He believed that animals had a descending evolution, evolving 'downwards' from their archetypal origin, the spiritual human form, and hardening into specialization. Human beings descended and condensed or incarnated later. Evolution is also ascending towards greater conscious spirituality as it increases in complexity. His time scales were very short even in terms of contemporary geological and anthropological knowledge, but the huge time spans established by more recent radiocarbon dating have made many of his statements look shorter still. His follower, Guenther Wachsmuth, surmounted the problem through 'establishing' that radioactive decay itself first began between 15,000 BC (the entry of the Platonic year into Libra) and 13,800 BC (when it entered into Virgo).[15]

Occasionally, the possibility that Steiner made a mistake may be contemplated. Deep ocean exploration has made his siting of Atlantis look impossible. Some Anthroposophists reputedly believe he erred, and Steiner himself admitted the possibility of a few minor mistakes. But others defend the revelation through disputing the validity of the backwards projection of findings made by oceanographers: for it is thought that at the time of Atlantis the earth was more fluidly spiritual. It has also been held that Steiner's descriptions of Atlantis were not intended literally.

Steiner revived *Projective Geometry* in order to understand realities of movement and metamorphosis which, he thought, were not well served by conventional geometry. This initiative is continued by some of his followers.

As has been stated, Anthroposophical science is not about applying 'Occam's razor'. It seems to presuppose Steiner's cosmology and then amplify it spiritually. Life on earth derives from chains of supernal and immanent beings. Thus the First Spiritual Hierarchy are said to be so pure that they are separated from their 'selfhood', which constitutes the Second Anthroposophical Spiritual Hierarchy. In Anthroposophy some of the latter (the Powers) form plants, animals, man and planets, while others (the Mights) govern the growth of living beings. The Third Anthroposophical Spiritual Hierarchy directly affect life on earth, thus flowing water is said to contain the Angels. Wind and fire are infused by other spirits, and *Zeitgeists* (or Spirits of the Age), which are taken literally, are thought to be the manifestation of the Principalities. These and other spirits have 'offspring', which are the 'nature spirits' of air, water, earth and so on. In Anthroposophy there are also, as already stated, 'elemental beings' such as goblins, sylphs, undines, salamanders, and gnomes, all of which are said by

Steiner to consist of body and soul only and to have been left behind in evolution. A man who takes sixteen false paths in his incarnations may become one. The earth itself is seen as a living organism with 'spiritual sheaths'. It 'breathes', exhaling in the morning and inhaling in the afternoon. The Anthroposophical universe is inversely related to the sociologist Max Weber's description of the modern world as disenchanted.

Astrosophy

Anthroposophical astrology, known as *astrosophy,* has been considerably developed from the 'indications' given by Rudolf Steiner. Its purpose, in the tradition of gnostic astrology, seems to be to help followers transcend necessity. For the Anthroposophist, this is a question of knowing and transcending one's karma. The small ring at the centre of the Goetheanum serpent has twelve lines radiating outwards, pointing towards the macrocosm represented by the serpent itself. This may represent the overcoming of the tight ring of the everyday self through knowing how the twelve signs of the zodiac affect one's biography or karma. The ultimate purpose of the transcendence seems to be to 'redeem the planets'. Some members refer to this in terms of the Bodhisattva ideal of Mahayana Buddhism.

In Anthroposophical cosmology, the physical planets are broken or crushed spirit. They are at the edge of a sphere governed by a Spiritual Hierarchy. There are resonances with Ptolemaic cosmology, with the influence of the Angels, for example, extending to the Moon, the Archangels to Mercury, and the Principalities to Venus. The earth is the centre of the spiritual solar system. Moons are the corpses of planets. Comets or meteors are trying to collect harmful astral material and remove it from the planetary system. The Sun is the external appearance of the 'Christ-Being'. The foregoing is only a brief summary of insider statements which derive their meanings from wider Anthroposophical contexts, and thus pays the reductionist price of creating a 'potted' Anthroposophy.

Much of what has just been described is considered more 'esoteric' than the overarching cosmology available generally in *Occult Science*.[16] The cosmological gradations from asleep to awake, from exoteric impurity to the purest of the Spiritual Hierarchies, or even to the Trinity, to some extent correspond with the realities of belonging to the Rudolf Steiner movement. The search for collective spiritual awareness legitimises the School of Spiritual Science as the main institution. Membership of the external shell, the General Society, does not carry so much status. The cosmology and the social structure have correspondences with each other.

My notes of an astrosophical weekend[17] at an old mill in the West of England convey something of the realities of living the cosmology. 'At the mill, we don't feel outside, but inside everything . . .'; 'If all these planets move retrograde, there is the most intense development of consciousness . . .'; 'The Epoch Chart awakens within you memories of pre-earthly existence . . .'; 'One Anthroposophical doctor said contraceptives cause tremendous suffering in the spiritual world since they stop souls from incarnating . . .'; 'What one does in the world will shape the future physical body'. This last comment, as it turned out, in an esoteric way anticipated the new science of epigenetics (in which the expression of genes is affected in short time by the environment) by two decades. A visiting American Theosophist, who misjudged the ambience, committed a wisecracking *faux pas:* at teatime he said, 'Meditate on the meals, then they will materialise on the table.' None of the Anthroposophists smiled.

Bio-dynamics

Though Anthroposophical agriculture and horticulture have much in common with the ecological awareness of organic farming, their *bio-dynamic* rituals and preparations give them a further identity of their own. Bio-dynamic farming involves much more than being conventionally organic. Nature is theurgically 'dynamised' in the making of manures, compost harmonisers and so forth. Similar magical practices govern the mode and timing of application. Rhythm and direction are both prescribed in the ritual preparation. For example, a mixture mysteriously known as 'formula 500' – to conventional chemical analysis it is cow manure – is left in a cowhorn in the ground in winter (when the earth is said to be most 'alive'), then stirred in water according to a prescribed rhythm and direction for an hour. The final stage is the carrying out of the spraying procedures. '501', which to conventional chemical analysis is powdered quartz, is on the other hand left in a cowhorn in the earth during summer. It becomes a crop nutrient. Yarrow, dandelion, chamomile, nettle, valerian and oak-bark are used as bases for six preparations which 'harmonise' fermentation in manure and compost. They are enveloped in specific animal organs and exposed to seasonal soil or atmospheric influences. Quantitatively, yields are said to be comparable to chemical methods, but their quality is claimed to be much better.

Anthroposophical ritual and natural magic, which are intended to produce a different order of quality, involve heartfelt participation from those involved in the rites. Nor is technical knowledge a mere question of book-learning, for Imagination is a necessary aspect of farming. Without it, for example, the farmer will not know whether to use a given preparation. The biodynamic approach is thus perceived as a qualitative step beyond more usual organic agriculture. I have heard that in Australia there are farmers who use some biodynamic methods because they perceive them as working, and who disclaim any belief in mysticism or Anthroposophy.

Steiner gave his first agricultural course in 1924. By 1982 as many as 560 people, mostly from Germany and Switzerland, attended a conference held by (invitation only), the Agricultural Circle of the Natural Science Section of the School of Spiritual Science.[18] Later, in 2005, a national newspaper article stated that 'biodynamic food is beginning to penetrate the mainstream marketplace, albeit slowly, and gaining a reputation as it does so for exceptional quality'.[19] Steiner saw his bio-dynamics as a conscious advance from the atavistic instinctual wisdom of old peasant calendars. For him man has developed an independence that has given him partial emancipation from cosmic rhythms: thus human menstruation does not follow the exact dates of lunar cycles but only the same elapsing of time. For Steiner the conscious individuality of man needs to comprehend the cosmic rhythms outside him. Anthroposophy's anthropology is thus modern compared to the animism of primal cultures. In Anthroposophy plants reflect immediately what is taking place in the planets. Furthermore, the elemental beings termed gnomes, below the earth's surface, help plant roots to grow, and the astral aura of cows nourishes the gnomes. Again, cud-chewing animals have the important spiritual function of bringing cosmic forces down to earth, and the task of birds is to carry earthly substance out into the cosmos. Thus the Anthroposophical farmer is aware of much more than pressing financial realities. Through bio-dynamic knowledge and procedures Anthroposophical cosmology is re-created in social practice.

Medicine and Health

Only conventionally qualified doctors are said to become Anthroposophical medical practitioners. Rudolf Steiner's main approach to *healing* was frequently homoeopathic, though allopathic therapies are often also used, for example, with ailments of the kidneys and stomach. Physical symptoms are generally understood through a total Anthroposophical approach which respects the patient's wishes. The therapeutic aim is to convert imbalance to harmony, for example, to correct a 'metabolic-limb' system that is too strong, thus producing inflammation, or an over strong 'neuro-sensorial' system, which tends to result in thrombosis, sclerosis and angina. Cancer is seen as the symptom of an underdeveloped psychic state which is connected with, or perhaps derives from, the withdrawal of form-producing ('etheric') forces. To strengthen these, the sufferer is given a medication, Iscador, which is derived from mistletoe. This is believed to have abundant formativeness because it is perceived as independent of 'earth forces' and seasonal rhythms. It should also be noted, however, that to conventional chemical analysis some, though not all, Anthroposophical medicines are nothing but water.

Anthroposophical healing is not compartmentalised into a discrete medical model. Thus in the Christian Community sacrament of the Consecration of Man there is a reference to the 'sickness of sin'. Each member must come to terms with his own 'temperament'. Here again there are resonances with the Middle Ages. In Anthroposophy the 'sanguine' has the greatest correspondence to spirit; the 'choleric', 'phlegmatic' and 'melancholic' decreasingly so. In the case of the last, according to Steiner, the great danger is madness. Therapy involves many of the other applications. Thus painting, drawing and modelling may be prescribed. Colours are used homoeopathically, though not in small 'doses', to evoke responses.

Nutrition is also much considered. There is a vegetarian tendency that derives from Steiner's statement that those who eat meat cannot develop as well spiritually as those who do not, though he also wittily said it is better to eat meat than think meat. He would comment that the main inner hindrances of members – personal ambitions, illusions, petty jealousies, and so on – were a problem of nutrition.

Spiritual cults, unlike many world-rejecting sects on the Protestant model, have not usually come into major conflict with the states of liberal democracies and on most fronts Anthroposophy has been no exception. But because, on conventional scientific analysis, the efficacy of many of its medicines (which are branded under the name of 'Weleda') is difficult to establish, conflict has occurred in some countries. In Great Britain there was a massive fund-raising appeal so that the movement could conform to stringent regulations concerning the premises in which medicines are made.

Arts and Education

The social being of the movement is inseparable from its arts. With the possible exceptions of eurythmy and speech formation, Anthroposophy has not created new art forms; instead it spiritualises established forms.

Eurythmy and Speech Formation

Steiner thought that *eurythmy*, his spiritual movement, would be comprehensible to everyone because it expresses the Word of the universe. As in Hindu cosmology, God himself is perceived as involved in a cosmic dance; as a result there arises the form of man. This is related to the beginning of St John's Gospel, though Anthroposophy does not have an orthodox theism. The lengthy physical training is the outer aspect of what are seen as the inner dynamics of music and language: unlike ballet teaching, there is a meditative preparation so that the dancer, as microcosm, expresses the appropriate aspects of the macrocosm. The performers enact the essence of legends, stories and even of characters such as Dickens' Sam Weller.

There are now several hundred or more expert performers, and most Anthroposophists have probably taken up eurythmy at some stage or other. It is linked with *speech formation,* which is particularly associated with Steiner's second wife, Marie von Sievers. These processes are demanding. A report on two members looking back stated that there were 'glimpses into the endless hours of rehearsals, hours of despair when they could not grasp what Marie Steiner was calling for, moments of joy when a temporary acceptance had been achieved'.[20]

Steiner had been the original moving spirit behind eurythmy, at first receiving no response. It was also he who gave 'indications' for a new way of declaiming, a hieratic speech which was developed by Marie Steiner and has thereby become the content of speech formation. Consonants are related to the signs of the zodiac and vowels to the planets. Each temperament is thought to have a special relationship to particular vowel sounds. These and other Anthroposophical arts are widely used in its educative and curative applications.

As part of the anniversary celebrations for the late Marie von Sievers there was a *music* workshop with the theme 'Becoming Conscious of the Threshold in Musical Experience'.[21] The short intervals of modern music are thought to presage an ascent towards spirit, when we will learn to perceive from inside the single note. Clairaudience is an aspect of Inspiration: Pythagoras' music of the spheres is considered to be a reality. A divinely inspired instrument such as the lyre, harp or violin is thought to have resonances with the form of the human being.

Visual Arts

Cosmologically, there is an Anthroposophical hierarchy of the arts. Eurythmy, speech formation, music and Anthroposophical dramas are most spiritual. Painting, sculpture and architecture are, in descending order, expressions of less spiritual realities, the astral, etheric and physical worlds respectively. But in the practice of the arts there seems to be no sense of one being superior to the other.

Anthroposophical *painting* works with Goethe's colour theory to introduce colours as living spiritual entities, and the forms arising out of colours as a new impulse. It has typically flowing forms and pale colours, though in West Germany I saw some Anthroposophical impressionist and expressionist work. The preferred medium is watercolour; oils are thought to be too heavy. Many later artists, including Joseph Beuys, who is said to have been influenced by Steiner's use of blackboards, and Paul Klee, who is reputed to have been an Anthroposophical member, are claimed to have been influenced by it. It contrasts with the modernist Bauhaus.

Steiner stated that when we project the organisation of the human body into the space outside it, then we have *architecture*. As described in chapter one, he lived in Vienna during most of the penultimate decade of the nineteenth century and met people there who were in the forefront of European architectural development. Unlike most of them, he was able to build his major design. From a reductionist point of view, it has been said that the Art Nouveau of the period was, in Steiner, to find its most unusual exponent.[22] There has already been some description of his main buildings, the old and new Goetheanums. Anthroposophical architecture has developed very strongly, especially in the Camphill movement, and organic architecture is now a mainstream genre in current building design, paradoxically aided by the computer. Steiner saw the artist as needing to recognise the governing tendency in the 'intention' of nature, and to help it towards its realisation in the material world.[23]

Philology

The writings of Owen Barfield, who, as previously mentioned, was associated with the Oxford 'Inklings' circle, developed Steiner's revelation. A committed Anthroposophist, his main subject was philology. Anthroposophy seems not to be much mentioned and it has been said that his many non-Anthroposophical readers might, if they were fully aware of Steiner, consider Barfield to have been the superior thinker. He believed that Anthroposophy is Romanticism grown up.[24]

Camphill 'Curative' Education

One of the main contacts of the movement with the outside world is through Anthroposophical *education*. Indeed many people mistakenly seem to think of Steiner as a modern educationalist similar to Montessori. As a young man Steiner spent many years helping a hydrocephalic boy, the experience forming the basis of his later commitment to *curative education*. He understood pathology to be the result of imperfections in the hereditarily derived body. The individuality, he thought, is intact. There may be karmic reasons why an imperfect body is chosen before birth. A genius often goes through such an incarnation, apparently, or the defect may be the straightforward result of actions in a previous life.

Those suffering from Down's syndrome are considered to have 'a particular mission, bringing the gift of their own heart forces unhindered by intellect and ambition to compete. Their very posture when in repose is like that of the Buddha.'[25] Steiner saw it as a special grace to be granted the gift of such a child. Because of their gaiety and warm love, Down's Syndrome people are seen as the archetypal Gestalt of man before the Fall and consciousness of good and evil. They have a special meaning for Camphill members.

Camphill children in need of special care often begin the day with music from flute or lyre and then, after breakfast, form a circle for morning song. Rhythmic intervals of silence arising from inner stillness are said to be essential therapeutically. These children 'go to school': there are classrooms, which are distinct from the substitute families with whom they live. A powerful therapeutic factor is said to be the interaction of those with diverse ailments, for example, the hyperactive and aggressive with the frail and physically handicapped, or withdrawn autistics with outgoing Down's Syndrome children. In the evening there is 'story-hour' and a period when 'house' or 'dormitory parents' can spend time in close conversation with the individual child. The week as well as the day is given an ascending and descending rhythm.

Waldorf and Adult Education

Many dissertations seem to have been written from teacher training colleges about Anthroposophical 'Waldorf' education. However, significant further dimensions arise when this is understood as part of Steiner's cosmology. As will be much more fully explained, he believed that everything tangible in the solar system has condensed into matter from an original state of spirit. The cosmos is, by no means smoothly, starting to respiritualise and we are now just beyond the turning point, which was marked by the coming of Christ. This respiritualisation is a return with a difference, for its end is the heightening and extending of the consciousness of one's spiritual individuality. As already stated, the whole process is depicted in the circular path of the Goetheanum serpent.

In Anthroposophy the individual as a microcosm is part of this evolutionary spiritual progress. Through the path of knowledge, through Imagination, Inspiration and Intuition, the future respiritualisation can be anticipated to some extent on earth now. Much of the Steiner adult education – in the School of Spiritual Science, in the individual reading of his path of knowledge, probably also at the Goetheanum, in Stuttgart, Zeyst, Sacramento and at Emerson College – is directly concerned with transformation and cosmic respiritualisation. It is considered essential that this is undertaken with free will as a conscious individual. Analogously perhaps, the Goetheanum serpent has a great eye and its mouth encloses but (just) remains separate from its tail.

In Anthroposophical adult education the cosmic, social and individual come together. The world outlook is maintained through specialised vocational courses on, for example, bio-dynamic agriculture and education. Emerson College alone, by 1981, had about 200 students who came from thirty different nations. There were Chinese and Japanese students, but no Arabic ones.[26]

In 2005 there were 894 Steiner schools in 45 countries. This included young schools and initiatives in China, Lebanon, and Tanzania.[27] More recently, it seems that Anthroposophy has become a more acceptable subject to cover in conventional higher education. Public funding is a major issue. It seems there is public funding in Germany, Norway, New Zealand, Sweden, and Finland, though governments often try to avoid funding Waldorf schools. In France there is even said to have been an attempt to ban Waldorf schools, but it was not possible to prove that they were sectarian.

In 1999 'People for Legal and Non-Sectarian Schools, Inc (PLANS)' issued a press release with a headline:

> California group sues public schools over adoption of "Waldorf" education movement's weird spiritualism and pseudo-science. . . . PLANS does not object to private Waldorf schools, and supports freedom of religion in private. But PLANS objects vigorously to anything Waldorf in public schools because of its inseparability from the religion of Anthroposophy. . . . At the Rudolf Steiner College, public school teachers were indoctrinated in Anthroposophy as a mandatory part of their training for the adoption of the Waldorf method in their public schools. Teachers who voiced objections to occult spiritualism and pseudo-science instruction were ostracised.

The two Waldorf schools being sued stated there were no religious or unconstitutional elements in either the method or the curriculum.[28]

Steiner's revelation is not taught directly at primary or secondary level, though it is said that Waldorf/Steiner schools offer Anthroposophical study groups outside the standard required curriculum, and that parents as well as students are encouraged to join. Teaching the revelation directly would, it is thought, preclude later free choice as an individual. But, inevitably, the social context and the ambience are Anthroposophical. In this sense the macrocosm is seen as being faithfully reflected to pupils. It seems, for example, that rebirth is not taught explicitly, but the soul may be compared to a butterfly which has developed from a chrysalis.

Steiner believed that, reflecting the macrocosm, human beings develop in seven-year stages. At the birth of the physical body there is a spiritual nature (the 'etheric') in an 'envelope' around the baby assisting its growth, just as, before birth, the mother enveloped the foetus. At about 'the change of teeth', or seven years, the etheric nature is no longer needed by the organism and so becomes 'freed' into imagination (it is said that a child whose teeth have not yet begun to change may not be allowed to move on with the others of the same age). Similarly, a higher spiritual nature (the 'astral') is 'freed' during puberty, at about fourteen years. At twenty-one or so the essential human individuality (known as the 'I') is said to become liberated, with a resulting capacity for idealism, judgment and independence. From this point on development seems to depend largely on conscious intervention as revealed in Steiner's path of knowledge.

Anthroposophical education starts from the pre-natal preparation of the mother. Up to the age of three a strong and healthy will is encouraged; then, up to seven, the capacity for imitation and example will probably be considered most important. From seven to fourteen the child at a Waldorf school belongs to a group who keep the same basic class teacher throughout to satisfy the need at this stage for 'veneration' and 'reverence'.

After a two-hour lesson with the class teacher, who should teach in an Imaginative way, the late morning curriculum ideally contains rhythm and movement, languages (not regarded as a 'subject') and singing. Here the child can experience other teachers, as also in the afternoon, which is given to arts and crafts, gymnastics and eurythmy, practical activities and sport. At nine years old, Old Testament stories will be told; at ten, Norse sagas and myths; at eleven, Greek history, and at twelve, Roman and medieval history.

In teaching teenagers, attempts are made to adapt to the outside world. In 2004 the first Waldorf school (in Luxemburg) was represented in the International Baccalaureate Organisation (IBO).[29] In France and, to some extent, the Netherlands, there have been official curriculum requirements. Nevertheless, no one should go to a Steiner school if they want competitive intellectual training. An ex-pupil of Michael Hall, the oldest Steiner school in the UK, started a research project questioning her old classmates, who had been teenagers there in the early 1950s. She found that, unlike her, they had been happy but that they tended to have a sense of academic inferiority later in life.[30] It seems that some Steiner schools are making computer training available to a limited extent, but that the use of computers is not as early or widespread as it is in conventional schools. The advent of computers adds to the educational differences in the event of a child wishing to transfer from a Steiner education.

The Threefold Commonwealth

The Threefold Commonwealth emerged in the apocalyptic days of German collapse after the First World War. It was Steiner's hope for the future organisation of Europe, if not the world. The Anthroposophical NPI is based on it; also, in the early 1980s, there was an action group in Stuttgart with their own building. The Threefold Commonwealth is seen as a description of the social dynamics to be incarnated, the details to depend on the particular context.

There will be a 'spiritual-cultural function' which is to be funded by 'gift-money'. Also there will be a 'rights-body' which will be distinguished by independence, impartiality and democracy. This should govern wages and education. The blueprint, in advance of

EU regionalism, provided for more states than had been the case so that nationalism could give way to more local allegiances. Thirdly there will be the 'economic function'. Steiner proposed associations of producers, distributors and consumers. Money is not to be based on gold but instead on a perishable commodity such as wheat. At the heart of the idealistic blueprint is Steiner's good-natured belief, perhaps reflecting pre-Holocaust optimism, that every exploiter of his fellow men would naturally much prefer his victim not to suffer.

5. Man Today, Karma and the Macrocosm

Out of this wood do not desire to go:
Thou shalt remain here, whether thou wilt or no.

And I will purge thy mortal grossness so
That thou shalt like an airy spirit go.[1]
— William Shakespeare, A Midsummer Night's Dream

The social being of Anthroposophy has been described as spiritually informed. In a rainbow-like way the applications are meditations and vice-versa. Coherence comes from shared seeking based on Steiner's work. The Anthroposophical mind is on a perpetual quest to realise the spirit that is already in matter through attaining the higher states of Imagination, Inspiration and Intuition. Following the path to these sublime states, Steiner's followers increasingly perceive the cosmos as he revealed it. These 'objective spiritual truths' are the ultimate justification for everything Anthroposophical.

They are rarely systematised[2] or seen as culturally relative. Getting to know the revelation is like entering an enchanted wood. There is no allowable way of seeing it as a mapped whole and the attempt to do so (as in this book) is close to a profane, or Ahrimanic, act. There are none of the linear, sharp perspectives that belong to the outside, contemporary 'Ahrimanic' world. This and the following chapter go into the wood as far as possible in an attempt to give an overview of the cosmology.

The way in has largely been through English-speaking Anthroposophy. The poetic, mythic, and lived processes whereby Anthroposophy is communicated are an important part of the message and are noticed briefly at the end of the chapter and through quotations in this and the following chapter. However, no structural analysis of Steiner's revelation seems to exist. As will be seen, its structures can be interpreted as corresponding to the meanings of the Goetheanum serpent and of Anthroposophy's social being, which has already been described.

Members have greatly helped me to understand the cosmology and they, as much as written sources, have – without being in any way responsible for it – contributed to this Ahrimanic version.[3] Told as a whole it is inevitably intricate.

The Nature of Man Today

Rudolf Steiner's simplest description of man was to compare him to a plant. The stalk is analogous to the soul, which 'takes root' in the physical world and 'blossoms', through the 'I', in the spiritual world. The familiar splitting into body, soul and spirit is the starting point from which he opens out his vision.

A ninefold division arises through subdividing the three primary realities of body, soul and spirit into three subtle entities (or 'natures') each. The body of man is described as consisting of 'physical', 'etheric'[4] and 'soul' natures or 'bodies'. Of these, only the physical contains matter in the everyday, sense-perceptible use of the word. The etheric nature is what gives the physical form and shape; the latter decomposes when (as in 'death') this etheric nature leaves it. There are, for example, etheric fingers and hearts, all in flow and movement and much more complicated than the physical organs. Steiner's revelations about the etheric nature have been related to the beginning of energy field theory in modern biology. The etheric nature is the passer on of heredity. The soul nature is the rouser of consciousness; nevertheless, it is seen as part of the body of man.

The second of the three main divisions, the soul of man, also consists of three natures. The first subdivided aspect is the 'sentient soul', which is barely distinguishable from the soul nature of the body. Steiner often grouped them together, calling them the 'astral body'. The sentient soul responds through the senses to the stimuli of the outside world; it is also the area of human subjectivity, that is to say, feelings, passions, and instincts. The other two natures of soul, the 'intellectual' and 'spiritual' souls, are implicitly spiritual principles. The intellectual soul arises when thinking is brought to bear on sense perception to change the physical world, thus creating technology and material civilisation. But such thinking, even when unconscious of its origins, is, Steiner states, really spiritual because it is connected with the transcendent individuality of man, the 'I'. The spiritual soul is formally part of the basic soul reality of man, but is implicitly spirit because it is the God within, at the developmental stage when the soul comes to know the 'I'. It is, in Anthroposophy's ethical intuitionism, identified with the good, the true, and inner duty.

The eye in the head of the Goetheanum serpent as it coils round to enclose its tail-end suggests the guiding theme of the three spirit natures. Consciousness becomes aware of the lower bodies in a process that remarkably resembles the path of knowledge, with its stages of Imagination, Inspiration and Intuition. 'Spirit-self' arises when the astral body is transmuted to a higher state. 'Life-spirit' is the similar transformation of the etheric nature. 'Spirit-man' is the conscious penetration and complete transmutation of the physical organism itself. These spiritual states are considered to belong generally to the future but, it seems, are anticipated in the Imagination, Inspiration, and Intuition of the path of knowledge.

In Steiner's *Theosophy* the threefold approach, having been expanded as described into one that is ninefold, is then contracted to seven and, finally, four aspects (see Table 2). The nine subtle natures (three each for the body 'root', the soul 'stalk' and the spirit 'blossom') contract to seven. The last of the body and the first of the soul natures constitute the astral body; and the last nature of the soul, the spiritual soul, is combined with the first of the spirit natures, spirit-self, and takes the latter's name. There is a further contraction to four entities. The last two soul natures have become spirit since the higher one has become spirit-self while the other one, the intellectual soul, has become identified with the 'I'. Thus all is spirit until the astral body; then there are the etheric and physical natures. This fourfold division seems to be the one that is most significant for Anthroposophists, for the physical body is what man today has in common with minerals, plants and animals; the etheric corresponds to the life of plants and animals, the astral to that of animals, while spirit is within humanity and other 'Beings'.

Apart from the present physical body all the natures of man are considered to be supersensible. Furthermore, of the original nine natures, five are related to what Steiner terms 'spirit'. This illustrates the importance of spirit in his cosmology. Subjectivity and affects are represented in the astral body alone, as what is formally 'soul' (our 'stalk') loses two of its natures to spirit.

Given that technical advances such as scanning brain processes have now made it possible to link states of consciousness with physical correlates, it is interesting to compare Steiner's revelation with one of the most down to earth yet poetic expositions of the new neuroscience. Antonio Damasio in *The Feeling of What Happens* distinguishes between a minimal proto-self and wakefulness, core consciousness with a sense of self which involves a 'second order map of organism-object relationship', and extended consciousness which is uniquely human, involving autobiographical memory and conscience.[5] There appear to be similarities between these and, if the macrocosmic dimensions are momentarily ignored, Steiner's etheric body, astral body and intellectual soul.

Karma and Repeated Earth Lives

In Anthroposophy man has a destiny that far transcends his present limitations. After explaining the nature of man Steiner goes on to describe karma in what is perhaps the best example of his translated style.

> By means of its actions, the human spirit has really brought about its own fate. In a new life it finds itself linked to what it did in a former one. . . . The physical body is subject to the laws of heredity. The human spirit, on the contrary, has to incarnate over and over again; and its law consists in its bringing over the fruits of the former lives into the following ones. The soul lives in the present. But this life in the present is not independent of the previous lives. For the incarnating spirit brings its destiny with it from its previous incarnations. And this destiny determines its life. What impressions the soul will be able to have, what wishes it will be able to have gratified, what sorrows and joys shall grow up for it, with what individuals it shall come into contact — all this depends on the nature of the actions in the past incarnations of the spirit. Those people with whom the soul was bound up in one life, the soul must meet again in a subsequent one, because the actions which have taken place between them must have their consequences. When this soul seeks re-embodiment, those others, who are bound up with it, will also strive towards their incarnation at the same time.[6]

In Anthroposophy death is considered to be a process similar to, but going beyond, sleep. In sleep, if it is dreamless, the astral nature or body and the 'I' separate from the physical and etheric bodies of the sleeper. The former return to replenish the latter and the sleeper awakes. On death, the (formative) etheric as well as the astral body and 'I' are believed to leave the physical body, which thereby disintegrates.

Dying, usually at least, is perceived to be gradual and not confined to the physical body alone. The etheric and astral bodies also become 'corpses'. After the death of the physical body, the etheric and astral bodies and the 'I' are joined together. The etheric body, freed from the memory-limiting physical body, is believed to make the past life appear in a vivid, all-embracing simultaneous tableau, then (after a few days) to die. The essence of the memory tableau is retained.

Following the death of the etheric body, the next process begins. It takes about as long as the time spent sleeping in the previous incarnation, and involves the purging of the astral body, which then becomes a corpse itself. This takes place in the 'soul-world'. The past incarnation is purged by being lived backwards to the time (at birth or conception?) when spontaneous experience of the 'spirit-world' had been lost. This purging results in a spiritual 'seed', which then grows in the spiritual world of the freed 'I'.

Anthroposophically, the soul-world occupies the same planes as the physical world but, as described, has different essences: passions and higher feelings. The forces of 'sympathy' overcome those of 'antipathy', which are concentrated in the two lowest of the seven 'regions' of the soul-world. (The three highest contain no antipathy at all.)

In the lowest region, that of 'Burning Desire', cravings form actual beings which to the spiritual eye cause pain and ghastly horror. They are greedy and avaricious, determining the lower sensual impulses and dominating selfish instincts in animals' and men's souls. This purgatory is related to the Hindu Kamaloca. The next region, that of 'Flowing Susceptibility', consists of the external glitter and worthless trifles of life. Its successor, 'Wish Substance', purges wishes. In 'Attraction and Repulsion' there is the special trial of losing the illusion of bodily self. The highest three regions purge lesser goods: that of 'Soul Light' removes sensuous enthusiasm, whether for natural, educational or welfare ideals; 'Active Soul Force' disposes of (among other things) aestheticism; the highest, 'Soul Life', frees man from any lingering attachments to the physical world.

The 'I' is progressively freed after the death of the physical body to grow in the spirit-world with a purged and spiritualised memory tableau and astral body. The 'I' grows rather than undergoes purgation. Steiner states that 'to avoid confusion'[7] a careful distinction must be made between what can be purged in the soul-world and what can only be redeemed through the karmic law of reincarnation; but having made the abstract distinction he does not seem to give it any content.

The spirit-world is 'woven out of the substance of which human thought consists'.[8] Steiner tells us that initially it is bewildering: it consists of continuous creative activity expressed, for example, in spiritual colour, taste and sound (hence the Pythagorean 'music of the spheres'). Like the soul-world, it has seven interpenetrating regions; these Steiner refers to by number. The first three are the spiritual forms of what are, on earth, life in the sense-world, feeling and emotion. In the first, it appears, family and those closest to us are rejoined. The fourth region contains the archetypes of the arts, sciences, technology, the state, and of thoughts generally. The fifth consists of the archetype of Wisdom. In the sixth, man will fulfill that which is most in accord with the true being of the world. The seventh leads man to 'Life-kernels' that give him a complete survey of the spirit, soul, and material worlds.

The regions of the spirit-world have been working with the 'I' to change the conditions of earth for the next incarnation. After a discarnate period of, it seems, about 500 to 1,000 years, the 'I' is believed to gain a new astral and etheric body and to be guided by spirit-beings towards its choice of mother and father. Usually the rebirth is as the opposite sex to that of the previous incarnation. On re-entry into physical life the 'I' is said to experience a prevision of the coming life, a tableau which shows all the obstacles to be removed.

Anthroposophical development is thus macrocosmic, unlike psychological theories such as Stern's or Erikson's. Here the mystery of the macrocosm tends to become contracted to the mystery of the infant's experience, or at most to that of the individual lifespan. Subject to this there are some structural similarities between Stern's developmental schema (which is based on sense perception) and Steiner's. For Stern, the infant is endowed with observable capacities that mature. 'When these become available, they are organised and transformed, in quantum mental leaps, into organising subjective perspectives about the sense of self and other. Each new sense of self defines the formation of a new domain of relatedness. While these domains of relatedness result in qualitative shifts in social experience, they are not phases; rather, they are forms of social experience that remain intact throughout life. Nonetheless, their initial phase of formation constitutes a sensitive period of development'.[9] After the sensitive periods there may be regression or, alternatively, development, for example through the psychotherapeutic process of reconstructing a past.

The Macrocosm

At this stage, in his seminal *Occult Science,* Steiner reveals the most far-reaching visions of all: he describes the beginning, nature, and future of the macrocosm.[10] The preceding account of man, karma and rebirth is more or less confined to the present; it is merely a contemporary aspect of the Anthroposophical esoteric synthesis.

Steiner's revelation is about spiritual experience, not 'Ahrimanic' intellectual analysis of the structures. If this book were to reflect only the insider experience of Anthroposophists, the analysis which follows would not be made. They do not experience structures. What follows are interpretations made here. They are not 'Anthroposophy' but represent an external attempt to make sense of the revelation from the point of view of the history of ideas. Only an outsider could contribute such a perspective, and in the very giving of this added perspective much of the spirit of Anthroposophy is inevitably lost.

Anthroposophy's cosmological structures have already been suggested in the interpretation given here of the macrocosmic serpent. Some introduction has also been made in chapter two, in order to explain the movement's attitude towards education, and elsewhere. As will be suggested in the next part of the book, the revelation's prototype is 'Syrian-Egyptian gnosis'. This term, as used in this book, extends a description of a controversial historical (and loosely boundaried) variant of gnosticism into an ideal-type. It thereby provides a schema for an understanding of the structures of Steiner's revelation.

Cosmological Structures

1. In the beginning all was spirit and at the end it will mostly or entirely become spirit again.

In orthodox Christian cosmogony God creates a finite world and mankind. Similarly, in Judaism and Islam there is a creator God who is utterly other. In contrast, spirit for Steiner is the original state of everything: he reveals no self-sufficient, pre-existing creator God comparable to that of the Judaeo-Christian-Islamic tradition. The Anthroposophical Trinity consists of spiritual essences outside the solar system; yet they are also the ultimate identity of man and the world. Spirit gradually becomes matter in cosmic embodiments. In Anthroposophy this is accompanied by an 'abnormal' or pathological development in which matter becomes 'too' hard or gross. This is sometimes in Anthroposophical explication linked to the idea of a 'Fall'.[11]

In this Syrian-Egyptian pattern – usually somewhat before the 'present age', whenever that may be – there is a turning point. This inaugurates a reverse process, one of spiritual restoration or redemption. All matter has gradually formed as the result of the dynamic activity of spirit; but after the turning point most, or perhaps all of it is due to respiritualise. Pictorially this can be interpreted as being expressed at the point where the Goetheanum serpent, like other serpents in Western Gnosticism,[12] starts to coil round so that its head approaches its tail-end. The macrocosmic idea that matter or, at least, gross or 'too hard' matter needs to be redeemed is different from traditional Christian eschatology with its judgment for human beings only and everlasting heaven or hell.

In the Anthroposophical beginning there were no earth, moon, sun, stars or solar system as we know them; instead, the macrocosm consisted of undifferentiated essences in states of 'spiritual warmth'. Steiner gave the macrocosm at this stage the name of 'Saturn'.

A benign spiritual tension occurred between the essences of which Saturn consisted. The tension led eventually to a rather denser cosmic embodiment consisting of 'spiritual air', which is known as 'Sun'. The tension increased, leading to the 'liquid' cosmic embodiment of 'spiritual water': this stage of the macrocosm is called 'Moon'. With further tension solid matter itself began to form and the present solar system hardened out. Accompanying this was a development in which matter 'fell'. Steiner gave this present cosmic embodiment the name of 'Earth'. (The earth − with a small 'e' − on which we live is just a part of the macrocosmic Earth, our present solar system.) The densest part of the descent from spirit is reached in Earth, the fourth and middle of the seven macrocosmic planetary embodiments.

However, there is also an 'abnormal' development whereby matter becomes too solid. This is linked to a rebellion by Lucifer, who is the karma of Ahriman, the spirit of hardening. As a result of this rebellion and excess hardening the turning point within the planetary embodiment of Earth is just after the middle point. It takes place in the fifth, not fourth, of the seven 'epochs' or sub-divisions of Earth[13].

The turning point, the start of the reverse process which respiritualises the macrocosm, has just begun. This is marked by the redeeming descent of Christ. Steiner devotes far less space to the future than to the past. The macrocosmic embodiment to follow is known as 'Jupiter'. It is more spiritual than Earth, corresponding, though in a more consciously developed way, with the 'spiritual water' of Moon. Thus the fifth planetary period is a restoration − though with greater conscious differentiation − of the spirituality of the third period. Similarly, the sixth, respiritualised embodiment (known as 'Venus') differentiates 'spiritual air' and so corresponds to Sun, the second stage. In the seventh, final embodiment (that of 'Vulcan'), the macrocosm − apart from a possible 'irreclaimable moon' – has circled back round again to differentiate the pristine 'spiritual warmth' of Saturn, the first stage, into ineffable spiritual individuality.

Thus there is a fundamental structural symmetry: increasing tension leads to a macrocosmic descent to an apogee, just after the middle point, when matter is too solid. Then there is a gradual return of most if not all matter to its source through respiritualisation. This pattern is basic to Anthroposophy. Steiner's description of the nature of man and repeated earth lives only applies to the current stage of our Earth embodiment.

Steiner infused it with another structure which has correlates with Theosophy and Indian cosmology.[14] There are great pulsating rhythms of collapse into spirit and manifestation (Theosophically and Anthroposophically known as pralaya and manvantara respectively). The collapses into spirit occur between the 'planetary' embodiments: for example, between Saturn and Sun, Sun and Moon, Moon and Earth, and so on. The manifestations reach their peaks at the middle of each embodiment, for example, at the middle of Saturn, Sun, Moon, Earth, etc. These major rhythms are indented with minor rhythms which go in the opposite direction, so that there is an exceedingly complex rippling effect. This resonates with Hinduism. Steiner named the present period after the lesser Hindu cycle of Kali Yuga, though for him this has a duration of only a few thousand years and not the Hindu 432,000 years. This is consistent with the tendency for revealed time-scales in Western tradition – for example, in Genesis – to be much shorter than Hindu ones, and also much shorter than those of contemporary science.

A further correlate with the structures of Steiner's revelation has been said to be the theory of thermodynamics. Differentials of temperature are fundamental to the description of the origins of the Anthroposophical cosmos (i.e. its cosmogony). This may, of course, have its origins in Steiner's scientific training.

2. Man is a microcosm of the macrocosm

Today it is conventional in the secular West to perceive the natural environment in a post-Kantian way as unknowable 'in itself'. Thoughts manifesting through mental processes are not conventionally thought to have a literal correspondence with essences in the outside world. To Anthroposophists this outlook is, philosophically, a residue of undeveloped positivism.

In Anthroposophy concepts are understood to have literal

correspondences with what is perceived as being outside. Indeed, 'inside' and 'outside' are not sharp distinctions. If they appear to be so, this is because the person concerned is thought to be uninitiated, not realizing that he is a microcosm, a miniature of the macrocosm.

During the Saturn phase the prototype physical body was more or less universal and largely undifferentiated into individual physical bodies. This was, to a lesser extent, the case with the etheric body common to all living organisms which began to develop in its Sun phase. It was also somewhat the case with the astral body, common to all animals, which began to develop on Moon. Thus the present physical, etheric and astral bodies of man have evolved out of and so correspond to the physicality, ether and astrality outside man. Only the 'I' itself, the spiritual spark which is individual for each human being, is truly a unique activity, though even this is also macrocosmic spirit. The 'I' has in Anthroposophical evolutionary time only descended to the level of its physical, etheric and astral 'sheaths' around the middle of the Earth era. The redeeming Christ, who also descended at this time, is the archetypal 'I'. Man is not a discrete creation out of dust, as in Christian orthodoxy, but is composed of a pantheistic, living nature and, through the 'I', is of the same essence as Christ himself, though individual at the same time.

As will be seen, this anthropology has many correspondences with gnosticism. The latter incorporated Babylonian astrology and developed magical practices based on planetary correspondences between 'inside' and 'outside'. The aim was to experience transcendence through the spark of spirit, which, it was thought, had become entangled in passion (soul) and overlaid by matter in an original cosmic fall.

It was said that in Anthroposophy the prototype physical body of man was present on Saturn, the first planetary embodiment. How can this be if, as has also been stated, the macrocosm only condensed into matter in the present, fourth embodiment of Earth? Can the physical body be other than matter as we know it?

Steiner states that it can be. It just so happens that the physical body is our kind of earth-bound matter at the present. The physical body has been spirit before; it can exist immaterially as warmth and archetypal form. This doctrine does not seem to be Theosophical: a Theosophist with a Ph.D. could only mutter with astonishment when I tried to explain it to him. However, as with much else in Anthroposophy, there is an antecedent in Valentinian gnosticism (see chapter seven).

3. Hardest matter is a negative organizing principle

Dynamic spirit has come to rest in matter, which is frozen or crystallized spirit, just as architecture is considered to be frozen music. Anthroposophists believe in a need to realise the spirit that they perceive as already in matter (there is nowhere Christ did not go), and so they state that matter for them is not a negative organising principle. Ahriman, the opponent representing hardening, is not a force to be overcome but to be redeemed. An outside interpretation that Anthroposophy uses hardest matter as a negative organising principle depends on interpreting their situation differently, that implicit in the mission of realising the spirit which is in matter is a sense that spiritually unrealised matter is in a lower state.

Furthermore, there is an explicit Anthroposophical concept (stated in Steiner's *Occult Science*) of over-hardened matter. The cold necessity of Ahriman, who imprisons everything, and the rebellious Lucifer, who is considered to be the karma of Ahriman, intervened in the evolution of the planetary embodiments so that matter condensed too much. This is apparent not only from present sclerotic aspects of the world but also from the specialised forms of animals. Thus hardest matter is the turning point – and so, cosmologically, the negative organising principle – for the serpent, which redemptively coils back round towards its own tail; and also for humans, who develop spiritually once they recognise their microcosmic correspondence with the macrocosm.

To non-Anthroposophists, matter's degrees of hardness are not central to existential, moral or cosmological issues. Anthroposophy's emphasis here is unlike orthodox Christianity, Islam, Judaism, Zoroastrianism, many[15] schools of Hinduism and, strictly, Buddhism. Anthroposophical salvation seems to consist in part of transcending and transmuting over-hardened identifications through finding the true 'I' of objective spirit. In Anthroposophy, as with the most sophisticated (Valentinian) form of gnosticism, the path entails mild asceticism, or at least a marked moderation. In other gnostic systems it has sometimes been severely ascetic, or occasionally, in the attempt to free the self from perceived imprisonment in a material body, orgiastic and antinomian.

Hardened matter is negative with a seed of spiritual promise (and so also ambivalent) because individually fashioned redemption is put centrally on the agenda by the fact of the hardening. Steiner rejected the excessive hardening caused by Ahriman but nevertheless saw the condensation of matter as a gift that enables man to evolve. There are analogies between Ahriman and the Satan of Valentinian gnosticism:

he is structurally necessary to make sense of the situation. Understood psychologically, there seems in Anthroposophy to be a cosmological ambivalence towards matter which expresses the experience of many spiritually-minded and creative people, not least of Steiner himself, towards the world. This can be perceived as pervading its many social applications, whose 'embeddedness' gives a means of living in spiritualised enclaves of the material world.

Anthroposophists believe that we can find within ourselves the capacity to release the frozenness. We can remove ourselves from this local, temporary level of hardness. So Anthroposophy is not internally perceived as dualistic − with a spirit/matter split − because it is the Anthroposophical view that matter can be redeemed, and that this is the direction the cosmos is going and its true nature. Indeed, Steiner wanted to break out of the idealism/materialism dichotomy. However, from external ontological perspectives it is the here and now perception from which Anthroposophy is starting, not its internally believed-in redemption, which is the frame of reference. Hence non-Anthroposophical perspectives will interpret its cosmos as dualist.

4. There is development towards spiritual individuality

An ascending spiritual individuality which evolves through transmuting the world in which it lives is the ultimate meaning of Steiner's cosmos. This is the purpose of the tension which starts in the Saturn phase and gathers momentum, with rhythmic respites or pralayas, until about the middle of the Earth era. There is a tension between two poles of reality. These are the pristine world of spirit, including the Trinity and many of the Spiritual Hierarchies, and the over-condensing world, which includes other Spiritual Hierarchies. This 'abnormal' 'fall', in becoming gross and more rebellious − as with the 'Luciferic' spirits in the Moon phase − also becomes more independent and developed. With the polarization at its apogee in the Anthroposophical Earth era there has arisen individualism. Ahriman's domineering hardness has given man an overriding need to control. Nevertheless, individualism gives man the freedom to choose to develop spiritual individuality. This, as has been seen, lessens the tension by infusing hardness with spirit through a cosmic ascent of consciousness, which arrives back at its origins in an ever more differentiated, aware state. The Goetheanum serpent's large head and eye can be interpreted as depicting this aware ascent.

In the Anthroposophical beginning − its Saturn phase − one part of the original macrocosmic essence, aided by self-sacrificing Spiritual

Hierarchies, began to rotate around the other. This rotation causes the development of prototype physical bodies. The greater rotation and differentiation of the Sun phase, together with grace emanating from spiritual beings, result in the physical bodies, which are not matter but a form of rudimentary consciousness, ascending to a higher level of organization: that of etheric bodies. In the Moon phase there is a further ascent from the rather less rudimentary consciousness of the etheric bodies towards the more differentiated picture-like consciousness of the astral bodies. This ascent of consciousness accompanies the condensation into subtle matter and 'fall' into 'abnormal' or gross matter. In the Earth era there is a further ascent of consciousness to the intellectual stage: that is, intellectualism where it is unaware of its identity with the 'I'. At the same time there is the furthest possible separation and fall, whereby the most Ahrimanic matter hardens furthest. This fall is paradoxical in nature: it is not the 'true purpose' of evolution, yet its alienation enables man's freedom of choice.

The ascent continues, after the Earth era, in the Jupiter phase. Here, consciousness will become aware of the astral world (this is the spirit-self stage). In so doing, some of the tension will be reduced and the macrocosm will be partly restored from the fall into grossness. In the next stage of the ascent of consciousness – the Venus phase – life-spirit represents the extension of awareness to the etheric world; as a result the polarized tension is further reduced and there is a further respiritualisation. In the final phase – Vulcan – the rudimentary, diffuse, physical consciousness of the Saturn phase is penetrated by individual consciousnesses ascending to 'spirit-man' and becoming aware of their 'I's. The tension is entirely abolished and the macrocosm saved and respiritualised at a higher level. Man has redeemed the planetary phases through becoming entirely aware of and responsible for his nature. Perhaps this is close to the meaning of Paracelsus' motto, 'Let no one be another's who can be his own'.[16]

There are some more detailed ascending structures in the notes[17] and tables 3 and 4. Steiner's is probably the most complex example of what the French occultist Edouard Schuré called the glory and incomparable splendour of the esoteric synthesis.

Knowledge

The cosmological 'structures' are here interpreted as the organising principles of Anthroposophy. Knowledge such as karma and rebirth, modern astronomy, evolution and the Atlantean epoch is synthesised through these structures, increasing the integration.

In Anthroposophical experience, as explained earlier, the revelation is true as a whole: it coheres without analytical distinctions between 'structures' and 'knowledge'. Thus the Indian idea of karma becomes identified with what has been termed here a structure, the ascent of consciousness to transmute the world and thereby realise spiritual individuality. Albert Steffen wrote, 'Consider well the symbol of the serpent that forms a circle and bites its own tail. It admonishes us to view the whole world in accord with the laws of Karma and reincarnation.'[18]

The 'Christian' Trinity in Anthroposophy transcend yet permeate the macrocosm, except within gross matter. The macrocosm is identical to the solar system; the Trinity have their abode beyond it. Thus Steiner assumes the astronomical finding that the cosmos extends beyond what has been identified as the solar system. However the presence of the Trinity, rather like that of Bhagvān in Hinduism, is pervasive. They are not, as has been seen, sharply separated from man as creative forces. The Trinity have correspondences with the gnostic Pleroma. They are the greatest ultimate described, and in one aspect, that of Christ, descend as the archetypal 'I' to fallen matter to mark the turning of the macrocosm towards restoration. Conventional Christian doctrine is absent. The 'Trinity' is a familiar name applied unusually to the spiritual essence(s), the 'Crystal Heaven', beyond and yet partially penetrating the solar system. The 'I' is divine because of its identity with Christ.

Darwinian evolution is fused with the structures. Thus the facts on which the Darwinian hypotheses are based are, in Anthroposophy, fused with the idea of a spiritually descending specialization and ascending complexity. Animal forms hardened first and most grossly, hence early fossil remains. Steiner stood Haeckel's materialistic evolutionism on its head.

The optimistic evolutionism of Steiner's age (until 1914 or so) is in accord with the great emphasis in Anthroposophy on the upward ascent of consciousness to realise spiritual individuality. This has some correspondences with Syrian-Egyptian gnosis, but in Anthroposophy it seems to have been much reinforced by the progressive evolutionism of the later nineteenth century.

The enormous contemporary hopes for – and prestige of – science also correspond with the nomenclature of Steiner's spiritual path. He called his system 'spiritual science'. Unlike most similar spiritual leaders he trained successfully as a scientist. L. Ron Hubbard of Scientology only claimed to have done so. Blavatsky, who – if Goethe is not included in this more recent company – perhaps pioneered the notion of 'spiritual science', and Mary Baker Eddy, with her Christian Science, had no scientific training. A frequent doctrine of modern spiritualities is the claim to be based on scientific research. Similar claims can also be seen in Freudian, Jungian and other psychological revelations: these convey an atmosphere of scientific credibility, despite the devastating sociological and epistemological critiques by Gellner, Grunbaum and Popper,[19] because of their medical provenance.

The arrangement of Steiner's revelation is not predictably symmetrical. The turning point does not occur exactly halfway through the Earth era, which is itself the middle planetary state. It occurs slightly later. In his early days as General Secretary of the German Section of the Theosophical Society, Steiner was identified with Blavatsky's teachings. Earth, itself the middle planetary embodiment, has seven 'epochs' and we are now (according to both Blavatsky and Steiner) in the fifth, not the fourth. Before Anthroposophy had evolved to be an independent thought form from Theosophy, Steiner had repeated Blavatsky's clairvoyant finding that there were four epochs, including Lemuria and Atlantis, before the present one. The specifically Anthroposophical Christ was revealed to have descended in the fifth epoch and not the half-way point.

The Anthroposophical explanation of this is that Christ could not intervene in the central, fourth, epoch because of the 'abnormal' intervention of Lucifer and Ahriman. To balance them, Christ descended to Palestine in the fifth epoch. There is perhaps an analogy with Wagner's *Ring* in that necessity, symbolised by the three Norns, is overridden by the birth of freedom from the moment Brunnhilde lovingly and courageously differentiates herself as more than merely the blind will of Wotan. The Norns' ropes of fate, that is, the predictability of things, eventually break. Abnormal interventions break the predictable symmetry provided by necessity. *Occult Science* and Wagner's *Ring* are vastly different in many important ways, but it will be suggested later that there is a common matrix of nineteenth century German culture.[20]

Language

Inseparable from the structures and knowledge of Anthroposophy is its mode of expression. In the foregoing analysis this 'feel' has all but disappeared, but, in its English-speaking form, it will emerge rather more in the following chapter.

The rainbow-like social being of the Rudolf Steiner movement corresponds to the literalness of Steiner's prodigious revelation. He wrote many books and there are − often unreliable − notes of about 6,000 of his lectures. If there is an essential metaphor, this is only because he is having to reduce his perceptions from Intuition and Inspiration to their less spiritual manifestations. Thus his Imaginative pictures of high, supersensible realities are necessarily modelled on his tangible contemporary world. There is an unusual synecdoche in which the spiritual whole is described by means of the more condensed Imaginative part. For example, 'warmth' (on 'Saturn'), 'air' (on 'Sun'), and 'water' (on 'Moon') are not mere metaphors, nor are they absolute literal truth: they are a partial, synecdochal truth. Perhaps this is what Steiner's translators are trying to convey by 'half-metaphorically' and 'as it were'.[21]

Anthroposophists see the older English translations as poor. Nevertheless the Anthroposophical spiritual world with its movement of forms and processes outside conventionally perceived boundaries makes an impact. 'If we imagine something intermediate between the nutrition and breathing of today, we shall have a fair idea of what is taking place in this direction.'[22] Or 'the second kingdom of the Sun is endowed with the character of personality'.[23] Or again, 'That which remains behind when the soul departs from the body is no longer merely like a seed, to be kindled to life by the returning soul;'[24] here, the apparent mixed metaphor of 'kindling' a 'seed' to 'life' is Anthroposophically synecdochal, because fire and seeds are spiritually close as essences.

The imagery, whether sustained or casual, is nearly always taken from nature and tradition, with very little from contemporary technology (even the spread of railways). 'Seed', 'kernel' and 'fruits' are much used, as is the elemental 'raying back'. 'Kingdom' and 'domains' are frequent. Those artefacts used to provide immediate metaphors have a long human history, for example, 'thread', 'coin' and the frequent 'veil'.

Contemporary translations of main works have been produced. The older translations evoke the sacred through everyday words or syntax that may have been in keeping with popular Edwardian poetry but are now out of use. Examples are 'nay', 'partake but feebly', 'perforce', 'bedecked', 'one needs must have', 'now therefore the souls, formerly translated onto Mars, Jupiter. . .'. Biblical resonances tend to occur strangely in Hellenic contexts, as with 'sinning against the law of harmony' and 'the altar of humanity'. There are occasional poetic evocations, for example, the quasi-Coleridgean 'wondrous magic scenes'. Mixed in is some residual Theosophical terminology from the East, such as pralaya and manvantara. Capital letters are used for hypostasised qualities such as 'Thought', 'Wisdom', 'Event of Palestine', 'Imperishable Reality'. Hyphens are pressed in aid, as in 'being-of-will', 'warmth-of-soul'. There is repetition, for example, 'first foundation', 'in that age of time', 'first harbingers', and circumlocution, as in the sentence: 'It is by no means out of keeping with the facts to say that in those pristine ages the Earth underwent a day-time and a night-time.'[25] Especially because of the difficulties of translation, the trees are difficult to understand without having first taken the Anthroposophical wood as the unit for comprehension.

6. The Evolution of the Macrocosm

*I am most vividly conscious that what I have undertaken to do far
exceeds any human powers and their duration on earth.[1]*
— *Goethe*

Rudolf Steiner thought that Goethe hesitated before the supreme
reality of spirit. Anthroposophists think that their founder's vision
completes the task that Goethe began.

The account of the revelation that follows in this chapter mainly
draws on Steiner's *Occult Science*.[2] Throughout it is based on
Steiner's published material as available to English-speakers, and as
stated previously does not reflect the author of this book's personal
perceptions or convictions; this disclaimer will not be repeated,
in order that the reader might, in the pages ahead, develop some
experiential sense of the immediacy and immersion of the original.
The version that follows is more strictly chronological than Steiner's
exposition but more or less preserves his emphasis, with most space
being given to the immediate past (for example, Lemuria), less space
to the remote past, and least space to the future. Steiner quite often
wrote about the past in the present tense because he was describing
it through the findings of his contemporary research. The summary
here tries to retain this sense of immediacy.

Anthroposophists and gnostics assume that the development
of each human being reflects the cosmological evolution of the
anthropomorphic macrocosm. Within a biologically boundaried frame
of reference this has analogies with the ontogenetic/phylogenetic
thinking, prevalent around the time of Steiner, in which the evolution
of the individual is seen as recapitulating that of the species. From a
'psychologism' perspective (one with the intra-human assumptions
of psychology), Steiner's macrocosm will seem to be a projection
of his personal biography. For example, the phase of Saturn might
be interpreted to correspond to womb-like experiences, Sun to early

infancy, and Moon, with its Luciferic rebellion, to the struggles for independence of later infancy (or of adolescence). Early Earth, with its giants, floods and 'overhard' animals, could be considered as the attempt in early childhood to consolidate a consistent consciousness that distinguishes reality from fantasy. Or it might, together with the controlling egotism of Ahriman, be interpreted to represent the fantasies and turmoil of adolescence. The turning point of the cosmos, the descent of Christ, might be understood as a projection of the crucial moment when human nature starts to know itself. The planetary phases of Jupiter, Venus and Vulcan could be seen as future intra-psychic integration.

This psychological perspective does not alter the macrocosmic account that follows, the main aim of which is to present Anthroposophical cosmology. But references to Steiner's life are made from time to time so that possible correlations with the seer's biography, however they may be interpreted, are drawn to the reader's attention.

Steiner's revelation about how the solar system evolved is here presented chronologically in the sequence of the planetary phases or embodiments (Saturn, Sun, Moon, Earth, Jupiter, Venus and Vulcan). The first section reveals the macrocosmic situation before the start of the solar system and the cosmogonic development of Saturn.

Before the Solar System

Beyond the solar system, in starry space or the 'Crystal Heaven', are the transcendent Trinity. Also in their (or its) presence are the three highest Spiritual Hierarchies, the Seraphim, Cherubim and Thrones. The two highest of these seem to have completed their evolution. The Thrones, not yet pure being, have a little further to go. The Crystal Heaven consists of the deeds of evolution that took place before the evolution of our present solar system. The foregoing is highly 'esoteric' knowledge. In a gesture of systemic containment *Occult Science* discourages the pursuit of origins.

A psychologist's perspective would reduce the Crystal Heaven to some intuitive recall of a blissful state of being before the troubles of infancy develop. This could be linked with the Steiner family's sense of a past paradise, their roots in the Lower Austrian forest district north of the Danube, before they experienced the marginalities involved in working for the new railway. More generally, it is another of mankind's frequent myths (the word is used here in the sense of 'not necessarily untrue') on the theme of paradise lost.

Saturn

Duration

From this state of already evolved being, the solar system begins to develop. Saturn and the Crystal Heaven seem ambiguously related to the view of Henri Bergson, Steiner's French contemporary and a philosopher with some parallels to Steiner, who held that there is no eternity standing in contrast to time. Spirit very gradually starts the condensation that eventually results in the hardening of matter on Earth and its later respiritualisation. The Seraphim, Cherubim, and Thrones are in the zodiac outside the embryonic solar system, but the Dominions, Mights and Powers are within it. Steiner described this early Saturn as 'chaotic, undifferentiated substance'.[3] This is a phrase, reminiscent of the psychologist William James' contemporary evocation of the infant's experience as a 'blooming, buzzing confusion', which could perhaps also apply to the dawning of individual human consciousness, or even to sensations in the womb. There is some difference between these two groups of Spiritual Hierarchies that causes Saturn to rotate. It seems to be expressed in terms of temperature. As already stated, Steiner, a trained scientist, is said to have had full command of the laws of thermodynamics.

The Anthroposophical Spiritual Hierarchies are essential forces expressing qualities such as love, harmony, wisdom, form and movement: for example, the Thrones consist of courage. Here Steiner is consistent with the Christian tradition that accepted the Pseudo-Dionysian adaptation of the gnostic Pleroma (see table 4). Anthroposophists often use the familiar Pseudo-Dionysian names.

The rotation is the start of separation and, eventually, of Luciferic and Ahrimanic conflict. This increases in the following planetary phases or embodiments of Sun, Moon, and the first part of Earth. With the accompanying condensation into harder states comes also the ascent of consciousness: here is the purpose or ultimate 'karmic' meaning of evolution. In the first stages, at least, the rotation is an altruistic process. In the beginning the Thrones give their being of 'heat substance' to the 'Saturn substance' which, united with the Dominions, mirrors or 'rays' it back.

The Spiritual Hierarchies, through giving their being unselfishly, themselves ascend in awareness. Thus the Principalities on Saturn are enabled to become aware of their 'I' since it is rayed back by the warmth of Saturn and so brought home to their consciousness. As a result they go through their 'human' stage (see table 4): 'To see this fact in its true light, we must be ready to conceive that a being can be a "human" without necessarily having the form and figure man has today.'[4]

Until the end of Duration – a translated term which has been used not only in relation to Bergson but also, in various senses, in relation to Augustine, Aquinas, Spinoza, Locke, Newton, Leibniz and William James[5] – the 'pure warmth-of-soul' on Saturn has no inner life of its own, and time has not started.

Time

Saturn consists entirely of 'warmth-bodies' which are 'delicate, tenuous and ethereal'. 'They are the first beginnings of the present physical-mineral body of man, which has evolved out of the old warmth-body by receiving into it the gaseous, liquid and solid substances that developed only at a later stage.'[6] As stated in the previous chapter, only on the present hardened planetary embodiment of Earth is the physical body made of matter.

Anthroposophy is pan-psychic. Towards the middle of Saturn, when Duration ends and Time begins, the warmth-bodies develop consciousness. These 'phantoms of man' become endowed with the simplest awareness that is 'yet more dim than that of dreamless sleep. Under present-day conditions the minerals possess this consciousness.'[7] The rotation of the Saturn substance and interaction with the Spiritual Hierarchies enable the warmth-bodies to become more differentiated, though, as throughout all evolution in the planetary embodiments, not all life achieves the highest complexity possible. Through the influence of the different regions of the zodiac, prototypes of physical organs emerge, for example the heart in Leo; the rib-cage in Cancer.

A play of light is added to warmth, then, 'though it may well seem quite mad to some people . . . something like sensations of taste begin to go surging to and fro'.[8] Nutrition, excretion and smell begin to develop. Macrocosmic man, or 'the seed of man', is evolving. Here the parallels with human infancy are obvious. Warmth is experienced before light. Consumption and excretion are processes that in another contemporarily nascent German-speaking myth were to be systematised by the psychoanalyst Abraham into supposed 'oral' and 'anal' infant stages. Other cultures find other human processes to describe cosmogenesis. For example, Hinduism holds that *sruti,* or what is heard, is even more sacred that *smriti*, or what is seen, and indeed, research today finds that the foetus hears before it sees.

The condensation and descent of spirit, so that it gradually evolves into matter, is to continue. But, as stated in the previous chapter, Steiner's cosmos is also pulsating (Theosophy and Hinduism have parallels). The planetary embodiment of Saturn is succeeded by that of Sun, but between the two – and between all the planetary embodiments – there is a *pralaya* in which everything becomes primal spirit again. The later part of the planetary embodiments or manifestations *(manvantaras)* consists of rhythmic recessions back into spirit. Thus Saturn, after its peak of manifestation (around the middle), begins to recede.

Steiner describes the *pralaya* before the emergence of Sun thus:

> A kind of interval of rest begins. The germ or seed of man passes as it were into a state of dissolution; not that it vanishes entirely – rather it is in the condition of a plant seed which, resting in the earth, will ripen by and by into a new plant. . . . And when the time for its awakening has come, then the Spiritual [Hierarchies] have acquired – under different conditions – the faculties to work still further upon the seed of man.[9]

Sun

Recapitulation

During the second planetary embodiment, that of Sun, the condensation of spirit into matter and the ascent of consciousness continue. But macrocosmic man (the 'seed of man'), emerging from *pralaya,* first of all recapitulates the development of Saturn in a rhythmic way, refining and adapting what has already evolved. The recapitulation of previous embodiments is the first occurrence after entering subsequent embodiments.

Differentiation

Once the recapitulation of Saturn's evolution is completed and it has adapted to the conditions of Sun, there is a condensation from 'warmth' to 'air'. With this hardening there is further differentiation: the 'physical' body becomes more refined and to it is added (for the first time) the etheric body. The Dominions are instrumental in this; indeed, the Spiritual Hierarchies intervene as crucially in Sun and subsequent planetary embodiments as they do on Saturn. There is rotation as on Saturn, but it is more pronounced. Steiner's teleological approach has analogies with primary and secondary human education:

> In the course of a given epoch not all the beings attain the goal of their evolution. Some fall short of it. During Saturn evolution, for example, not all the [Principalities] attained the "human" stage appointed for them. Nor did all the human physical bodies that developed upon Saturn reach the degree of maturity which would enable them to become the bearers on Sun of an independent etheric body. As a result, beings and structures are present on Sun unsuited to the conditions that obtain there. These must now make good what they missed on Saturn.[10]

These retarded substances divide into two when the etheric body is 'in-poured' by the Dominions. 'One is as it were absorbed by the human bodies, and constitutes henceforth, within the human being, a kind of lower nature'; the other forms 'a second kingdom, developing a fully independent, but purely physical body – a body of warmth'.[11] This, together with Spiritual Hierarchies who have affinities, becomes a separate cosmic entity, a new Saturn on Sun. In our Earth embodiment, two *manvantaras* on, this new Saturn has developed enough to differentiate into the physical planets of our present-day solar system.

Higher consciousness and respiritualisation

During the rotation of Sun and its rhythmic interaction with the Spiritual Hierarchies, macrocosmic man develops further than on Saturn, adding primitive reproductive and glandular organs, sense perceptions and taste. The Saturn consciousness, more dim than dreamless sleep, is advanced to that of sleep (equivalent, Steiner says, to that of plants on earth today).

Sun, like all the planetary embodiments, ends in respiritualisation or *pralaya*. The rotation slows down and the differentiation again collapses to a condition similar to that of a plant when its forces of growth are resting in the seed. The new Saturn fuses once more with the remainder of the Sun embodiment.

Moon

Recapitulation

The *manvantara* or planetary embodiment of Moon follows the
same pattern as that of Sun, but is more differentiated and also more
developed in its ascent of consciousness.

Moon's first two epochs (out of seven, the same total as the number
of planetary embodiments) recapitulate Saturn and Sun. Thus the
most successful macrocosmic men refine the physical body for the
third time and the etheric for the second. These prototypical men are
prepared to receive the astral body and its picture-consciousness for
the first time. As they do so, Moon condenses from 'air' to 'water'.

Differentiation

> But now, as on Saturn, so in the Sun stage too, not all the forms
> attain the corresponding maturity. Hence we find upon Moon
> forms which are even now still at the Saturn stage, and some also
> which have reached but remain at the stage of Sun. Two other
> kingdoms thus emerge besides the properly developed human
> kingdom. One consists of beings which, having remained at the
> Saturn stage, have physical body alone; and this physical body
> is not yet able, even now on Moon, to become the bearer of
> an independent [etheric] body. These beings form the lowest
> kingdom.

They are 'plant-minerals', the semi-live ground mass of Moon.
'A second kingdom is composed of beings who have stopped
short at the Sun stage, and are accordingly not ready on Moon to
incorporate within them an independent astral body.' They are 'plant-
animals', mobile like a turgid sea. 'They constitute an intermediate
kingdom between the aforesaid and the normally advanced human
kingdom.'[12]

The latter, or 'animal-men', are permeated by the two lower
kingdoms: thus the most advanced men on Moon also have a Sun and
Saturn nature. As with Sun, during the middle epochs Moon splits
as part of its differentiation. One part (the forerunner of the earth
we now live on) 'is occupied by man, together with the two lower
kingdoms . . . and also certain higher beings'. It has 'warmth', 'air'
and 'water'. Another part, which 'is taken for their dwelling-place'[13]
by other higher beings, becomes a newborn Sun of 'warmth' and 'air'
but no water. Other heavenly forms, the forerunners of our present
planets, also split off. The Spiritual Hierarchies associated with these

split-off portions cause them to move; Moon itself moves round the new-born Sun.

> Spiritually and materially, the Moon body now contained within it two kinds of life – one that was in intimate union with the Sun's life, and another which, having "fallen" from this, went on its own independent way. This division into a twofold life comes to expression in all the succeeding events of the Moon embodiment.'[14]

An abnormal Luciferic rebellion by some of the Spiritual Hierarchies gives rise to a coarse independence (perhaps from a psychological perspective this can be compared with the turmoil of adolescence). The most advanced men are especially involved in rebellions against the Spiritual Hierarchies who remain fine and pure. These men are divided within themselves because they also contain the Sun nature within them; at times they are dependent on the new-born Sun, becoming frailer and less conscious, and at other times the Moon aspect revives with independence of mind and a more material physical body. Here are the forerunners of our present sleep and waking.

Steiner saw this development of duality as 'of the very deepest significance for all succeeding evolution'.[15] On Moon, differentiation has descended into rebellion and conflict. Biographically, this could be related to his childhood sense of being an outsider, and the tension he felt in adolescence between his intuition and contemporary materialist philosophy.

Higher consciousness and respiritualisation

As Moon rhythmically pulsates towards *pralaya*, the split portions of Moon reunite and man becomes redeemed from his fallen state of rebellion. However, he retains something of the more developed consciousness his new-found rebellious independence has evolved. Here the Anthroposophical spiritual path in the succeeding Earth embodiment, which is a more vigorous *manvantara* than the three preceding it, is anticipated.

The good Angels make the physical body a physiognomical image of the newly independent astral body (there is not such a close relationship between the two on Earth.) Through this altruistic sacrifice these Angels attain the 'human' stage (see table 4). The Archangels endow the etheric body with a kind of memory. Men grow nobler and stronger and are 'able increasingly to preserve the picture-consciousness even on into the Sun periods, with the result that this consciousness gains influence on the formation of the physical and the etheric bodies'.[16] Through long epochs the fallen beings on Moon are gradually overcome by the more spiritual beings of the Sun. The Moon periods become shorter and shorter, the Sun periods longer and longer. Then, in the final two epochs, Sun, Moon and the two lower kingdoms form a single cosmic entity. Man is no longer twofold but one. But he is not as fully individual and free as he is after the coming of Christ, the archetypal 'I', on Earth; on Moon he has a Group-Ego and feels himself to be the instrument of the Angels.

Earth

Recapitulation: the Polarian and Hyperborean epochs

The Goetheanum serpent has three bumps on the top of its head. Perhaps these are intended to represent the previous planetary embodiments of Saturn, Sun and Moon. The fullness of its circle also suggests that the serpent refers to the condensation of spirit into matter in our present Earth embodiment, the most condensed point of the seven planetary embodiments.

During the first two epochs within the Earth phase of Steiner's system and at the beginning of the third, Saturn, Sun, and Moon are recapitulated and man prepares to receive a consciousness that is higher and more objective than the astral picture-consciousness of Moon. The Spiritual Hierarchies have been continuing to develop as a result of their former deeds. The first two epochs are known as the Polarian and Hyperborean respectively. Steiner may have adapted Polarian from the geometrical and scientific uses of the word. The fabled Hyperboreans lived in the extreme north.

Differentiation: the Lemurian epoch

During Lemuria, the third epoch of our Earth embodiment, the differentiation develops further than it does on Moon. The portions that split off are the immediate predecessors of our present planets (Saturn, Jupiter and Mars, etc.) and of the Sun, which is the centre of the ineffable Christ-Being.

The condensation into matter continues. The 'water' of Moon solidifies into 'earth'. The occult meaning of earth is that it bears death. This is the time of the expulsion from the Biblical paradise, as Lucifer intervenes. The Lemurian continent solidifies south of our present Asia and extends approximately from contemporary Sri Lanka to Madagascar. Lemures in Roman myth referred to the shades of the dead, and Linnaeus had used the stem 'lemur' to name a genus of nocturnal mammals found chiefly in Madagascar. The influential German biologist Haeckel thought that Lemuria was the original habitat of the lemur. Lemures are described by Mephistopheles in *Faust Part Two* as 'patched up, shambling demi-creatures' who have been 'cobbled from sinew, bone and skin'.[17]

Steiner states that the human bodies were 'like plant and flower forms of the most delicate texture', 'for only in a very rarified state did "earth" enter into their composition'.[18] Man floats and soars above the earth. Because of the increased hardening of the Earth more and more souls leave for the 'planets', so that there are Sun souls, Saturn souls, Jupiter souls and so on.

During Steiner's Lemurian epoch Man is still relatively macrocosmic and undifferentiated. Thus his influence can cause a surging of waters over the surface of Earth. His perception of the difference between inside and outside is not yet very developed: to give one example, according to Steiner's interpretation, the Cyclops had a single eye.

With the increased hardening comes specialised animal life. 'It befell that . . . a portion only of the human bodily descendants became vehicles for Earth men. Another portion, owing to their hardened form, could only receive souls that were at a lower level than the souls of men.'[19] These are animals.

The hardening into earth comes far on in Steiner's evolving macrocosm. It occurs in the middle or fourth planetary embodiment during the third epoch, only two epochs before our own. Biographically, this could be correlated with the improvement in his sense perception when he was thirty-five, about a decade before he revealed his full 'esoteric' synthesis. In his *Autobiography* he realized that this normally occurred to others at a much earlier age. In the revelation man is still very largely macrocosmic at this time, for example (as mentioned above) being able to cause surges of water. From a psychoanalytic perspective this is reminiscent of fantasies of omnipotence. Steiner disliked the modern urban conditions of Berlin and, after a struggle, inwardly escaped the contemporary philosophical materialism. Correspondingly in the revelation, more sensitive souls leave for the planets as conditions become more solid.

The 'lower' level of animals suggests that drives such as sex or aggression are lower. Similarly, Steiner's emphasis in the *Philosophy of Freedom* is on thinking which transcends passion. Indeed, in gnostic myth the Sophia (the same word as the '-sophy' after the 'Anthropo-'), a feminine vessel for every kind of feeling to assail mankind, was held to be cast out from the Pleroma or spiritual fullness, and it is said that from her afterbirth were derived human passions.

The hardening on Lemuria relents as our present (physical) Moon splits off from Earth. In the course of time the souls who have left Earth for the 'planets' return and multiply. Thus some men are essentially 'Mars' men, others 'Jupiter' men and so on; on the other hand, some are descended from bodies that have managed to remain on earth. Here are the origins of individual karmas.

Steiner seems to have answered two potential questions by his revelation that souls gradually returned to earth. The fact that the hardest forms had been animal explains how it is that human fossils are dated much later than animal ones. Also the rebirth of individual souls can be reconciled with population increase, because souls continue to return.

Fear, illness and death arise with the increased power of Luciferic Spiritual Hierarchies, who have 'an abnormal evolution of rebellion'. They use man's astral body, which is developing the sentient, intellectual and spiritual souls, to dominate his 'I'. As a result, 'man became entangled, more than had been predestined for him, in the realm of earthly matter.'[20]

Through the Luciferic influence man acquires a sense of independence. The Lemurians communicate by thought-reading. The boys have to endure fierce pain to become hardened, or perish; the girls develop strong imaginations. From these arise the first ideas of good and evil. Their memory is almost unlimited but their logical thinking is very undeveloped. They erect buildings instinctively. The greater part gradually decline and become stunted. Steiner, in accord with the European supremacy of his times, stated that the 'savage' tribes of his time were their descendants. Those returning from vulnerable planets are influenced by the Luciferic powers and 'so far extend the arbitrary power of the fiery spark of the "I" which was within them as to be able to call forth in their environment mighty workings of fire, of a harmful nature. This eventually led to a stupendous Earth catastrophe.'[21]

This disaster consumes much of the Earth and with it those who have erred. Only a very small number are pure enough to be able to take refuge on the safe land of Atlantis. They are the ancestors of the 'root-race' who inherit the middle, fourth epoch of Atlantis. In myth, as mentioned by Plato, Atlantis was an extensive island in the Atlantic before it was overwhelmed by the sea.

Differentiation: the Atlantean epoch

Atlantis is in the middle of the evolution of the solar system. It is the fourth of the seven epochs of Earth embodiment, which is itself fourth of the seven planetary embodiments. Steiner stated that Christ would have descended in the middle of Atlantean evolution had it not been for the rebellion of Lucifer. As has been stated his chronology was consistent with Blavatsky's. Blavatsky gave no special meaning to Christ, unlike Steiner, who had been converted to esoteric Christianity in Berlin just before he became General Secretary of the German Section of the Theosophical Society.

The harm done by Lucifer on Lemuria is made worse by Ahriman on Atlantis, though as a result man gains independence and the possibility of inner freedom. A few Initiates progress spiritually. They cultivate secret knowledge at Oracles. Most spiritual and comprehensive – they know Christ – are the Initiates of the Sun Oracle. Apart from this inclusive Oracle, there are others corresponding to the planetary origins that increasingly differentiate men, for example, a Saturn Oracle, a Mars Oracle, and so on.

The Initiates, however, do not protect their secrets carefully, and many become corrupt.

> The evil grew to wider and wider dimensions. . . . Now the forces of growth and reproduction, when torn from their mother-soil and independently employed, stand in a mysterious relationship to certain forces that work in air and water. Mighty and ominous powers of Nature were thus let loose by the deeds of men, leading eventually to the gradual destruction of the whole territory of Atlantis by catastrophes of air and water.[22]

These catastrophes start around the middle of the Atlantean epoch.

There is a change from the earlier sub-epochs within the Atlantean epoch, when man is wholly related to nature and property is held in common. A settlement at these times resembles a garden, the houses being built of trees with artfully entwined branches. Furthermore, the Atlanteans have vehicles that float in the air. Steiner's clairvoyant perception of this came just after the first petrol powered aeroplanes. 'Depravity of passion, or of instinct or desire brought with it a monstrous enlargement of the material in man.'[23] Thus there arise giants. (Steiner himself was physically short.) Through the power of Ahriman (seen also in the form of Mephistopheles) man becomes more and more identified with matter. The sub-races – the Rhmoahls, Tlavatli, Toltecs, Primal Turanians, Primal Semites, Akkadians and Mongols – harden into egotism and power-seeking. Memory of ancestors is lost, except in sleep, hence there arises the mistaken idea that one is the reincarnation of an ancestor. As a result of this condensation into matter there is further differentiation: thought and self-consciousness begin to awaken in the human body.

The companions of Manu, the Christ-Initiate, are saved from the floods. They are men of highly developed intellect but have less knowledge of the spiritual than any other people of that time. Here, perhaps, Steiner drew on his experience of dry philologists at the Weimar archives and of metropolitan intellectualism in Berlin. They withdraw to the south of Asia as Atlantis finally sinks in the tenth-millennium BC. Situated between the present Europe, Africa and America, Atlantis lasts for about a million years.

The Post-Atlantean epoch: the turning point in the solar system

At the middle of the fifth, Post-Atlantean epoch, Christ, the archetypal 'I' or Sun-Being, descends to Earth. After this the basic movement of the solar system as it evolves is not to harden further but to respiritualise.

The Post-Atlantean epoch is itself divided into 'culture-epochs', which seem to be spiritual archetypes of historical periods. Manu, in the first, *ancient Indian culture-epoch,* contributes to archetypal Vedas (not the historical ones that came to be recorded in writing). Caste arises because these prototype ancient Indians are descendants of Atlantean men from the different planetary karmic streams, for example, Saturn men, Jupiter men and so on.

Unlike these Indians, the archetypal Persians of the second *Persian culture-epoch* are well fitted for the physical world, loving the earth. They use nature to serve the personal interests of man. This is the start of the Dark Age or Kali Yuga, which in the mythology of the Hindu Vaishnavas is the last, shortest and nastiest age in each world cycle. Anthroposophically it ended at about the beginning of the twentieth-century, when Steiner first began his optimistic public spiritual teaching, and, so it seems, before the 1914-1918 and 1939-1945 World Wars and the horrors of the twentieth-century.

Because of Kali Yuga, spiritual faculties are largely lost in the *Egypto-Chaldean culture-epoch.* 'To a man of the Chaldean and Babylonian peoples the world of the senses was no longer an illusion'. Hermes, influenced by the Zarathustra Mysteries, teaches that he who most zealously 'employs his forces upon Earth to work it in accordance with the aims of the Spirit Powers . . . will be united with Osiris, even with the sublime Being of the Sun'. There developed a popular misconception about astrology: 'instead of the Spirit of the star, the star itself was placed in the foreground.'[24]

As man turns more and more to the physical world in the middle, *Graeco-Latin culture-epoch*, Ahriman finds his way ever further into men's souls. With this increased differentiation the intellectual soul develops.

The Orphic, Eleusinian and, especially, the Pythagorean Mysteries are successors to the Atlantean Oracles. Here is revealed 'what had been veiled by the impulses of Lucifer and Ahriman':[25] The Initiates in the Mysteries are, as much as Moses, prophets of Christ. A summary only of Steiner's Christology[26] can be outlined here. He thought that many of the differences between the accounts and perceptions of the evangelists were the result of their diverse planetary karmic streams. Christology has special importance in Anthroposophy, especially for the Christian Community, because it marks the redemptive turning point of the evolving solar system.

Steiner reveals that there were two Jesuses. Anthroposophically, the main purpose of the Hebrew people from the time of Abraham is to prepare a body that can receive the Christ. This culminates in the Jesus of St Matthew's account. He is ascribed uniquely great wisdom and called the 'Solomon' Jesus. But there is also another Jesus, the 'Nathan' Jesus, who is full of love: the Spirit of the Buddha Gautama fills him with compassion from the heavenly choir. This is the Jesus of St Luke's differing account.

At the time of the discourse with the priests at the Jerusalem Temple, the two Jesuses fuse into one, the wisdom-filled Solomon Jesus uniting with the love-filled Nathan Jesus. At this point the 'Cosmos of Wisdom' is preparing to turn into the 'Cosmos of Love': in other words, the second half of the ascending evolution of the solar system is taking over from the first. The Solomon Jesus – other than his prepared body – and the young mother of the Nathan Jesus die. The transformed Jesus is brought up by the relatively old mother of the Solomon Jesus.

In lectures, including a series entitled *The Fifth Gospel*, Steiner revealed details of the eighteen years between the event in the Temple and the baptism by John. By this later time the transformed Jesus is sufficiently evolved to bequeath his newly spiritualized nature to the archetypal 'I', or Christ himself. It seems Christ does not take himself fully into matter. In orthodox Christianity, this is the docetic heresy (Conventional Christology recently has moved far from this possibility). The temptation is not by one devil alone but by two, Lucifer and Ahriman. Golgotha itself is direct Reality, the turning point of the evolution of the solar system as the Cosmos of Wisdom transforms into the Cosmos of Love.

Christ leaves the body before it dies, hence the residual cry, 'My God, my God, why hast thou forsaken me?' Because the body is spiritual, the death on the cross is quicker than would be expected from a normal healthy man. The earth begins to shine when Christ's blood flows on it, and is transmuted. Christ becomes the spirit of the earth and also of man's physical and etheric bodies, bounding Ahriman in hell. As Christ's being has never incarnated before, his form disintegrates at once, becoming visible as light. Man's body on the final planetary embodiment of Vulcan is similar. His form is seen by those visiting the sepulchre on the third day, and also by those receiving forty days' subsequent esoteric teaching. The descent of the tongues of fire at Pentecost gives man the possibility of understanding these happenings through his own spiritual efforts.

The Graeco-Latin culture-epoch ends by about the fifteenth century. The redemptive, respiritualising coming of Christ, who is the archetype of our 'I', or highest-nature, works very gradually. Men with very different karmas find through Christ the ideal of a universal humanity. There is, however, a growing separation between this ideal and the growth of individualism. This is reflected in Aquinas: Thomism does not allow differentiated human thinking to cross over into spiritual reality.

We are now in the fifth, *Post-Atlantean culture-epoch* (the name is the same as the Post-Atlantean epoch). It emerges fully in the fifteenth-century and is marked by duality of soul, resulting in 'the antagonism between external science and spiritual knowledge.'[27] It seems to be centred on Europe, whose fairy-tales and sagas, Steiner stated, do not say with assurance that the God of Light will conquer Lucifer. This duality is now seen as being overcome by Anthroposophy and similar esoteric movements, especially those which stress its variant of karma and reincarnation. The latter starts fully on Atlantis; 'death' relieves souls from excessive exposure to hardness. Steiner saw his spiritual science as a twentieth-century development, through Goethe, of Thomism.

The *sixth culture-epoch* (it has no name) is now developing and it will bring harmony. The darkened age of *Kali Yuga* has ended and gradually people are awakening to see Christ on the etheric plane, or the Second Coming. The separated and accelerated intellectual development of man will, imperceptibly at first, accept higher spiritual knowledge, or the Knowledge of the Grail. The present, fifth culture-epoch repeats the contribution of the third, but in a new way.

Instead of perceiving the spiritual world as external to him, man feels
it as a world into which he himself is growing.

> The fifth and sixth are the decisive culture-epochs. In the *seventh
> culture-epoch* the souls who have reached the evolutionary goal
> of the sixth will go on evolving. For those who have not, the
> surrounding world will be too greatly altered. They will find little
> opportunity to recover their lost ground, and must await a more
> distant future when the conditions will again be favourable.[28]

After the seventh culture-epoch there will be another great convulsion
comparable to the catastrophe between the end of the Atlantean and
the beginning of the Post-Atlantean epochs.

The last two epochs: Higher consciousness and respiritualisation

In the last two Earth epochs an ascending consciousness accompanies
respiritualisation. The present Moon will reunite with our Earth.

Some men will be victims of the Azuras,[29] very wicked beings
who, on Earth, steal men's 'I's. There will also be souls who have
burdened their karmas with so much error, ugliness and ill-doing
that they will constitute a special group on their own. But the better
developed humans will help transform them and so enable the Earth,
already reunited with the moon, to reunite with the sun and planets.
This essentially benign vision of the future corresponds to Steiner's
good-heartedness. There is a respiritualisation or *pralaya,* then the
emergence of the Jupiter planetary embodiment.

Jupiter

Jupiter, the fifth planetary embodiment, correlates to the third, Moon,
but in a more conscious, individual form. Analogously, Imagination
(in Steiner's path of development) is an increase of consciousness
into the astral body, which develops on Moon.

Thus the Cosmos of Wisdom is being transformed into the Cosmos
of Love. The Wisdom that is prepared in the Saturn, Sun and Moon
evolutions lives in the physical, etheric and astral bodies of man
and manifests as wisdom of the world. Then, with the descent of
Christ or the archetypal 'I', there starts of process whereby it will
be transmuted. From about the Post-Atlantean epoch of the Earth
embodiment onwards, the Wisdom of the outer world is realised as
inner Wisdom, Wisdom in man himself. When thus 'resurrected'
in the inner life, in the 'I' of man, it grows into the seed of Love.

Wisdom is the premise, the forerunner of the more conscious Love. Love is Wisdom brought in to the 'I' of man.

In the first four Jupiter epochs there is a recapitulation of Saturn, Sun, Moon and Earth embodiments, but in a more spiritual way. In the fifth epoch, mineral forces become plant-like, the lowest form of life; above this is a new animal life, then a stratum of human life descended from the bad humanity on Earth. The higher humanity are as evolved as the Angels are on Earth. They have attained spirit self, the Jupiter equivalent of the Imaginative stage on the current embodiment of Earth, and are without physical bodies because no body is evolved for a fifth time. The better humanity works to redeem the lower stratum. After Jupiter, as with the other embodiments, there is *pralaya.*

Venus

The ascent of consciousness towards conscious individuality continues in Venus, the sixth planetary embodiment, which corresponds to the second or Sun. It first five epochs recapitulate Saturn, Sun, Moon, Earth and Jupiter. However, this recapitulation is even more spiritual than Jupiter's and so does not seem to involve condensation into matter. Animals are the lowest form of life; above them there are three human strata of differing spiritual attainments. The highest is at the stage of life-spirit, which is analogous to Inspiration on the current embodiment of Earth.

Man is free to oppose evolution. The effects of Lucifer and Ahriman on Earth evolution have resulted in man having free will. Those that persist in opposition are detached into an irreclaimable moon. Otherwise humanity, after *pralaya,* ascends into the Vulcan embodiment, the seventh and last, which corresponds with the first, Saturn. The mouth of the macrocosmic serpent is enclosing its tail.

Vulcan

In *Occult Science,* Steiner states that any description of Vulcan would be beyond the compass of the book. Its first six epochs recapitulate Saturn, Sun, Moon, Earth, Jupiter and Venus in a refined, spiritual way.

In the final epoch the ascent of consciousness is completed. Vulcan becomes a chain of Beings like the First Spiritual Hierarchy, advancing to new creative tasks in the universe. Man in the solar system has developed from taking to giving in an evolution that leads to the ultimate in spiritual self-development. In terms of conventional Christianity this seems close to the Pelagian heresy. Psychologically this ultimate might be interpreted as an 'inflation' or 'grandiosity' in which excessive emphasis is placed on the potential for self-development, in contrast to the natural and cultural constraints placed on us without and within. Alternatively or additionally it might be interpreted as generativity, Erikson's final human stage of development in which the nurturing of children is extended to the cultural sphere.

Steiner's revelation from the Post-Atlantean epoch of Earth onwards perhaps corresponds to his own life after making this revelation. As described earlier, during his final, Anthroposophical period of life he gave 'indications' for founding Anthroposophical activities and for spiritualising the earth. On his deathbed, perhaps in Vulcan-like mode, he stated that somehow he had lost contact with his physical body.

Part Three

Gnosis in the West,
or the Western 'Esoteric Tradition'

7. From Gnosticism to Rosicrucianism

Or let my Lamp at midnight hour,
Be seen in som high lonely Towr,
Where I may oft out-watch the Bear,
With thrice-great Hermes, or unsphear
The spirit of Plato to unfold
What Worlds, or what vast Regions hold
Th' immortal mind that hath forsook
Her mansion in this fleshly nook.[1]
— Milton, *Il Penseroso*

In describing the Rudolf Steiner movement, frequent references have been made both to gnosticism and the Western 'esoteric tradition' (as gnosis has also been called in the modern period). This background to Anthroposophy is summarised here and in the following chapter in an attempt to outline what is probably the most profound imaginative 'tradition' of the West, influencing Shakespeare, Goethe and W.B. Yeats, amongst many others. Also, unless some recent scholarly doubts are well founded, it was the matrix from which modern science emerged. Through Aleister Crowley and Gerald Gardner, Western gnosis has also, much more immediately, influenced punk, rock, Wicca and the recent revival of witchcraft and paganism (though as will be explained each of these also has major differences from the transcendence provided by gnostic thought systems).

It is not easy to judge how fully the Western 'esoteric tradition' truly constitutes a tradition. This is either in terms of temporal continuity, though there have certainly been very active times and periods of quiescence, or in terms of cosmological and other thought structures. There may be enough continuity to justify the use of the term 'tradition', but if so it should be understood as one which is loose, fissiparous and constantly resynthesising.

The overview of this 'tradition' attempted here is provisional, a first step summary. It is also intentionally selective: the focus is on those aspects of Western 'gnosis' (the general term used here for the content of the 'tradition') which are relevant to Anthroposophy. Thus there is little or no mention of texts, such as the Nag Hammadi finds, which would have been unknown to Steiner.

The focus here is on cosmology. This has the potential to reveal much about the social and cultural conditions in which a revival occurs. At the same time, historical and literary connections are indicated in this introduction to the 'tradition'. The concluding part of this book is concerned with abstracting leading themes from the material summarised in this part. One has already been discussed in relation to Anthroposophy: 'hardest' matter is a negative organising principle for gnosis. In the remaining chapters there is a contrast with 'mysticism', which, as a response which is more accepting of matter, will be distinguished from 'esotericism'.

Another main theme to emerge is understanding the two main gnostic episodes in the West, the first during the Renaissance and the other around the turn of this century. Both occurred when the contemporary orthodox cosmology was split into two contending outlooks. These were, crudely, Protestant versus Catholic Christianity, and modern science-based secularism versus Protestantism. The gnoses at these times of crisis have generally functioned as deep level syntheses and intuitive reconciliations of rival world views for many. Nevertheless, despite their synthetic nature, both major episodes have been accompanied by heavy bloodshed. The Thirty Years War in the early seventeenth century in central Europe bequeathed a devastating legacy for generations to come, while the 1914-1918 war was the first stage in terrible intra-European and northern hemisphere conflict.

The influences on recent Western esotericism are traced back in part to the gnosticism (to be explained) of the early centuries of the Christian era. But a fuller perspective would also summarise the very complex situation around the Mediterranean at that time and earlier. Gnosticism's origins have been variously linked to a great many causes: for example, the influence of Greek thought on Christianity; an other-worldly shift resulting from worldly misfortune, such as the conquests of Alexander the Great in the fourth century BC; influence by Hindu and Buddhist contemplation; influence from the Iranian area in the early centuries before Christ; probable influence by the mystery religions of late antiquity, such as those of Isis and of Mithras (itself an offshoot from Zoroastrianism).

The prophet Zoroaster,[2] somewhere between 550-1500BC, provides a significant and relatively little-publicised part of the cultural backdrop. His cosmology had dualist potential – Zoroastrianism holds that in the beginning there were two wholly independent and opposed twins, one good, the other evil. This was probably connected with the social situation, because Zoroaster was defending the values of settled, agricultural communities (in what is now Iran) against marauders who were perceived as delighting in strife for its own sake. The good spirit was held to have created the world to help in the struggle against, and the eventual victory over, the evil spirit. The birth of Zoroaster was believed to have begun the process whereby evil was to be overthrown. It was later believed that there would be a succession of three saviours, each to be born by the seed of Zoroaster from a virgin after bathing in a lake.

It is highly likely that from the many Zoroastrian doctrines about this final victory are derived, through Judaism, the similar Christian teachings on God and the Devil, individual judgement at death, the Last Judgement, resurrection of the body, heaven and hell, and life everlasting. Thus Zoroastrianism seems to have been a seminal factor in the development of Judaeo-Christian orthodoxy. The gnostics generally were alienated from the development of that orthodoxy.

The Zoroastrian dualism is that of spiritual good versus spiritual evil. It encourages a positive view of the world of matter, which was created by the good spirit. This is different from the dualism in gnosis, where spirit tends to be identified with liberation, matter with limitation.

Gnosticism

As stated earlier, making ideal-types out of 'gnosticism' and other worldviews in order to decide on the inclusion and exclusion of a given system within the categories thus created is, in one sense, misleading. Every transcendental system is a synthesis, and every individual who seems to subscribe to one is no doubt a complex jumble of very many different kinds of synthesis and cognitive dissonance, including heretical ones. Hans Jonas, in relation to gnosticism, refers to 'half-tones' beyond a 'hard core' of gnostic thinkers and the need to have a 'musical ear'.[3] However, without positing ideal types at the level of culture (i.e. generalising from the aggregated experience of unique individuals) it is difficult to identify analogies coherently.

Gnosticism emerged in the first two centuries of the Christian era, in the Roman Empire's increasingly complex mass society. As has been stated, there is considerable dispute about its origins.

From the borders of India to Egypt, after the conquests of Alexander the Great between 334-323BC, there arose an overarching Hellenistic culture. The Greek 'cosmos', which originally meant 'order', had in classical antiquity been identified with the city-state. Plato thought it a living creature with soul and reason. With larger, more complex polities acquired through conquest, the ideal of cosmos became more abstract, meaning the order enjoyed by citizens of the universe, or cosmopolitans ('cosmopolites'). Later, especially under the Roman Empire, the old ideal of cosmos came to appear more and more oppressive and threatening.

During the time of Alexander, when the Persian polity was overcome by the Greek, cosmos with a negative connotation is thought to have replaced the Zoroastrian positive evaluation of the world. Zoroastrian dualism may have shifted to a spirit/matter dualism, forming the forerunner of gnosticism in what the scholar Hans Jonas has termed an invisible, antagonistic East, which rejected the oppression of the Greek cosmos.[4]

During the large structures of the later Roman Empire, astrology, which had developed into a more abstract form from its origins in Babylonian religion, came to be identified with the repressive 'cosmos'. The universal fate or 'heimarmene' dispensed by the planets was no longer potentially benign. It was seen by many as inimical, as a terrifying necessity which was rigidly unaware of the divine. The divine now existed transcendentally, outside the seven planets. Astrology became the truth of the cosmic or natural man from which the spiritual man sought to escape. The transcendent way out was through an increase of intuitive knowledge or 'gnosis'. This Greek word means 'knowledge', and the 'gn' stem through common Indo-European origins has similarities to the word 'knowledge' itself, to the Latin 'cognoscere', and to the Indian 'jnana'(jnana yoga is a path of spiritual knowledge.) Gnosis, often achieved through the practice of magic, provided freeing self-knowledge through explaining – in a characteristic way, as will be described – man's relationship to the threatening planetary cosmos and the transcendent reality beyond it.

Manicheism

Gnosticism is mythic, and feeling, in the form of yearning, is central to its cosmic story. Steiner's is a more conceptual revelation. It has more analogies with the Syrian-Egyptian variant (to be described further on in this chapter) than with the Iranian type which culminated in Manicheism. Mani (216-c.276CE) based his myth on the Zoroastrian dualism of two eternally opposed principles. In Syrian-Egyptian gnosis, darkness and matter are the result of a fall from an original fullness of light, whereas in Manicheism they are dualistically co-eternal with the light. The darkness perceives the light and then, in hate and envy, aggressively tries to mingle with it. The light is fearful and pacific in the face of the onslaught of the King of Darkness, who eats the five sons of the Primal Man. The latter has been emanated by the light through the Mother of Life to defeat the aggressor. The five sons are mingled with the darkness of the present world, which is an embodiment of the evil principle, or Ahriman (a use of the name which predates Anthroposophy's). The light uses the mingling to restore the *status quo ante,* to free the five sons and their light, which is gradually being redeemed through being borne aloft by the revolution of the spheres.

In Manicheism the eating of the Tree of Knowledge by Adam is a positive act. It enables the spiritual Jesus, the suffering form of the Primal Man, to warn him against touching Eve and so perpetuating through reproduction the dispersal of the light. Adam and Eve's having had offspring made necessary the historical revelations of Buddha, Zoroaster and, most universally of all, Mani himself. Mani taught that through self-restraint, including non-reproduction, in the end light will be separated from darkness and the original dualism restored.

This does not have the more optimistic, progressive quality of Syrian-Egyptian gnosis in which the darkness or matter, the result of a fall from light, is − in part at least − redeemed. Though systems such as Steiner's, which are cyclical and ascending, have more in common with the latter, there are also some correspondences with Manicheism. For example, as just noted the Anthroposophical demon, Ahriman, is similar in name to the Manichean King of Darkness, though the Anthroposophical Ahriman does not seem to be co-eternal with Anthroposophy's good spiritual evolution.

In Christian gnosis, in a reversal of the meaning of the Old Testament, there is a positive rather than negative (Greek rather than Hebrew) evaluation of knowledge. Adam did well to eat of the Tree and thereby know good and evil. Asceticism is generally another feature of gnosticism, as in the Manichean myth. The synthesising from many sources is also typical, though Mani's is unusually wide: his cosmogony resembles Zoroastrianism; his asceticism and ethics, Buddhism; and his 'eschatology', Christianity and Zoroastrianism. Atypically, perhaps, he intended to found a universal religion rather than initiate a select circle of initiates.

Manicheism was a much more widespread historical force than Syrian-Egyptian gnosis. It spread rapidly from Mesopotamia to Palestine, Syria, Asia Minor, Egypt, North Africa and, by the fifth

century, to Rome, Dalmatia, Southern Gaul, and Spain. By the sixth
century, severe repression had removed its threat to Christianity from
the northern territories of the crumbling Roman Empire, though it
spread to the eastern provinces of Iran, Chinese Turkestan, and China,
where it survived until the fourteenth century or later. Manicheism,
though not its co-eternal principle of evil, seems to have influenced
Catharism. This spread from the end of the tenth century to Orleans,
Toulouse, Milan, Florence, and through much of Europe. It probably
derived from the Bulgarian Bogomils, or from a residual gnosticism
surviving in the Pyrenees. However, in the Christian Middle Ages the
accusation of being a 'Manichee' heretic covered heretical doctrines
that did not derive from Mani.[5] It seems that the Templars were not
Manichean or even particularly gnostic.

Syrian-Egyptian gnosis

Syrian-Egyptian gnosis was by no means all Christian, though most
Christian gnosis seems to have been Syrian-Egyptian: Valentinianism
was its culmination. Valentinus, whose system is known largely
through his disciples, was educated in Alexandria and taught his
variant of Christianity in Rome between about 135 and 160CE, about
a century before Mani.

   In the Syrian-Egyptian gnostic ideal-type (see the explanation
of 'ideal-type' earlier in this section) there are prototypes of the
four cosmological structures described in chapter five: that in the
beginning matter was spirit and at the end it will mostly become
spirit again; that man is a microcosm of the macrocosm; that (hard)
matter is a major negative organizing principle; and a seed of the idea
that there is a development of spiritual individuality.

   In Valentinianism, unlike Manicheism, matter and darkness are the
result of a fall of part of the spiritual fullness, or Pleroma, from itself,
because it strives yearningly for gnosis. After the fall much of the
descended part of the Pleroma is redeemed, but that which is not
redeemed descends further. There is further partial salvation, and a
fall towards matter-creation of the remnant, until the present world
is created. There are structural similarities with Anthroposophy's
planetary embodiments.

   Ignorance, far from being bliss, is identified with lostness,
darkness, and matter. Salvation is the condition of having gnosis, or
intuitive revelation about how the self is related to the macrocosm.
Through gnosis, which is an ontological state, it is held that much
of the present world will be redeemed, though what is irredeemably

matter will (as in Anthroposophy) be consumed by fire and cease to exist. The rhythmic descent and striving for gnosis are prototypes for Anthroposophy's more conceptual condensation from spirit, and its reformation in spirit through an ascending development of awareness. However, the Valentinian fall is as much the result of a tragic imbalance in the godhead as the working out of a purposeful ascent towards fuller consciousness.

The fallen principle, Sophia, is female and unpaired while unredeemed. The other spiritual principles are harmoniously in male-female pairs or 'syzygies'. In Valentinianism, Anthropos is the spiritual principle that is the syzygy of Ecclesia, or the ideal Christian Church. In other Syrian-Egyptian myths such as the *Poimandres*, Anthropos – macrocosmic, archetypal Man – and not Sophia, is the spiritual principle that falls.

Syrian-Egyptian gnosticism was not just fatalistic. Those capable of being redeemed from the astrological necessity ordained by the dread planetary rulers (or 'Archons') could strive to achieve gnosis here and now. Because of man's macrocosmic origins even spiritual people were thought to be caught in the world and so trapped by the Archons, but through a detailed understanding of means such as magical passwords, and the appropriate moments to use them, they could seek to struggle free. Transmigration of souls was also often a feature of gnosticism.

Essential to gnosticism was its attitude to existence, with a dualism between transcendence and the world, a dualism which also existed within man. Steiner, in *Occult Science*, refers to a dualism of soul in the fifth civilization epoch, 'a dualism which has lasted on to this day and shows itself in many ways'. For Steiner the current era is the time of finding the thread which will unite the two.[6] Students of the experiential qualities of gnosticism have also made analogies with existentialism.

The Valentinian myth, a brief account of which follows, has a feeling of pathos[7] whereas Steiner's *Occult Science* comes more from a standpoint of spiritual 'science'.

In invisible and nameless heights, there is a perfect spirit or 'aeon', the Father. With him is Silence.[8] In Valentinianism she bears him, as if from his seed, Mind ('Nous') and Truth. From these original four, the root of all, come forth more spirits (including Anthropos and Ecclesia) until there are thirty. They constitute the 'Pleroma', or fullness. It is worth noting that Irenaeus, the hostile Church father whose accounts of gnosticism have nevertheless often been corroborated by other evidence, stated that the thirty original spirits of the Pleroma were related to the thirty years during which Jesus did not teach in public.

The spirits are held to long to behold the begetter of their seed, but only Mind knows the Father. Silence restrains him from spreading this knowledge. The last and youngest of the spirits, Sophia (or Wisdom) plunges forward in the attempt to comprehend his greatness, thereby losing the embrace of her consort (or syzygy), and falls victim to Suffering. The nature of Suffering is separation from the Father. With Suffering comes Limit, which keeps Sophia separated from her desire to comprehend the Father's greatness, and purifies and strengthens her. As a result she – apart from what she leaves behind – is reunited with her syzygy in the Pleroma.

Mind emits two further spirits, Christ and the Holy Ghost, to prevent other spirits from falling into Suffering. Christ teaches that it is enough for them to know that syzygy by its very nature means an understanding of the unbegotten Father. He teaches gnosis: the Father is Inconceivable, Incomprehensible and is only known from Mind. Through the Holy Ghost the spirits come to partake in each other's qualities, so that they become equal in form and mind.

Outside the Pleroma there remains an amorphous birth from Sophia, alternatively, her 'becoming'. This, the 'Lower Sophia', is given form by Christ but prevented by Limit from attaining the Pleroma or Light. The Lower Sophia suffers in ignorance. The spirits take pity on her and, because Christ cannot leave the Pleroma a second time, send their common front, Jesus, to be her syzygy just outside the Pleroma, in 'the Centre', so that he can cure her through gnosis. The Lower Sophia, in turning towards Christ (though also deprived of Christ), brings about the soul or 'psyche' of the world through her son, the world's creator or 'Demiurge'. From her shock, terror and perplexity eventually comes the matter or 'hyle' of the world; however, at this stage it is non-corporeal (in this specific there is also a resonance with Anthroposophy).

The Demiurge, in ignorance and unconsciousness, presumption and conceit (but guided without his knowledge by his mother, the Lower Sophia), is Creator of the seven planetary heavens and of the physical, which solidifies into matter. The Old Testament prophets are his creation and mouthpiece, though his mother also has frequently spoken through them. She has incarnated in the historical Jesus (again, Steiner's system seems to have resemblances, on this occasion in his Christology).

The Demiurge is composed of soul; but there is also Satan who is a spirit of evil and knows about the Pleroma. Despite Satan's existence, there are men who are informed with spirit (the 'pneumatics') and are assured of salvation. These most 'perfect' Valentinians, according to Irenaeus, did everything forbidden by Holy Scripture, assuming that they, like gold, could not be harmed through being cast into the mud. Others were considered to be 'psychics': because those thus described do not have perfect gnosis they can be saved by works and faith alone. Good psychics may eventually be able to receive the seed of gnosis; but others are by nature evil. Those people who are 'hylic' perish because they are of the gross nature of matter.

Thus salvation is according to selective grace. The 'pneumatics', putting off their souls, enter the Pleroma. The 'psychics' and the Demiurge ascend as far as the Centre, the abode of the Lower Sophia, but cannot enter the Pleroma. The 'hylics' and unjust 'psychics' are consumed, together with matter (which is irredeemable), by the fire which is hidden in the world.

The rise of orthodox Christianity

Pagan gnosticism often differed radically from Valentinianism: a few circles even ritually ate aborted foetuses. Christian gnosticism itself seems to have been varied and as much a powerful climate of thought as a group of systems with definable social boundaries.

The Church, which in the centuries of the gradual decline of Rome was becoming the organisational inheritor of Caesar, was battling with this multiform and influential gnosticism. The instruments of approved sacred literature, or canon (ironically, first used by Marcion the gnostic), and dogma were fashioned for the fight. 'Orthodoxy' was spelled out by Augustine, the first to define the Church as a necessary condition for grace. The 'organisation men', the faithful who looked up to the institution of the Church, prevailed against the intuitive and often élitist Christian gnostics who frequently belittled the Church, seeing it as a manifestation of the ignorant Demiurge. Frequently, they ignored the social conventions of the orthodox: for example, the Christian gnostics sometimes practised sexual equality. Those they opposed may have been, in the scathing words of *The Gospel of Philip,* waterless canals, but, possibly for this very reason, they had the power of social organisation behind them.

Christian orthodoxy was influenced by Neoplatonism, which is discussed in the context of the Renaissance in the following section. Augustine, for example, was influenced by the Neoplatonist, Plotinus. Neoplatonism, though it is contemplative, is not gnostic because it does not strive against matter or the planetary cosmos.

Perhaps because Augustine was also affected by Manicheism, Christianity has had a tendency towards ascetic rejection of the world. However, Christian contemplation, unlike gnosticism, does not explicitly reject matter; furthermore, it tends to affirm the Church as an institution. The suppression of Christian gnosis appears to have been a near-complete success. There seems to be little or no trace in the West of its Syrian-Egyptian ideal-typical form until the Renaissance.

Hermeticism, Kabbalism, Alchemy, and Rosicrucianism[9]

After a millennium, at the time of the Renaissance and Reformation, some people in the West discovered gnosticism. Less specifically, a mythic and magical climate of thought tended to subvert the guard of conventional Christianity, both Catholic and Protestant. The emergence of this climate of thought is summarised here. A brief account is given of some main components – Hermeticism, Kabbalism and alchemy – and of their later, more composite form, Rosicrucianism.

In general, the four cosmological structures described in chapter five and mentioned in relation to Syrian-Egyptian gnosis should probably be qualified in any attempt to summarise Renaissance magical thinking. Conventional Christian cosmogony and eschatology may often have modified the belief that matter in the beginning was spirit and in the end will mostly become spirit again. However, the Renaissance magus placed great stress on the idea that man is a microcosm. Compared to the gnostics, there appears to have been less sense that matter is a major negative organising principle. Indeed, Renaissance magic with its frequent hubris is believed to have led directly to the rise of the scientific exploration of matter and so of the modern period, whose esotericisms, much more than preceding ones, are often dynamically centred on the evolution of spiritual individuality.

Hermeticism and Ficino

In the Renaissance there were new syntheses of gnosticism, Neoplatonism and magic. They were often connected with the name of Hermes Trismegistus (or, as he was known, 'Thrice Great'), who was identified with Thoth, the ancient Egyptian God of Wisdom.

In about 1460 a collection of disparate astrological treatises came from Byzantium to Florence, where they were translated by Ficino and ascribed to Hermes, becoming known as the *Corpus Hermeticum.* The first, the *Pimander* (or *Poimandres)* is a gnostic cosmological myth of the Syrian-Egyptian type. Here it is Anthropos who falls. Other tracts were concerned with the secret virtues of plants and stones used in sympathetic magic, the making of talismans, alchemy and the occult generally.

It was only gradually, from 1614, as a result of the work of the classical humanist scholar Isaac Casaubon, that it was realised that the treatises do not derive from the era of Hermes in pre-Christian Egypt but are broadly gnostic, dating from the second to third century after Christ.[10] The erroneous dating had allowed the *Corpus Hermeticum,* and an earlier known, analogous treatise, the *Asclepius,* to be reconciled with the Christian teachings of the times. No less an authority than the Church Father Lactantius had considered Hermes Trismegistus to be one of the most important gentile seers, a prophet who had foreseen the coming of Christianity. To the unhistorical Renaissance mind the treatises seemed to hark back to a golden age. Affinities were discovered with the Christian scriptures. Hermeticists seem scarcely to have noticed the profound differences, though many of their conventional Catholic or Protestant contemporaries were not only aware of them but also disapproved.

Hermetic cosmology generally seems to have lacked the dualism of gnosticism. The *Corpus Hermeticum* treatises were interpreted in the context of the richness of contemporary Neoplatonist thought. Plotinus' mystical approach was not in opposition to matter. 'One should not concede that this Cosmos is evil by nature because there are many abominable things in it', he wrote.[11] More monistically, he envisioned the universe as a single emanating being that lives differently in each of its aspects. He held man to be a microcosm corresponding to the three principles from which the world has been derived, the One, the Intelligence and the World-Soul. In the Renaissance they were synthesised with the Trinity. A part of our soul belongs to what is most spiritual, another part is intermediate while a third part is mundane.

Ficino, a priest as well as a physician, reconciled the cautious practice of magic with pious religious observance. His aim was not the gnostic, transcendent one of escaping the dread planetary Archons. It seems to have been immediate and natural, though altruistic. The magician creates an effect on the macrocosm through altering corresponding aspects of the human microcosm, or vice versa, often through the use of talismans. Frances Yates suggests that Boticelli's 'Primavera' is a complex talisman to draw down spirit from the star Venus and transmit it to the beholder of Venus in the painting. A cameo (a two-coloured talismanic gem) was sometimes used to confine an astral or demonic force; with a 'virtue' thus captured, the magus united it with the corresponding constituent within himself, and thereby achieved effects in the world outside.

Kabbalism and Pico della Mirandola

During the Renaissance and later, Christian Hermeticists synthesized Jewish Kabbalah. It probably derived in part from Syrian-Egyptian gnosis, though in the Middle Ages it was thought to be part of the law given to Moses at Sinai.

In the thirteenth century this tradition was becoming thought of as such, hence it was called tradition or 'Kabbalah'. The *Sefer-ha-Zohar* or 'Book of Splendour' expressed its main aspects, which were Jewish gnosticism, recently synthesized Neoplatonism and magic. It was written about 1280 but not widely disseminated until after the use of printing.

Kabbalism was strong in Provence in the mid-twelfth century. It shared with Catharism the doctrine of rebirth. Somewhat later, it became established on the other side of the Pyrenees, in Gerona and Castile; then, in the fourteenth century, despite considerable opposition from within Judaism, it spread through most of the Jewish communities in Spain, to Italy and the east. From 1492 the shock of the Spanish expulsion of the Jews made Kabbalism, which became more widely available, place more stress on the coming of the redeeming Messiah.

The different variants of Kabbalah seem to have been in the Syrian-Egyptian gnostic pattern, but made much less dualist through the influence of Neoplatonism, though the Lurianic Kabbalah, based on the teachings of Isaac Luria (1534-1572), was more dualistic. From the Neoplatonist infinite One, or 'Ein-Sof', emerge the 'Sephiroth', divinities who contain the archetypes of every finite thing. The cosmic tree has its roots in them and grows downwards (Anthroposophy also depicts plants with roots upwards); or, analogously, Adam Kadmon, the macrocosmic man, starts his descent from them. Beneath the Sephiroth is the 'Merkabah' or Throne of God. Lower down are the planetary spheres, then the terrestrial world.

Many Jewish esotericists believed that in the future every finite being would ascend to the source from which it had emanated. The *Sepher-ha-Zohar* is not definite about whether evil finally disappears or survives as a place of eternal punishment for the wicked. Evil was sometimes understood merely as inadequate influx from the Sephiroth, or it was seen as the consequence of an inessential attribute of God or, most powerfully of all, as a complete 'emanation of the left'. (Leftness here suggests all that is not ordered or 'right'; similarly our word 'sinister' is derived from the Latin word for left.)

It was held that man's final purpose is to reunite the divine and human wills. Adam Kadmon's fall and separation from the Sephiroth has resulted in multiplicity and individuality. Rebirth, originally thought of as a punishment, came to be seen as offering opportunities to the soul, which was believed to have free will, to make up for previous failures. It was assumed man is a microcosm and can influence the macrocosm; however, magic used for personal ends was thought of pejoratively as sorcery.

Each part of the soul and the physical body were thought to correspond to aspects of the Sephiroth. The *Sefer-ha-Zohar* states that the lowest soul is that of animal vitality. The two others rise above this and may (as in Anthroposophy) develop post-natally; the highest is the divine spark of intuitive apprehension. After death, the lowest part remains below by the grave and is punished. The intermediate soul is also punished but then enters the 'Garden of Eden below'. There was no settled opinion on which sin was punished thus and which by a further life. The highest part of the soul is not subject to sin and returns to its source in the 'Garden of Eden above'. The gnostic categories of men, the 'pneumatics', 'psychics' and 'hylics', or the spiritual, soulful and matter-bound, seem in Kabbalism to become differing aspects of the same individual human being. Later, two even higher parts of the soul were added. So sublime is the highest that the chosen few who attain it are free from further rebirth. The Lurianic Kabbalah introduced further refinements.

The structural similarity with Steiner's Anthroposophy is striking. There are also detailed analogies. There was a variant of Kabbalism which held that each of its seven planets rules in turn during a coming into being, after which the world is destroyed by God; then there is another cycle, and so on. Also of interest is the modification, from about 1250, that makes the Sephiroth rather than the stars influence the world. The first three Sephiroth remain concealed (analogously, the first three Spiritual Hierarchies are beyond the solar system in Anthroposophy). The other seven Sephiroth 'activate' seven cycles. These constitute a cosmic cycle, after which there is chaos, then renewal in another cosmic cycle.

Pico della Mirandola (1463-1494), a Christian Florentine who was connected with the Platonic Academy, which was endowed by the

Medicis, believed he could prove the doctrines of the Trinity and the Incarnation using the Kabbalist axioms. Pico was the seminal figure who perceived the structural similarities between the Kabbalah and the *Corpus Hermeticum.*

Any magus who, unlike the piously and ascetically Christian Pico, understood the essential paganism of the Syrian-Egyptian gnostic and Neoplatonist sources of both the *Corpus Hermeticum* and the Kabbalah, received no encouragement to voice his thoughts. Some magical practitioners were too explicitly pagan or just unlucky. Campanella was held in prison for twenty-seven years and tortured; Giordano Bruno was burned at the stake.

The fusion of Kabbalism with Hermeticism resulted in a synthesis which was close to paganism, though as the historian Frances Yates remarks of Bruno, it did not break the Christian ethic of love; instead, it transcended the bloody categories of Reformation and Counter-Reformation. Hermetic-Kabbalism spread in both Catholic and – especially later – Protestant lands, notably Italy, France, Germany and, to a small but influential extent, England. It was in contrast to intolerant contemporary events, which included the sixteenth-century wars of religion in France and the devastating Thirty Years' War in middle Europe.

The non-magical devotees, though they incurred the disapproval of the more critically-minded humanists such as Erasmus, avoided the danger of being completely rejected by theologians, provided they also justified Hermetic-Kabbalism in terms of Christianity. The Kabbalah was integrated with the Christian doctrine that had been grafted onto the *Corpus Hermeticum.* The Sephiroth were identified with the Christian angelic hierarchies (which much earlier, despite their gnostic origins, had been made palatable by Pseudo-Dionysius), even though there were ten Sephiroth and nine Christian hierarchies, ten being an important number in Kabbalist numerology. Bruno exuberantly solved this problem by adding a tenth 'hero' order to the nine Christian hierarchies.[12]

A powerful body of theological opinion, both Catholic and Protestant, opposed the tendency among Hermetic-Kabbalists to use magic. Pico added the magic of 'practical' Kabbalah on to Ficino's cautious 'natural' magic. This resulting 'astral' magic attempted to escape from astrological determinism. It was given special emphasis in Agrippa's forthright *De Occulta Philosophia* (published between 1531 and 1533). This may have been the source for Dürer's 'Saturnian talisman', the 'Melancholia'. Though the power of conventional Christianity made seeking astral experience dangerous, Renaissance magi practised astral magic and experienced themselves, if they were in Bruno's heroic cast, as making ascents and descents through the spheres.

Hermetic-Kabbalism and alchemy enjoyed a golden age towards the end of the Renaissance, in the late 1500s and early 1600s; in part this occurred because powerful patrons, such as the Medicis, Borgias, and Protestant monarchs, often became personally involved protectors. As late as 1628, Campanella, the last of the Italian magicians, made magic with Pope Urban VIII, who had forebodings about his impending death.

It was not theologians, but the rise of the modern mentality associated with Descartes which dated the micro/macrocosmic correspondences which were the essence of magic.

Alchemy and Paracelsus

The magical tradition of alchemy was integrated with Hermetic-Kabbalism in the Renaissance. Spiritually centred alchemy was not so much concerned with the transmutation of metals for the mundane motives of commercial profit, as with transmutation as a method of salvation.

Alchemy had spread to Christendom in the eleventh to thirteenth centuries as a result of contact between Europeans and Arabs in Spain and Sicily. Albertus Magnus, who may have been a practitioner, Roger Bacon, and others compiled alchemical knowledge into their encyclopaedic works. Alchemy came, often via Byzantium, from two main sources.

Gnostic Alexandria blended Aristotelian thought, Egyptian technology and Mesopotamian astrology in an alchemical synthesis. Aristotle believed that from 'prime matter', matter and form produce the 'four elements' of fire, air, water and earth, which, through multi-form combinations, result in the diversity of the material world. Egyptian metal workers attempted to reverse this process by transmuting 'base' substances such as lead into 'higher' ones such as gold. Their thinking was magical: macrocosmic astrological influences were all important. Steiner was to accept the traditional belief that gold corresponds with the sun, silver with the moon, copper with Venus, lead with Saturn, iron with Mars, tin with Jupiter and quicksilver with Mercury.

Alchemy's other main source was Taoist. Use had been made in China of a 'medicine', that is, a substance added to mercury to bring about a transformation which was believed to cure illness and even to bestow immortality. This 'medicinal' alchemy influenced Nestorian Christians and Arab thinkers. The 'medicine' eventually became the 'philosophers' stone' of later European alchemy. The 'stone', alias the 'elixir of life', was held to heal 'sick' (base) metals by turning them to gold.

Titus Burckhardt writes, 'Spiritually understood, the transmutation of lead into gold is nothing other than the regaining of the original nobility of human nature.'[13] Gold and silver are the macrocosmic correspondences to the original condition of the soul. The aim of the spiritually-minded alchemist was the 'chemical marriage' of Sun and Moon (King and Queen, or gold and silver) using himself as a microcosm. The consciousness in precarious control of the transformation was understood as masculine. It was considered to be the active agent in the process of *solve et coagula,* of reducing base metals, and so unacceptable aspects in the microcosm of the alchemist himself, to 'prime material'. Only through this disintegrating preliminary could there be a transmutation and coming together into silver and gold. Thus the first colour to be experienced, when mundane defences were deliberately destroyed, was despairing darkness (or the *nigredo);* later came the washing or whitening (the *albedo),* then − if the alchemist was fortunate − divine grace or reddening (the *rubedo).*

The 'bible' of the alchemists, the *Emerald Tablet,* was attributed to Hermes Trismegistus. In the Renaissance a new wave of Byzantine alchemy reached the West, and interest reached a peak. The seminal, idiosyncratic figure, who used to threaten to put both the Pope and Luther in their places, was Paracelsus (1493-1541).

The problem of disease was the starting point for this physician, who was not conceptually systematic. He had sufficient confidence to reject much of the anatomical understanding of the times. Instead, he created a 'Christian' magical philosophy which was influenced by Ficino, Agrippa and other contemporary Hermeticists.

Paracelsus' 'prime matter' is the ideal pattern and spiritual prelude of the material world. Matter's multiplicity he saw as a process, which he termed 'cagastrum', in which simplicity and unity become split. Though his God may be a theistic creator, Paracelsus' cosmology seems essentially to be Neoplatonist. Disease is evil or disharmony resulting from separation of the 'salt', 'sulphur' and 'mercury' which are intrinsic to human beings. Some ailments, for example, pleurisy, plague and fevers, he thought to be the consequence of cagastric seed possessing the body from outside.

Liberation from disease is an aspect of the redemption and

reunification of the soul, Paracelsus believed. He held that the evil cagastric seeds and demons that attack man can be overcome by physician and patient through micro/macrocosmic magical work. Crucial to success in this are the physician's arcane understanding, self-knowledge and other, more conventionally Christian, virtues.

Rosicrucianism

The many-sided genius of John Dee (1527-1628) reached far back into the past and yet sowed the seeds of the future. He synthesized Paracelsus in a Platonic-Pythagorean cosmology that directly influenced late Renaissance Hermeticism-Kabbalism-alchemy. This became identified with the Protestant cause and with a popular 'Rosicrucian' craze that was the prototype for many subsequent Western 'esoteric' outbreaks. At a less popular level, major syntheses (also known as 'Rosicrucianism') continued well into the seventeenth century.

Dee inspired the Protestant poet-warrior, Sir Philip Sidney, and his small but influential courtly circle, who were at the centre of the cult of Elizabeth, the Virgin Queen, and the revival of medieval chivalry. This was even identified with by the Neapolitan Giordano Bruno. The atmosphere is reflected in Shakespeare's creation of Prospero, the magus of his magical, valedictory *The Tempest*. He may well have added its nuptial masque two years after the play's first performance in order to celebrate the marriage in 1613 of Elizabeth, daughter of James I of England, and Frederick, the Elector Palatine. Out of the tense contemporary religious and political situation, as will be described, came the first popular 'esoteric' craze. The existence of independent printing presses and of greater lay literacy were also powerful enabling factors.

The marriage seemed to seal a Protestant alliance between England and the Palatinate, with Venice potentially sympathetic. But after Frederick made his disastrous acceptance of the Bohemian crown, challenging the formidable Counter-Reformation powers, his father-in-law, James I, failed to support him. In 1620, at the start of what came to be known as the Thirty Years' War, the Catholic forces won a crushing victory at the Battle of the White Mountain. They were only defeated much later through the intervention of the Swedes, led by Gustavus Adolphus.

During this time Hermeticism-Kabbalism-alchemy, henceforth to become known as 'Rosicrucianism', was much practised in the Palatinate and Bohemia and enabled by Frederick and Elizabeth's tolerant Protestantism. A popular Rosicrucianism, which perhaps became so because it was being manipulated for Protestant political purposes, swept the Palatinate, Bohemia and much of Europe from 1614-1618. In the 1620s, however, it was persecuted as the victorious Counter-Reformation powers searched for Rosicrucians.

Popular allegorical pamphlets, such as the *Fama Fraternitatis,* or 'a Discovery of the Fraternity of the most Noble Order of the Rosy Cross' and the *Confessio Fraternitatis,* or 'the Confession of the Laudable Fraternity of the Most Honourable Order of the Rosy Cross, Written to All the Learned of Europe', revealed the supposed existence of an Order or Fraternity of hidden esotericists founded by 'Christian Rosenkreuz', or 'Rose Cross', who supposedly died in 1484 aged 106. His 'vault', which many people sought out, was said to be lit by an inner sun; his teachings were in 'Book M'. (This, as stated in chapter one, is reminiscent of Steiner's 'M'.) The 'Fraternity', which was almost certainly fictional, was presented as a secret order moving in the world in ordinary clothes.

Immense excitement radiated out from the Palatinate, where the pamphlets were first published, to much of continental Europe. However, Rosicrucianism made little impact across the Channel in contemporary England.[14] As political propaganda which created identification with the tolerant Protestantism of Frederick, the pamphlets were brilliantly successful. As religious allegories they failed, because they were taken so literally. When the Catholics, continuing the literal interpretation, took them as evidence of witchcraft, J.V. Andreae, one of the leading inside figures, cast doubt on their literal truth.

Andreae's *Chemical Wedding* was a Rosicrucian work of genius. After the Battle of the White Mountain, 'esotericism' of this profounder type, as much as any other, was forced underground. Hence, perhaps, Jacob Boehme's pessimistic idea of a negative as well as positive energy in the Godhead, or the 'nay in God', with its Manichean resonances. The general despair is reflected in Comenius' *The Labyrinth of the World.* Comenius witnessed the vigorous Baconism, which had some resemblances to Rosicrucianism, flourishing in England in 1641, just before the abyss of the Civil War. He correctly forecast that this rosy dawn was also the prelude to bloodshed.

By about the second half of the seventeenth century, the continuation of the Hermetic-Kabbalist-alchemical tradition through Rosicrucianism seems to have been approaching intellectual rigor mortis. The energies of this early modern age were increasingly creating science as we understand it conventionally today. The English physician, Robert Fludd (1574-1637), had synthesized Pico, Paracelsus and Dee around a pre-Copernican esoteric cosmos. His compatriot successor, Thomas Vaughan, who produced *Anthroposophia Theomagica* in 1650, seems to have innovated little. Newton was obsessed by alchemy, but became better known for other work. The farcical, demotic aspect of the popular esoteric craze originating in Frederick's Palatinate was a forerunner of much superficial, rootless occultism in succeeding centuries, and of the mass-marketing of some cults and thought systems today.

Yet Rosicrucian thought was still to have a strong mainstream imaginative influence. It has significant analogies in German Idealism. Goethe's *Fairy Tale* seems to have been a recast *Chemical Wedding*, though his work as a whole far transcends any one source, Western esotericism included. Lessing had written very favourably about the superior kind of knowledge that informs Paracelsus' medicine. Hermeticism also directly influenced the external symbolism and − more than critics often allow − the meaning of the *Magic Flute* (not only Schickeneder's libretto).

William Blake was thought by W.B. Yeats to have been an initiate. Blake was influenced through his upbringing by the Anglophile eighteenth century Swede, Emmanuel Swedenborg, who proclaimed a spiritual world. Blake's symbolism, whose obscurity may have arisen simply because he was not formally educated, has been interpreted by Kathleen Raine through her own synthesis of Blake experts. She describes a spiritual cosmology which has many analogies with gnosticism: indeed, his Urizen, the spirit of materialism and of cruel law-making and rigid morality, emerges as the main negative organising principle.

Some of Coleridge's thought, such as his theorising about 'primary' and 'secondary' imagination and 'fancy', also appears to have Rosicrucian resonances. The subject matter of Rosicrucianism was perhaps understood by the mainstream − though not by Blake, for whom the human imagination was cosmic − more as interior experience, less as literal cosmology.

Jewish Kabbalism, unlike Rosicrucianism, had been changing. The more dualist, messianic and complex Lurianic type replaced the older, more Neoplatonic form. There may have been a general Kabbalist influence on the pantheism of Spinoza and of Hegel. Franz Molitor (1779-1861) brought the Lurianic type − without a critical historical approach − into a completely new Christian Kabbalist synthesis.

Frances Yates suggests the august Royal Society in the UK, which historically was the prototype for modern scientific bodies, may have been inspired originally by Rosicrucian ideals. Rosicrucian meanings also became embedded in the ritualism of Freemasonry. This had first developed in 1638, or even earlier, in Great Britain, and in about 1710-1720 was established in France and Germany. The tone of Rosicrucianism seems to have become generally reduced, during the eighteenth-century, to fraternising at a social and fashionable level. This is suggested, for example, by Pope's *Rape of the Lock* (1712-1714). Frederick-William II himself belonged to the Gold-und-Rosenkreuz Freemasonry.

The Comte de Saint-Germain in the 1720s and Cagliostro in the 1780s had an immense success in persuading much of French Society that they possessed extraordinary occult powers and enjoyed unnatural longevity. The polarised social conditions of Versailles could have been as favourable a ground for synthetic spiritual activities as they were for the celebrated revolutionary bloodshed that was to follow. It was in this atmosphere that, in the 1770s, Court de Gebelin claimed that the Tarot pack derived from the ancient Egyptians. The claim flies in the face of post-Renaissance critical scholarship; this does not prevent it, however, from still finding many believers.[15]

It appears that little continuous Hermetic-Kabbalist-alchemical activity survived into the eighteenth-century. If there were Rosicrucian practitioners of long standing who were more than Freemasons they concealed themselves very effectively, in an extended interval of what adepts term 'silent activity'. The knowledgeable A.E. Waite stated that 'it is a complete blank', as far as the Rosy Cross in Germany is concerned, from the time of Frederick William II 'till Rudolf Steiner began to use the name and symbol of the Rosy Cross in his reproductions of a qualified modern theosophy'.[16]

8. Modernity and Gnosis

For us eternal life is death – not in the bosom of Jesus – but just death, no more being born again to endure life to die again. Yet people come in increasing numbers to India to be born again with the conviction that in their rebirth they will relearn to live.[1]
— Gita Methta, *Karma Cola*

Chronologically this chapter follows on from the last. But the late nineteenth and early twentieth century revival of gnostic-like thought forms (in relation to these times, often called 'esoteric') was temporally and doctrinally discontinuous with Renaissance Rosicrucianism. The lessened intensity of eighteenth-century Rosicrucianism correlated with the easing of the Catholic/Protestant conflict and the development of science. Though the late nineteenth-century revival was a powerful influence on the arts, it was often thought frivolous by intellectuals during this time, the heyday of scientific materialism.

One way of understanding the occurrence of this revival is to relate it to the overriding theme of modernity. To summarise what is well-known, the radical social innovations associated with the Industrial Revolution and urbanisation coincided, after the publication of Darwin's challenge to Genesis, with secularism and increasing religious doubt. Perhaps even more significant was the growth of a cultural relativism in which other spiritual and religious traditions became better known. As a result of such comparative religion more and more people were loosened from traditional legitimacies of thought and in perplexity became comparatively religious. The industrially-based middle class was growing rapidly, and with it secular liberal-democracy, with individualist ideals. The demand justified the publication of translations; thus Plato, Plotinus and Proclus became available in English. It seems to have been during the nineteenth-century that the 'Western esoteric tradition' came to be thought of as such. This in itself suggests an historical sense, a conscious looking back from what was perceived as a new situation.

Anton Mesmer (1733-1815) conducted spectacles in which, using magnets, he put people into trances; they were frequently cured of intractable complaints. It was later realised that the magnets he used were superfluous and so what had been called 'animal magnetism' became 'hypnotism'. The trances were accompanied by sensations such as knocks and lights. It seems that at least nine journals devoted to magnetism appeared in France alone from 1815 to 1850. Mesmerist societies held meetings and congresses and conferred prizes and awards.[2] This activity prepared the way for the subsequent popularity of spiritualism (see chapter two), one of the first cultural exports from the New World to the Old. From about the 1850s it spread in France and England.

Cosmological perplexity was added during the last quarter of the nineteenth century and later. The geology of Lyell (and others), and especially the new Darwinism, seemed to many to spell out the death of God because of their conflict with the accounts of creation in Genesis. The *machina* of the eighteenth-century *deus ex machina* consensus was perceived to be dispensing with the *deus*. The cosmological consensus was split into options of fundamentalist Protestantism and scientific materialism with uneasy compromises in-between. An influential minority committed themselves to a third, transcending and synthetic alternative, the gnostic, 'esoteric' or 'occult' (as it has also been called) revival.

The conflict between fundamentalism and scientific materialism is transcended by gnostic cosmology. Science is affirmed but made spiritual, for matter is not embraced positively. Darwinism is affirmed but made to conform to a descending, spiritual evolution. Divine revelation is confirmed, but time scales in the creation story are greatly expanded. Scholarly research into differing religious traditions is affirmed but often reduced to vague syncretism.[3] These visionary systems probably satisfied intuition and feeling more than the divide and conquer method of much post-Enlightenment thinking. The first section of the chapter describes this revived Western esotericism, with a focus on Anthroposophy. The revival was a newly expressed synthesis which contained modernity within some traditional thought forms.

The esoteric fashion died down after the 1914-1918 World War. This coincided with the rise of psychoanalysis and, less specifically, depth-psychology. These latter became partial explanations of reality and sometimes practical paths of salvation. Jung, who was fascinated by gnosticism and alchemy, saw them as deep truths about the 'psyche'. However, at least in his explanations of his 'analytical psychology' to the general public, he emphasised the reductionist interpretation of gnostic cosmology as a psychological projection. In this interpretation, modern scientific cosmology contains the insights of gnosticism: the latter's truth is seen as experiential and subjectively mystical. The second section of the chapter explores this situation. The third section briefly assesses the influence of Eastern thought on this gnostic revival.

Gnosis Containing Modernity

The 'occult' revival[4] around the turn of the twentieth century is outlined in this section. It is intended to portray some of the context accompanying the life of Rudolf Steiner and to trace immediate influences on the Anthroposophical cosmological structures described in chapter five.

There are other, parallel influences in Romanticism and nineteenth-century German culture. To name but one, a distillation by a musical genius of a great many largely German or pan-German cultural sources, Schelling and Hegel among others, the cult of Wagner's *Ring* has many underlying gnostic resemblances. Wagner, a central influence in German culture, is rooted in the latter's early to mid-nineteenth century preoccupations and anticipates much in its apocalyptic mid-twentieth century. In the *Ring* (reflecting perhaps Schelling's cosmogony, which Wagner knew),[5] an original bliss or innocence turns into a dualism when a dwarf, dwelling in subterranean night and longing for love, is turned away from it because of his repulsive qualities. Redemption of the cosmos from the egoism of the world, symbolised by the curse of power shaping a ring out of innocent gold from the Rhine, only becomes possible because of the consciousness and love displayed by the redeeming figure (Brunnhilde).[6] The world of power and status (Valhalla) is finally transformed into its elements by a consuming fire. Other themes in Wagner have gnostic resonances: for example, the antinomian, redemptive love-death (as in *Tristan und Isolde)*; and the originally pure state of things (as in *Parsifal* and the later stages of the *Ring)* which has been almost totally usurped by an alien force, a false underworld.

The late nineteenth century gnostic revival owed much to Eliphas Lévi, the *nom de plume* of a Frenchman who was a major source for the generation of occultists who lived after him. He experimented with alchemy and may have been the first to connect the Tarot with the Kabbalah. He was familiar with Knorr von Rosenroth's *Kabbala*

Denudata (c. 1680), a vast compendium of ancient and Lurianic Kabbalism.

Lévi was influenced at one stage by English Rosicrucianism. The Societas Rosicruciana in Anglia (or 'Soc. Ros.') was founded in 1866 and still exists. John Yarker was a member of the Soc. Ros.'s Manchester college. He later founded Masonic lodges, including the lodge which Steiner led within the Ordo Templi Orientis from 1906 to the outbreak of war. Bulwer Lytton was the Soc. Ros.' Grand Patron in 1871; his Rosicrucian novel *Zanoni* had, in about 1840, anticipated the coming revival.

The *Kabbala Denudata* was translated by MacGregor Mathers (as *Kabbala Unveiled)*. It seems to have been a strong influence on The Hermetic Order of the Golden Dawn, which was founded in 1888. Alchemy, astrology and Tarot were also important in this magicking movement. The Golden Dawn member was initiated through a series of grades corresponding to Gold-und-Rosenkreuz Freemasonry. Part of the ritual consisted of the reading out of an account, based on the Rosicrucian *Fama,* of the life of Christian Rosenkreuz. The first eight English Anthroposophists became so when they seceded from the Golden Dawn in 1912, after having listened to Steiner lecture in London.

The rise of the eastwards-looking Theosophical Society (described at the beginning of chapter two) occurred as part of a wider 'esoteric' revival. In contrast to the Golden Dawn, Theosophy renounced magic. It was largely based in the English-speaking world and India; as has been seen, it spread little in Germany, except as transformed by Steiner's Rosicrucian Anthroposophy. In France, Theosophy at first made little headway against the more Western, native occultism inaugurated by Lévi and continued by charismatic and colourful leaders such as Papus (Gérard Encausse), Stanislas de Guaita and Joséphin Péladin. The French Section of the Theosophical Society was led by Lady Caithness, the Duchesse de Pomar, who believed she was the reincarnation of Mary Queen of Scots.

The effect on the arts was considerable. The 'Celtic Twilight' movement in Ireland looked back, through Kabbalism and Rosicrucianism, to pagan roots. Yeats' *A Vision*, as well as the poet G.W. Russell's (alias 'A.E.'s) *The Candle of Vision* – and, later, the poetry of Edwin Muir and, perhaps, of Kathleen Raine – assume that stupendous visions are objectively real. For otherwise, 'We are but critics, or but half create' (W.B. Yeats, *Ego Dominus Tuus).* *The Phases of the Moon,* perhaps Yeats' most developed gnostic statement, has resonances with Lévi's phases of the moon. The

Robartes of the poem is a 'Master' analogous to Blavatsky's. The spiral ladder of Blake's 'Jacob's Ladder' was associated by Yeats with the winding, ancient stair of his high, lonely tower where, unlike Milton's Hermetic-Platonist, he could keep watch with the subsequently incarnated spirits of Goldsmith, Berkeley and Burke. In the tower is 'the lonely light that Samuel Palmer engraved'. (W.B. Yeats, *The Phases of the Moon.*) Later artists, including Kandinsky and the French Symbolists, such as Gustave Moreau, were strongly influenced by the esoteric revival.

Yeats retained his Golden Dawn membership until 1909. He had been expelled from the Theosophical Society for practising magic, having been a critical and cool member of its Esoteric Section. Aleister Crowley's Anti-Christ sign of the 'Great Beast', which anticipated the historical heart of the twentieth century, resonates with Yeats' 'rough beast' in *The Second Coming*. Satanism was also an important resource for Huysmans after his despairing *A Rebours*. In 1907 Crowley seceded from the Golden Dawn and, conducting magical warfare with Mathers, founded his Order of the Silver Star. After the First World War the gnostic revival was approaching its old age. T.S. Eliot consigned Madame Sosostris' Tarot pack to the wasteland. Charles Williams and Evelyn Underhill, later to be well-known in the UK and beyond, had briefly been members of the Golden Dawn but left this for mystical Christianity. The most prolific manifestation, Theosophy, had peaked by 1930. It was instead the Rudolf Steiner movement, despite vicissitudes after Steiner's death, which grew in the longer term.

Theosophy[7]

There can be no doubt that Theosophy's karma and much of its cosmology derive from Eastern traditions. Blavatsky and Besant seem to have been considerably influenced by Mahayana and Tibetan Buddhism and by Hinduism. Much of the terminology is certainly from India; thus there is 'jnana yoga' rather than gnosis (though as stated earlier the two words have a common Indo-European root), and use of words such as 'rishi' and 'avatar'. Members see Theosophy as more Eastern in spirit than Western; however, the basic structures seem also to have analogies with Syrian-Egyptian gnosis.

In the first four years, from 1875-1879, the core influence on Theosophy was Western. Indeed, in *Isis Unveiled,* which was published in 1877, Blavatsky stated that reincarnation is as rare as a two-headed infant. Theosophists admit these facts but explain that the public was not yet ready for the full revelation and that, in dismissing reincarnation, Blavatsky had a specialised meaning.

A bequest by a Baron Palme, at whose funeral Theosophists sang Orphic hymns, was used for Theosophical relocation to India. In 1879 the headquarters were settled at Bombay and in 1882 at Madras. From this time through to the 1890s, despite damaging allegations of fraud, membership expanded dramatically. The revelation came increasingly to be expressed in Indian terms. It was imparted in 1888 through the eagerly awaited publication of *The Secret Doctrine.* This consists of Stanzas from the 'Book of Dyzan', which Blavatsky supposedly received in an extrasensory way from Tibetan 'Masters', and her commentaries on them.

In 1893, W.E. Coleman, who was preparing an expose of Theosophy as a whole, published a painstaking analysis of Blavatsky's sources.[8] This gives the appearance of being objective, though his motive in writing it was probably personal. He concluded that *The Secret Doctrine* is 'permeated with plagiarisms and is in all its parts a rehash of other books. . . . I find in this "oldest book of the world" [the 'Book of Dyzan'] statements copied from nineteenth-century books.' Apparently, in Theosophy's beginnings, most was derived from Eliphas Lévi. A large part of the revelation came from spiritualism (Blavatsky had been a medium) and Western esoteric sources. Hinduism later came to constitute 'one of the larger portions', with Wilson's *Vishnu Purana* contributing most of the Hindu terminology. Buddhism was not so important as Hinduism, and, if Coleman is correct, the Western influences on Theosophy have often been underestimated.

Theosophists have not adopted many characteristically Indian concepts. Thus the Eastern idea that human beings can be reborn as animals has been rejected. The mysteriousness of Blavatsky may also be subtly different from the socially embedded spiritual elitism of India; Blavatsky was perhaps more in accord with the Christian Rosenkreuz furor. Her dedication of *The Voice of the Silence*[9] 'to the Few' appears to have been abandoned in recent editions. She generated no reformist zeal about India's social system. But in the later stage of Besant's Theosophy, when it was infused with liberal social concern, members disapproved of the Hindu legitimization of the caste system through use of karma, and through the campaigning of Besant and others influenced on the political stage what was to become Hindu separatism from British rule.

The cosmology comes across as amorphous and not as conceptual as Anthroposophy. The summary that follows is to a considerable extent taken from a codification published by the Theosophical Society.[10] There are strong resonances with Anthroposophy.

In the beginning there is an Absolute Whole, or 'full plenum' of the 'nature of the Self within', or 'svabhavat'. This whole differentiates into absolute consciousness and also ultimate matter, which is feminine or the 'Mother'. There is a rhythmic periodicity in which a ray drops into this germ of matter and the 'Golden Egg' of cosmic manifestation (or *manvantara)* descends. The egg is surrounded by seven elements or planes of decreasingly subtle matter, in which evolution occurs. The concept of the egg is probably Hindu in origin[11] but otherwise this cosmogony is compatible with Syrian-Egyptian gnosis.

Furthermore, there is individual development in accordance with the Syrian-Egyptian pattern of a descent into matter and a return with a more complete, spiritual awareness, though this pattern could also have been derived from aspects of Indian cosmology. The dynamic parts of the cosmos are spiritual essences or 'monads' which spiral further and further down the seven elements and then up again. The monads belong to one of seven spiritual hierarchies, in our case, the human kingdom, and are microcosmic, containing within them some of the seven elements. The highest element is spirit (or 'atma'), then there are 'buddhi' (which, microcosmically, corresponds to the spiritual soul), the higher mental element ('manas'), the lower mental element ('kama rupa'), the astral, etheric and physical elements. Within their hierarchies, some monads are 'laggards', while others are advanced. Higher hierarchies help lower ones in their evolutionary ascent.

There are seven static 'chains' round which the monads spiral. Evolution proceeds through the seven elements or kingdoms of nature. In each chain life evolves through one of these kingdoms; for example, present men were animals on the 'Moon', the previous chain. The fourth, our Earth chain, touches the lowest element, the mineral, and is 'the Turning Point and the Crucial Fourth', after which there is an 'arc of return' to the highest elements.

The cosmology relating to 'chains' was elaborated by Besant, who had been studying Hinduism. Each chain has seven 'globes', which, though thought of as invisible planes, are given planetary names, such as Mars and Mercury. The first three globes form a descent down towards the lowest element of the particular chain, where the fourth globe is situated; then there is an ascent up the last three globes, which correspond to the first three. The monads circuit the globes.

We are at present on the fourth globe of chain four. Globe four of our chain has been the cosmic turning point, the lowest descent of evolution. The Darwinian theory that humans and animals have common ancestors has truth Theosophically: spiritual monads incarnate as human beings after having been animals on a previous globe.

Each monad, which becomes individual at about the human stage, has to reincarnate (perhaps 800 or so times) into each of the seven globes of each chain. Within each globe there are seven time-periods, known as 'races', which replace each other through continental cataclysms. Atlantis, the last, fourth race, lingered on (in the form of the island described by Plato) until it sank about 11,500 years ago. We are at present in the fifth race.

In the arc of return there is increasing unity. In chain five the animal kingdom becomes human; they are followed by the plant kingdom on chain six and the mineral kingdom on chain seven. At the end, the seven elements become unified in their relationship to perfected consciousness.

Anthroposophy

It is now possible to relate Anthroposophy to Theosophy, seeing the broad similarities as well as the differences. Steiner's revelation almost certainly has analogies with the Theosophical as well as the Renaissance and Rosicrucian syntheses. Anthroposophists, Theosophists and others see their cosmologies as the truth that underlies world religions and so as independent of cultural sources.

In the foregoing summary of Theosophy many similarities with Anthroposophy stand out. Theosophy also has the four cosmological structures identified in chapter five, though with variations of emphasis. Steiner's system, synthesising the individualism of modernity, probably places more stress on the evolution of spiritual individuality. Both have broadly similar teachings about the sevenfold nature of man.

Steiner, as well as Blavatsky, synthesised the myth of Atlantis. This followed the success of Donnelly's *Atlantis: the Antediluvian World,* which was first published in New York in 1882 and had run into eighteen editions by 1889. In 1894 it was translated into German.[12] Donnelly's and Steiner's later Atlantis is in the Atlantic, opposite the Strait of Gibraltar. Blavatsky and Steiner also tell of three earlier 'continents', including Lemuria.

Theosophy and Anthroposophy adopt the very important Indian doctrine of karma. The rebirth revealed by both seers rules out the transmigration of human souls to animals and so is closer to the

Kabbalist tradition, for example, as expressed by Giordano Bruno, than to oriental teachings. Besant's Jesus had similarities with Steiner's in that a spiritual Christ entered him in the last three years. Neither was incarnated in a theologically conventional way.

With so much in common, the frequently stated view that Theosophy is Eastern while Anthroposophy is Western is rather misleading. Theosophy may well be more Western than is generally thought, whereas Anthroposophy has more in common with the Eastern aspects of Theosophy (such as karma and, perhaps, the pulsating Hindu kalpas) than appears in Steiner's *Autobiography.* Having said this, Anthroposophy does have Western features which are absent in Theosophy. Anthroposophy makes Christ central; Blavatsky gave more attention to the Buddha. Also, Anthroposophy's spiritual 'science' is more developed than that of Theosophy. The influence of Goethe, German Idealism and Rosicrucianism has been strong.

Instead of 'chains', 'globes' and 'races', Steiner's system has 'planetary embodiments', 'epochs' and 'culture-epochs'. It is strikingly similar to variants of Kabbalism (see the previous chapter) and perhaps owes much to Rosenroth's compilation, the *Kabbala Denudata.*

Theosophical cosmology seems to be more statically spatial and Anthroposophical more dynamically based on time. The Theosophical chains and globes, though these can die, are located in space and it is mainly the monads that move, giving rise to time; their spiralling circuits are the focus of spiritual evolution. In Anthroposophy rhythmic movements through time govern the planetary embodiments as a whole; the successive movement from one to another constitutes a progressive evolution. 'Moon', 'Sun' and 'Saturn' are past states spiritually deducible from the present, 'Earth' situation. In contrast, the Theosophical chains still exist after monads have moved on.

The effect, as Edwin Muir has pointed out in relation to novels,[13] is that the spatial system is more extroverted and the temporal more introverted. Anthroposophy's succession through time stresses the ascent of consciousness towards spiritual individuality. Theosophy's anthropology has one fewer spiritual body than Anthroposophy's. There are analogous temperamental differences between German idealism, with its historicity, as in Hegel's belief that the process of reality is one in which the Universal Spirit (Geist) progressively becomes conscious of the object-world as its own product,[14] and Anglo-Saxon empiricism.

Steiner, in contrast to Blavatsky, stressed his reve-lation's affinities with Rosicrucianism. Rosenkreuz, according to Steiner, was present at the Mystery of Golgotha and is the fulcrum of historical development. Reborn in the thirteenth-century, as a child he synthesised twelve world-conceptions held by twelve initiates. He was also reborn in the fourteenth-century and later as the Comte de Saint-Germain. This only scratches the surface of Steiner's Christian Rosenkreuz mythology,[15] which seems to be more prolific than the fables produced in the seventeenth-century.

Unlike Blavatsky, Steiner, as a professional researcher with a doctorate, was closely involved with contemporary science and philosophy. Scholarly reflexes may have led him to study original Western gnostic works in medieval Latin. He is said to have taught himself Latin in Vienna as a young man so that he could tutor it. In addition, his knowledge of Western gnosticism presumably derived from German translations, including perhaps the second-hand sources of the late nineteenth-century esoteric revival, for example, Eliphas Lévi's compilations.

The Threefold Commonwealth and the Goetheanum have Rosicrucian rather than Theosophical antecedents. Campanella's *Citta del Sole* (c. 1602) is a vision of an ideal state based on astrology; in the centre is a marvellous temple. Andreae's *Christianopolis* is a city Utopia with a predominantly scientific culture; its sciences and arts are based on 'theosophy' or divinised natural science (the word was appropriated by Blavatsky). It is both more mathematical and angelical than Bacon's *New Atlantis.* Late Renaissance macro/microcosmic work is harmoniously ordered round a higher unity, such as Bruno's 'Temple of Wisdom'.

In these descendents of Plato's *Republic,* astral magic seems to be at the centre of all activities. Correspondingly there is some higher magic in Anthroposophical activities: in the 'dynamising' of nature in biodynamic farming, for example. The many Anthroposophical applications seem to be the most extensive enactments of Rosicrucian utopianism. Theosophy, which is non-magical, is relatively inactive.

Anthroposophy has other detailed correspondences with Rosicrucianism which it seems not to share with Theosophy. Fludd's 'quintessential wheat' is similar to Steiner's suggestion that wheat should be the currency in the Utopian future of the Threefold Commonwealth. Steiner revealed that since 1879 we have been in the 'Michael Age'; this seems to derive from the magus Trithemius (perhaps through Eliphas Lévi). The Kabbalist linking of the Hebrew alphabet with the signs of the zodiac has similarities with Anthroposophical Speech Formation. Steiner may have been aware of a light-hearted work, *Le Comte de Gabalis*

(1670), which theorises about elemental spirits called, as in his later system, gnomes, sylphs and salamanders. The latter at least were alchemical symbols.

Western gnosis during the twentieth century

The decline of Theosophy and slow growth of Anthroposophy have been described in chapter two. With the fading of the occult fashion after the 1914-1918 war, it was not until the 1960s that it seems to have come into its own again.

Theosophy has been the alma mater of other movements, for example, the Buddhist Society and the Astrological Society. It has inspired other structurally similar revelations, such as that of Alice Bailey. Also claiming to be in communication with Tibetan Masters, Bailey seems to have synthesised onto a Syrian-Egyptian gnostic core some of the psychological ideas that have spread since the First World War.

The various Rosicrucian organisations today generally derive from the esoteric wave of about a century ago. The Lectorium Rosicrucianum of Haarlem, Holland, founded in 1924, has branches in Europe and America. The Ancient Mystical Order Rosae Crucis ('AMORC') was formed in 1915 by an advertising executive, H. Spencer Lewis, who had been a member of Péladin's movement in France. Its Supreme Temple is at San Jose, California. Mass-marketing techniques have helped boost its membership in Europe and America, where around 1980 it had about 60,000 people enrolled.[16] This is much more numerous than Anthroposophy at the time. However, there are reasons for believing that Anthroposophy is much more qualitatively differentiated.

Gurdjieff's 'Institute for the Harmonious Development of Man' at a Fontainebleau chateau attracted many famous literati in the 1920s, including Aldous Huxley, Katherine Mansfield, J.B. Priestley and, briefly, D.H. Lawrence. The 'Work' was spread in America (from New York) by A.R. Orage. Gurdjieff's thought seems to correspond with gnostic, Neoplatonic and Rosicrucian sources, and also Sufism and Buddhism. The 'Work' has been described as leading to an intuition of not knowing. Here the Buddhist analogy is strong. Later followers have included Gurdjieff's populariser, Colin Wilson.

The 'Work' was developed considerably by P.D. Ouspensky, who broke with Gurdjieff in 1924. The *Psychological Commentaries* on both by Maurice Nicoll, who was also influenced by C.G. Jung, synthesise Darwinism and depth-psychology, in a relatively non-extravagant way, onto gnostic cosmological structures.[17] An English follower of Gurdjieff, J.G. Bennett, recognised the former's 'Awakener of Conscience', the Messiah of the Second Coming, in 'Bapak', who founded the Subud movement.

After the time of Steiner, Western gnosis has often felt a need to synthesise depth-psychology. It has also accommodated itself to changing sensitivities. The privileged, traditional world of the 'Inklings' followed Steiner in time in a contemporary way, yet they are now themselves part of English speaking Anthroposophical lore.[18] C.S. Lewis, who with J.R.R. Tolkien was the best known of the four Inklings, conducted a 'Great War' with his friend Owen Barfield, perhaps the most distinguished English Anthroposophist, in which they crossed metaphysical swords. In contrast, Saul Bellow has mingled Steiner with the blank and pitiless modernity of Chicago. In *Humboldt's Gift,* with contemporary disenchanted sensibility, he tells of Kafka being disgusted when Rudolf Steiner worked his handkerchief deep into his nostrils with his fingers.

Western occultism revived in the counter-culture of the 1960s. However, as science after Einstein and the new physics have become much less identified with philosophical materialism, so the spiritual need to react against them has decreased.

Utopianism and existentialism

This section on gnosis containing modernity would not be complete without noticing how acclaimed scholars have regarded utopianisms such as Marxism and Nazism, and also existentialist philosophy, as having underlying gnostic structures. Hegel's philosophy, a source of modern secular utopianisms, is seen by Voegelin and others as having an essential core which is the same as in Valentinian gnosis.[19]As Levy states, the Hegelian reconciliation of subject and object is when the subject becomes conscious that the object is a manifestation of the subject. Marx completed this by adding in the material world. 'Nature is transformed by human activity and, to the extent that the problems of immediate scarcity are overcome, the being on which man and human consciousness are said to depend itself becomes a being structured or produced by human activity'[20] The notion of the final withering away of the state (Marx), or of the beginning of the thousand year Reich (Hitler), became ends which justified means such as the Holocaust, so Hegelian philosophy and gnosticism are perceived as potentially dangerous. In relation to existentialism and Heidegger, Jonas draws attention to the ontologically unsupported world of both gnostic and existentialist man.[21]

However, these scholars in pointing to the similarities do not stress the significant difference between the transcendence of gnosticism and the immanence of Marxism, Nazism and existentialism. This section of the book, which relates Anthroposophy to modernity, has as its subject other transcendent systems.

Modernity Containing Gnosis

The cosmological structures (described in chapter five) which underlie Syrian-Egyptian gnosis have been made to look increasingly implausible by the development of modernity.

The magical view of man as a microcosm has, in a great many minds, become increasingly ousted by the scientifically observed cosmos: macrocosmic thinking not only seems redundant but erroneous as a description of the world. Man's physical link with the cosmos has more and more come to be understood in terms of Darwinian evolution. This is difficult to integrate with a descending spiritual evolution, the Western esoteric explanation of the origin of macro/microcosmic correspondences.

Spirit has tended to be seen more as subjective experience which is immanent in matter and less as transcending the world. Spiritual evolution has generally been divested of the dualist Western esoteric structures: a mystical sense of earth itself becoming self-aware seems to have been replacing the pattern of primordial consciousness becoming trapped in matter and gaining redemption through gnosis. There has been a spread of psychological perspectives whereby gnostic cosmology is interpreted as a psychological projection.

Teilhard de Chardin and C.G. Jung, two most significant twentieth-century spiritual thinkers, are used here to illustrate the tendency of modernity to contain gnosticism.

Teilhard de Chardin

Maritain said that Teilhard's cosmos is just one more Christian gnosis.[22] This dismissive statement probably stresses the gnostic resemblances too much.

Teilhard de Chardin (1881-1955) had the theistic idea that divine initiative, or the grace of God, draws matter in a convergence towards consciousness and union in the differentiated whole he called 'point omega'. This is different from the gnostic fall into matter, the Sophia's afterbirth, and redemption from it. De Chardin seems to have experienced the world itself as filled with the divine absolute, and his idea of the 'super-material' does not seem to have led to a dualist approach to matter. Unlike ascetic gnostics he accepted sexual energy as a legitimate part of the great cosmic force, though he thought it should be transformed for a full flowering of mysticism. Also, his sense of spiritual progression through Darwinian evolution seems to have been without micro/macrocosmic correspondences.

It is in this overall context that de Chardin's system's resonances with the esotericism of his early life should probably be placed. One similarity is that he seems to put little emphasis on the problem of evil. Linked with this is his optimistic evolution of consciousness towards greater awareness: a turning-in of developing consciousness is crucial to the aim of being 'united, while remaining oneself', to the 'convergence of multiple elements' in a differentiated union. He interpreted history as an ascending spiral in which patterns recur in new ways. But these seem not to be the cosmological and anthropological structures that developed from Syrian-Egyptian gnosis. In de Chardin's thought these have been either omitted or contained within the cosmology and anthropology of 'modernity'.

De Chardin was influenced by the esoteric revival of his youth, but not as much as by non-esoteric evolutionary thought. He read the occultist Schuré's *Les Grandes Initiés* in 1918 and told of 'the joy of finding a mind extremely sympathetic to my own', though he soon found Schuré unreal and out of date.[23] He also read Maeterlinck and Emerson.

De Chardin criticised the static mysticism expressed in Aldous Huxley's *The Perennial Philosophy* because he was opposed to mystical experiences of 'cosmic consciousness' which were not integrated into an evolution of consciousness leading to a higher, 'person-centred' mysticism based on love. He seems to have believed in an ultimate *personhood* (analogous to the Pleromatic Anthropos) which is identical with love. This, the 'Road of the West', is the essential contribution of Christianity; for him the incarnation of Christ was the 'spearhead of monotheism'. His system seems to be mystically Christian and evolutionary. It also has something in common with secular evolutionary theories such as Julian Huxley's.

Carl G. Jung[24]

Though Freud, Adler, Rank and Jung seem ultimately to have been concerned with transcendence,[25] the psychological assumptions from which they worked largely reflect modernity, not gnostic cosmology. Jung's profound involvement with alchemy and gnosticism was, for professional consumption at least, from a psychological perspective.

Depth-psychology, which developed from medical science at the turn of the century, has thought of itself as scientific, though as already stated this self-conception has been much criticised. Its crucial insights about the formation of the mind in infancy and childhood, especially the underlying power of parental influence, and its techniques for allowing consciousness to experience unconscious energies have been accompanied by highly specific modern myths. Instead of being kept as secondary and speculative, the specific myths (such as the nature of the Oedipus complex) were in the twentieth-century often made primary and tenaciously defended. Though these positions are not held in common by the different schools, historically their legitimisation has been clinical experience, not scientifically gained evidence.

After his break with Freud, Jung (1875-1961) endured a profound crisis during the First World War, his 'ego', in the Jungian sense of the centre of the field of consciousness, just managing to ward off his 'psychosis'. He believed he was experiencing objective, archetypal areas of the psyche. Beside a Swiss lake he restored himself through assimilating these powerful irruptions, his consciousness asserting itself in his building of a tower by the water's edge at Bollingen. Its sombreness makes it a fitting modern successor to Milton's 'high lonely Towr' of the Hermetic tradition, or Yeats' tower.

These experiences did not lead to an immersion in the revival of Western esotericism. Jung wrote that Theosophy is 'indescribably cheap, impoverished and lacking in creative energy' because it reduces everything to metaphysics, which explains as little as a purely materialistic approach. Nor did he approve of the so-called 'scientific' esotericism of Anthroposophy.[26] Conversely, Steiner thought (the early) Jung was unspiritual and Anthroposophists tend to see him as understanding soul but not spirit.

His 'analytical psychology' does not see matter as problematic. Jung emphasised the need to be well adapted to the world. Steiner's own sensation function seems to have been extremely undeveloped, at least until the close of his Weimar years. Jungians would probably understand him as an 'introverted intuitive' type. Here in Jungian typology are found the mystical dreamer and seer as well as the artist and crank. The moral variant transforms his vision from aestheticism into his own life, making it symbolic, adapted to inner but not to outer reality.

Titus Burckhardt criticises Jung's approach to alchemy as too psychological and as insufficiently spiritual. But mostly the criticism of Jung is the other way round: it is assumed he became immersed as an alchemist himself. Jung undoubtedly saw alchemy and gnosticism as psychologically true, limiting them to the psyche only, whatever the extent to which he also saw them as expressing cosmological truths. In no sense did he reduce the felt experience of what he was studying, dismissing it as relatively unreal, as 'only' the psyche. Alchemy seemed to him to be as uncontaminated an expression of psyche as it was possible to find in culture, with its tendency to refine spontaneous experience into acceptable packages. Walter Pagel, an expert on alchemy, has written that Jung's is a largely successful attempt to understand it.[27]

Jung understood the alchemist as projecting his unconscious onto the outside world. The *nigredo,* or reduction to 'prime material', he saw as the blackness, negativity and depression within the practitioner himself. It is largely analogous to the 'shadow' of analytical psychology. Then the *albedo,* or whitening, is dominant; this is a process of washing which Jung related to the continual attempts to assimilate irruptions from the unconscious through reliving the trauma producing them. This purification as understood by Jungians involves the acceptance of one's psychological projections. If all goes well, it brings a transcending peace. From now on, the alchemists say, one has simply to feed the fire to keep it going. In this process there is the *conjunctio,* or coming together, as in Andreae's *Chemical Wedding*, of male and female. Jung saw this as the projected recognition of the contra-sexual in the psyche. Men have an unconscious archetypal 'Eve', known as the 'anima'; women have a corresponding 'Adam' or 'animus'. The philosophers' stone is, for Jungians, the transcendent experience known as the 'self'. The *rubedo,* the final alchemical state, is compared by Marie-Louise von Franz to the hoped-for end result of analysis, an experience that grips or falls upon one as from above.

Similarly, though there are ambivalences, Jung interpreted gnostic (and other) cosmology as projected psychology. He understood the Syrian-Egyptian fall from spirit and subsequent struggle for gnosis as an unconscious form of what, in his analytical psychology, he termed 'individuation': that is, the re-finding of the 'self' by an adult, individual consciousness which, since infancy, has become differentiated and so alienated. His 'self' archetype has psychological affinities with Manichean and Zoroastrian dualism, since for Jung there is darkness (or 'shadow') even at this ultimate of experienced reality. The descent of the Sophia, or the cosmic 'anima' figure falling into matter, represents the moment when the individual projects this archetype into matter. That it is sometimes the Anthropos who falls accords with the contra-sexual aspect of Jung's system, the 'Eve' or 'Adam' within. The syzygies or pairings off of the Pleroma are also consistent with this. The rhythmic emanations of much Western gnosis seemed to him to express the recapitulations that accompany psychological development.

Jung did not interpret all as projection. His idea of 'synchronicity', or the mutual influence between psyche and what is outside, is a limited instance of magical thinking. It seems he was influenced by Taoism more than by the micro/macrocosmic correspondences of Western esotericism. He thought that the unconscious probably has a material aspect, which would be why it knows about matter; conversely, he seems to have believed that there is a dim or vague phenomenon of consciousness even in inorganic matter. But the correspondences of synchronicity in his published thought system are approached through the psychological assumption that all is projection.

Jung also seems to have embraced the possibility that the 'archetypes of the collective unconscious' in one person can affect those in someone else by processes which are beyond the use of the five familiar senses. Many followers are committed to this position. The 'self' is a transcendent experience which corresponds to the 'carbon' or ultimate substance of the cosmos at large, much like the relationship between the Hindu *atman* and *brahman.*

Jung assumed no descending spiritual evolution into which Darwinian evolution is fitted. Such an assumption is not implicit in his distinction between the 'actualised' archetype and the 'archetype *per se*'. The former is a culturally conditioned manifestation. The latter is analogous to the uniform axial system informing the myriad different shapes of crystals; he saw it in a Lamarckian way as having been phylogenetically conditioned through the evolutionary past. He made references to 'Mendelian units' though his concept of the collective unconscious and the archetypes that transcend personal genetic history has become a mystical and not a scientific notion.[28] Thus his archetypes, apart perhaps from his ultimate 'self', do not descend from a gnostic Pleroma in which matter does not exist. Instead, for him they are forged by the material and biological circumstances of evolution (to others they may seem to derive from German culture). Similarly, the Jungian development in which the individual is thought to recapitulate the archetypal evolution of the species is not based on Western gnostic macro/microcosmic correspondences; instead, his ontogenetic/phylogenetic link-up is related to biological evolutionary theory. Indeed, his archetypes are instincts which become spirit through the activity of knowing them.

Jung was sufficiently identified with modernity to base himself on Kant's theory of the unknowability of reality in itself. His descriptions of the collective unconscious seem to have been epistemologically pragmatic, from an 'as if', and so generally avoid literalism (i.e., from a Kantian point of view, transcendental illusion). He occasionally contradicted this Kantian outlook by saying that science will make the collective unconscious more knowable, but here − however erroneously − he seems to have been placing his trust primarily in empirical scientific method, not in revelatory 'spiritual science'. His cultural evolutionism is in many ways complementary, in a psychological, introverted way, to Teilhard de Chardin's more extroverted approach.

Jung's theory of culture was based on the evolution of consciousness or the developing relationship of 'ego' and 'self'. He understood Christian culture as having gradually swung from an over-emphasis on spirit in the gnostic era to its opposite, the highly differentiated materialism of the twentieth-century. Unlike de Chardin, he greatly stressed the existence and problem of evil in the psyche and the 'self'. In no way did he equate modernity with moral progress, which he identified with the right use of self-knowledge. He criticised the dissociation of modern consciousness from its archetypal foundations and understood contemporary astrology and flying saucer mythology as the projected search of modern man for a soul.

Jungian analytical psychology has become rather insulated from the mainstream of psychological research and even from its own cousin, the MBTI (Myers Briggs Typology Indicator), a psychometric which is widely used in large corporations without any reference to Jung's seminal book *Psychological Types*. Analytical psychology's main growth seems to have been in its broad cultural associations. After Jung, Fordham produced a more concrete synthesis, and others such as Hillman more symbolist syntheses. For example, a connection has been made[29] between the 'new physics', 'superspace' and the archetypes; in this development the biological model has been subsumed within one that is cosmological.

The Influence of the East

In seeking renewal, twentieth-century Western man frequently turned his eyes to the exotic and sometimes 'esoteric' East. The death of his own gods encouraged him to dream about foreign ones. But his longing often returned to him his own East, a Western fantasy.

Ironically, those who live in the actual East were often modernising fast.

As already suggested, in the late nineteenth century the 'East' became popularised in the West. For example, *The Light of Asia* compared Buddha to Christ. Karma and rebirth are important teachings in gnosticisms of our times, notably Theosophy and Anthroposophy. Theosophy brought to India liberal-democratic Western ideals and helped stimulate the renewal of Hinduism, but it seems not to have taken away from India much that altered the fundamentally Western state of mind with which its pioneers first arrived.

An aspect of this Hindu revival which has analogies with the Western gnostic renewal is the success of Advaita or non-dualist Vedanta. It has been adapted by Indians to the needs of the West. In New York during the 1890s, leading members of the influential New Thought and Christian Science movements attended lectures by the Vedantist Swami Vivekenanda. In this century the non-dualist Vedantist synthesis has been very pervasive, reaching its climax, perhaps, in the one, divine Reality celebrated in Aldous Huxley's *The Perennial Philosophy.*

The success of the perennial idea was not merely a function of the need to reconcile different religions. There were good reasons for thinking its phenomenology sound. Non-dualist Vedantism is in many ways in accord with the philosophical Idealism that once had a powerful grip on European and American imaginations. It is also superficially compatible with Western esoteric cosmology, though there is a difference between dualistically rejecting excessive hardness (as in Anthroposophy), and declaring the phenomenal world relatively illusory (as in Advaita Vedanta). The oneness that self-styled non-dualist Vedanta, unlike Theravada Buddhism, sees as all-encompassing reality, is in its affirmation of primal substance not radically different from the emanating originality of the gnostic Pleroma; that is, if one does not notice that it inherently develops dualism through its partial fall into matter. The West's East has tended to be represented as monistic spirituality. The actual variety within the Vedanta school and elsewhere has not been widely appreciated in the West. De Chardin, for example, considered pantheistic 'cosmic consciousness' to be the 'Road of the East'. Hesse's *Siddhartha* perhaps expresses quite recent Western expectations, but to a swami, it probably appears 'typically Western'.

Some Anthroposophists are concerned that various Westernised Eastern practices and meditative cults are much more numerous and better financed than the Rudolf Steiner movement. It is suggested at the end of this book that much Eastern mysticism such as T.M. (Transcendental Meditation) has succeeded in the West because factors in the contemporary Zeitgeist have allowed it to be adapted and marketed well, sometimes through world famous champions such as the Beatles. Eastern spiritual practices as brought to the West often share some hinterland with gnosticism, though they are less dualist, and so seem accessible in a way Anthroposophy may not. Some cults, such as those based on Guru Ji, Meyer Baba or Krishnamurti, have become long-standing. Furthermore, the West has become aware of cults, such as the feminist Brahma Kumari or Sri Aurobindo's evolutionary Advaita Vedanta, which reflect the influence of modernity on India itself. Such cults have been matched to Western expectations yet still seem to bring with them the allure of the pre-modernised East.

Part Four

Different Perspectives

9. Interpretive Visions

A spiritual theory of man is a necessary presupposition for cultural sociology.[1]
Max Scheler, *Problems of a Sociology of Knowledge*

This book attempts a broad-based approach to a very large and complex subject. The value adopted here is to be inclusive of as many levels of reality as possible, and to aim to avoid understandings that are reductionist: in other words, to avoid attempting to fully explain one area of reality in the terms of another. Each major perspective, whether gnostic, sociological, psychological or positivist, has inherent reductionist assumptions.

Gnostic Reduction of the Social to Spirit

The reduction of social reality to spirit is a hazard for the Anthroposophical cosmological structures defined in chapter five. For the reasons stated earlier 'Syrian-Egyptian gnosis', used as an ideal type – extending its historical and disputed use by Hans Jonas – seems close to the main cosmological features of Anthroposophy. This section suggests that there are thought forms inherent in Anthroposophy and Syrian-Egyptian gnosis which can in practice limit full appreciation of the distinctive quality of socially emerged reality (analogously, these revelations understand some matter to be over-hard). It also suggests that the distinctively beneficial effects of Anthroposophy may not be achievable without this reductionism.

It is not easy, after induction into Anthroposophy, to see it from many different perspectives at the same time. 'Openness' can consist of identifying with Steiner's life and thought as faithfully as possible. The argument *pro hominem* is deployed: biography, implicitly if not explicitly, becomes hagiography. The rainbow-like social being of the movement seems to confirm everything he revealed. It tends to encourage a progressively developing Anthroposophical identity, in which the gaining of knowledge itself becomes an act of commitment. One has to belong in order to know what happens in the elite School of Spiritual Science: to belong, it is necessary to take responsibility for Anthroposophy. However, there are signs that Anthroposophists are becoming increasingly open to outside perspectives now that those who heard Steiner are no longer around to speak of the experience.

The non-absolute quality of Steiner as a man influenced by the varying currents of his times is suggested by humanly understandable discrepancies. Steiner opposed esoteric secrecy but later set up his own closed circle. He stated that his revelation should be read before trying his meditative exercises yet denied that such reading would affect the experience itself. He stressed the need to think for oneself, yet there is a taboo against coherent intellectual analysis of his cosmology, this being considered 'Ahrimanic'. Anthroposophy's fit with Western esotericism and turn of the century German culture has to be interpreted as confirmation of Steiner's world outlook, for it is considered 'Ahrimanic' to suggest that the doctrines he revealed were in part at least conditioned by his time.

From another point of view these enclosures can be seen as illusory. If the revelation is objectively true and at some level known by everyone, reading about it can only be a superficial influence. The privacy for the meditations and other activities of the School of Spiritual Science is likewise not fundamental, but merely a temporary protective filter. Indeed, the gnostic idea that that which spiritually is of the nature of gold cannot be contaminated by mud tends to be perpetuated within Anthroposophy through a highly idealistic understanding of, and expectation from, the movement's social forms.

Anthroposophical reality is maintained by the movement's social organisation because this is based on Steiner's revelation. From within one aspect, such as eurythmy, or bio-dynamics, or a study group on *Occult Science,* there radiates reverence for its wide-ranging whole. To see it entire from a spiritual point of view would be for one to become reality itself, to realize one's spiritual individuality through Intuition. No ordinarily modest Anthroposophist could envisage such a situation in this incarnation. To approach this visionary state it is seen as necessary to take responsibility first, perhaps by participating in the research of a section of the School of Spiritual Science, and so sharing in its knowledge of one specific aspect of Anthroposophy as a whole. With growing commitment, thoughts are increasingly unlikely to occur if they are outside Anthroposophical boundaries.

The movement's spiritual absolutes are also maintained by a certain licence on small matters. It has been possible to think that Steiner was incorrect in some minor areas of his spiritual research, as long as more is not threatened. His imputation of European seasons world-wide is clearly a slip. Here an Anthroposophist can identify with him as a fallible person like oneself. But this cannot extend to examining whether the asymmetricality of his revelation – because the coming of Christ is slightly off centre – was the result of his acceptance of Blavatsky's system; this kind of cultural analysis is too disturbing to be likely to emerge from within the movement's social rainbow. Assimilation is also used. Other knowledge can be syncretised in a non-threatening way, as in making depth-psychology apply to soul only, not spirit. Rudolf Steiner's thought can also be confirmed through being further developed by others, as with astrosophy and most of the applications.

Steiner insisted that his language was unimportant and that his intention was to convey the spiritual reality itself, not to give a linguistic illusion of the transcendent. This raises an issue about the epistemological and ontological status of his revelation: if all his language is completely unrelated to spiritual reality, his doctrines concerning karma, rebirth, Saturn, Sun, Moon and so on might just as well be replaced by the thirty-nine articles of the Church of England. How is one to know where his language is a mere metaphor, a pointer towards the ineffable, and where, however necessarily imperfectly, it has some literalism in it?

It is almost impossible to pin the revelation down to specific facts (let alone refute it) because its words are justified by Anthroposophists in terms of leading one towards experience of spirit. However, its statements may also be seen as related to material facts. The result is an ambiguous position: for example, it is difficult to know whether 'Atlantis' describes a geographical landscape as well as a metaphysical one. Neither Steiner's statements nor anything in the Anthroposophical belief system provide internal rules which enable one to know when the words connect literally with observable matter and ordinary concepts, and when and how they do not.

As has been seen, the gnostic cosmos is one which seeks the spiritual and is ambivalent about the material world, unlike Protestantism, where commercial success in the world has been linked in the minds of believers with divine grace. The blind spot in the world views subscribed to by intuitive idealists is likely to be the material world, just as the self-legitimations of those who identify with the material world are likely to be pragmatic.

Reduction of Spirit to Society in the Social Sciences

In defence of the spiritual

People worldwide have a sense of the spiritual, yet this can be excluded from contemporary secular understanding about what draws people to belong to spiritual organisations. This is partly because the spiritual cannot be identified to the five senses as distinctive, and so from a positivist perspective it is meaningless.

From the point of view of social theory, spiritual experience tends implicitly to be reduced to its phenomenology. For much contemporary social theory there seem to be no such things as 'mysticism' or 'esotericism', only culturally conditioned mysticisms or esotericisms. Meditative systems can be interpreted reductively, using an exclusively linguistic focus, in terms of their verbally expressed end-states of being or non-being (this form of reductionism is the converse of the spiritual reduction of the social described in the preceding section). Thus Buddhism, according to Edwin Arnold, seeks a ceaseless, lifeless, timeless bliss; Vedanta's ultimate is the 'one'; Jewish Kabbalism thinks of the emanations from the Godhead in terms of values; some Christian mystics speak of an ineffable love. These affirmations are understood by some interpreters to be entirely culturally conditioned.

However, not all the many attempts at cross-cultural understandings have been spiritually reductionist. Some, indeed, through using a spiritual perspective, seem to fall into the opposite trap of reducing cultural differences. Thus Aldous Huxley stated that his revelatory 'perennial philosophy', which contains 'hardly anything' from the professional philosophers, is primarily concerned with 'the one, divine Reality substantial to the manifold world of things and lives and minds'.[2] However, to later scholars the expressions of difference between religious traditions are more pronounced than they were for Huxley. Few contemporary students of religion would wish to defend the phenomenology through which Huxley appears to derive his mystical 'X'. To many it appears to be the high-water mark of Vedantism.

Using a more differentiated approach, Ninian Smart suggests[3] the term 'mysticism' be restricted to contemplative experience and not be used to cover what Rudolf Otto calls the 'numinous': the awful, submerged feeling of nothingness in the face of thunderous outer might that is characteristic of prophetic experience in Judaism, Christianity and Islam.

Stace also proposes a cross-cultural ideal-type of mysticism related to the language used. He claims that mystical language has an underlying core which is, *inter alia,* non-spatial, non-temporal, beyond language and ineffable, paradoxical, sublime and joyful. In his and similar analyses the words used by the contemplative are treated as having meaning outside the context in which they arise: for example, after making careful linguistic and cultural allowances, it would be thought valid to compare an Anthroposophist's description of supersensible experience with that of a Japanese Buddhist or of an Eastern Orthodox monk.

It is a reductionist step to conclude that contemplative experience, such as Steiner's stage of Intuition, is nothing but a social product, the end result of the cultural path followed. Steven Katz states that there are no pure or unmediated experiences. He seems to mean by this that there are no non-social 'X's' which can be experienced through (or beyond) the filters of the social; for him contemplatives come to know no more than the 'x^1', 'x^2', 'x^3' that are the ends of the specific meditative path with which they have identified.

Because Katz disagrees that descriptions (for example, 'ineffable', 'paradoxical', 'sublime') have any meaning outside their contexts, he claims that the cross-cultural comparative approach from which Stace derives his common core is misconceived. From a perspective which places such emphasis on context, if there is a common core or there are cross-cultural cores, its or their expression may well be masked by the linguistic context. In this case the apparent diversity of the ends of specific contemplative paths should not be used to suggest there is no common core. However Katz inconsistently states, comparing Buddhism and Jewish Kabbalism,

> there is no intelligible way that anyone can legitimately argue that a 'noself' experience of 'empty' calm is the same experience as the experience of intense, loving, intimate relationship between two substantial selves, one of whom is conceived of as the personal God of Western religion and all this entails.[4]

If words cannot have meaning outside their cultural context, the comparative approach is irrelevant in considering whether common realities beyond the social enter into the experience of the specific contemplative end. If words can have meaning outside their cultural context, the cross-cultural analogies make it more likely than not that such realities do enter in. Supersensible experience has been taken for granted by a large portion of mankind, even in secular, hedonistic societies: for example, research in Britain shows that over a third of the population studied have admitted they have been aware or influenced by a 'presence or power' (though many felt inhibited about discussing their experience).[5] It is by no means obvious that the onus of establishing plausibility is, on the analogy of a null hypothesis and its specific epistemology, on those who propose the existence of experience beyond the social. For it seems, using sociological sceptics' own assumptions, that most doubt on this question is an Enlightenment social construction: incredulity is probably rare outside the culturally conditioned influence of modernity.

Similar intangible thinking is also inherent in the working models of sociology itself. In sociological assumptions about the origins of society it is broadly necessary (breaking the rule of logical priority) to adopt Durkheim's explanation that society emerged from an 'instinct to be social' which was unconscious; otherwise a Darwinian model has to be abandoned. Social scientists, however, seem reductively to assume that this emergence was once and for all, taking place only in the primeval mists. However, on a Darwinian model, it is not likely that 'an instinct to be social' within people created society but then stopped emerging in succeeding generations. Such an important developing emergence would only halt very slowly, taking far longer than the few million years in question. This barely conscious or unconscious instinct to be social, if it was with our ancestors a minute or so ago (in evolutionary terms), is likely to be with us now, in addition to the society that is obviously 'out there'. Society is presumably emerging all the time. Thus from sociology itself there seems to be an ongoing metaphysical social causative factor which cannot be analysed. By analogy, the fact that no one is able to measure the spiritual does not mean it exists only as a social or linguistic construction.

Variation in predisposition to spiritual experience

A further point, independent of the question of in which senses the spiritual dimension exists, is whether people vary in their capacity to have spiritual experience. Variation in predisposition is independent of the debates about whether spiritual reality is nothing but a social or linguistic construction, or whether it is outside the skin as well as inside.

It has already been suggested that it is likely, beyond the influence of the social, that some people are more predisposed to experience the spiritual than others. This argument is not based on the metaphysical belief in the grace of God as an independent factor, on ideas of karma, or on gnostic elitism. It derives from biological analogy.

Variation in predisposition within the population as a whole is not typically treated as an independent variable in sociological explanations of spiritual conversion, whether this is at the level of groups or of individuals. If spiritual energies are seen as a significant independent factor they are treated as a constant; if not, they are implicitly reduced to social factors. Yet, as in the case of other sense organs, it is more reasonable than not to believe that spiritual receptivity does vary between individuals.

Reductionism in the social sciences

As has been seen, gnosticism and, to a lesser extent, mysticism are essentially movements away from the constraints of social conditioning (this behaviourist word seems appropriate in this context), and towards the spiritual. Hence an interpretation of them in terms of social organisation has a hollow, superficial ring. It is a mistake to deny the very considerable influence of culture on contemplative experience; but it is equally mistaken to implicitly strip the spiritual factor from this experience. Gnosticism and mysticism are distorted by the usual 'scientific' practice of considering social factors alone.

Furthermore, otherwise excellent sociological studies often step over the ill-defined border between not concerning oneself with the spiritual and subtly denying its power. Thus Berger and Luckmann claim, 'To have a conversion experience is nothing much. The real thing is to be able to keep on taking it seriously; to retain a sense of its plausibility.'[6] Smelser states that esoteric cults stem from the convergence of like souls who see the world as hostile because of essentially independent personal experience (for example, a rejecting father). For Smelser, when alternative means of reconstituting society are perceived to be unavailable, such 'value-oriented' beliefs arise, the potential for violence being always present in them.[7]

As already suggested, if the methods of the sociology of knowledge are applied to social science itself, the implicit denial of the spiritual can be traced to its origins in positivism and the Enlightenment. A scientific or scientistic method has tended to have an *a priori* legitimacy even in the limiting case of studies of experiences of the spiritual. In explaining conversion, the hypothesis chosen cannot be fully separated from the observer's own reductive myth, though the attempt needs to be explicitly made. The three main explanatory concepts, those of community-seeking, deprivation and the need for meaning, exclude the spiritual as a separate factor.

It is often difficult to distinguish these concepts if the aim is to provide refutable hypotheses which do not overlap. For example, Glock subdivided[8] 'deprivation' into abstract categories. His 'psychic' deprivation can scarcely be distinguished from that which is 'organismic', since this (for him) includes mental traumas. Glock defines 'ethical' deprivation as a feeling the dominant values of society no longer provide a meaningful way of organising life. This surely is also traumatic. He specifies that deprivation should be perceived as such by the subject. In the case of the eighteen Anthroposophists to be discussed in the appendix, this would rule out of consideration those early hard experiences which they interpret in terms of karmic desert and opportunity. In the absence of refutable hypotheses, explanatory secular concepts become an alternative metaphysics to the spiritual.

The sociology of religion is still much influenced by its origins in Western society, concerning itself mainly with the study of orthodox or sectarian Christianity. This tends to be institutional in nature and so much more amenable than mysticism and esotericism to sociological assumptions. Troeltsch, a seminal figure, was concerned with the creative tension between Christian orthodoxy and Protestant 'sect' (as he termed it); his study of mysticism and 'technical mysticism' (broadly, what is here termed 'esotericism') was peripheral to his task yet it acknowledged spiritual energies. Since his time the Western secular democracies have become more pluralistic and mysticism and gnosticism have increased. For decades it has been widely agreed that, outside the lessening traditional 'church'/'sect' (as it is termed in the sociology of religion) tension, classification in the sociology of religion has, as one expert put it, fallen apart 'in a morass of conflicting and arbitrary definitions'.[9] These classifications tend to rule out spiritual energies as an irreducible factor in understanding contemplative experience.

Social Evolutionism

Technological progress and distraction from the spiritual

In discussing the tension between the social and spiritual, change over time has not so far been considered. Technological dynamism, what Hans Jonas called the signature of modernity, has increasingly distracted attention from the spiritual. This 'development' is ambivalent, combining progress in a technological sense with ontological loss.

Such an interpretative approach needs to separate itself from the legacy of the social evolutionism of the nineteenth century. Though Comte was not unsympathetic to religion, the culmination of his Law of the Three Stages of Intellectual Development, propounded in the 1830s, was scientific thought. Later, Spencer understood the history of religion as consisting of 'progress' out of superstition towards an enlightened present. This general outlook reduces the spiritual to the scientific world-view of the European nineteenth-century. Also, the patterns produced tended to be based on 'armchair' fieldwork and linguistic distance. They sometimes forced 'primitive' societies into preconceived European moulds. For example, a single category of 'ancestor worship' was constructed in a one-sided attempt to explain the origins of religion.

The later reaction was to throw out the baby with the bathwater of imperialism and racism. Any overall analysis of the development of religion tends to be rejected as Western bias and so as 'ethnocentric'.

Robert Bellah's social evolutionary theory[10]

Robert Bellah's theory, despite its many drawbacks, will be expounded in some detail in the pages that follow because after major changes it provides the framework for the approach proposed towards the end of this chapter.[11]

The pattern, at its most basic, consists of an initial, dream-like world acceptance which gradually develops, in about the first-millennium BC, to a religious mentality of world rejection. From Protestantism to modernity, this split between religious and worldly institutions and outlooks, or dualism, then changes to a new general world acceptance. Bellah distinguishes five stages, which are never completely abandoned.

In the first, 'primitive' stage there is a 'hovering closeness of the world of myth to the actual world'. Thus the Australian aboriginal word for their symbol system is 'the Dreaming' (or 'the Dreamtime'). The mythical world is very closely related to the detailed features of the actual world and such myth is the beginning of man's capacity to transcend and dominate suffering and the other limitations imposed by the conditions of existence. There is considerable fluidity: dreams may lead to a reinterpretation of myth, causing ritual innovation.

In the ritual the participants become identified with the mythical beings represented; at these moments the distance between man and mythical being – which was at best slight – disappears altogether. There is as yet no 'religious' organisation in a social institution which is separate from the social differentiations of age, sex, kin and so on.

The religious systems of much of traditional Africa, Polynesia and some of the New World, as well as the earliest religious systems of the ancient Middle East, India and China, are placed in Bellah's second 'archaic' stage. Here, though the individual and his society are still merged in a natural-divine cosmos, there is increased complexity and with it a new sense of freedom and, perhaps, anxiety. Mythical beings have become gods: they are more distinct and, in a vast cosmology, actively control aspects of the natural and human world. The need for a mediating communication system is much more acute and is met in worship and, especially, sacrifice; there may also be priests and divine or priestly kingship.

Religious organisation is still by and large merged with other institutions: the functionally and hierarchically separated groups in archaic society tend to have their own cults. Agriculture makes a two-class system possible. The 'upper status group', which tends to monopolise political and military power, usually claims a superior religious status as well. There is little tension between religious demands and social conformity.

In the great transformations of the first-millennium BC, Bellah sees the breakthrough to his 'historic' or third stage. The relative integration of 'religion' with the world in the preceding stages, especially the first, becomes a dualism: through religion there is world rejection and perception of a need for salvation in a transcendental, universal reality. Connected with this is the emergence of various conceptions of hell. Salvation through understanding and participating in the fundamental structure of reality becomes, for the first time, the central religious preoccupation.

Bellah holds that devaluation of the empirical world and the empirical self highlights the conception of a responsible self, a core self or a true self, deeper than the flux of everyday experience, facing a reality over against itself, a reality which has a consistency belied by the fluctuations of mere sensory impressions. For the first time, instead of a diffused sense of identity, there is a clearly discriminated self, and it is possible to conceive of man as such. Salvation becomes a quest to escape, through religious action such as contemplation or asceticism, basic flaws in one's nature, for example, greed and anger.

Bellah sees this core self facing the flux of everyday experience not only (it seems) in the *atman/brahman* idea of post-Vedic Hinduism, but also in the *nirvana* of Theravada Buddhism, even though the latter is often described as a void or nothingness. This is because it serves 'fundamentally as an identity symbol' and because 'for practical and ethical purposes at least, a distinction between the true self and the empirical self is made by all schools of Buddhism'. Furthermore,

> even when, as in the case of Judaism and Islam, the religion enjoins types of worldly participation that are considered unacceptable or at least doubtful in some other historic religions, the devout are still set apart from ordinary worldlings by the massive collections of rules and obligations to which they must adhere. The early Christian solution, which, unlike the Buddhist, did allow the full possibility of salvation to the layman, nevertheless in its notion of a special state of religious perfection idealised religious withdrawal from the world. In fact the standard for lay piety tended to be closeness of approximation to the life of the religious.

This dualism is also found in the social realm: the single religious-political hierarchy of archaic society tends to split into two at least partially independent hierarchies, one political and one religious. The roles of subject and believer become distinct. Bellah points out that this is the practical result in Islam, though it is not supported by religious norms. This religious development, which is closely associated with the growth of literacy, is accompanied by differentiation into a four-class system; this consists of a political-military elite, a cultural-religious elite, a generally archaically minded peasantry or lower-status group, and a religiously innovatory urban group of merchants and artisans, also of lower status. The dualism of this 'historic' stage results in a new tension, in which political acts could be, and have been, judged in terms of standards that the political authorities could not finally control.

The fourth, 'early modern', stage is based on the Protestant Reformation. For Bellah the defining characteristic of early modern religion is the collapse of the hierarchical structuring of both this and the other world. With more direct confrontation between the two worlds, religious action is identified with the whole of life. Salvation, which is now potentially available to everyone, is to be found in the midst of worldly activities while retaining the self as the centre of one's identity, and not in an indirect (or 'mediated') way, through conformity to religious law, participation in a sacramental system or performance of mystical exercises. The separate self of the 'historic' stage is discriminated still further. After the Reformation, the service of God became a total demand in every walk of life. Much of the cosmology of medieval Christianity was dropped as superstition.

The stress was on faith, an internal quality of the person, rather than on particular acts clearly marked 'religious'.

The four-class system in Europe began to break up. Especially in the English-speaking world, Protestantism greatly contributed to its replacement by a more flexible, many-centred mode of social organization based more on contract and voluntary association. The old religious distinction between two levels of religious perfection was lessened in the new division between the elect and reprobates. In this stage there are, for the first time, institutions which are set up to reform the *status quo*. For Bellah, liberal, voluntary, democratic society is the result of this self-revising social order. There have been close analogies to the early modern situation, Bellah stated, in many of the developing countries.

Bellah terms his fifth and last stage 'modern religion'. Its central feature is the collapse of the dualism so crucial to all the historic religions. However, there is no return to the relative integration of the primitive stage. The split, in the historic stage, between religion and world, is replaced by multiplicity. Life has infinite possibilities. The analysis of modern man as secular, materialistic, dehumanised and in the deepest sense areligious seems to Bellah to be fundamentally misguided. This is because he believes such a judgement is based on standards that cannot adequately gauge the modern temper.

Bellah cites the attempts of the Protestant theologians Tillich, Bultmann and Bonhoeffer to come to terms with modernity, and sees parallels in Japanese Mahayana Buddhism. He points out that in American religious adherence the obligation to be doctrinally orthodox sits lightly indeed. (This observation was written before the advent of the Moral Majority and fundamentalism.) No longer do groups explicitly labelled 'religious' monopolise the symbolisation of man's relation to the ultimate conditions of his existence. Bellah believes that modern religion is beginning to understand the laws of the self's own existence and so to help man take responsibility for his own fate.

Bellah holds that the search for adequate standards of action, which is at the same time a search for personal maturity and relevance, is in itself the heart of the modern quest for (non-dualist) salvation. Culture and personality have come to be seen as endlessly revisable: knowledge has opened up almost unlimited new directions of exploration and development. Bellah states that at each stage the freedom of personality and society has increased relative to the environing conditions: in the last two stages world rejection has been mitigated by the possibility of remaking the world to conform to values.

Bellah's Evolutionism

As a preliminary, it needs to be noticed that 'religion', a word whose roots are in Roman and Christian worship, is arguably out of context if applied to Bellah's 'primitive' stage or to much of the secular symbolising of modernity, such as Marxism and depth-psychology; indeed, it is questionable whether it is inclusive enough even to cover Confucianism and Theravada Buddhism.

There is perhaps moral progressivism in Bellah's questionable metaphysical liberalism, in his optimistic belief that freedom is increasing and that a deeper understanding of the laws of the self is being attained. Calling his earliest stage 'primitive' rather than, say, 'primal' also suggests an evaluative position. However, modern 'religion', as much as old, can be disintegrating and disruptive. In the case of neuroscience, for example, it seems that ancient perspectives and dilemmas are being opened up again in new ways, with no final resolutions. 'Evolution' explicitly need mean nothing more than generalisations about sequences of human culture, and this is the sense in which it is adopted here.

Furthermore, Bellah's evolution of freedom and understanding could be taken to imply an implicit or immanent progress analogous, though in a much more secular vein, to Teilhard de Chardin's. Despite possible contrary hints in his account, it seems clear, however, that his stage of 'modern religion' has almost entirely spread through the social influence of diffusion, not through intrinsic and parallel independent developments. He does not explore the pessimistic paradox that the increase in complexity, which he sees as accompanying his hypothesised development of freedom, also makes the individual more and more dependent on the social environment. Indeed, whether social complexity has increased with technological development is disputed by sociologists. A distinction here needs to be made between the individual's complex reality, whatever the society (whether primal or post-modern), and the higher volume of overall complexity in specialised, modern, populous societies.

Bellah's Californian-style modernity may be criticised because his emphasis on the self and freedom are not to be found convergently emerging in all rapidly growing economies. Other cultural models, as arguably in Chinese collectivism, may focus on being carriers of an increasingly rapid technological progress. The same might also be said about Christian fundamentalism in the US. Admittedly, the culturally singular development from Protestantism to modernity, his final stage of 'modern religion', has had considerable global impact as a model for societies – excepting some Islamic ones – with no history of Protestantism. Secular, pluralistic, liberal ethics are enshrined, for example, in the UN Charter and are paid lip-service by many a tyrant. They have become the 'virtue' to which, in Oscar Wilde's aphorism, 'vice' pays hypocritical tribute. Western societies have had considerable success in institutionalising these norms and they are now, despite religious fundamentalism, more prevalent than they were fifty or a hundred or so years ago.

Bellah's 'modern religion' seems to put horror in the past. There is no sense from him of the shadow side of 'progress'. With his increase of freedom has come the increase from muskets to nuclear weapons; within a shorter time-scale, the development from the concentration camps used at the turn of the century to contain Boers to Belsen, the gulags and Guantanamo Bay; or again, the cross-cultural increase of terrorism practiced on civilians. He pays no serious attention to materialism and distraction from nature and spirit, an existential dualism which may be an aspect of his fifth, modern stage itself. Shadow might be an inevitable accompaniment of the transition to 'modern religion', or belong to it.

Envisaging the development of the social in terms of its interplay with the spiritual puts the above issues in a new light. Understanding materialistic technological dynamism as a force which distracts from the ground of being, the spiritual, is a less optimistic scenario than Bellah's 'modern religion'.

The Spiritual, Changes in Collective Consciousness and Western Gnosticism

A crucial modification being made in this book to Bellah's thesis is to introduce the spiritual. Its interplay with the development of society is the broadest interpretative context suggested here, and is the basis for the interpretation of Western gnosticism given in the next chapter. Indeed, in several other ways the interpretation which follows transforms Bellah's approach, which nevertheless is useful as a point of departure.

In the dawn of culture, society and consciousness seem to be (compared to modernity and its alienation) relatively unemerged.[12] In this general respect, it seems reasonable to generalise about our neolithic ancestors from recent primal society survivals. There is more access to and immersion in 'the Dreaming' and the spiritual. Perhaps this state has some relationship with the early paradise of which so many myths tell. Though individual consciousnesses within primal societies are highly differentiated, such societies as a whole are nothing like as complex or differentiated as modern ones.

As consciousness and society become more consolidated and emerged (the 'archaic' stage) there is greater distance and tension between them and the spiritual. There is already evidence of dualism. Distinct gods in a vast cosmology are beings held apart and there is more of a contrast to the immersing effect of primal ritual. Access to the supersensible depends more on intricacies of worship and sacrifice and also on social status: one's relationship to the divine king, for example.

In Bellah's 'historic' stage, religion – an institution devoted to the cult – separates from the political hierarchy. Society has become more differentiated with the increase in different status/occupational groups, and everyday consciousness is more separated from the spiritual as it adapts to, manipulates and becomes identified with increasingly emerged social realities. Religion plays an ambivalent part, sometimes supporting this separation and deferring a direct meeting with the spiritual to a life after death, and sometimes attempting a contemplative reconciliation with the spiritual, in or through existing social institutions.

The massive rules and obligations of Judaism and Islam prevent consciousness from seeking relief from its separation through contemplative integrations with the spiritual; instead the pious must have faith in the reward of the life to come. Orthodox Christianity also has the same effect. The meeting of consciousness with the spiritual ultimate is held off until the resurrection of the subtle body or, in its Hellenic form, the survival of the soul. Breaching these boundaries is taboo. Contemplative, homeostatic tendencies are dubiously on the margins. Thus Kabbalism has had a precarious relationship with Judaism and Sufism with Islam. Though Christian gnosis in the first-centuries CE acquired considerable legitimacy, it was then suppressed with only the Neoplatonist mystical tradition just managing to avoid censure. The boundaries had also (arguably) been maintained in the seminal inspiration of the Judaeo-Christian-Islamic prophets. Being licensed as a prophet was only possible for the very few, in a certain form (the 'numinous', a thunderous, awesome revelation coming apparently from outside), and in specific historical conditions. The tendency towards monotheism alongside the emergence of increased overall social complexity probably was associated with a general separation of consciousness from the spiritual.

However, the religion of the 'historic' stage also contains reactions towards contemplative homeostasis, or integration with the spiritual. These are the dominant philosophical elements in Upanisadic Hinduism and Buddhism. The admired specialists − though a tiny minority of the population as a whole − achieved meditative salvation in one life, anticipating what most people in the historic East hoped to attain eventually. Common experience shows, most unsurprisingly, that Hindu villagers are not philosophical contemplatives. This is not the same thing as denying the overarching importance of philosophical contemplation for Hindu village culture. The Hindu *atman* and Theravada Buddhist *nirvana* are similar in that they are returns to what is deemed to be the ground of being, whether this is expressed as oneness or as nothingness. This attitude is profoundly different from the barriers against contemplation set up by the prophetic religions.

There is much in popular Hinduism (especially in its *bhakti* form) and Buddhism which corresponds to Judaeo-Christian-Islamic orthodoxy, but the big difference seems to be that in the Indian traditions contemplation holds a central legitimacy. Spiritual homeostasis as much as socially crystallised theism integrated society.

The specialisation and separation of consciousness seem to have been most pronounced in Christian, especially Protestant cultures. The two main periods of Western gnostic emergence have coincided with the impact of the 'early modern' and 'modern' stages, that is in the Renaissance/Reformation and in the late nineteenth-century. The gnostic responses seem to have been minority reactions embracing radical spiritual transcendence at times when orthodox consciousness was caught up in cosmological conflicts. At the same time, modern gnosticisms have incorporated the Protestant cultivation of individual spirituality through emphasising the development of spiritual individuality.

This need for spiritual union is perhaps reflected in the long cosmogonies and eschatologies (what Hans Jonas has termed the historical sense) of gnostic systems. It will be suggested in the next chapter that they reveal how emerged the social has become, and that many consciousnesses experience that emergence as alienation. The perceived path back, whether through magical passwords or Steiner's Imagination, Inspiration and Intuition, is correspondingly arduous.

10. Western Orthodoxy, Mysticism and Gnosis

Now by Liberalism I mean false liberty of thought, or the exercise of thought upon matters, in which, from the constitution of the human mind, thought cannot be brought to any successful issue, and therefore is out of place. Among such matters are first principles of whatever kind; and of these the most sacred and momentous are especially to be reckoned the truths of Revelation.[1]
— John Henry Newman, Apologia pro Vita Sua

This chapter attempts to interpret the timing of Western gnostic outbreaks more closely and to make some sense of the patterns of occurrence of contemporary gnostic (or 'esoteric') and mystical cults.

Gnosticism, Catholic orthodoxy and Neoplatonism

The mystery religions of the ancient world reflected the increasing complexity of consciousness and society. Bellah understands them as transitions between 'archaic' and 'historic' religion. The participants were less and less locals and more and more educated cosmopolitans with the means to travel. Presumably those who were not just going through a conventional rite of passage were seeking release from the world through spiritual experience. Thus the Orphic motto was 'the body a tomb' *(soma semi)*. Its early enactment of rite became mythological and philosophical: the rites were approached more consciously as they became symbolised. In an analogous development in the sixth-century BC Pythagoras revealed that there is an underlying, harmonious unity of numbers.

The initiations in the mysteries seem generally to have been supportive of the social and political order, or cosmos. After his experience of the goddess Isis, Lucius Apuleius, who was a Roman citizen, practised in Rome at the bar. The revelation of the goddess gave authority to Apuleius' function as a legal upholder of the social system. He playfully wrote, 'I will record as much as I may lawfully record for the uninitiated, but only on condition that you believe it.'[2] But revelation was also used by his more other-worldly contemporaries to legitimize world rejection in gnostic systems.

Their sense of the oppressiveness of the social world, expressed in their rejection of matter and the universal fate dispensed by the planets, seems to have been greater than that felt by the Hindu Upanisadic contemplatives a few thousand miles to the east in the Indus and Ganges basins. Perhaps this was because the Roman Empire was on a much grander scale than the Aryan. Nevertheless, there are similarities in some schools of Hinduism.[3]

The felt oppressiveness of a complex world is also suggested by the protracted gnostic cosmogony and – to a lesser extent perhaps – redemptive respiritualisation. There is, as previously mentioned, pathos in the lengthy fall of the Valentinian Sophia and a sophisticated discrimination in the relativity of her salvation: while in part she is more aware through attaining gnosis, an aspect of her, the irredeemable matter that is her shapeless abortion, is consumed by fire.

Though in 'archaic' societies (in Bellah's sense) there may well be sophisticated cosmology, it seems that stories of the origins of the cosmos (cosmogony) and of man are usually relatively brief. This could be because it is with increased separation of consciousness (and consequent increased emergence of the social) that the question of *how* the cosmos and mankind arose becomes more obviously meaningful and pressing. For example, cosmogony seems to have become more important in the 'historic' stage of Hinduism, in the latest hymns of the *Rig-Veda,* when there was a displacement of old gods and a developing contemplative tradition. Likewise the creation story of the first chapter of Genesis seems to have been derived from Mesopotamia and Egypt, and to have been added on later than the account (in chapter twelve) of Abraham sensing a divine call to leave Mesopotamia. Ling[4] associates the story in the first chapter with the rise of the Hebrew priestly tradition occurring after the 'historic' breakthrough into ethical monotheism and the special destiny of being a chosen people. The Israelites at this later stage appear to have been influenced by the cosmogonies of the hydraulic-agrarian civilizations of the ancient Near East, as well as by their latest technologies, such as the highly conscious one of tree-grafting to start producing our present-day unnaturally large apples (as in the story of Eve's attaining new knowledge). The use of irrigation and the complex social organisation that was needed to work it was an obvious achievement which perhaps required mythic answers to many basic questions of origin and maintenance. A further instance of cosmogony correlating with increased social complexity arises with Zoroaster's dualistic cosmogony and eschatology: these made sense of the complications caused by waves of lawless marauders across the Iranian plateau. Similarly, by the time of Augustus the 'historic' discrimination of Roman identity was very considerable. Virgil's *Aeneid* reflects this sophistication in being very long-drawn out and not so much a cosmogonic myth as a very lengthy aesthetic and moralising fable for the origins of the Roman empire. Cosmogony and the story of the origins of man thus seem to become more prominent with the developing complexities of society, and function to legitimise a specific constellation of socially circumscribed meaning.

Analogously, the need to be saved in an afterlife does not seem to be prominent before development into Bellah's historic stage. The need for salvation implies events leading to a present predicament from which man needs to be saved, hence there is a close relationship between the theme of salvation and the themes of cosmogony and the origins of man.

In gnostic systems, unlike the mysteries described by Lucius Apuleius, cosmogony was no longer used to legitimise the social order. On the contrary, it came to have the inverted function of vilifying the phenomenal cosmos. Cosmogony was necessary, for otherwise the experience of being trapped in the world could not be explained; it legitimized rejection of the world. The creation of the world becomes tragedy, the fall of spirit into matter; the only hope is the possibility of salvation, sometimes only for a spiritual elite, through gnosis. Cosmogony without eschatology thus becomes a situation for despair, not a this-worldly creation which calls for joyful celebration.

That the 'trap' of the emerged social order – and so, it might be presumed, of the gnostic's own accreted consciousness – was experienced as extensive is also suggested by the many micro/macrocosmic correspondences in gnostic thought. Through the adoption and development of Babylonian astrology, the extent to which the 'inside' corresponds with constraining planetary influences on the 'outside' became a highly discriminated, specialised body of knowledge. Furthermore, escape from the adverse Archons depended on correct timing. Salvation is a developmental process. Those called to gnosis, or intuitive awareness of the structures of reality, can only experience their escape from the hard world through an arduous change of consciousness. The Sophia who, in her ardent desire for gnosis of the Father, falls out of the Pleroma, is the youngest; her initial energy seems to come from a sense of being behind, of wishing to be fully mature. This leads to a complex, alienated state of fallenness. Salvation can only come from further movement forwards. Gnosis is a more self-aware, insight-giving state than the one she left behind. The potential for dynamism makes this Syrian-Egyptian pattern qualitatively the prototype of modern gnosticisms which stress the development of conscious individuality.

The victory of the Augustinian church and Catholic orthodoxy was, as has been seen, an intolerant one. It represented the interests of the urban many, not the world-despair of a spiritually-inclined relative few. Gnosticism was suppressed, not just voluntarily abandoned. This churchly barricade of canon and dogma has perhaps played an ambivalent part in the survival of Catholicism. It claimed a monopoly of salvation: objective grace through its institutionality became all. Unlike Judaism, it was not the repository of a logically coherent, ethnic, prophetic tradition whose main concern was with everyday practice; instead it was attempting to define the good news of what it claimed was the Son of God. In the battle against approaches it deemed heretical, closely worded theological positions were taken, such as on the Trinity. These, in their tortuous balancing of logical and other inherent tensions, lead to the mentality of Tertullian's famous 'I believe because it is impossible'. The Christian emphasis on belief as a boundary has perhaps made possible the modern liberal idea that everyone should think for themselves.

The brittly defined thought of the Church cannot be separated from the purple of Caesar which it had taken over into its own social practices. The new doctrines often, implicitly or explicitly, legitimised the stability of its hierarchy. For example, what the Church came to define as the 'heresy' of docetism tended to lead to a priesthood of all believers, for in maintaining that Christ was entirely spiritual and had no physical body, docetism implicitly denied the exclusiveness of the appearance of Christ after the crucifixion to the disciples and hence, through the doctrine of apostolic succession, denied the Church hierarchy.

The anti-gnostic development that started with orthodox canon and dogma eventually led to the events of the Reformation and, through Protestantism, to modernity. It has enabled the Church to survive for an enormous stretch of time, but at the price of schisms from its carefully controlled position. In the cosmological crises of the Renaissance and Reformation, and of modernity, the development of epistemological individualism left Catholic institutionality behind. At these two (early modern and modern) breakthrough points there have been pronounced Western spiritual reactions away from the world. The availability of gnostic revelations and the spiritual syntheses around them attracted many during these times of cosmological crisis.

The survival of Catholicism may be partly due to its tolerance towards some kinds of contemplative experience. Sometimes it has accepted the authenticity of recent visions of the kind that Otto terms 'numinous'. The saints, where they have become living symbols, have contributed much to its stability. Also, the Neoplatonic current in Christian intellectual history has produced what have become more or less official Christian mystics, such as Eckhart, Tauler and Suso. Though this unitive Christian mysticism has often been in an ambiguous relationship with orthodoxy, it seems to be just about tolerated, if only because – unlike in gnosticism – there is no ultimate rejection of the world. As a result, mystics can accept the institutional claims of the Church even if at the same time they criticize it for lacking the right spirit. Thus the self-deification that can accompany unitive contemplative experience such as the Neoplatonic is, in Christian mysticism, less threatening to the status of the Church than it is in Christian gnosis. Mysticism of all kinds may have functioned as a safety-valve, drawing off potential rejection of the Church as an institution.

The Renaissance and Reformation

During the Renaissance and the late nineteenth- and early twentieth-centuries cosmological crisis has been accompanied by an increase in neo-gnostic affiliation.

At those times in the Christian West when cosmological orthodoxy has not been much questioned, the spiritually inclined can genuinely be mystics more or less co-existing within the church, but at times of cosmological questioning alternative templates are more likely to be sought. The questioning of the Renaissance was partly the result of the new availability of gnostic texts, so this alternative template itself helped produce the questioning. The gnostic vision with its astral magic and micro-macrocosmic links not only offers, as has been described, an alternative cosmology, but also has its own built-in path of salvation.

The conceptual distinction between mysticism within an unchallenged Christian consensus, and cosmological crisis requiring an alternative spiritual template, may be difficult to apply in particular instances. The ambiguities of any one person's experience may make it unclear, for example, how far they are influenced by cosmological crisis. The intention here is to apply this distinction at a more general, structural level in order to describe cultural trends.

The recorded, retrospectively termed 'esoteric tradition' seems to have started with the arrival of the *Corpus Hermeticum* in Florence in 1460. Availability and contemporary plausibility as a stock of knowledge seems to have been a precondition for the numerically significant spread of Western gnosis. In the case of the Cathars the social stock of knowledge appears largely to have been communicated by word of mouth and by personal example. The availability of gnosis since has largely been through the written word, and the public exposed to it has gradually increased with the spread of printing and literacy.

Catharism derived from the Bogomils and/or gnostics in the Pyrenees. After Catharism was suppressed, gnosis, until the arrival of the broadly Syrian-Egyptian *Corpus Hermeticum,* was not plausible, for access to it was largely through the Church Fathers' refutations. Although later textual discoveries suggest that Christian writers such as Bishop Irenaeus were factually accurate in describing the gnosticism they were refuting, the context in which they were writing was that of triumphal Catholicism. The erroneous attribution of the *Corpus Hermeticum* to Hermes, however, gave it plausibility in many Renaissance minds and legitimized it, thus making it more available.

The plausibility of the Renaissance macro/microcosmic magician was probably also heightened by the rift in cosmological orthodoxy. The Protestant quarrel with Catholicism involved questions of doctrine and dogma. The contemporary Hermeticism tolerantly reconciled these rigidly confined disputes in its widely enfolding arms. For example, Catholic/Protestant disputes about the workings of grace become doctrinally inessential once gnostic cosmology is adopted. Later, Hermeticism − when it came to be called Rosicrucianism − was increasingly identified with the breakthrough to early modernity or Protestantism. After this strife it lost its creative impetus, but not before − some think −being the direct progenitor of modern science. However, the spiritual movement towards a new synthetic gnosis, despite its cultural importance, was only a minority one. For numerous others the tension was experienced in the more mundane and bloody French wars of religion and Thirty Years' War. Rosicrucianism's cosmological synthesis was an aspect of the onward thrust of Western consciousness towards, as it turned out, greater rationality, materialism and emergence.

Modernity, Gnosticism and Mysticism

The eighteenth-century consensus, the cosmology of the *deus ex machina,* had its surface ruffled by esoteric ripples, but there were no waves comparable to Rosicrucianism, or to the occultism of the late nineteenth-century. Western gnosticism was influential mystically on Romanticism and Idealist philosophy, but no longer was it so seriously taken as an undiluted cosmology.

Mesmerism and spiritualism provided relief from the boundaries inherent in nineteenth-century Protestant orthodoxy. In contrast to formality and repression, there was the exciting encounter with split-off aspects of the self, and also with supposed spirits of the dead. This seems to have functioned as a safety valve for the pressure of conventional practices, such as church-bound worship.

The spiritual reaction away from late nineteenth-century rigidities became more pronounced, more gnostically inclined to reject philosophical materialism, when to a large section of the middle class there seemed to be a conflict between 'Christianity' and 'science' (identified with Darwinian materialism). Many felt an acute conflict at the level of cosmology and some solved it through gnosis or 'spiritual science'. At this stage the breakthrough to modernity seems to have been making its greatest intellectual impact on the increasingly educated, urban middle classes.

Systems such as Anthroposophy, however, did not abandon the increased awareness in the Protestant West of people as separate individuals with the self becoming more and more discriminated. Late nineteenth-century gnostic syntheses, like any others, were creations of time and place. The Syrian-Egyptian gnostic structure, the basis of Kabbalism and Rosicrucianism, was suited to a graft of evolutionary progressiveness. Contemporary individualism, with its materialist connotations, tended to be reflected in an ascending 'esoteric' individuality. For the ancient gnostic, the mythic story of the fall into matter seems to have been a cosmic disaster, an explanation of all the suffering, spiritual and otherwise, in the human condition. The redeeming feature, gnosis, was an advance from the *status quo ante,* but one for which a terrible price had been paid. In turn of the twentieth-century gnosticisms in Europe, the development of an emerged social order – and even the contemporary materialistic individualism – tended to be seen optimistically: for as a result the self has become discriminated, and so is available for the free ascent towards spiritual individuality. Up to the First World War, it was a time of social optimism. In the individual gnostic pattern typified by Anthroposophy, the fall into what is perceived as extra hardness, though it may also be overlaid by spiritual opponents outside the scheme of things, is an essential part of the overall cosmic meaning. In the return to the ultimate, the self is not only conceived as merged with the Pleromatic All as if it were – in the Hindu phrase – a drop of water in the ocean. Instead there is a paradox: the self is infused with the macrocosm and yet heightens its individuality through retaining a purified essence of its worldly experience.

This spiritual individuality is located within the relatively high social complexity of Anthroposophy, which is considerable compared to other 'cults'. (There is no attempt here to define 'cult' inclusively, if such a thing is possible. In this book it is used to distinguish non-church-related spiritual/religious identities from 'sects', which typically deviate from mainstream churches on relatively few, though fiercely defended, points.) Cults generally appear to lack stable, continuing social institutions. Anthroposophy's established, post-Second World War stage seems to be exceptional. The genuine Anthroposophist, whether a teacher, secretary or farmer, is in part defined in terms of trying to infuse the work with the intuitive Anthroposophical totality. As has been suggested in chapter four, sense-based rationality is subordinated to one of spirit even in the performance of specific tasks.

The great increase in literacy and the book market during the nineteenth century made gnosticisms available as never before, especially towards its close. Connected with this is the move towards populism which first became apparent with the Christian Rosenkreuz craze in the early seventeenth-century. The scholarly were generally repelled by Blavatsky. However, Theosophy attracted intuitive minds through and despite its exotic terminology, occultism and aura of fraud, and, as in the cases of the poets 'A.E.' and W.B. Yeats, it appealed to intuitives of a very high order. Anthroposophy, in some contrast, has been described as 'the intellectual's esotericism'. As already described, Steiner in *The Philosophy of Freedom* prioritised thinking. The contemporary expansion of scholarly knowledge about non-Christian religions was accompanied by loosely gnostic syntheses. In London just before the First World War, Theosophy, the Societas Rosicruciana in Anglia (or Soc. Ros.), the Golden Dawn and even Anthroposophy were available.

The Protestant/Catholic wars of the Renaissance were, in part, explicitly about cosmology, while the First World War was not. Nevertheless, it is interesting that the breakthrough into modern as well as early modern consciousness in the Western world was accompanied not just by neo-gnosticism but also by terrible bloodshed. At around the time of the First World War, Christendom – an overarching consensus based on Christianity – had become an outdated idea. Instead there was a conflict between residual Christian thinking and Darwinian social evolutionism, with Einstein just becoming known for having relativised everything except for the speed of electricity.

During the mid-twentieth century Protestant fundamentalism receded and was generally replaced by increasing acceptance of the scientifically or scientistically derived cosmos. With the popularisation of Einstein and the new physics this has become less associated with philosophical materialism. Theosophy in particular slowly faded from Western consciousness as the cosmological conflict became less acute.

Scientific materialism, unlike turn of the nineteenth-century esotericism, has often been accompanied by a bleak subjectivism in the arts, literature and philosophy. Depth-psychology (outside the USA) has generally stressed the negative side of human nature. The darkness of much modern mysticism has functioned as a support of the scientistically derived cosmos. Where, as with Teilhard de Chardin, there is an optimistic spirituality, it is generally rooted in the earth, affirming matter.

In the modern psychological climate, esoteric cosmogony and revelations about the future tend to be interpreted from the point of view of personal, adaptively minded psychology. This perspective was discussed in chapter six in relation to Rudolf Steiner's revelation. The cosmogony of a gradual, recapitulating fall into matter is seen as deriving projectively from the early development of personal consciousness. The gnostic rejection of matter is likely to be understood as fear of an effective adaptation to external reality. The future return to spirit is interpreted as the hope of personal integration or individuation; however, because of its transcending of the current, emerged world, it is seen to be accompanied by the danger of grandiosity, or possession by unconscious contents, or psychological splitness.

Depth-psychologists seem to understand themselves as pushing back the frontiers of the unknown. What was formerly thought of as the 'divine' or 'macrocosmic' has tended to be made internal to the individual, hence the idea of the 'unconscious'. Though its energies are thought of as very powerful, psychological culture no longer perceives them as if they were not part of the person; instead it tries to integrate them. The aim is to produce a more energetic consciousness, one which is extended and fully individual. This can be seen in the names for the desired end: 'autonomy', 'ego' and the Jungian 'individuation' suggest a self-sufficient monadism through assimilating the mysterious material of the unconscious (though the development and influence of 'object relations' brings in more human inter-relationship). Just as modernity has led to 'individual-gnosticism', so, in depth-psychology, biographical self-knowledge has produced forms of 'individual-mysticism'.

These are ideal types because there is a large and difficult to pin down area in-between 'individual-gnosticism' and 'individual-mysticism'. For example, Scientology and EST (Erhard Seminars Training) seem to show some parallels with the individual-gnostic ideal-type but also seem to be more psychological, internalising macrocosms and spiritual involutionary patterns where there is a descent or fall, then a respiritualisation. Nicoll's *Psychological Commentaries on the Teaching of Gurdjieff & Ouspensky* are similarly in-between.

Another tendency, often coinciding with the above and in line with the move towards democratisation of the spirit mentioned earlier, has been to enroll a volume of members. As stated in chapter eight, one Rosicrucian organisation alone, the Ancient Mystical Order Rosae Crucis (the 'Soc. Ros.'), had a total of about 60,000 European and American members enrolled in the mid-1970s, more than twice the number of Anthroposophists then enrolled. Popular gnosticism is likely to be far more numerous than Anthroposophical affiliation and influence suggests, even though those strongly influenced by Anthroposophy are a much larger number than the formal membership figures. Thus Anthroposophy appears to be the most intellectually and socially differentiated and distinctive form of contemporary Western 'individual-gnosticism', but not the most popular gnostic system.

Qualifications to the above theory

The structures implicit in Anthroposophy (here called the Syrian-Egyptian pattern) have in practice been taken in this book as an ideal-type, because the focus has been on Anthroposophy. There is a good question how well this ideal-type covers modern gnosticisms which are non-Anthroposophical. Pending further research, generalisation from this ideal-type is hypothetical. The main theoretical distortion is probably that gnoses such as Theosophy are less thought-through than Steiner's revelation, so that a looser ideal-type may fit them better. Also, Anthroposophy follows a Syrian-Egyptian cosmogonic pattern, whereas some other gnosticisms have a Manichean cosmogony.

A claim is made here that Anthroposophy, though less numerous than contemporary esotericisms such as the Soc. Ros., the outreach of Gurdjieff and the influence of the dualistic aspects of the 1960s counter-culture, is qualitatively more developed. This claim rests upon Anthroposophy's differentiation, both in terms of the revelation and its embedded community. However, esotericism, broadly interpreted, also seems to have been important amongst, in overall Western terms, relatively uneducated and non-privileged people whose numbers are well in excess of Anthroposophy, The Soc. Ros. and the outreach of Gurdjieff combined. The experience and meanings of such people might seem to be devalued if Anthroposophy is taken as the model for the ideal-typical benchmark. While Anthroposophy should not necessarily be dismissed as a starting point for hypothesis formation, it should also be borne in mind that it is at the elite end of the spectrum. It seems to have few social overlaps with and to be much less widespread than Aleister Crowley's influence on the punk approach of Johnny Rotten, the kabbalism popularised by Madonna, or the neo-pagan, earth-centred practises of Wicca. The analysis linked to Anthroposophy might help locate other movements in terms of broad cultural context, but at the level of the individual, 'structures' or any other analytical framework should not be allowed to take anything away from the richness, and other often paradoxical qualities, of personal experience.

Similarly, the distinction made in this book between 'mysticism' and what has been extrapolated here as 'gnosticism' (also termed 'esotericism' in the modern period), has also depended for its clarity on having studied the highly differentiated example of Anthroposophy. In summary, the ideal-type of gnosis (whether Syrian-Egyptian or Manichean) is described as dualist with a strong urge for liberation from the bonds of matter and the world. This typically involves micro- and macrocosmic thinking and elaborate cosmogonic myth. The ideal-type of mysticism is described in contrast as either supportive of, or as a safety valve to, prevailing culture. It involves the spiritual or emotional but is not dualist, and it may be minimalist in its specific supporting cosmology. Its myth may well be internalised: that is, seen as true at the level of biography without any application to the world outside human skin. In the modern period especially, as in Anthroposophy, the differentiation of individuality is often pronounced, and where this applies it has here been indicated by prefixing 'individual-' to gnosticism (esotericism) or mysticism as appropriate. However empirical reality might be too loose-textured to make the ideal-typical distinctions between gnosticism and mysticism, and between individual- and non-individual gnosticism and mysticism, useful for general social analysis. For example, the widespread but casual dissemination of kabbalism through a magazine story about Madonna might not be a good fit with these ideal-typical distinctions.

The analysis has been Eurocentric in that the history of gnosis has been described in terms of its two main manifestations in the European Renaissance and the Western world around the turn of the twentieth-century. In summary, the occurrence of gnosis has been understood to correlate with cosmological turmoil which prevents mysticism sufficing as a homeostatic solution. Gnosis at these times has provided a necessary extra factor of cosmological synthesis. Occurrences of gnosticism outside the European context have been outside the scope of this analysis, though Anthroposophy is no longer almost entirely Western.

The modern prevalence of mysticism over gnosticism

The modern world has frequently been described as 'secularised'. This difficult concept with its many complex ramifications is often condensed into meaning the decline of religion. It is suggested here that religion (inclusively defined) has not so much declined as fragmented. A common polarisation has been between self-conscious fundamentalisms which avoid the perceived atheistic abyss of (post-)modernity, and mysticisms which support adaptation to global technological dynamism with its social opportunities and disintegrations. Since the First World War Anthroposophy has co-existed in an environment which has been more favourable to easy-going mysticisms than to approaches which are perceived as dualist and totally enveloping and challenging. It has done well to thrive. Without its community it is doubtful whether it could have.

Over a very long period standard thinking in the West reversed itself. From a pre-Catholic position in which gnosticism and Neoplatonism were acceptable, orthodoxy became more and more defined; it developed from Catholicism through to Protestantism and then to post-Christian modernity. Around the end of the nineteenth century, the new orthodoxy of scientific materialism seemed to explain life away, depriving it of its enchantment. To many then both materialist science and the conventional religion it opposed seemed like aspects of the relentless planetary fate which was the dread of the gnostics. Since then, pure science has become less materialist but, in part through the engine of global consumerism, the practical social consequences of experiential materialism and cultural relativism have increased. Man's very humanity seems to have been contracted 'to a self imprisoned in its selfhood'.[5] There have been two prominent reactions to this situation: the fundamentalist and the immanentist.

The fundamentalist reaction has become very apparent over three or so decades in relation to Christianity, Islam, Hinduism and Judaism. In the US, sophisticated as well as naive thinking is employed in attempts to overturn Darwin and restore a literal interpretation of the Genesis creation story. The 'world rejecting'[6] new religious movements, for example, the Jesus People and the Unification Church (or 'Moonies'), are also traditional in a manner reminiscent of early modern Protestantism. In these sects there is a strong puritanical moral code, an authoritarian social structure and an ethic of service rather than consumerism. Both traditional Abrahamic religious forms and liberal, tolerant spirituality have been well represented in new religious movements since the 1970s.

Another widespread modern reaction has been to bring the Judaeo-Christian-Islamic transcendental dualism down to earth, to make it immanent. Instead of the hope of heaven, the potential enlargement of the shrunken self is projected in a utopian way onto an earthly future. In the ideologically endangered twentieth-century Voegelin pointed out that

> some imaginative constructions of history, designed to shield the contracted self, as for instance those of Comte, or Hegel, or Marx, even have grown into social forces of such strength that their conflicts with reality form a substantial part of global politics in our time.[7]

Thus, with Marxism, Christian 'pie in the sky' became collective pie on earth on an eternal day after tomorrow. The Marxist 'withering away of the state', its utopia, can be interpreted as a this-worldly application of Judaeo-Christian eschatology, which in turn appears to have been in large part ultimately derived from Zoroastrianism. Protestant orthodoxy has been invaded by this immanentist tendency.

A development related to this has been the cult of experience. The immanentist development of modernity has produced a pervasive mysticism. Goethe's self-description as an odd creature, sometimes Dives and sometimes Lazarus, is a forerunner. This tendency can be seen in the arts and literature as well as in the individual-mysticisms of depth-psychologies.

Often what is sought is not so much spiritual as a manipulation for the purpose of achieving worldly ends, such as succeeding in business, making friends or good public relations through thinking positively. Wilson's 'manipulationist'[8] response usefully sums up this individualist tendency. However, other groups are, as Martin states,[9] mystical rather than self-adjusting to society. Psychotherapy might be thought of as 'manipulationism' where it is primarily concerned with adaptation to the outer rather than inner world, 'individual-mysticism' where it leads consciousness to an individual integration with the biographical self, and 'individual-gnosticism' where this integration leaves the world behind. Gnosticism here does not imply specifically Syrian-Egyptian thought forms.

Wallis' 'world-affirming' category has much in common with 'manipulationism'. He includes here Transcendental Meditation (T.M.), Scientology and the nationalist Buddhism of the Japanese Sāka Gakkai. Wallis states that these movements offer the means to achieve the world's benefits more easily, and also that their salvational 'commodity' releases the self from conventional restraints, inhibitions and repressions. Much of the 'cultic milieu'[10] is probably on the borderline between manipulationism and mysticism.

Far from principally reflecting negatives such as alienation and anomie, and being a dependent and temporary response to secularisation, the milieu of many new religious movements seems well adapted to express man's spiritual nature in a complementary contrast to so-called 'post-modern' circumstances. The survival characteristics have been summarised as immanence rather than transcendence, pragmatism in relation to religious authority and practice, syncretism and tolerance, monism rather than dualism, a lack of total social immersion (i.e. compatibility with the social order around us), an inner-worldly mysticism compatible with scientific orientations, and reliance on experience.[11] Excepting perhaps the last criterion, Anthroposophy looks different.

It has transcendence at its core as well as immanence, a cosmological syncretism based on Steiner's revelation more than experimental individualism, a claimed monism which from the outside appears dualistic, and through the 1923 Laying of the Foundation Stone (see chapter two), a total, challenging social foundation requiring commitment. Unlike Anthroposophy and other gnosticisms, many mysticisms imported from the East and adapted to the West meet the Zeitgeist described by the above criteria well. Many have caught the spirit of the moment and so have recruited more numerously than Anthroposophy.

An important reaction to the collapse of Christian transcendence has been to import spiritual religion. There has long been a melting pot of religions and quasi-religions in much of the West. The influence of the East has already been discussed at the end of chapter eight. Non-dualist Vedanta, one of the main imports, is loosely reconciled with Western mysticism though historically at least it lacks spiritual individuality.

Western gnosticism was in general decline from about the 1920s until the counter-culture of the 1960s. This may well be connected with post-war pessimism, the development of depth-psychology and the waning of scientific materialism into the ambiguity of the 'new physics'. The latter is seen by some scientists themselves as the conceptual complement of pantheistic experience. Transcendentally spiritual itself, Western gnosis in the twentieth-century has been increasingly exposed to a modernity whose mysticism tends to exalt matter. As the conflict between scientific materialism and (in Europe) Christian fundamentalism has faded towards the end of the twentieth-century, and the new science has presented a mysterious universe to the imagination (however conceptual it is at the level of mathematics), cosmological reaction towards spirit has been less and less called for. Nineteenth-century materialism seems to have become reflected in the twenty-first century lived experience of consumerism and technology, not in its cosmological thought. The decline of gnosis (Anthroposophy excepted) from its pre-First World War peak may well be closely connected with the lack of clear-cut cosmological conflict within orthodoxy, which seems to have taken doubt up into itself.

With the coming of the counter-culture of the Western 1960s there was a return of interest in gnosis, but this seems to have been an aspect of a diffuse interest in immanent mysticism rather than a revival of transcendence specifically. Taking a long-term moving average, Anthroposophy has been recruiting slowly but steadily. This is against the flow, given that the post-World War One Zeitgeist described above seems to favour mysticisms more than gnosis. The reasons for this expansion, as well as probably having much to do with Steiner's social foundation of Anthroposophy in 1923 and the movement's embedded community, may also include the model of Steiner as a paternal alternative (for an illustration of this see the appendix 'Some Ways In'). Also, its continuing success should be interpreted in the light of increased 'market share' given the decline of its main alternative, Theosophy.

Looking ahead, assuming Anthroposophy continues to develop roots in Asia, Africa, and South America, its implicit Eurocentric stance, and also that of this book, will increasingly be open to question. This could increase tensions between the centre and the periphery. Also, it remains to be seen how climate change and the rise of concern about environmental catastrophe will relate to Anthroposophy. In the face of the major uncertainties likely to accompany this huge global threat, cosmologies with spirit/matter dualisms may benefit, especially those which, like Anthroposophy, are environmentally friendly.

Appendix: Some Ways In

'Mercy on us!' –
'We split, we split!' – 'Farewell my wife and children!' –
'Farewell, brother!' – 'We split, we split, we split!'[1]
      – William Shakespeare, *The Tempest*

Anthroposophy lives within people: it is not a mere abstraction. It could be misleading just to describe it as a metaphysical system, or solely at the level of social organisation. This appendix gives an inevitably subjective impression of some of those who have been committed to it. It attempts to generalise about how a few individuals became Anthroposophists. To help the reader see through some of my subconscious distortions in carrying out this broadly inductivist research, I have included certain personal reactions. The account which follows focuses on a particular group, drawing on biographical interviews with eighteen members in London around the mid-1970s. The eighteen were not a representative sample of Anthroposophists as a whole, and this should be constantly borne in mind. Also, much has changed since.

    Thus my access was at one particular time and through one slice (among many others) of Anthroposophical reality. I had one-to-one meetings[2] of about three hours each with the eighteen. I guaranteed them anonymity.[3] They were ten men and eight women, all of English-speaking origins. A substantial minority came from the USA, Canada and New Zealand, though most were from the UK. The members were all mature students at Rudolf Steiner House, the British headquarters near Baker St, London. The focus of their day was training in Anthroposophical spiritual movement ('eurythmy') or declamation ('speech formation'). Since they were being 'officially' influenced through their courses I hoped to gain insights into British Anthroposophy and Anthroposophy as a whole; also, they were interesting as part of the then-younger adults in the movement. As probably with most registered members, they joined after childhood rather than being brought up as followers.

In addition to the uniqueness of each, there appeared to be some common patterns which are the focus here. All can be seen to have begun from an original 'normality' in ignorance of Rudolf Steiner. Then some generalisations seem possible concerning the convergence on Anthroposophy of their hearts, minds, and everyday lives. At the time of our meeting they generally seemed to me to be identified with something other-worldly, beyond appearances. At the end of the chapter, partly drawing on the experience of the eighteen, suggestions are made as to who is most likely to be converted.

Eighteen convergencies towards Anthroposophy

All the eighteen people I met saw Steiner as a great initiate from whom they could only learn: thus he was described as a 'man of tremendous moral stature and integrity' and was ranked with Aquinas. At the same time, an Anthroposophist who was born into the movement told me, 'I get fed up with "Steiner says . . ." People always have quotations by the arm's length.'

There was a tendency for their backgrounds to be professional or managerial; but there was also a broad spread of paternal occupations. Four described artisan origins. Rather over half the parents were perceived as not especially committed spiritually or ideologically, but the opposite was clearly the case for about a quarter. Only a few of these were themselves members of cults or sects. Factors that could correlate with their later veneration of Steiner may lie elsewhere.

The future Anthroposophists, who were widely distributed in order of birth,[4] generally saw themselves as unusual within their families. Their siblings, in contrast, were typically seen as 'very much carrying on what's come through': they conformed to the parental pattern of non-commitment or commitment.

Some recalled a stable and happy early family life. However, at least a third came from homes that were broken in childhood or adolescence by parental death, separation or divorce. Many described themselves as unhappy children, often turned in on themselves, well-behaved and alone. They did not see this in psychological terms as a situation resulting from family dynamics. They saw it Anthroposophically in terms of karma continuing from their previous births on earth, for this was the sense in which they quoted the saying 'As ye sow, so shall ye reap'.

There was considerable criticism of their mothers, especially from the women; however, half of the men were generally positive. Nearly all the eighteen reacted against their fathers. Perhaps Steiner became in part a projected, ideal father. This remains possible even though none of the eighteen seem to have linked their spiritual experience to this psychological explanation. However, 'paternal deprivation' cannot explain away the Rudolf Steiner movement. For example, there are others with similar backgrounds who have nevertheless not identified themselves with the movement.

All the women were in some way negative about their father-figures. These were described in terms of antagonism, weakness, coldness, the misfortune of death or in one case, forcing the family to subsist on stolen food. One woman said, without acknowledging the improbability, that her first words were, 'Why do we have to have a Daddy?' Though the men's reactions were less conclusive they were negative in their main comments on their fathers or remembered them as remote. Only one man seems ever to have modelled himself on his father through following his occupation.[5]

I met a woman in her early thirties with a father she described as 'strict, authoritarian and cold'. She had been very influenced by Steiner when about fifteen. 'Very impressed by the wholeness of his outlook', she felt he combined things 'that would normally be 'hived' off' and 'looked at the individual as an eternal being'. Though she has retained good feelings about Steiner, she has also felt on several occasions, 'O Lord, I must be careful. I mustn't join this': 'I have an extreme revulsion about commitment to groups: I can't become a member of anything'. At an interview with an Anthroposophical community she had been told she 'had to give up everything for the movement at £400 p.a.' (a very small amount even in the 1970s).

Another woman I met, who described her step-father as a 'horrible man', encountered Anthroposophy in her early thirties. She had many friends who were mediums and psychic.

> I was very fascinated by Steiner for about three to four weeks. Then probably my work took over. Some things were not right. ... The tone of defence was not necessary. Steiner's evolution is all back to front ... very good ideas on education ... [Anthroposophy considers][6] only a third of the world ... Steiner's face was wrong ... I wonder if we are not much more dominated by physical things than he thinks ... I'm not sure about reincarnation.

Somehow these two women resisted conversion despite negative feelings towards their father figures.

The two women above, like many of the Anthroposophical women in the sample, had been to university. All but one of the latter seemed to have completed some form of higher education, generally studying languages or social sciences. By the 1980s women members under forty seemed generally to have been much better educated than those who were older.

Nearly all the men were accepted for university or college courses, generally in the humanities, for example, philosophy or religious studies, but no more than three completed their chosen course. Academic specialisation tended to be rejected as meaningless. There had also been a tendency for the men, four of whom boarded at fee-charging schools, to feel dissatisfied with their secondary schooling. The women, only one of whom had boarded, had not been so opposed.

The conversions of the eighteen generally occurred when they were in their early to mid-twenties. The world, far from beckoning with opportunities, seemed to them to be alienating and bleak; conventional work roles were seen as imprisonment. Despite the uniqueness of each experience leading to the Rudolf Steiner movement, there seemed usually to have been a gradual but often painful struggle during which there was a transformation of what William James terms 'the habitual centre of personal energy'.[7]

One told me:

> Until a lot of things happened I was typically materialistic. . . . The period . . . was a trial by fire . . . terrible despair, apathetic, alienated and drab. I asked a lot of questions.
>
> The turning point was when I read a book knitting it all together. . . . In my inner life at this time I had a tremendous feeling of what I'd now recognise as divine presence. I felt all right with the world, at one with it. . . . The greatest joy became to open oneself to others' needs and give. I felt less separated and not so superior.
>
> Amazing coincidences happened at this time. I would read a passage in a book which was a direct description of what I was feeling, or the same happened when I turned on the radio. Things in practical life went like clockwork. I was aware of something 'very real' in life and totally at peace with the world.
>
> Later, an Anthroposophist told me about Steiner. For two or three months I read Steiner at an enormous rate and was convinced. In him all threads are drawn together and knowledge is extended. I wrote to the Society and joined a funny old local group. I became an Anthroposophist despite the group.

I started to come down out of the clouds and realised there were human problems in Anthroposophy. But I felt united with people there. I had never felt so close to people before, except perhaps in early childhood. If you embark on Steiner's path proof comes and continues to do so through its esoteric and moral exercises. I've felt I've had to bring my moral conduct into line, for example, no lying, doing harm . . . trying not to think negatively.

This man, after a long experience of 'Ahrimanic' intellectual alienation, was, like most of the eighteen, plunged into darkness. The external occasion for him, as for some others, was the break-up of a sexual relationship. Other 'triggers' included ruptures with parents, bereavement and bad experiences with psychedelic drugs (the eighteen had matured during the 'counter-culture': at least four men and two women seem to have tried psychedelics). At this stage there was a general feeling that 'inner substance' was lacking. A vibrant, intense person recalled feeling like a marshmallow inside; depression, anxiety, apathy and loneliness were also described.

The negativity was sometimes mild (for example, being 'in a vacuum'). At the other extreme, a woman told how she was at 'zero point' through taking heroin: during this 'Luciferic' experience she did not know 'what was true or false'. For another woman the negativity consisted of feeling degraded through wearing provocative clothes. Most began to feel positive only after they had been through some experience of darkness. About twelve of the eighteen had experimented elsewhere before finding the Rudolf Steiner movement. They mentioned Scientology, the Swedenborg Society, astrology, Findhorn, Ouspensky, yoga, Buddhism and a flirtation with Marxism. Several were married; their spouses tended to be Anthroposophists also. None gave any hint that they were likely to move on from Rudolf Steiner.

For some the turning point of their spiritual/emotional experiences occurred before they encountered Anthroposophy and its interpretations. Probably more came across Anthroposophy, often accepting it gradually, while they were enduring dark experience.

One woman seemed to be at a spiritual/emotional turning point at the time of our meeting. She had avoided the folksy style of dress Steiner women sometimes adopted. (The men then in the UK tended to wear pullovers and cords or, if in later middle age, tweed jackets and baggy trousers). But her style, involving subtle natural colours, seemed to me to identify her with the movement. She told me:

Anthroposophy is just beginning to get me. I resisted it for a long time. Then I realised that Rudolf Steiner was a giant, a genius. Through eurythmy it begins to make sense, to work in me. It is so all-embracing and links up with everything, a complete way of life.

A minority admitted to little or no sustained negative feeling but instead seemed to have experienced something more like a gradual ripening. They were not the most active of the experimenters with non-Anthroposophical cults and identities.

A woman told me:

As a child I was secure. I longed to be committed to something in youth. Later I read a book about Steiner. . . . On my first coming to Anthroposophy I felt so much to be true. There's such openness once you've developed trust.

I feel Anthroposophy is a path to work with. Steiner's exercises develop the soul life: I used to live the day backwards [in my imagination]; I don't know why it is backwards. To know yourself better is an excruciating process. I've felt since adolescence that negative emotions can be worked with, transformed. Anthroposophy has overcome my impatience and opened up the world of art.

Of the eighteen, about six – mainly men – were first introduced to Anthroposophy through reading. Usually the initial contact was through another person, including sexual partners and strangers.

After conversion to the Steiner movement the eighteen were on convergent tracks. They had come to 'know' – rather than view as belief – that Steiner's revelation is true: for them Anthroposophy had become real through the course being followed, community life, the books they had read and so on. For example, one man told me he had been in a community looking after a very difficult boy who was subject to severe fits. He dreamt that he saw this child's body together with William Blake. Later he was inclined to interpret this to mean that the boy was the reincarnation of Blake. This idea, which is in keeping with the spirit of Steiner's teachings on rebirth, reinforced his commitment to help this child and others Anthroposophically.

The sense of totality of the eighteen seemed to be completely identified with Rudolf Steiner's vision though, at the most conscious level, the principle of critical independence was given importance. Steiner himself used to speak of its importance. But a deeper level of identification sometimes became obvious. After I asked if she

believed in Darwinian evolution, a woman replied: 'I could refer you
to every volume of Steiner's if you want to know.'

As a result of their 'Anthroposophicalness' their pasts became
connected, deeply meaningful. It was generally accepted that Christ
taught that there is rebirth. Several cited the Biblical statement that
John the Baptist was Elijah 'come again'. I was told: 'Moral justice
works through karma, whereby we have to compensate for the harm
we do.' They often quoted Plato's myth of Er, for the belief that
they had chosen their parents before being born on earth was vitally
important to them. Steiner taught that the choice is made in the
'spiritual world', usually on the basis of karmic compensation: for
example, someone self-contained in the present rebirth might well
have been aggressive in the previous one. Each life on earth provides
karmic opportunity – and the freedom of choice – to remedy past
spiritual failings. Those with whom one has close links in 'repeated
earth lives' tend to be the same individualities.[8]

At a cognitive level, some had a much more sophisticated knowledge of
Steiner's teachings than others. Very few, if any, of the Anthroposophists
I met (not just the eighteen) seemed to have looked at the complex
revelation in a detached, intellectual way so that they perceived what,
in my opinion, are its implicit structures. Instead, I sensed that it was as
if these structures contained them. Some serpents ('uroboros' symbols)
in the Western 'esoteric tradition', unlike the turquoise one in the
Goetheanum, have teeth that hold the tail that has coiled round in a
circle. This perhaps suggests a sharper, more intellectually aggressive
attitude than that fostered within the Rudolf Steiner movement, where
such an attitude might be deemed 'Ahrimanic'.

As already stated, followers of Rudolf Steiner absorb the essential
idea that the world condensed from spirit and that its destiny is to
become spirit again. As microcosms with free will, human beings
are central to the development of the cosmos from an over-hardness
of matter. The head of the Goetheanum serpent is identified with
original macrocosmic spirit through having the tail within its gums.[9]
Anthroposophists strive to leave materialism and individualism
behind and to develop spiritual identity instead. The pattern of the
serpent can be interpreted as behind and within the meanings of
Anthroposophical social life,[10] especially the School of Spiritual
Science, to which about six of the eighteen belonged. However, not
all members see the serpent itself as a significant symbol.

Unusually for followers of Rudolf Steiner, the eighteen lived in
London, typically in single-room apartments (or 'bed-sits') north of
Rudolf Steiner House. The process leading into Anthroposophy was

described as like 'being in a cocoon and being fed riches', or being delivered from the 'trap' of one's body. The eighteen either shut out modern culture, which was generally regarded as Ahrimanic or Luciferic, or modified it through assimilating it into Steiner's revelation. Television was rarely watched, for it was thought to be Luciferic in transmitting flickering fantasies, not true imagination. This was not just a question of programme content but, more fundamentally, of the nature of the medium itself. They believed that society should be reshaped to accord with Steiner's 'Threefold Commonwealth', his hopeful blueprint for social life: hence contemporary politicking was perceived as an aberration. Knowledge of the outside world came from infrequent reading of quality newspapers (*The Guardian* or *The Times*). Though there were differences of emphasis and opinion, there was a common background in Rudolf Steiner's revelation.

Thus, some approved of differentials in earnings and some did not; but all, more basically, deplored a wage mentality. Their own financial turnovers seemed to be very low. There was considerable, though undogmatic, sympathy with pacifism, more among the men than the women; partly, at least, this was because of the karmic consequences of killing. The strong tendency towards vegetarianism was largely for the spiritual reason that eating meat could lead to the incorporation of the animal's will. Also, I was told that some students deny themselves meat in order to induce ecstatic experience. The reading that was not Anthroposophical or esoteric was generally compatible, being either high quality or respectably middle-brow. 'Detective or sexy stories' were not – as one woman said – included. Some at least looked up to Shakespeare, that 'great Anthroposophist'.

They carried some of the attitudes of what was then, the younger generation into the movement. Compared to their elders the admitted sexual mores of the eighteen were more liberal. Also, they probably were more opposed to racial discrimination. However, Steiner's teaching that the races have different group souls does not – at least, outside South Africa – seem to have been used to justify discrimination. However, this was a question of abstract attitude only because nearly all members at this time were white.

As already stated Steiner saw spiritual development as the meaning of the evolution of the world. The condensation of the cosmos into matter has enabled this development of consciousness to begin. But the result is some separation between consciousness, which becomes increasingly important, and the macrocosm. Despite their common life and immersion in Anthroposophy many of the eighteen seemed to have a certain sense of seclusion about them.

How did People become Anthroposophists?

The eighteen stories give clues about which kinds of people have been most likely to become adherents of Anthroposophy. To non-Anthroposophists, including psychologists and sociologists of religion, the term 'conversion' will seem appropriate. Anthroposophists do not use the term, perhaps because they see 'conversion' as rooted in the different context of conventional Christianity, and perhaps because use of the term suggests epistemological scepticism.

A major problem related to the inevitable subjectivity, and so bias, of the researcher is the reduction of interpretation to whatever one is able to understand in oneself, or to the academic discipline to which one is committed, a difficulty discussed in chapter nine. As an analytical distinction, in contrast with social science assumptions, it was suggested there that it is likely that, over and above the influence of the social, some people are more innately predisposed than others to join spiritual movements. With theoretical reservations[11] 'the social' is intended to mean nurture, and 'innate predisposition' heritable nature. Social explanations of conversion have tended either to be negatively focused or to be based on needs. As previously stated, there have been three main hypotheses: deprivation; the need for community; and the need to construct a meaningful world. These are very significant factors, and it has been suggested that community is specifically pertinent, but they are too limited to be the only ones which apply. One of the hypotheses used here is that converts to Anthroposophy tend, through innate predisposition, to be especially imaginative, creatively inclined people. Of course, from birth (perhaps conception) onwards, social factors will also have shaped them.

Practical psychological categorisations, such as the DSM-IV, assess symptoms, not causes. The DSM-IV is driven by pathological diagnosis and so using it for present purposes would be one-sided and pejorative. However, the DSM-IV 'schizotypal' category could be close if, as some have suggested it should be, it is conceived that there can also be a positive 'schizotypy' for spiritually minded people.

Most people predisposed to conversion have no awareness of Anthroposophy in particular, just as Anthroposophists have no awareness of many other spiritual identities. Membership of the Rudolf Steiner movement in the Third World was very limited in the late 1970s. Also, those born into societies with a Protestant tradition, especially the Netherlands, New Zealand, West Germany, Switzerland, the UK and USA, were much more likely to become aware of Anthroposophy than people whose ascribed culture was completely Catholic or totalitarian.

At their conception there was probably a screening out of those not capable of absorbing considerable education, however favourable their innate predisposition, for Rudolf Steiner's revelation is complex and intellectual. Connected with this is the availability of education: the eighteen Anthroposophists (and my further experience) suggest that membership is more likely to be from backgrounds favouring education.

The eighteen may be typical in tending to be imaginative, creative and spiritually inclined. They seem to have reacted against the fragmented social contexts characteristic of modernity, sometimes including their family of origin. This sort of background perhaps made the eighteen and others like them particularly averse to the academicism of higher education. For women there may have been an added advantage: Anthroposophy enabled them to be liberated while retaining their femininity.

Very many people must still have been eligible; yet, in terms of the larger society, Rudolf Steiner membership has remained limited numerically. Even where the movement is most strongly represented, the vast majority would not have been sufficiently aware of it to consider joining. There were many other mystical identities to satisfy them. Many others who were eligible and aware of Anthroposophy may, like the two women mentioned earlier, have chosen not to become involved with an unusual cult.

About two-thirds of the eighteen considered other cultic and esoteric identities before selecting the Rudolf Steiner movement. Theoretically a drift model, in which seekers come to rest according to factors such as the number of movements tried, may apply. However, in general they did not strike me as fickle. This suggests Anthroposophy has provided something which the others lack. In some cases this could be the challenging spiritual environment. In others it may be the patriarchal figure of Rudolf Steiner. The difficulty experienced with fathers is probably not confined to the eighteen and may often be a very important factor tipping the scales in favour of Anthroposophy. Alternative cults, such as Theosophy, Christian Science, and the Alice Bailey movement, may attract others because of their female founders. Another factor, one that is unusual in an esoteric cult, is the extent of community in Anthroposophy. It may be especially attractive to some and not others because of the commitment and dedication called for by its many applications, such as caring for the disabled, 'bio-dynamic' agriculture, and 'Waldorf' education.

Notes

Prologue

1. Saul Bellow, *Humboldt's Gift,* Penguin, 1973, p. 469.
2. I have never hidden my independence from Rudolf Steiner's revelation and have often been explicit about this to his followers. Commitment to it is not necessary for membership of the Anthroposophical Society in Great Britain (as contrasted with membership of the School of Spiritual Science); it is on this basis that I became a member of the society.
3. Hans Pusch, 'Thoughts on the seal', foreword to the English translation (Steiner Book Centre, 1973) of Rudolf Steiner's *Der Seelen Erwachen* Rudolf Steiner Verlag, Dornach, Switzerland, p. 4.
4. See Erich Neumann, *The Origins and History of Consciousness,* Princeton University Press, New York, 1969.

Chapter One

1. C.S. Lewis, *The Pilgrim's Regress*, Fount Paperbacks, Glasgow, 1980.
2. The main source for this chapter is *Rudolf Steiner. An Autobiography,* ed. Paul Allen, Rudolf Steiner Publications, New York, 1977. My account relies heavily on the background notes provided by Paul Allen, an Anthroposophist. The very frequent drawings from this book are not, except for quotes, page referenced.
3. Yasna 46.1, trans. J.H. Moulton, *Man's Religious Quest,* ed. Whitfield Foy, Croom Helm, London, 1978, p. 633.
4. For example, J. Hemleben's *Rudolf Steiner,* Henry Goulden, East Grinstead, 1975. This simple book, however, is well-written and produced. A.P. Shepherd's *A Scientist of the Invisible,* Hodder and Stoughton, 1971, is a hagiography from a typically English point of view.
5. M. and F. Kirchner-Bockholt, *Rudolf Steiner's Mission and Ita Wegman,* Rudolf Steiner Press, London, undated, pp. 7-12 and 121-123.

6. The frequency of the number seven in Anthroposophy might well be traceable to Zoroastrian and, ultimately, Indo-European myth.

7. A. Storr, *Feet of Clay*, Harper Collins, 1997, pp. 211, 270, 81.

8. The translation in J. Hemleben's, *Rudolf Steiner*, Henry Goulden, East Grinstead, 1975, p. 9. In the *Autobiography,* 'to which I rightly belong' is rendered as 'from which my family came'. There is a photograph of Steiner's mother in *Rudolf Steiner,* p. 9. For the following quote see *An Autobiography* (see. note 1), p. 18.

9. Her maiden name was Franziska Blie. She died at Horn (1834-1918).

10. His father (1829-1910) reverted to Catholicism later. He retired to Horn.

11. Rudolf Steiner, *Self Education. Rudolf Steiner's Childhood and Youth up to the Weimar Period,* typescript trans. of lecture, Berlin, 4 February 1913, p. 118 *sic.*

12. *An Autobiography* (see note 1), p. 28.

13. As above, p. 52.

14. As above, p. 44.

15. As above, p. 54. For a rare reference to this period while he was still a youngish man, see his *Goethe the Scientist,* Anthroposophic Press, New York, 1950, p. 98.

16. *An Autobiography* (see note 1), pp. 61 and 444 (n. 86). Steiner remembered that above Felix's door were the words, 'God's Blessing is Everything' ('Gottes Segen ist alles gelegen').

17. Felix became a full-time factory worker. See Emil Bock's interesting 'The Search for Felix' in *The Golden Blade,* 1961.

18. Rudolf Steiner, 'Autobiographical Sketch' (written for E. Schuré), reproduced in *The Golden Blade,* 1966.

19. Sinnet's *Esoteric Buddhism.* See *Autobiography* (see note 1), pp. 468 (note 210), 124-5,141-2, 340 and 344, *Self Education* (see note 9), pp. 167-8 and 'Autobiographical Sketch' (see note 16), p. 3.

20. Professor Josef Kuerschner's edition.

21. Edouard Schuré, 'The Personality of Rudolf Steiner and his Development' in *The Golden Blade,* 1966, p. 13.

22. *An Autobiography* (see note 1), p. 109.

23. H. Ellenberger, *The Discovery of the Unconscious*, Basic Books, US, 1970.

24. Hemleben in his *Rudolf Steiner* states (p. 73) 'Anna Eunicke had moved to Berlin already before Steiner left Weimar. When he followed her shortly afterwards, he first of all took a place of his own.' Steiner states *(Autobiography,* p. 326), 'The practical aspect of my private life had become entirely satisfactory because the Eunicke family had moved to Berlin, and I could live with them under the best of care after having experienced for a time the utter misery of living alone.'

25. *Autobiography,* p. 117. Schroer introduced him but, offended by the circle's antipathy to Goethe, never returned. In this circle Steiner met theology professors. He was particularly struck by a Cistercian, Wilhelm Neumann whom he admired. Occasionally also in the circle were a

philosopher, Adolf Stohr; a future well-known novelist, Maria G. von
Berlepsch; 'the sensitive story-teller', Emilie Mataja (nom de plume
'Emil Marriot'); a poet and writer, Fritz Lemmermayer; and a composer,
Alfred Stross. The contact with this pessimist circle encouraged Steiner
to develop his contrast between human ideals and necessity in nature.
Steiner also moved in the circle of Alfred Formey, an evangelical pastor
Lemmermayer described as 'drunk with faith in God and blessedness'
(p. 129). He would visit the house of an actress, Frau Wilborn, 'where
people laughed till the chairs shook' (p. 131).

26. As above, p. 129.
27. W.M. Johnston, *The Austrian Mind,* University of California Press,
1972, pp. 156-158.
28. A contemporary satire *(Homunculus,* by Hamerling) roused Steiner's
interest; it parodied the situation through using extremes which perhaps
had some influence on the later formation of the Anthroposophical
demons Ahriman and Lucifer.
29. *An Autobiography* (see note 1), pp. 205-6.
30. 'Spiritism today is a wrong path to the spirit sought by souls who wish
to find the spirit in an external way even by means of experiments
— because they have lost all feeling for a real, true, genuine path.' *An
Autobiography*, p. 256.
31. The thesis, which attempted to show how human consciousness can
come to an understanding of itself (with special reference to Fichte), was
passed by Heinrich von Stein.
32. This was the circle of Conran Ansorge, pianist and pupil of Liszt.
(Steiner was out of sympathy with Wagner because of the latter's lack
of pure tone; pure tone to Steiner was akin to thinking). The circle of
an ironical playwright, Hans Olden, wished to live in 'the present'.
Anthroposophical painting was influenced by Steiner's opposition to
the naturalistic art taught in Weimar.
33. *An Autobiography* (see note 1), p. 223. Frau Förster-Nietzsche asked
the empathetic Steiner to arrange Nietzsche's library. Later she was
in serious conflict with him.
34. As above, p. 277.
35. As above, p. 294.
36. This found expression in Steiner's *Christianity as Mystical Fact and
the Mysteries of Antiquity,* Rudolf Steiner Press, London, 1972.
37. *An Autobiography* (see note 1), p. 302.
38. *The Fairy Tale of the Green Snake and the Beautiful Lily.*
39. He gradually revealed his esoteric synthesis. His *Theosophy* was
published in June 1904. In 1909 he published his fully Anthroposophical
works *Occult Science* and *Knowledge of the Higher Worlds*. His books
were often more formal versions of themes he had already lectured about
or taught.
40. Steiner's autobiography, which was being published in serial form for
Anthroposophists, was cut short at about 1907 by his death in 1925. A

devoted follower, Guenther Wachsmuth, has published a detailed and verbose continuation, *The Life and Work of Rudolf Steiner,* Vols. 1 and 2, tr. O. Wannamaker and R. Raab (New York, Whittier Books, 1955). For Steiner's death, see pp. 560, 563, 569 and 577-8.

41. Rom Landau, *God is my Adventure,* Unwin Books, 1964, p. 174. Landau, a connoisseur of spiritual leaders, disagrees and writes favourably about Steiner.

42. Keyserling stated that Steiner died of cancer; others rumoured that he was poisoned. Wachsmuth (see note 37) denies the latter charge and states that it is the duty of eyewitnesses (he was one) to set the record straight. He then fails to do so, beyond stating that every meal caused Steiner renewed suffering.

43. 'Letters of Rudolf and Marie Steiner', ed. G.C. Bosset, in the *Anthroposophical Quarterly,* Vol. 13, No. 1, Spring 1968, pp. 14-15.

Chapter 2

1. Ninian Smart, *The Religious Experience of Mankind,* Collins, 1981, p. 683.

2. See generally, G.K. Nelson, *The Development and Organisation of the Spiritualist Movement in Britain,* PhD thesis, London University, 1966.

3. R.F. Gombrich, *Precept and Practice*, Oxford University Press, 1971.

4. David Martin, *A General Theory of Secularization,* Blackwell, Oxford, 1978, p. 179.

5. *Rudolf Steiner. An Autobiography* (see chapter three, note 1), p. 365 and A. Nethercot, *The Last Four Lives of Annie Besant,* Rupert Hart-Davis, London, 1963, generally (for Theosophy) and p. 177.

6. *Rudolf Steiner. An Autobiography* (see chapter three, note 1), p. 401.

7. Marie Steiner, 'Foreword' (1931) to *The Anthroposophic Movement* (eight lectures by Rudolf Steiner, Dornach, 10-17 June 1923. Unrevised short-hand notes available to members at Rudolf Steiner House, London).

8. *The Spiritual Beings in the Heavenly Bodies and in the Kingdoms of Nature* (see chapter two, note 12), p. 177.

9. *Rudolf Steiner. An Autobiography* (see chapter three, note 1), pp. 372-373.

10. *The Last Four Lives of Annie Besant* (see note 5), p. 134.

11. *Theosophical Society. Thirty-Seventh Anniversary and Convention Report* 1912, p. 16.

12. *Mitteilungen,* January 1913, p. 5 and 'Translator's Note', p. 4.

13. *Mitteilungen,* December 1912, p. 9.

14. Albert Steffen, *Meetings with Rudolf Steiner,* Verlag fur Schonewissenschaften, Dornach, 1926, p. 36.

15. 'Transforming' leadership is used here in the humanistic psychology sense, propounded by James Burns, of a relationship of mutual stimulation and elevation that (inter alia) converts followers into leaders.

16. *Anthroposophic News Sheet,* 26 July 1942.

17. J. Steyrer, 'Charisma and the Archetypes of Leadership', in *Organisation Studies,* Winter 1998, p.4.

18. M Maccoby, Narcissistic Leaders' in *The Harvard Businesss Review,* Jan 2004.

19. For the above quotations see: 'Rudolf Steiner. Recollections by some of his Pupils' in *The Golden Blade,* 1959, pp. 35, 37, 40, 41, 27 and 77 and 1958, pp. 79,17,24 and 35; 'Incidents in Rudolf Steiner's Life' in *The Anthroposophic Movement,* Vol. 4, London 1927, p. 243; A. Heidenreich, 'Rudolf Steiner, Initiate, Christian and Human Being' in *The Christian Community Journal,* Vol. 15, London, 1961, pp. 2 and 4; 'Personal Memories of Rudolf Steiner' in *The Present Age,* Vol. 2, No. 1, 1936, pp. 51 and 55 and Vol. 2, 1937, p. 13; 'Rudolf Steiner and Community among Men in the Future' in *Anthroposophical Quarterly,* Vol. 6, No. 4, Winter 1961, p. 78. These journals are available through the movement. Also: F. Rittelmeyer, *Rudolf Steiner Enters My Life,* The Christian Community Press, 1963, pp. 145 and 148-149; and G. Wachsmuth, *The Life and Work of Rudolf Steiner,* Whittier Books, New York, 1955, pp. 7-8, 10, 16 and 156-157.

20. There is an apocryphal Anthroposophical story that Steiner briefly drank very heavily as a young man in order to rid himself of atavistic clairvoyance (so that he could develop conscious clairvoyance).

21. See, for example, D. Buchanan and A. Huczynski, *Organisational Behaviour. An Introductory Text,* Prentice Hall, Harlow, 2004 pp720-723.

22. Given that, in the sense of Hersey Blanchard, his followers were not 'mature' in the Anthroposophical context.

23. C. Wachtmeister, *Reminiscences of H.P. Blavatsky and the Secret Doctrine,* Theosophical Publishing House, 1976, p. 35.

24. See Nicholas Goodrick-Clarke, *The Occult Roots of Nazism.*

25. *The Last Four Lives of Annie Besant* (see note 5), p. 230.

26. Perhaps the term 'cult' would be more appropriate. However, what has been translated is 'sect' (with its deviant Protestant connotations). Rudolf Steiner, *The Anthroposophic Movement,* Lecture VI, Dornach 10-17 June 1923 (typescript available at Rudolf Steiner House, London), p. 173.

27. *Anthroposophic Movement,* December 1935, p. 185.

28. See for example www.social-ecology.org/article by Peter Standenmaier 'Anthroposophy and Ecofacism'

29. www.defendingsteiner.com/misconceptions/r-race. It is said that in 1995 there was a scandal in the Netherlands over Dutch Waldorf Schools allegedly teaching racial ethnography. In 2000 the Anthroposophical body in the Netherlands was apparently involved in a legal conflict over denied allegations of Steiner's racism: see www.bruisvat.vol/english/racism

30. *Anthroposophical Movement,* 23 November, 1930, p. 371.

31. James Webb, *The Harmonious Circle,* Thames and Hudson, London, 1980, p. 186.

32. www.social-ecology.org/article

33. Theosophical membership in 1925 and 1981 (brackets); USA 7333 (52, 58); UK 6158 (2360); India 6395 (10,063); France 2923 (1357); Holland 2673 (891); Dutch East Indies 1939 (Indonesia 795); Australia 1564 (1188); Sweden 1073 (289); New Zealand 953 (1528); Cuba 805 (487); Germany 650 (279); Canada 635 (86); Italy 623 (911); East and Central Africa (1320); Brazil (896). The 1981 statistics are from a photocopy from official records. See also C. Jinarajadasa, *The Golden Book of the Theosophical Society 1875-1925*, Theosophical Publishing House, Adyar, 1925, p. 262, and *The Theosophical Society in England. Report of the General Secretary for the Year 1982*, p. 6.

34. *The Last Four Lives of Annie Besant* (see note 5), pp. 438 and 447. My main sources for Theosophy, as for Anthroposophy, are members who might prefer to be anonymous. When I found a younger member and put to him the assertion of my Scandinavian colleague that Tantric sex yoga is practised in the Esoteric Section (currently 10-20 per cent of members), he replied that he doubted 'they could find a sufficient number of people who were capable'. However, the past may have another story to tell. Blavatsky was involved with esoteric Mahayana Buddhism and claimed contact with Tibet.

Chapter 3

1. W.B. Yeats, *Collected Poems,* Macmillan, London, 1950, p. 280.

2. Throughout this and the succeeding chapter I have relied on various Anthroposophical sources who would not wish to be singly acknowledged.

3. For these, see the Bibliography.

4. It is possible to belong to the General Anthroposophical Society without joining a national society.

5. The only commitment for membership seems to be that the existence of an institution such as the Goetheanum in its capacity as a School of Spiritual Science is considered justified. Its purpose (whatever its practice) is 'undogmatic spiritual research': it seems to be accepted, at any rate in the UK, that membership of the national society is possible without accepting Steiner's revelation. This is not seen as a 'religion' but as the spiritual foundation of all religions.

6. Rudolf Steiner, *The Anthroposophic Movement,* Lecture VII, Dornach, 10-17 June 1923 (trans. typescript Rudolf Steiner House, London), p. 166.

7. The national membership figures that follow for 1996-2001 are taken from Anthroposophy Worldwide, No 6, July 2003. Otherwise they are usually estimates from anecdotal sources.

8. J.W. Montgomery, *Cross and Crucible* Vol. 1, M. Nijhoff, The Hague, 1973, p. 162.

9. Rita Bultemann's research.

10. Dietrich Goldschmidt and Peter Roeder *Alternative Schulen? Gestalt und Funktion nichtstaatlicher Schulen im Rahmen offentlicher Bildungssysteme* (Klett-Cotta Sonderdruck), *Ubersicht uber die nach der Pedagogik Rudolf Steiner's Arbeiten Schulen* (Juni 1981) and *Internationale Vereinigung der Waldorfkindergarten E.V.* (Mai 1982). Some Camphill schools are included.

11. Rita Bültemann's research.

12. Rita Bültemann's conclusion (after talking to the head of the training department of a large company).

13. Rita Bültemann. She commented: 'The Anthroposophists claim that they don't want to be an élite group but are open to everybody. That is why I don't understand why they spread an air of mystery around the whole thing.'

14. These include many of the increasing numbers of those members who are dying. There are also, however, Anthroposophical nursing homes.

15. Rudolf Steiner House was valued at £400,000 in the 1981 accounts. The cost of its upkeep is large.

16. See *Anthroposophy Worldwide*, No 4, May 2005 for the information in this paragraph.

17. *Anthroposophical Weekly*, No 7, Sept 2004.

18. I was told in the early 1980s that there were many applications to the Anthroposophical Society in GB from Nigerians. It was surmised that they were made to support efforts to obtain UK visas.

19. *Anthroposophical Weekly*, No 4, May 2004

20. *Anthroposophical Weekly*, No 9, Nov 2004

21. *Anthroposophical Weekly*, No 7, Sept 2004

22. *News from the Goetheanum*, Vol 14, No 6, Nov/Dec 1993.

23. 2005, www.camphill.org.uk

24. *Camphill Directory,* Camphill Press, Botton Village, Yorkshire, Spring 1981.

25. This was said to me in 1980 during a visit to the Camphill centre at Delrow, Hertfordshire, England.

26. A socialist acquainted with Camphill vehemently told me it was based on 'capitalist exploitation'. My participant-observation at Botton was in late spring, 1973.

27. This is derived from my visit to Delrow.

28. Bernard Nesfield-Cookson, *Rudolf Steiner's Vision of Love,* Aquarian Press, Wellingborough, 1983, see title page. My information on the Christian Community has been very largely derived from listening to priests and my own observation.

29. 2005, www.thechristiancommunity.org

30. *Anthroposophical Weekly*, No 8, Oct 2004.

31. Joachim Kohler, *Richard Wagner. The Last of the Titans*, Yale, 2004, pp. 529-38.

Chapter 4

1. Goethe, *Faust.* Part 1, tr. Philip Wayne, Penguin, 1972, p. 71.
2. G. Ungen, *Flying Saucers*, New Knowledge Books, East Grinstead, 1958.
3. My sources include participant observation and meetings with Anthroposophists. There is not space here to note all my detailed written references. These can be found in my *The Anthroposophical Movement in the UK; its gnosis and the thought world and identity of its members* PhD thesis, London School of Economics, 1981.
4. Rudolf Steiner, *Occult Science. An Outline,* tr. George and Mary Adams, Rudolf Steiner Press, London, 1972, pp. 233-234.
5. Rudolf Steiner, *The Philosophy of Freedom. The basis for a modern world conception,* tr. Michael Wilson, Rudolf Steiner Press, London, 1970.
6. As in Gary Lachman's *Rudolf Steiner. An Introduction to his Life and Work,* Penguin, New York, 2007. This is an accessible, informed and unusually independent account of Steiner's thought and revelation.
7. *The Philosophy of Freedom* , Rudolf Steiner Press, 1964, p. 84.
8 *The Philosophy of Freedom* , Rudolf Steiner Press, 1964, p. 114.
9. *The Philosophy of Freedom*, Rudolf Steiner Press, 1964, pp. 119-20.
10. An established member's words to me.
11. *Occult Science* (see note 4), p. 236. An introduction to Steiner's occult path can be found in *Occult Science. Also see his *Knowledge of the Higher Worlds. How is it achieved?,* Rudolf Steiner Press, London, 1973, and his *Methods of Spiritual Research,* Rudolf Steiner Publications, New York, 1971.
12. Hans Pusch (see Prologue, note 4), p. 3.
13. *Occult Science* (see note 4), p. 27.
14. Rudolf Steiner, *Goethe the Scientist* , Anthroposophic Press Inc., New York, 1950, p. 10.
15. Guenther Wachsmuth, '*How old is the earth?*', article in *The Golden Blade,* 1954, pp. 20-23 (available through the Rudolf Steiner movement).
16. I found it in copies of Rudolf Steiner's translated lectures in the archives of Rudolf Steiner House (London) library. See *The Influence of Spiritual Beings upon Man,* eleven lectures, Berlin, 8 January to 11 June 1908, Anthroposophic Press Inc., New York, 1961, *The Spiritual Beings in the Heavenly Bodies and in the Kingdoms of Nature,* ten lectures, Helsingfors, April 1912, Rudolf Steiner Publishing Co., London, 1951,and *The Spiritual Hierarchies and their Reflection in the Physical World-Zodiac, Planets, Cosmos,* ten lectures, Dusseldorf, April 1909, Anthroposophic Press, New York, 1970.
17. 10-11 November 1973.
18. The Anthroposophical Society in GB, *News Sheet for Members,* Vol. 59, No. 3, Ascension-Midsummer 1982, p. 2.
19. *The Guardian,* G2, 15.06.2005, p.8
20. *News from the Goetheanum,* Vol. 3, No. 3, May/June 1982, p. 3.

21. As above, p. 2.
22. I am grateful to Desanka Rowell-Ozim for her expert help.
23. Hagen Biesantz and Arne Klingborg, *The Goetheanum. Rudolf Steiner's Architectural Impulse*. Rudolf Steiner Press, 1979, pp. 83-84.
24. R.J. Reilly, *Romantic Religion,* University of Georgia Press, Athens, 1971.
25. The Anthroposophical Society in GB, *News Sheet for Members*, Vol 59, No 1, mid-February-March 1982, p.7.
26. *News Sheet for Members* (as note 24), p. 7.
27. *Newsletter* Summer 2005, Steiner Waldorf Education
28. Press release September 29, 1999, www.waldorfcritics.org
29. *Anthroposophical Weekly*, No 6, July 2004.
30. She called Anthroposophy a '1984 thinkstop' and bravely fought her way to Oxford University. I would like to record my gratitude to the late Gillian Mullins for her help.

Chapter 5

1. William Shakespeare, *A Midsummer Night's Dream,* III, i.
2. This is no longer as much the case as it was two decades ago. An example of a highly schematic Anthroposophical description of Steiner's revelation is Reaugh Smith, E *The Burning Bush: Rudolf Steiner, Anthroposophy and the Holy Scriptures. An Anthroposophical Commentary on the Bible. Terms and Phrases*, Vol 1, Anthroposophic Press, Great Barrington, 2001.
3. Very many written sources have contributed to this account. The two outstanding ones (both by Steiner) are *Occult Science. An Outline* (see chapter two, note 4) and *Theosophy,* Garden City Press, Letchworth, 1970.
4. Steiner disclaimed any connection with the 'ether' of past scientists.
5. Antonio Damasio, *The Feeling of What Happens,* London, Vintage, 2000.
6. *Theosophy* (see note 2), pp. 63-65.
7. As above, p. 81.
8. As above, p. 88.
9. Daniel Stern, *The Interpersonal World of the Infant,* Karnac, London, 1998, p 34.
10. His meditative path is described after the lengthy cosmogony and before the relatively brief 'eschatology'.
11. For example, in Roy Wilkinson, *Rudolf Steiner. An Introduction to his Spiritual World View*, Anthroposophy, 1998.
12. As stated in the Prologue, their details – head, eye, teeth or gums, whether the tail is within or across the mouth, or touching or not – all differ. For a phenomenology and an interesting post-Jungian interpretation of the meaning of such 'uroboric' serpents, see Erich Neumann, *The Origins and History of Consciousness* (New York, Princeton University Press, 1969).

13. Lachman describes this turning point as taking place at the half-way stage, in the fourth epoch. He does not differentiate between Steiner's 'epochs' and his 'culture-epochs'. Lachman, G, *Rudolf Steiner. An Introduction to his Life and Work*, Penguin, New York, 2007, p147.

14. Its *kalpas* or 'day of Brahmas'. A.L. Basham, 'Hinduism', in R.C. Zaehner ed., *The Concise Encyclopedia of Living Faiths,* Hutchinson, London, 1977, pp. 223-224. Anthroposophy's rhythms seem to go beyond the emanations of Neoplatonism.

15. In Advaita Vedanta matter is considered relatively unreal rather than rejected, though the distinction is probably more theoretical than concerned with social practice. Thus Christian Science asserts that physical treatments of illness are unreal, yet confirms their reality as a negative organizing principle by banning them.

16. 'Alterius non sit qui suus esse potest'.

17. Some ascending sub-structures:
a) Each body, e.g., the physical or etheric body, recapitulates itself four times, refining its nature (see Table 3). There is a maximum of one refinement each planetary embodiment and not all bodies manage to achieve this. Thus physical bodies on 'Earth' have had the chance to develop four times. After four developments the body is shed. Thus human beings who have always made the grade will not have physical bodies on 'Jupiter' (the phase after 'Earth'). They will be the ones who develop spirit-self. See Table 3.

Man is one hierarchy down from the lowest of the Spiritual Hierarchies (Steiner renamed them but in this book I use the Pseudo-Dionysian terminology). Each Hierarchy has passed through the 'human' stage. (The Hierarchies themselves have an ascending evolution.) Man is passing through the 'human' stage on earth. See Table 4.

Spiritual Hierarchies sacrifice themselves (and so evolve) to help man or other Spiritual Hierarchies ascend. The particular Hierarchy sacrificing itself so that the 'human' stage can be reached is always four hierarchies higher than the Hierarchy or life-form (currently man) attaining the 'human' stage. See Table 4.

The planetary embodiments, such as earth, are themselves divided into sub-epochs and sub-sub-epochs in multiples of seven. The first epochs of any phase tend to recapitulate, the middle ones to innovate and the final ones to retreat into the *pralaya,* pulsating back into spirit.

18. *Meetings with Rudolf Steiner*, p. 65.

19. Ernest Gellner, *The Psychoanalytic Movement. The Cunning of Unreason*, Blackwell, UK, 1985; Adolf Grunbaum, *Validation in the Clinical Theory of Psychoanalysis*, International Universities Press, Connecticut, 1993; Karl Popper, *Conjectures and Refutations. The Growth of Scientific Knowledge*, Routledge and Kegan Paul, London, 1963.

20. See Joachim Kohler, *Richard Wagner. The Last of the Titans*, Yale University Press, London, 2004, p386.

21. *Theosophy,* p. 107. The quotations which are not referenced here are referenced in my thesis (see chapter two, note 3).
22. *Occult Science,* p. 142.
23. As above, p. 134.
24. As above, p. 169.
25. As above, p. 167.

Chapter 6

1. Goethe, Letter to Schiller, 27 August 1794 in M. von Hersfeld and C. Melvil Sym tr., Stephen Spender ed., *Great Writings of Goethe,* Meridian, New York, 1977, p. 34.
2. The main source, *Occult Science,* is not specifically referenced here, except for quotations. More detailed references can be found in my PhD thesis.
3. *Occult Science,* p. 119.
4. As above, pp. 121-122.
5. W.L. Reese, *Dictionary of Philosophy and Religion,* Humanities Press, New Jersey, 1980, pp. 138-39.
6. *Occult Science,* p. 118.
7. As above, p. 124.
8. As above, p. 123.
9. As above, p. 128.
10. As above, p. 133.
11. As above, pp. 133-134.
12. As above, p. 140.
13. As above
14. As above, p. 155.
15. As above
16. As above, p. 155.
17. Goethe, tr. Philip Wayne, *Faust. Part Two,* Penguin, 1959.
18. *Occult Science,* pp. 169-170.
19. As above, pp. 177-178.
20. As above, p. 184.
21. As above, p. 192.
22. As above, p. 196.
23. As above, p. 197.
24. As above, pp. 209-211.
25. As above, p. 214.
26. For a summary, see S.C. Easton, *Man and World in the Light of Anthroposophy,* The Anthroposophic Press, New York, 1975.
27. *Occult Science,* p. 220.
28. As above, p. 308.
29. Steiner presumably had the Asuras of the Hindu Vedas rather than the Iranian Ahuras (who were good) in mind. Both derive from a common Indo-European root.

Chapter 7

1. John Milton, 'Il Penseroso', in J.T. Shawcross ed., *The Complete English Poetry of John Milton* , Anchor Books, New York, 1963, ll. 85-92.
2. My main source is Mary Boyce, 'The Continuity of the Zoroastrian Quest' in W. Foy. ed., *Man's Religious Quest. A Reader,* Croom Helm, London, 1978, pp. 603-619. She opposes Zaehner's view.
3. Hans Jonas, 'The Gnostic Syndrome' in *Philosophical Essays. From Ancient Creed to Technological Man,* University of Chicago Press, 1974, p.276.
4. Hans Jonas, *The Gnostic Religion. The Message of the Alien God and the Beginning of Christianity,* Beacon Press, Boston, 1958. Jonas' approach and my analysis of the Rudolf Steiner movement are similar in many ways; however, I read Jonas only after I had completed this work on these lines. Another major source used here is Robert Haardt, ed., *Gnosis. Character and Testimony,* E.J. Brill, Leiden, 1971.
5. S. Runciman, *The Medieval Manichee. A Study of the Christian Dualist Heresy,* Cambridge University Press, 1947, pp. VII, 67 and 117; P. Partner, *The Murdered Magicians. The Templars and their Myth,* Oxford University Press, 1982, p. 84, and Jacques Madaule, *The Albigensian Crusade,* tr. Barbara Wall, Burns and Oates, London, 1967, pp. 31-32, 33-38 and 53.
6. Rudolf Steiner, Occult Science An Outline, tr. G&M Adams, Rudolf Steiner Press, London 1972, pp. 220 & 221.
7. Even through the main traditional source, the hostile Church Father Irenaeus. *Gnosis*, pp. 120-151, and *The Gnostic Religion*, pp. 174-199.
8. Or 'Thought'.
9. The main works consulted: Frances Yates, *Giordano Bruno and the Hermetic Tradition,* Routledge, London, 1964, and *The Rosicrucian Enlightenment,* Paladin, St Albans, 1975; G. Scholem, *Kabbalah,* Keter, Jerusalem, 1974; Titus Burckhardt, *Alchemy. Science of the Cosmos, Science of the Soul,* Stuart and Watkins, London, 1967; Walter Pagel, 'The Prime Matter of Paracelsus' in *Ambix. The Journal for the Study of Alchemy and early Chemistry,* Vol. IX, No. 3, October 1961, and 'Paracelsus and the Neoplatonic and Gnostic tradition', as above, Vol. VIII, No. 3, October 1960; R. Alters, 'Microcosmos' from *Traditio,* Vol. II, 1944; A. Debus, *The Chemical Philosophy. Paracelsian Science and Medicine in the Sixteenth and Seventeenth Centuries,* Vol. I, Science History Publications, New York, 1977) and *Robert Fludd and his Philosophicall Key* (same publisher, 1979); J. Jacobi, ed., *Paracelsus: Selected Writings,* Routledge, 1951; J. Hargrave, *The Life and Soul of Paracelsus,* Gollancz, London, 1951, I.R.F. Calder, *John Dee studied as an English Neoplatonist* , PhD thesis, University of London, 1953; J. W. Montgomery, *Cross and Crucible,* Vol. I, M. Nijhoff, The Hague, 1973; P. Allen ed., *A Christian Rosenkreuz Anthology*, Rudolf Steiner

Publications, New York, 1968, Mervyn Jones, 'The Rosicrucians' and 'Freemasonry' in N. Mackenzie ed., *Secret Societies,* Aldus Books, London, 1967; A.E. Waite, *The Brotherhood of the Rosy Cross,* Rider, London, 1924; H. Jennings, *The Rosicrucians,* Chatto and Windus, London, 1879; Christopher McIntosh, *The Rosy Cross Unveiled,* Aquarian Press, Wellingborough, 1980, and G. Knight, *A History of White Magic,* Mowbrays, 1978.

10. It is now thought that the treatises themselves are composites.
11. Plotinus, 'Enneads', 11, 9, 4, 22-24, quoted in *Gnosis*, p. 177.
12. Steiner seems to do much the same in stating that man can be seen as a tenth Spiritual Hierarchy.
13. *Alchemy. Science of the Cosmos, Science of the Soul*, p. 26. The insights of Jung (surely misunderstood by Burckhardt himself?) have been my major source in attempting to understand alchemy.
14. Speculations about the source of the Red Cross symbolism are legion. It is possible (only) that the Red Cross Knight of Spenser's *Faerie Queene,* which was inspired by the Order of the Garter, was an influence.
15. Even more bizarre was the association, in the minds of many French royalists, of Rosicrucianism and the Templars. After 1815 there was a persecution theory which supposed that the 'Templars', under the guise of Rosicrucianism, fomented the Revolution in order to avenge the judicial murder of their Grand Master, Jacques de Molay, by a medieval ancestor of Louis XVI, the Bourbon king executed in 1792.
16. *The Brotherhood of the Rosy Cross* (see note 9), p. 618.

Chapter 8

1. Gita Mehta, *Karma Cola,* Fontana, Glasgow, 1981, p. 105.
2. Henri Ellenberger, *The Discovery of the Unconscious*, USA, Basic Books, 1970, p. 83.
3. Max Müller stated that 'nothing has injured Buddhism so much in the eyes of scholars and philosophers in Europe as what goes by the name of esoteric Buddhism'. Quoted in R.F. Gombrich, *Precept and Practice,* Oxford University Press, 1971, p. 54.
4. *Kabbalah* and *The Rosy Cross Unveiled*, Christopher McIntosh, *Eliphas Lévi and the French Occult Revival*, Rider, London, 1972, Kathleen Raine, *Yeats, the Tarot and the Golden Dawn,* The Dolman Press, 1972, and *The Sword of Wisdom.*
5. Joachim Kohler, *Wagner. The Last of the Titans*, Yale University Press, New Haven, 2004, p.296.
6. See Rudolph Sabor, *Richard Wagner. Das Rheingold,* Phaidon Press, Hong Kong, 1997, and the continuing series on *Die Valkure, Siegfried, Gotterdamerung* and *Der Ring des Nibelungen* for material relating to the fascinating analogies between the Ring and gnosticism, developing which would be the subject for at least one PhD thesis!
7. My sources include contacts with Theosophists. Works consulted

include: V.S. Solovyoff, *A Modem Priestess of Isis,* Longmans, Green and Co, London, 1895; H. P. Blavatsky, *The Secret Doctrine,* Vols. I and II, Theosophical Publishing House, London, 1888, *The Key to Theosophy* (as before, no date), *Isis Unveiled,* Vol. I, 'Science', Theosophical University Press, 1960; H. Murphet, *When Daylight Comes. A biography of Helen Petrovna Blavatsky,* The Theosophical Publishing House, India, 1975; Boris de Zirkoff, *How the 'Secret Doctrine' of H.P. Blavatsky was written,* The Theosophical Publishing House, India, 1977; Annie Besant, *Thought Power,* The Theosophical Publishing House, India, 1909; H.S. Olcott, *Old Diary Leaves. The True History of the Theosophical Society,* Putnams, New York, 1895; W.Q. Judge, *The Ocean of Theosophy,* The Theosophical Co, Los Angeles, 1937; C.W. Leadbeater, *A Text-Book of Theosophy,* The Theosophist Office, Adyar, 1912; W. Old, *What is Theosophy?,* Hay Nisbet, London, 1891; E.R. McNeile, *From Theosophy to Christian Faith,* Longmans, Green, London, 1919, and 'Preface' by Bishop Gore.

 8. W.E. Coleman, 'Appendix C in A. Lillie, *Madame Blavatsky and her Theosophy,* Susan Sonnenschein, London, 1895, pp. 353-366.

 9. H.P. Blavatsky, *The Voice of the Silence,* Theosophical Publishing House, 1892.

10. Corona Trew, *Studies in the 'Secret Doctrine',* The Theosophical Publishing House, London, 1972.

11. See H.H. Wilson, *Vishnu Purana,* Oxford, 1840, p. 214. The egg might also have been influenced by alchemical lead. See M-L von Franz, *Alchemy. An Introduction to the Symbolism and Psychology,* Inner City Books, Toronto, 1980, p. 82.

12. J.V. Luce, *The End of Atlantis. New Light on an old Legend,* Thames and Hudson, 1969.

13. Edwin Muir, *The Structure of the Novel,* The Hogarth Press, 1928.

14. David Levy, *Realism,* Carcanet Press, 1981, p.75.

15. *A Christian Rosenkreuz Anthology;* and Rudolf Steiner, *The Mission of Christian Rosenkreuz* , Rudolf Steiner Publishing, 1950, and *Rosicrucianism and Modern Initiation,* Letchworth, Garden City Press, 1965.

16. The Rosicrucian Fellowship has been active in America. It was founded by Max Heindel, who emigrated to the USA and adapted Steiner's ideas, apparently without acknowledgement.

17. J. Webb, *The Harmonious Circle,* pp. 18, 41, 544, 547, 557, 562, 571, 294 and 499-540, and M. Nicoll, *Psychological Commentaries on the Teaching of Gurdjieff and Ouspensky,* Vol. I, Stuart and Watkins, 1970.

18. See Lionel Adey, *C.S. Lewis' 'Great War' with Owen Barfield,* No. 14, ELS Monograph Series, University of Victoria, Canada, 1978.

19. Voegelin, E, *The Ecumenic Age,* Louisiana State University Press, Baton Rouge, 1974, p21.

20. Levy, D, *Realism*, Carcanet New Press, Manchester, 1981, p76.
21. Jonas, H, 'Gnosticism, Existentialism and Nihilism' in The Gnostic Religion, The message of the alien God and the beginnings of Christianity, 2nd ed, Beacon Press, Boston, 1963, pp320-340.
22. F.L. Baumer, *Modern European Thought. Continuity and Change in Ideas 1600-1950*, Collier Macmillan, New York, 1977, p. 451. My comments on Teilhard are largely based on Ursula King's *Towards a New Mysticism. Teilhard de Chardin and Eastern Religions*, Collins, London, 1980.
23. *Towards a New Mysticism*, p. 50.
24. Jungians themselves and my reading of translations of many of Jung's works have provided the basis for this summary. Of special interest are M-L von Franz, *Alchemy*, C.G. Jung, *Psychological Types*, Routledge, 1971, and E. Neumann, *The Origins and History of Consciousness*.
25. See Ira Progoff, *The Death and Rebirth of Psychology*, The Julian Press, New York, 1969.
26. C.G. Jung, *Psychological Types*, pp. 168 and 353-354 and C.G. Jung, *Psychology and Religion: West and East*, Routledge, London, 1973, pp. 518 and 525.
27. Walter Pagel, 'Jung's views on alchemy' in *Isis* No. 39, 1948, p. 48.
28. See Richard Noll, *The Jung Cult*, Princeton University Press, New Jersey, 1994, p.271.
29. C. Curling, 'Physics and Psyche' in *Harvest. Journal for Jungian Studies*, No. 26, 1980, pp. 62-72.

Chapter 9

1. Max Scheler, *Problems of a Sociology of Knowledge*, tr. M.S. Frings, Routledge, London, 1980, p. 35.
2. Aldous Huxley, *The Perennial Philosophy*, Chatto and Windus, London, 1946, p. 2.
3. Ninian Smart, 'Understanding Religious Experience' in S. Katz, ed., *Mysticism and Philosophical Analysis*, Sheldon Press, London, 1978, pp. 13-14.
4. S. Katz, 'Language, Epistemology and Mysticism' in *Mysticism and Philosophical Analysis*, pp. 39-40 (for quote) and generally.
5. David Hay, *Exploring Inner Space*, Pelican, 1982, p. 118 and generally.
6. Peter Bergman and Thomas Luckmann, *The Social Construction of Reality*, Penguin, 1966, pp. 177-178 (and p. 166).
7. N. Smelser, *Theory of Collective Behaviour*, Routledge, 1962, pp. 1-2, 12-18 and 313-364.
8. C.Y. Glock, 'The Role of Deprivation in the Origin and Evolution of Religious Groups' in R. Lee and M. Marty, eds., *Religion and Social Conflict*, Oxford University Press, 1964, pp. 24-36.
9. J.A. Coleman, 'Church-Sect Typology and Organisational Precariousness' in *Sociological Analysis*, Vol. 29, No. 2, 1968, p. 59.

10. Robert Bellah, 'Religious Evolution', in R. Robertson ed. *The Sociology of Religion,* Penguin, 1969, p. 263. Originally in the *American Sociological Review,* Vol. 29, 1964, pp. 358-374. The page references of the quotes in this section are, in chronological order, pp. 277-8, 278, 278, 280, 286, 288, 291 and 290.

11. The interpretative position taken in this book, in its skeletal way, owes much to the translated writings of C.G. Jung. Bellah's influence has been peripheral. (His approach seems to have affinities with Tillich and Eliade.)

12. It is not apparent that anthropological evidence contradicts the developmental approach taken here. This is a dynamic theory about the interaction of emerging social reality (defined on pp. 183-84) and the experience of spirit. In its social application it does little more than make explicit and join up academic assumptions latent within the boundaries of social anthropology, history and sociology.

    The theory here does not, so far as I can see, have any bearing on static, intra-social comparisons between 'anthropological' societies. 'Anthropological' societies have, *as societies,* a relative absence of social differentiation compared to modern societies; this is the important point. This is not to say that the experience of modern *individuals* is more differentiated than that of individuals in primal societies. Nor does it matter here that the differentiation primal societies have varies: that pygmies may have unusually little ritual, or that some aboriginals are exceptionally mobile, footloose and uncommitted.

    In her intra-social analysis in *Natural Symbols,* Barrie and Jenkins, London, 1970, Mary Douglas explicitly draws attention to the point that the dynamic, developmental approach is outside what she wishes to take into account (see p. 82). It is a path that does not seem to have been taken by twentieth-century anthropology.

Chapter 10

1. John Henry Newman, *Apologia pro Vita Sua,* Sheed and Ward, London, 1979, Note A, p. 193.
2. *The Golden Ass* (see Epigraph), p. 241. See also Ninian Smart, 'The Mysteries' in *Secret Societies,* pp. 84-94 and J.D.P. Bolton, *Glory, Jest and Riddle,* Duckworth, London, 1973, pp. 60-63.
3. R.C. Zaehner, *Hinduism,* pp. 231 and 219-221 and Mircea Eliade, *Yoga,* Princeton University Press, New Jersey, 1969, pp. 9-11.
4. T. Ling, *A History of Religion East and West,* Macmillan, London, 1968, pp. 56, 59, 19, 114-115 and 427. The short time spans and theism of Genesis cosmogony (compared to that of Hinduism) may be connected with the creative achievements of hydraulic-agrarian civilization.
5. Erich Voegelin, 'The Eclipse of Reality' in M. Natanson, ed. *Phenomenology and Social Reality. Essays in Memory of Alfred Schutz,* p. 185.

6. Roy Wallis, article in the *Times Higher Education Supplement,* 6 October 1978, pp. 11-12.

7. 'The Eclipse of Reality' (see note 5 above), p. 185. Unfortunately Voegelin terms immanentist philosophies 'gnostic' (despite their lack of transcendental dualism) because of the spurious certainty they share with gnosis. I am indebted to David Levy for helping me understand Voegelin. See David Levy's *Realism. An Essay in Interpretation and Social Reality,* Carcanet New Press, Manchester, 1981, especially chapter seven.

8. Bryan Wilson, *Religious Sects,* World University Library, 1970.

9. David Martin, *Pacifism,* Routledge, 1965, p. 5.

10. Colin Campbell's phrase.

11. Lorne Dawson, 'Anti-modernism, modernism, and post-modernism: struggling with the cultural significance of new religious movements', *Sociology of Religion*, Summer, 1998.

Appendix

1. William Shakespeare, *The Tempest,* I, i.

2. These meetings, which took place between 3 January 1977 and 4 March 1978, were by no means my first substantial contact with Anthroposophy. My approach throughout was essentially in the phenomenological tradition. I took contemporaneous notes after two trial runs with a tape-recorder (with other Anthroposophists) had shown that these machines were more than usually distrusted (because they were perceived as 'Ahrimanic'). I started a 'snowball' whereby one of my contacts would put me in touch with someone else. I sought the meetings on the basis that I was 'researching into the personal meaning of Anthroposophy' and had been 'sympathetically interested' for 'several years'. I generally made it clear that I was not committed to Steiner's revelation. I made the meetings as unstructured as possible while ensuring that about fifty points on a check-list had been covered.

3. Sometimes I have felt obliged to disguise identities by falsifying information which seems to me to be incidental to the main portrait.

4. Four were youngest, three only, and three eldest children.

5. The man who modelled himself on his father's occupation nevertheless totally rejected his ideas. The 'fathers' here include father-figures.

6. The square brackets within quotes indicate that I am supplying the context in my own words. I have occasionally added the definite or indefinite article, personal pronouns, etc.

7. Williams James, *The Varieties of Religious Experience,* Fontana, London, 1960, p. 200. The Humpty Dumpty of converted man consists, in an enormous literature, of anthropological, historical, sociological, psychoanalytical and theological fragments.

8. Nevertheless, contact between the eighteen and their relations and pre-Anthroposophical friends was generally infrequent.

9. '... the tail and face of the serpent are placed at the left side of the circular drawing. There is a certain orientation evident, which could be connected with the four main directions in which the altars of the Sun Temple as initiation centre are orientated, the Eastern altar in the zenith, the others clockwise, so that the Northern altar stands at the left side ... It has to do with the encounter of the forces of evil, in our time predominantly the Ahrimanic forces.' Hans Pusch, 'Thoughts on the Seal' Foreword to R. Steiner's *Der Seelen Erwachen*, , p. 5.

10. Anthroposophists reverse the image of Emile Durkheim. Instead of seeing religion as society they see society (especially their own movement) in terms of spirit.

11. Given recent scientific findings about the complex interactions (including epigenetics) between genes and the social environment, and the possibility of early biochemical, dietary and/or viral influences, the predisposition/nurture dichotomy made here is a distinction for making some fundamental points about social scientific assumptions about the causation of conversion, and is not intended to be theoretically watertight or operationalisable in terms of research. It need be no disproof of predisposition that about twelve of the eighteen future Anthroposophists had parents and siblings who were not especially spiritually committed. Predisposition is likely to be genetically conditioned (with scattered Mendelian distribution).

Tables

TABLE 1
The Human Aura
(compiled from Theosophy, pp. 115-124)

THE FIRST AURA (or lowest sheath)
(a mirror of the influence of the body on the soul):
The colours are opaque and dull.

Colour	Interpretation
Muddy yellow to brown	Lowest stage of egotism
Brownish and yellowish green	When desires are beyond the reach of capacities
Green	Inferior natures. Obtuse, enjoyment prone, exertionless
Obtrusive red	Sensual desires
Reddish blue spots and flecks	Excitement of external impression
Red to blue	Undeveloped impulses
Rose-red	Selfless natural impulse of mother love
Brown and grey blue	Cowardly fear of external provocations

THE SECOND AURA (or middle sheath)
(the life of the soul):

Colour	Interpretation
Bright yellow	Clear thinking and intelligence
Green yellow	Good memory
Green	Understanding of life and of the world
Red-yellow flecks	Inquisitiveness
Rose-red	A benevolent, affectionate nature
Brown and orange	Strong conceit, pride and ambition
Blue	Piety
Indigo blue	Idealism and higher earnestness
Violet	Religious fervour

THE THIRD AURA (or highest sheath)
(the spiritual in man):

Colour	Interpretation
Bright yellow	Thinking with lofty ideas, comprehending the divine World Order
Brilliant golden yellow	When the above is purified from all sensory conceptions
Green	Love for all beings
Blue	Selfless sacrifice
Light violet	Strong, willing, devoted to the service of the world

TABLE 2

The Natures of Man

The natures may interpenetrate

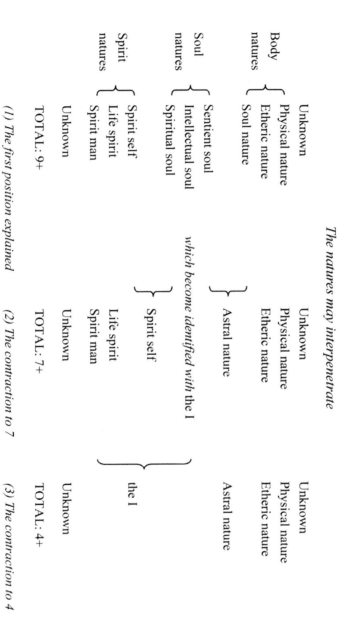

	(1) The first position explained	(2) The contraction to 7	(3) The contraction to 4
Body natures	Unknown / Physical nature / Etheric nature	Unknown / Physical nature / Etheric nature	Unknown / Physical nature / Etheric nature
	Soul nature	Astral nature	Astral nature
Soul natures	Sentient soul / Intellectual soul / Spiritual soul	*which become identified with the I* Spirit self	the I
Spirit natures	Spirit self / Life spirit / Spirit man	Life spirit / Spirit man	
	Unknown	Unknown	Unknown
	TOTAL: 9+	**TOTAL: 7+**	**TOTAL: 4+**

TABLE 3
The Natures of Man

PLANETARY EMBODIMENTS

	Saturn	Sun	Moon	Earth	Jupiter	Venus	Vulcan
Physical Nature	1	2	3	4	Shed		
Etheric Nature		1	2	3	4	Shed	
Astral Nature			1	2	3	4	Shed
The I				1	2	3	4
Spirit Self					1	2	3
Life Spirit						1	2
Spirit Man							1

The numerals show the number of times the nature has evolved at the end of the embodiment. After the maximum of four times, it is shed and a higher nature is added. The Table refers only to the most advanced men of each embodiment.

TABLE 4

Initiators and Initiated

The 'Human' Stage in the First Four Planetary Embodiments

(Pseudo-Dionysian names)			Saturn	Sun	Moon	Earth
(Seraphim)	1	Spirits of Love	Spirits of Love	Spirit of Love	Spirit of Love	Spirit of Love,
(Cherubim)	2	Spirit of the Harmonies	Spirit of the Harmonies	Spirit of the Harmonies	Spirit of the Harmonies	Spirit of the Harmonies
(Thrones)	3	Spirit of Will	Spirit of Will	Spirit of Will	Spirit of Will	Spirit of Will
(Dominions)	4	Spirit of Wisdom	Spirit of Wisdom	Spirit of Wisdom	Spirit of Wisdom	Spirit of Wisdom
(Mights)	5	Spirit of Movement	Spirit of Movement	Spirit of Movement	Spirit of Movement	Spirit of Movement
(Powers)	6	Spirit of Form	Spirit of Form	Spirit of Form	Spirit of Form	Spirit of Form
(Principalities)	7	Spirit of Personality	Spirit of Personality	Spirit of Personality	Spirit of Personality	Spirit of Personality
(Archangels)	8	Fire-Spirits	Fire-Spirits	Fire-Spirits	Fire-Spirits	Fire-Spirits
(Angels)	9	Sons of Life	Sons of Life	Sons of Life	Sons of Life	Sons of Life
	10	Man	Man	Man	Man	Man

The underlined higher beings are the beings initiating the 'human' stage. The boxed lower beings are going through the 'human' stage. The Spiritual Hierarchies are here given their Anthroposophical (rather than Pseudo-Dionysian) names. See left column for the latter.

Bibliography

1. On Anthroposophy or the Rudolf Steiner Movement

Adey, L., *C.S. Lewis' 'Great War' with Owen Barfield,* ELS Monograph Studies, University of Victoria, 1978.

Baditz, N. von, contributor to *Education as an Art,* Rudolf Steiner Publications, New York, 1970.

Barfield, Owen, 'The Art of Eurythmy', *The Golden Blade,* 1954.

——, *What Coleridge Thought,* 3rd printing, Wesleyan University Press, Connecticut, 1978.

Bellow, Saul, *Humboldt's Gift,* Penguin, 1978.

Bock, E., 'Religious Renewal', *The Golden Blade,* 1958.

——, 'The Search for Felix', *The Golden Blade,* 1961.

Biesantz, Hagen and Klingborg, *The Goetheanum. Rudolf Steiner's Architectural Impulse,* Rudolf Steiner Press, 1979.

Bosset, G.C. (ed.), *Letters of Rudolf and Marie Steiner. Anthroposophical Quarterly,* Vol. 13, No. 1, Spring 1968.

Bott, V., *Anthroposophical Medicine.* 1st English edition, Rudolf Steiner Press, London, 1978.

Compton-Burnett, Juliet, contributor to *Some Recollections of Rudolf Steiner. The Golden Blade,* 1959.

Compton-Burnett, Vera, contributor to *Some Recollections of Rudolf Steiner. The Golden Blade,* 1959.

Darcy, J. (ed.), *Work arising from the Life of Rudolf Steiner,* Rudolf Steiner Press, London, 1975.

Davy, John, 'The Movement that everyone tries to forget', *Times Educational Supplement,* 23 March 1973.

Easton, S.C., *Man and World in the Light of Anthroposophy,* The Anthroposophic Press, New York, 1975.

Emmichoven, F.W. Zeylmans van, 'Rudolf Steiner and Community among Men in the Future', *Anthroposophical Quarterly,* Winter 1961, Vol. 6, No. 4.

Grahl, V., *The Exceptional Child,* Rudolf Steiner Press, 1970.

Harwood, A.C., *Shakespeare's Prophetic Mind,* Rudolf Steiner Press, 1964

——, *The Recovery of Man in Childhood,* Hodder and Stoughton, 1971.

——, (ed.), *The Faithful Thinker,* Hodder and Stoughton, London, 1961.

Haas-Berkow, G., 'Experiences in the Realm of Dramatic Art', *The Golden Blade,* 1958.

Hausckka, M., *Rhythmical Massage,* Rudolf Steiner Press, 1979.

Heidenreich, A., 'Rudolf Steiner. Initiate, Christian and Human Being', *The Christian Community Journal,* Vol. 15, 1961.

——, contributor to 'Some Recollections of Rudolf Steiner', *The Golden Blade,* 1959.

Hemleben, J., *Rudolf Steiner,* Henry Goulden Limited, 1975.

Heydebrand, C. von, contributor to *Education as an Art,* Rudolf Steiner Publications, New York, 1970.

Hiebel, F., *Shakespeare and the Awakening of Modern Consciousness,* Anthroposophic Press, New York, 1940.

Kirchner-Bockholt, M. and F., *Rudolf Steiner's Mission and Ita Wegman,* Rudolf Steiner Press, London (no date).

Koepf, Pettersson and Schaumann, *Bio-dynamic Agriculture,* The Anthroposophic Press, New York, 1976.

König, K., *Rudolf Steiner's Calendar of the Soul: A Commentary,* Rudolf Steiner Press (no date).

——, 'The Camphill Movement', *The Cresset,* 1960.

Lachman, G, *Rudolf Steiner. An Introduction to his Life and Work,* Penguin, New York, 2007.

Lehrs, E., *Man or Matter,* Faber and Faber, London (no date).

Maier-Smits, L., 'The Beginnings of Eurythmy', *The Golden Blade,* 1958.

Mansfield, P., *An Examination of the Idea of the Threefold Social Order,* dissertation for BSc in Sociology, University of Bath, June 1978.

Marshall, A. (compiler), *Index to Bio-Dynamics 1941-1975,* Bio-Dynamic Farming and Gardening Association Inc., Illinois (no date).

Moore, V., 'Introduction', *The Arts and their Mission,* R. Steiner, Lectures 1923, Dornach, Christian Anthroposophic Press Inc., New York, 1964.

Nordoff, P. and Robbins, C., *Music Therapy in Special Education,* The John Day Company, New York, 1971.

Polzer-Hoditz, Count, 'Personal Memories of Rudolf Steiner', *The Present Age,* 1936, Vol. 2, No. 1 and 1937, Vol. 2.

Pusch, H., 'Thoughts on the Seal', Foreword to R. Steiner's *Der Seelen Erwachen,* Rudolf Steiner Verlag, Dornach, Switzerland.

Reaugh Smith, E, *The Burning Bush: Rudolf Steiner, Anthroposophy and the Holy Scriptures. An Anthroposophical Commentary on the Bible. Terms and Phrases.* Rev. ed. Anthroposophic Press, Great Barrington, 2001.

Rittelmeyer, F., *Rudolf Steiner Enters My Life,* The Christian Community Press, 1963.

Savitch, M., *Marie Steiner-von Sivers,* Rudolf Steiner Press, London, 1967.

Shepherd, A.P., *A Scientist of the Invisible,* Hodder and Stoughton, 1971.

Schindler, M., *Pure Colour,* Part I, New Culture Publications, London, 1946.

Schuré, Edouard, 'The Personality of Rudolf Steiner and his Development', *The Golden Blade,* 1966.

Steffen, Albert, *Meetings with Rudolf Steiner,* Verlag für Schonewissenschaften, Dornach, Switzerland, 1926.

Stein, W.J., *The British, Their Psychology and Destiny,* New Knowledge Books, East Grinstead, 1958.

Steiner, Marie, 'Foreword' to Rudolf Steiner's *The Anthroposophic Movement* (see below).

Steiner, Rudolf, *Agriculture,* 8 lectures, 1924, Kobernitz, Silesia, 3rd ed., Bio-Dynamic Agricultural Association, London, 1974.

——, *Anthroposophy and Psychoanalysis I & II,* Lectures, Dornach, 1917. Rudolf Steiner House Library (no date or publisher).

——, *Anthroposophy and the Social Question,* essay 1906-1908, printed by H. Collison, 27 Clareville Grove, London SW7 (no date).

——, *Architectural Forms,* Speech, Dornach, 1916, Rudolf Steiner Publishing Co., London (no date).

——, 'Autobiographical Sketch' (written for Edouard Schuré), *The Golden Blade,* 1966.

——, *The Course of My Life,* Revised tr. O.D. Wannamaker, Anthroposophic Press, New York, 2nd ed., 1951: later translated as *Rudolf Steiner. An Autobiography,* tr. R. Stebbing, ed., P. Allen, Rudolf Steiner Publications, New York, 1977.

——, *Carnegie and Tolstoi,* Lecture, Munich, 1908. H. Collinson, 1930 (private publisher).

——, *Christianity as Mystical Fact and the Mysteries of Antiquity,* Rudolf Steiner Press, London, 1972.

——, *Cosmic Memory,* Rudolf Steiner Publications Inc., Englewood, New Jersey, 1959.

——, *Connections between Organic Processes and the Mental Life of Man,* Lecture, Dornach, 1921. Typescript Rudolf Steiner House Library.

——, *Curative Education,* 12 lectures, 1924, Rudolf Steiner Press, 1972.

——, (et al.), *Education as an Art,* Rudolf Steiner Publications, New York, 1970.

——, *Eurythmy as Visible Music,* 8 lectures, Dornach, 1924, Rudolf Steiner Press, London, 1977.

——, *Friedrich Nietzsche. Fighter for Freedom,* R. Steiner Publications Inc., New Jersey, 1960.

——, (with Wegman, Ita), *Fundamentals of Therapy,* Rudolf Steiner Press, London, 1967.

——, *Goethe as the Founder of a New Science of Aesthetics.* Lecture, Anthroposophical Publishing Co., 1922.

——, *Goethe's Conception of the World,* Anthroposophical Publishing Co., London, 1928.

——, *Goethe the Scientist,* Anthroposophic Press, New York, 1950.

——, *Hidden Soul Powers,* Lecture, Munich, 1912. Typescript, Rudolf Steiner House Library.

——, *Human Values in Education,* 10 lectures, Holland, 1924, Rudolf Steiner Press, London, 1971.

——, *Knowledge of the Higher Worlds,* Garden City Press Ltd, Letchworth, Hertfordshire, 1973.

——, *Mysticism and Modern Thought,* Anthroposophical Publishing Co., and Anthroposophic Press, 1928.

——, *Occult Science. An Outline,* tr. G. and M. Adams, Rudolf Steiner Press, London, 1972.

——, *Occult Science. An Outline,* tr. M. and H. Monges, Anthroposophic Press, New York City, 1950.

——, *Reflections in the Mirror of Consciousness, Superconsciousness and Subconsciousness,* Lecture, Munich, 1912. Typescript Rudolf Steiner House Library.

——, *Rosicrucian Esotericism,* 10 lectures, 1909, Budapest, The Anthroposophic Press, New York, 1978.

——, *Rosicrucianism and Modern Initiation,* 6 lectures, 1924, Garden City Press Ltd., Letchworth, 1965.

——, *Self Education, Rudolf Steiner's Childhood and Youth up to the Weimar Period,* Lecture 4 February 1913, Berlin. Typescript Rudolf Steiner House Library.

——, *Spiritual Science and Medicine,* Rudolf Steiner Publishing Co., London, 1948.

——, *Spiritual Science and the Art of Healing,* 3 lectures, Arnheim, July 1924, Anthroposophical Publishing Co., London, 1950.

——, *Study of Man,* 14 lectures, Stuttgart, 1919, Rudolf Steiner Press, London, 1960.

——, *Supersensible Man,* 5 lectures, The Hague, 13-18 November 1923, Anthroposophical Publishing Company, London, revised ed., 1961.

——, *The Anthroposophic Movement,* 8 lectures, Dornach, 10-17 June 1923. H. Collison (private edition), 1933.

——, *The Birth of Christianity. Christianity and the Mysteries of Antiquity,* 2 lectures 1924, R. Steiner Publishing Co., 1950.

——, *The Education of the Child,* Rudolf Steiner Press, London, 1965.

——, *The Foundation Stone,* Speech, Dornach, 1924, Rudolf Steiner Press, London, 1979.

——, *The Four Seasons and the Archangels,* 5 lectures, Dornach, 1973, 2nd revised edition, Rudolf Steiner Press, London, 1968.

——, *The Four Temperaments,* 2nd ed., Anthroposophic Press Inc., New York, 1968.

——, *The Influence of Spiritual Beings upon Man,* 11 lectures, Berlin, 8 January to 11 June 1908, Anthroposophic Press Inc., New York, 1961.

——, *The Inner Aspect of the Social Question.* Lecture, Berlin, 1919, Rudolf Steiner Publishing Co., London and Anthroposophic Press, New York, 1935.

——, *The Inner Realities of Evolution,* 5 lectures, October-December 1911, Rudolf Steiner Publishing Co., 54 Bloomsbury Street, London WC1, 1953.

——, *The Karma of Materialism,* 9 lectures, Berlin, 1917. Typescript Rudolf Steiner House Library, London.

——, *The Lord's Prayer.* Lecture 1907. Anthroposophic Press Inc., New York, 1970.

——, *The Mission of Christian Rosenkreuz,* Rudolf Steiner Publishing Co., 1950.

——, *Theosophy,* Garden City Press Ltd., Letchworth, Hertfordshire, 1970.

——, *The Philosophy of Freedom,* Rudolf Steiner Press Ltd., 1964.

——, *The Redemption of Thinking,* 3 lectures, Whitsuntide 1920, Hodder and Stoughton, 1956.

——, *The Riddles of Philosophy,* The Anthroposophic Press, New York, 1973.

——, *The Social Future,* 6 lectures, Zurich, 1919. Anthroposophic Press Inc., New York, 3rd ed., 1972.

——, *The Spiritual Beings in the Heavenly Bodies and in the Kingdoms of Nature,* 10 lectures, Helsingfors, April 1912, Rudolf Steiner Publishing Co., London, 1951.

——, *The Spiritual Hierarchies and their Reflection in the Physical World — Zodiac, Planets, Cosmos,* 10 lectures, Dusseldorf, April 1909, Anthroposophic Press Inc., New York, 1970.

——, *The Theory of Knowledge Implicit in Goethe's World-Conception,* Anthroposophic Press, New York, 1940.

——, *Thomas Aquinas,* 3 lectures, Dornach, 1920. Percy, Lund, Humphries, 1932.

Strohschein, A., 'The Birth of Curative Education', *The Golden Blade,* 1958.

Treher, W., *Hitler, Steiner, Schreber. Ein Beitrag zur Phanomenologie des Kranken Geistes,* 1966.

Ungen, G., *Flying Saucers,* New Knowledge Books, East Grinstead, 1958.

Wachsmuth, Guenther, *The Evolution of Mankind,* Philosophic Anthroposophic Press, Dornach, Switzerland, 1961.

——, *The Life and Work of Rudolf Steiner,* tr. O.D. Wannamaker and R.E. Raab, Whittier Books Inc., New York, 1955.

——, 'How Old is the Earth?', *The Golden Blade,* 1954.

Whicher, O., *Projective Geometry,* Rudolf Steiner Press, London, 1971.

Wilkinson, Roy, *Rudolf Steiner. An Introduction to his Spiritual World View, Anthroposophy,* 1998, www.anthroposophy.org.uk

2. On Gnosticism, Esotericism, Mysticism and Depth-Psychology

Aagaard, J., 'Who is Who in Guruism', *New Religious Movements Update,* Vol. IV, issue 3, October 1980. Dialogue Centre, Klovermarksvej 4, D.K.-8200 Arhus N, Denmark.

Acyutananda, *Swami, '*Tantra: Can Sex be Yoga?', *New Religious Movements Update,* Vol. IV, December 1980. Dialogue Centre Klovermarksvej 4, D.K.-8200 Arhus N. Denmark.

Allen, Paul (ed.), *A Christian Rosenkreuz Anthology,* Rudolf Steiner Publications, New York, 1968.

Allers, R., 'Microcosmos', *Traditio,* Vol. II, 1944.

Apuleius, Lucius, *The Golden Ass,* tr. Robert Graves, Penguin, 1950.

Arnold, P., *Histoire des Rose-Croix,* Mercure de France, 1955.

Bailey, Alice, *Esoteric Psychology I,* Lucis Press Ltd., London, 1975.

——, *The Externalisation of the Hierarchy,* Lucis Press Ltd., London, 1972.

Barnes, Mary and Berke, J., *Mary Barnes. Two Accounts of a Journey through Madness,* MacGibbon and Kee, London, 1971.

Barter, J.P., *Toward Subud,* Gollancz, 1967.

Besant, Annie, *Thought Power: its Control and Culture,* The Theosophical Publishing House, 1909.

Blacker, Thetis, *A Pilgrimage of Dreams,* Turnstone Books, 1973.

Blake, J.A., 'Ufology: the intellectual development and social context of the study of unidentified flying objects', from *On the Margins of Science,* University of Keele, 1979.

Blake, William, *Poems and Prophecies,* Everyman, reprinted 1970.

Blakney, R.B., *Aleister Eckhardt. A Modern Translation,* Harper Torchbooks (no date).

Blavatsky, H.P., *Isis Unveiled,* Vol. I, Theosophical University Press, 1960.

——, *The Key to Theosophy,* Theosophical Publishing House Ltd., London (no date).

——, *The Secret Doctrine,* Vols. I and II. Theosophical Publishing Company Ltd., London, 1888.

——, *The Voice of the Silence,* Theosophical Publishing Society, 1892.

Bodkin, Maud, *Archetypal Patterns in Poetry,* Oxford University Press, 1974.

Bowlby, J., *Attachment,* The Hogarth Press and the Institute of Psychoanalysis, London, 1970.

Brown, J., *Freud and the Post-Freudians,* Penguin, 1971.

Bulwer-Lytton, *Zanoni,* Steiner Books, 1971.

Burckhardt, Titus, *Alchemy. Science of the Cosmos, Science of the Soul,* Stuart and Watkins, London, 1967.

Calder, I., *John Dee studied as an English Neoplatonist,* Ph.D. dissertation, University of London, 1953.

Carnegie, Dale, *How to Stop Worrying and Start Living,* Cedar Book, World's Work Ltd., 1962.

Chailley, J., *The Magic Flute, Masonic Opera,* Gollancz, 1972.

Coleman, W. E., 'Appendix C' in A. Lillie's *Madame Blavatsky and her Theosophy,* Susan Sonnenschein, London, 1895.

Colquhoun, Ithell, *Sword of Wisdom,* Neville Spearman, 1975.

Coomaraswamy, *On the Traditional Doctrine of Art,* Golgonooza Press, 1977.

Cooper, D., *Psychiatry and Anti-Psychiatry,* Paladin, 1972.

Corbin, H., *Mundus Imaginalis and the Imaginary and the Imaginal,* Golgonooza Press, 1972.

Curling, C., 'Physics and Psyche', *Harvest. Journal for Jungian Studies,* No. 26, 1980.

Dasgupta, S.N., *Hindu Mysticism,* Motilal Barnarsidass, Delhi. First Indian edition, 1976.

Damasio, Antonio, *The Feeling of What Happens. Body, Emotion and the Making of Consciousness,* London, Vintage, 2000.

Dawson, Lorne, 'Anti-modernism, modernism, and post-modernism: struggling with the cultural significance of new religious movements', *Sociology of Religion,* Summer, 1998.

Debus, A., *Robert Fludd and his Philosophicall Key,* Science History Publications, New York, 1979.

——, *The Chemical Philosophy. Paracelsian Science and Medicine in the Sixteenth and Seventeenth Centuries,* Vol. I, 1977 (publisher as above).

Donington, R., *Wagner's 'Ring' and its Symbols,* Faber and Faber, 1976.

Duncan, A.D., *The Fourth Dimension. A Christian View of Occultism,* Mowbrays, 1975.

Durand, G., *On the Disfiguration of the Image of Man in the West,* Golgonooza Press, 1977.

Dutton, E.P., *The Theosophical Movement 1875-1950,* The Cunningham Press, California. Revised edition, 1951.

Eliade, Mircea, *Yoga. Immortality and Freedom,* Bollingen, 1969.

Ellenberger, Henri, *The Discovery of the Unconscious,* US, Basic Books, 1970.

Filmer, P., 'Durkheim, Jung and Symbolism: the Necessity for a Sociology of the Unconscious', *Harvest. Journal for Jungian Studies,* No. 23, 1977.

Fisher, P.F., *Blake and the Druids,* Prentice-Hall Inc., New Jersey, 1966.

Franz, M.-L. von, *Alchemy. An Introduction to the Symbolism and Psychology,* Inner City Books, Toronto, 1980.

Freud, Sigmund, *The Interpretation of Dreams,* J. Strachey (tr.), Penguin, 1977.

——, *The Psychopathology of Everyday Life,* A. Tyson (tr.), Ernest Bean Ltd., second impression, 1972.

Fromm, E., *Psychoanalysis and Religion,* Bantam Books, 1972.

Gellner, Ernest, *The Psychoanalytic Movement. The Cunning of Unreason,* UK, Blackwell, 1985.

Grunbaum, Adolf, *Validation in the Clinical Theory of Psychoanalysis,* Connecticut, International Universities Press, 1993.

Haardt, R. (ed.), *Gnosis. Character and Testimony,* E.J. Brill, Leiden, 1971.

Hadfield, J.A., *Childhood and Adolescence,* Penguin, 1971.

Hammond, S., *We Are All Healers,* Turnstone Books, 1973.

Hargrave, J., *The Life and Soul of Paracelsus,* Victor Gollancz Ltd., London, 1951.

Heindel, Max, *Rosicrucian Philosophy in Questions and Answers,* L.N. Fowler, London, 1910.

Hesse, Hermann, *Steppenwolf,* Penguin, 1972.

——, *The Glass Bead Game,* Penguin Modern Classics, 1973.

Hone, J., *W.B. Yeats,* Pelican, 1971.

Howell, B.P. (ed.), *The Theosophical Society. The First Fifty Years,* The Theosophical Publishing House, 1925.

Huxley, Aldous, *The Perennial Philosophy,* Chatto and Windus, 1946.

Jacobi, Jolande (ed.), *Paracelsus: Selected Writings,* Routledge and Kegan Paul, 1951.

——, *The Psychology of C.G. Jung,* Routledge and Kegan Paul, 7th ed., 1968.

Jennings, H., *The Rosicrucians,* Chatto and Windus, Piccadilly, 1879.

Jinarajadasa, C., *The Golden Book of the Theosophical Society 1875-1925,* Theosophical Publishing House, Adyar, 1925.

Jonas, Hans, *The Gnostic Religion. The Message of the Alien God and the Beginning of Christianity,* Beacon Press, Boston, 1958.

——, 'The Gnostic Syndrome' in *Philosophical Essays. From Ancient Creed to Technological Man,* University of Chicago Press, Chicago, IL, 1974.

Jones, Mervyn, 'The Rosicrucians' and 'Freemasonry' from *Secret Societies,* N. Mackenzie (ed.), Aldus Books, London, 1967.

Judge, W.Q., *The Ocean of Theosophy,* The Theosophical Company, Los Angeles, 1937.

Jung, Carl G., *Aion,* Routledge and Kegan Paul, 2nd ed., 1974.

——, *Analytical Psychology. Its Theory and Practice,* Routledge and Kegan Paul, 1968.

——, *C.G. Jung: Psychological Reflections,* J. Jacobi (ed.), Routledge and Kegan Paul, 2nd ed., 1971.

——, *Civilisation in Transition,* Routledge and Kegan Paul, 1964.

——, (et al.), *Man and his Symbols,* Aldus Books, 1974.

——, *Memories, Dreams, Reflections,* Collins, 1972.

——, *Psychological Types,* Routledge and Kegan Paul, 1971.

——, *Psychology and Religion: West and East,* Routledge and Kegan Paul, 2nd ed., 1973.

——, *Symbols of Transformation,* Routledge and Kegan Paul, 2nd ed., 1970.

——, *The Archetypes and the Collective Unconscious,* Routledge and Kegan Paul, 2nd ed., 1971.

——, *The Development of Personality,* Routledge and Kegan Paul, 1977.

Katz, Steven (ed.), *Mysticism and Philosophical Analysis,* Sheldon Press, London, 1978.

King, Ursula, *Towards a New Mysticism. Teilhard de Chardin and Eastern Religions,* Collins, London, 1980.

Knight, G., *A History of White Magic,* Mowbrays, 1978.

Laing, R.D., *The Divided Self,* Penguin, 1973.

Landau, R., *God is my Adventure,* Unwin Books, New ed., 1964.

Leadbeater, C.W., *A Text-book of Theosophy,* The Theosophist Office, Adyar, 1912.

Lillie, A., *Madame Blavatsky and her Theosophy,* Susan Sonnenschein and Co., London, 1895.

Luce, J.V., *The End of Atlantis. New Light on an Old Legend,* Thames and Hudson, 1969.

Lucie-Smith, E., *Symbolist Art,* Thames and Hudson, 1972.

McIntosh, C., *Eliphas Lévi and the French Occult Revival,* Rider, London, 1972.

———, *The Rosy Cross Unveiled,* Aquarian Press, Wellingborough, 1980.

McKinley, H., *The Transformation of Faust,* Golgonooza Press, 1977.

McNeile, E.R., *From Theosophy to Christian Faith,* Longmans, Green and Co., London, 1919.

Madaule, J., *The Albigensian Crusade,* tr. Barbara Wall, Burns and Oates, London, 1967.

Marty, M., 'The Occult Establishment', *Social Research,* Summer, 1970.

Mehta, Gita, *Karma Cola,* Fontana, Glasgow, 1981.

Meyer, M.W. (ed.), *The Nag Hammadi Library in English,* E.J. Brill, Leiden, 1977.

Nelson, G.K., *Spiritualism and Society,* Routledge and Kegan Paul, 1969.

Nethercot, A., *The Last Four Lives of Annie Besant,* Rupert Hart-Davis, London, 1963.

Neumann, E., *The Origins and History of Consciousness,* Princeton University Press, 1970.

Nicoll, M., *Psychological Commentaries on the Teaching of Gurdjieff and Ouspensky,* Vol. 1, Stuart and Watkins, 1970.

Noll, Richard, *The Jung Cult. Origins of a Charismatic Movement,* Princeton University Press, Princeton, NJ, 1994.

Olcott, H.S., *Old Diary Leaves. The True History of the Theosophical Society,* Putnams, New York, 1895.

———, *Theosophy, Religion and Occult Science,* George Redway, London, 1885.

Otto, Rudolf, *The Idea of the Holy,* Oxford University Press, 1958.

Pagel, Walter, 'Jung's Views on Alchemy', *Isis,* No. 39, 1948.

———, 'Paracelsus and the Neoplatonic and Gnostic Tradition', *Ambix. The Journal for the Study of Alchemy and Early chemistry,* Vol. VIII, No. 3, October 1960.

———, 'The Prime Matter of Paracelsus', *Ambix* (as above), Vol. IX, No. 3, October 1961.

Pagels, E., *The Gnostic Gospels,* Weidenfeld and Nicolson, London, 1980.

Partner, P., *The Murdered Magicians. The Templars and their Myth,* Oxford University Press, 1982.

Perls, F. (et al.), *Gestalt Therapy,* Penguin, 1973.   '

Pirsig, R., *Zen and the Art of Motor Cycle Maintenance,* Corgi Books, 1976.

Post, Laurens van der, *Jung and the Story of our time,* The Hogarth Press, London, 1976.

Progoff, I., *The Death and Rebirth of Psychology,* The Julian Press Inc., New York, 1969.

Raine, Kathleen, *Berkeley, Blake and the New Age,* Golgonooza Press, 1977.

——, *Golgonooza, City of Imagination. Last Studies in William Blake,* Golgonooza Press, Ipswich, 1991.

——, *The Inner Journey of the Poet,* Golgonooza Press, 1976.

——, *What is Man?,* Golgonooza Press, 1980.

——, *Yeats, the Tarot and the Golden Dawn,* The Dolman Press, 1972.

Ransom, J., *A Short History of the Theosophical Society,* Theosophical Publishing House, Adyar, India (no date).

Reilly, R.J., *Romantic Religion,* University of Georgia Press, Athens, 1971.

Roberts, J.M., *The Mythology of the Secret Societies,* Secker and Warburg, 1972.

Rogers, C.R., *Encounter Groups,* Penguin, 1973.

Runciman, S., *The Medieval Manichee. A Study of the Christian Dualist Heresy,* Cambridge University Press, 1947.

Ryan, C.J., *H.P. Blavatsky and the Theosophical Movement,* Point Lorna Publications Inc., San Diego, California, 2nd ed. (no date).

Rycroft, C., *Anxiety and Neurosis,* Penguin, 1971.

—— (et al.), *Psychoanalysis Observed,* Penguin, 1968.

Saint John of the Cross, *The Dark Night of the Soul,* James Clarke, Cambridge, 1973.

Scholem, G., *Kabbalah,* Keter, Jerusalem, 1974.

Sinnett, A.R., *Esoteric Buddhism,* The Theosophical Publishing House Ltd., London, 1972.

Smart, N., 'The Mysteries', *Secret Societies,* N. Mackenzie (ed.), Aldus Books, London, 1967.

Solovyoff, V.S., *A Modern Priestess of Isis,* Longmans, Green and Co., London, 1895.

Stafford-Clark, D., *Psychiatry Today,* Penguin, 1967.

——, *What Freud Really Said,* Penguin, 1971.

Stern, Daniel, *The Interpersonal World of the Infant,* London, Karnac, 1998.

Storr, Antony, *Jung,* Collins, 1973.

——, *Feet of Clay. A Study of Gurus,* London, Harper Collins, 1997.

——, *The Integrity of the Personality,* Penguin, 1970.

Trew, Corona, *Studies in the 'Secret Doctrine',* The Theosophical Publishing House, London, 1972.

Underhill, Evelyn, *Mystics of the Church*, James Clarke & Co., Cambridge, 1975.

Voegelin, Eric, *The Ecumenic Age. Order and History*. Vol Four, Louisiana State University Press, Baton Rouge, 1974.

Wachtmeister, C. Countess (et al.), *Reminiscences of H.P. Blavatsky and the Secret Doctrine*, Theosophical Publishing House, 1st ed., 1976.

Waite, A.E., *The Brotherhood of the Rosy Cross*, William Rider and Son, London, 1924.

Webb, James, *The Harmonious Circle*, Thames and Hudson, London, 1980.

Westrum, R., 'Knowledge about Sea-Serpents' from *On the Margins of Science*, University of Keele, 1979.

Wilson, Colin, *The Occult*, Panther Books, 1979.

——, *The Outsider*, Picador, 1978.

Wilson, H.H., *Vishnu Purana*, Oxford, 1840.',

Winnicott, D.W., *The Child, the Family and the Outside World*, Penguin, 1973.

Yates, F.A., *Giordano Bruno and the Hermetic Tradition*, Routledge, London, 1964.

——, *The Rosicrucian Enlightenment*, Paladin, 1975.

Yeats, W.B., *A Vision*, Collier Books, 1972.

——, *Collected Poems of W.B. Yeats*, 2nd ed., Macmillan, 1973.

Zirkoff, Boris de, *How the 'Secret Doctrine' of H.P. Blavatsky was written*, The Theosophical Publishing House, India, 1977.

Zolla, E., *The Uses of Imagination and the Decline of the West*, Golgonooza Press, 1978.

3. General

Argyle, M., *The Psychology of Interpersonal Behaviour*, Penguin, 1968.

Asch, S., *Social Psychology*, Prentice-Hall Inc., 1962.

Barker, Eileen, 'Apes and Angels. Reductionism, Selection and Emergence in the Study of Man', *Inquiry*, Vol. 19, No. 3.

——, (ed.), *New Religious Movements: A Perspective for Understanding Society*, Edwin Mellen Press, New York, 1982.

Baum, G., 'Does the World Remain Disenchanted?', *Social Research*, Summer 1970.

Baumer, F.L., *Modern European Thought*, Collier Macmillan, London, 1977.

Beckford, J., *A Sociological Study of Jehovah's Witnesses in Britain*, PhD dissertation, 1972 (University of Reading).

Bellah, Robert (ed.), 'New Religious Consciousness and the Crisis in Modernity', *The New Religious Consciousness*, University of California Press, 1976.

——, 'Religious Evolution', in R. Robertson (ed.), *The Sociology of Religion*, Penguin, 1969 (reprinted from the *American Sociological Review*, Vol. 29, 1964).

Berger, P.L. and Luckman, T., *The Social Construction of Reality,* Penguin, 1966.

Berger, P.L., *A Rumour of Angels,* Pelican, 1971.

——, 'The Sociological Study of Sectarianism', *Social Research,* 21, Winter 1954, pp. 467-485.

Berlin, Sir Isaiah, *Against the Current. Essays in the History of Ideas,* Oxford University Press, 1981.

Blalock, H.M., *An Introduction to Social Research,* Prentice-Hall Inc., 1970.

——, *Methodology in Social Research,* McGraw-Hill, 1968.

Bolton, J.D.P., *Glory, Jest and Riddle,* Duckworth, 1973.

Boyce, Mary, 'The Continuity of the Zoroastrian Quest', in W. Foy (ed.) *Man's Religious Quest. A Reader,* Croom-Helm, London, 1978.

Buchanan, D., and Huczynski, A, *Organisational Behaviour. An Introductory Text,* Prentice Hall, Harlow, 2004

Campbell, C., 'An approach to the conceptualisation of irreligion and irreligiosity', *Actes de la 11e Conference Internationale de Sociologie Religieuse,* 1971.

——, 'Clarifying the Cult', *The British Journal of Sociology,* Vol. 28, No. 3, September 1977.

——, 'The Cult, Cultic Milieu and Secularization', *A Sociological Yearbook of Religion in Britain,* 5, 1972.

Clark, E.T., *The Small Sects in America,* Akringdon-Cokesbury Press, New York, 1937.

Cohen, P.S., *Modern Social Theory,* Heinemann, 1978.

Coleman, J.A., 'Church Sect Typology and Organisational Precariousness', *Sociological Analysis,* Vol. 29, No. 2, 1968.

Cupitt, Don, 'The Christ of Christendom', in John Hick (ed.), *The Myth of God Incarnate,* S.C.M. Press, 1977.

Davie, G. 'The Evolution of the Sociology of Religion: Theme and Variations', Michele Dillon (ed.) *Handbook of the Sociology of Religion,* Cambridge University Press, 2003.

Dillistone, F.W., *Traditional Symbols and the Contemporary World,* Epworth Press, London, 1973.

Douglas, M., *Natural Symbols,* Barrie and Jenkins, 1973.

Durkheim, E., *The Elementary Forms of the Religious Life,* Allen and Unwin, 2nd ed., 1976.

Eister, A.W., 'Towards a Radical Critique of Church Sect Typologising', *Journal for the Scientific Study of Religion,* VI, April 1967.

Eysenck, H.J. (ed.), *Readings in Extraversion-Introversion,* Staples Press, 1970.

Festinger, L., *A Theory of Cognitive Dissonance,* Tavistock, 1959.

Ford, J., *Paradigms and Fairy Tales 1.,* Routledge and Kegan Paul, 1975.

Garfinkel, H., *Studies in Ethnomethodology,* Prentice-Hall Inc., New Jersey, 1967.

——, in R. Turner (ed.), *Ethnomethodology,* Penguin Education, 1974.

Goethe, J.W. von, *Faust. Part Two*, tr. Philip Wayne, Middlesex, Penguin, 1959.

——, *The Fairy Tale of the Green Snake and the Beautiful Lily,* Floris Books, 1979.

——, Stephen Spender (ed.), *Great Writings of Goethe,* Meridian, New York, 1977.

Glock, C.Y., 'The Role of Deprivation in the Origin and Evolution of Religious Groups', in R. Lee and M.E. Marty (eds.), *Religion and Social Conflict,* Oxford University Press, 1964.

Glock, C.Y. and Start, Rodney, *Religion and Society in Tension,* Rand McNally and Company, 1965.

Gombrich, R.F., *Precept and Practice,* Oxford University Press, 1971.

Goodrick-Clarke, N. *The Occult Roots of Nazism. The Ariosophists of Austria and Germany 1890-1935*. Aquarian, Wellingborough, 1985.

Hardy, Sir Alister, *Science, Religion and World Unity,* Manchester College, Oxford, 1979.

Hay, David, *Exploring Inner Space,* Pelican, 1982.

Hudson, L., *Contrary Imaginations,* Methuen, 1966.

Jahoda, G., *The Psychology of Superstition,* Penguin, 1971.

James, William, *The Varieties of Religious Experience,* Fontana, 1971.

Johnston, W.M., *The Austrian Mind,* University of California Press, 1972.

Jones, David, *Use and Sign,* Golgonooza Press, 1976.

Kenny, A., *Aquinas,* Oxford University Press, 1980.

Kohler, Joachim (trans. Stewart Spencer), *Richard Wagner. The Last of the Titans*, New Haven, Yale University Press, 2004.

Kuhn, T.S., *The Structure of Scientific Revolutions,* University of Chicago Press, 4th impression, 1965.

——, *The Essential Tension,* The University of Chicago Press, 1977.

Küng, Hans, *Does God Exist?,* Collins, London, 1980.

Lewis, C.S., *Mere Christianity,* Fontana Books, 5th impression, 1958.

——, *The Pilgrim's Regress,* Fount Paperbacks, Glasgow, 1980.

Levy, David, *Realism. An Essay in Interpretation and Social Reality,* Carcanet New Press, Manchester, 1981.

Ling, T., *A History of Religion East and West,* Macmillan, London, 1968.

Lofland, John, *Analysing Social Settings,* Wadsworth Publishing Company Inc., 1971.

Lorenz, K., *On Aggression,* University Paperback, 1972.

Lowe, G., *The Growth of Personality,* Penguin, 1972.

Maccoby, M, Narcissistic Leaders' in *The Harvard Businesss Review*, Jan 2004

Mannheim, K., *Essays in the Sociology of Knowledge,* Routledge and Kegan Paul, London, 1952.

Martin, David, *A General Theory of Secularization,* Blackwell, Oxford, 1978.

——, *Pacifism,* Routledge and Kegan Paul, 1965.

——, 'R.D. Laing' in M. Cranston (ed.), *The New Left*, Bodley Head, 1970.

——, 'Revived Dogma and New Cult', in *Religion and America. Spirituality in a Secular Age,* Beacon, Boston, 1982.

——, *Tracts against the Times,* Lutterworth Press, 1973.

McCall, G.J. and Simmons, J.L., *Issues in Participant Observation,* Addison-Wesley Publishing Company, 1969.

McHugh, P., *Defining the Situation,* The Bobbs-Merrill Co. Inc., 1968.

Müller, Max, *Theosophy or Psychological Religion,* Longmans, Green and Co., London, 1893.

Nachmias, D. and Nachmias, C., *Research Methods in the Social Sciences,* Edward Arnold, 1976.

Needleman, Jacob, *Lost Christianity,* Doubleday, New York, 1981.

Nisbet, R.A., *Tradition and Revolt,* Vintage Books, 1970.

——, *The Sociological Tradition,* Heinemann, 1972.

Parsons, T., 'Introduction', *The Sociology of Religion* (M. Weber), Methuen, 1963.

Peel, J.D.Y., *A Sociological Study of Two Independent Churches among the Yorubas,* London School of Economics Ph.D. dissertation, 1966.

Pope, L., *Millhands and Preachers,* New Haven and Yale University Press, 1942.

Popper, K.R., *Conjectures and Refutations,* Routledge and Kegan Paul, 1976.

Priestly, J.B., *Literature and Western Man,* William Heinemann Ltd., 1960.

Pye, Michael, *The Buddha,* Duckworth, London, 1979.

Radhakrishnan (tr.), *Bhagavadgita,* Blackie, Bombay, 1974.

Rahula, Walpola, *What the Buddha Taught,* Gordon Fraser, 1978.

Ramsey, A.M., *Sacred and Secular,* Longmans, 1965.

Read, Herbert, *Coleridge as Critic,* Faber and Faber, 1949.

Reese, W.C., *Dictionary of Philosophy and Religion,* New Jersey, Humanities Press, 1980.

Rex, J., *Key Problems of Sociological Theory,* Routledge and Kegan Paul, 1976.

Richardson, James T., 'An Oppositional and General Conceptualisation of Cult', *Annual Review of the Social Sciences of Religion,* Vol. 2, 1978.

Robertson, R., *The Sociological Interpretation of Religion,* Blackwell, 1970.

Rookmaaker, H.R., *Modern Art and the Death of a Culture,* Inter-Varsity Press, 1971.

Rosjak, T., *Where the Wasteland Ends,* Faber and Faber, 1973.

Runciman, W.G., *Relative Deprivation and Social Justice,* Routledge and Kegan Paul, 1966.

Russell, B., *The History of Western Philosophy,* Unwin University Books, 2nd ed., 1969.

Sabor, Rudolf, *Richard Wagner. Das Rheingold,* Hong Kong, Phaidon Press, 1997.

Scheler, Max, *Problems of a Sociology of Knowledge,* Routledge, London, 1980.

Simmel, G., 'A Contribution to the Sociology of Religion', *The American Journal of Sociology,* May, 1955.

Smart, N., *The Religious Experience of Mankind,* Collins, Glasgow, 1981.

Smelser, N., *Theory of Collective Behaviour,* Routledge and Kegan Paul, 1962.

Sorokin, P.A., *Contemporary Sociological Theories,* Harper and Row, 1964.

——, *Sociological Theories of Today,* Harper and Row, 1969.

Stevenson, L., *Seven Theories of Human Nature,* Oxford University Press, 1974.

Steyrer, J. 'Charisma and the Archetype of Leadership' in *Organization Studies,* Winter 1998, p.4.

Storr, A., *Human Aggression,* Penguin, 1965.

Suzuki, D.T., *An Introduction to Zen Buddhism,* Rider and Co., 5th impression, 1977.

Tiger, L. and Fox, R., *The Imperial Animal,* Seeker and Warburg, 1971.

Troeltsch, E., *The Social Teaching of the Christian Churches,* Vols. 1 and 2, O. Wyon (tr.), Allen and Unwin, 1931.

Turner, J.H., *The Structure of Sociological Theory,* The Dorsey Press, 1978.

Vernon, M.D., *The Psychology of Perception,* Penguin, 2nd edition, 1971.

Voegelin, Erich, 'The Eclipse of Reality', M. Natanson (ed.), *Phenomenology and Social Reality. Essays in Memory of Alfred Schutz,* The Hague, 1970.

Wallis, R., *Salvation and Protest,* St. Martin's Press, New York, 1979.

——, Article, *The Times Higher Educational Supplement,* pp. 11-12, 6 October 1978.

Warburton, T.R., *A Comparative Study of Minority Religious Groups — with special reference to Holiness and related movements in Britain in the last 50 years,* London School of Economics, PhD dissertation, 1966.

Weber, Max, *From Max Weber,* H.H. Gerth and C. Wright Mills (eds.), Routledge and Kegan Paul, 7th impression, 1970.

——, *The Methodology of the Social Sciences,* (tr.) E.A. Schils and H.A. Finch, The Free Press, New York, 1949.

——, *The Sociology of Religion,* Methuen, 1963.

Whitworth, J., *Religious Utopianism: A Comparative Study of Three Sects,* Oxford University DPhil thesis, 1971.

Wilson, Bryan R., *Magic and the Millennium,* Paladin, 1975.

——, (ed.), *Patterns of Sectarianism,* Heinemann, 1967.

——, *Religious Sects,* World University Library, 1970.

——, 'The New Religions', *Japanese Journal of Religious Studies,* March-June 1979, Vol. 6, Kashiwaya Insatsu Sho, Tokyo.

Wright-Mills, C., *The Sociological Imagination,* Pelican, 1978.

Wuthnow, R., *Experimentation in American Religion,* University of California Press, 1978.

Yinger, J.M., *The Scientific Study of Religion,* Macmillan, 1970.

Zaehner, R.C., *Hinduism,* Oxford University Press, 1966.

——, (ed.), *The Concise Encyclopedia of Living Faiths,* Hutchinson, London, 1977.

Index

Abraham, 125, 135, 199
Adam, 145, 152, 153, 176, 177
Adolphus, Gustavus, 157
Advaita, 179, 180,
'A.E.' (G. W. Russell), 164, 205
Aestheticism, 32, 109, 175
Ahriman, 12, 21, 38, 40, 91, 112,
  115, 116, 119, 123, 133, 135, 136,
  138, 145; Ahrimanic, 105, 106,
  111, 117, 124, 183, 218, 220, 221;
  see also materialism; sculpture at
  Goetheanum, 12
Akkadians, 133; see also Sub-race(s)
Albedo, 156, 176
Alchemy, 150, 151, 155-157, 159,
  162-164, 174-175, 176; Arabs, 155;
  Aristotle, 155; chemical marriage,
  156; Conjunctio, 176; Philosophers'
  Stone, 156
Alexander the Great, 142-143
Alexandria, 146, 155
Ancient Mystical Order Rosae Crucis,
  The (AMORC), 171
Andreae, J.V., 67, 158, 170, 176;
  Chemical Wedding, The, 158-159,
  176
Angelic hierarchies; gnostic origins of,
  154
Anthropos, **13, 147,** 151, 174, 177
Anthroposophia Theomagica (Vaughan),
  13, 159
Anthroposophic News Sheet, 54, 228
Anthroposophical centres, 43, 58, 100-

103; education, 32; state funding of,
  9, 58, 75; see also Anthroposophists
Anthroposophical medicine, 52, 60, 67,
  72, 96-97
Anthroposophical Society, 12, **43, 46-
  47, 49,** 69, 79; 'English Section',
  54; formation, 46; General, 49,
  51, 54, 56, 58, 60, 64, 66, 73, 83;
  German, 56; in Great Britain,
  55, 57, 69, 79; members: Dutch,
  49, 54; English, 49, 54; German-
  speaking, 53, 54: President, 47, 48;
  publications; copyright issues, 47,
  61; reconciliation within, 55
Anthroposophists, 7, 9-10, **11-13,** 16,
  18-21, 28-30, 32, 37-39, 43, 44-49,
  51-58, 60-62, 64-83, 84, 86-87, 89-
  103, 105, 107, **109-116, 118-121,**
  122, 123-124, 129, 139, 145, 163,
  169-170, 172, 175, 179, 182-184,
  189, 205, 207, 214-215, 218-221,
  222-223; American, 66; British/
  English, **54-55,** 164; German, 56, 69;
  Swiss, 56
Anthroposophy (Rudolf Steiner
  movement), 3, 5 7, **9-11,** 13-15, 20,
  28-29, 31-32, 37-39, 43-46, 48-53,
  55-59, 61-62, 65-70, 72-81, 83-86,
  92-94, 96-98, 100-102, 105-106,
  108, 111, 113-119, 125, 135-136,
  141-142, 145-148, 152-153, 162,
  164, 166-171, 173, 175, 179-180,
  182-183, 204-205, 207-209, 211-

216, 218-223; Membership in Africa, 72-73; in Asia-Pacific, 72, 75-76; in Europe, 67-71, 73-75; in North America, 72; in South America, 75; behind the Iron Curtain, 75; at the Goetheanum, 69; dissensions in the movement, 47; movement, 37, 41, 43

Apuleius, Lucius, 9, 198, 199, 200

Aquinas, 125, 136, 215

Archetype, 11, 31, 33, 84, 91-93, 100, 110, 114, 118, 130, 134-137, 147, 152, **175-178**

Architecture, 51, 60, 84, 99, 115

Archons, 147, 151, 200

Argentina, 75

Asceticism, 18, 115, 145, 191

'Asia Pacific Round Table', 75; see also Waldorf Schools; education, Anthroposophical; Anthroposophical centres, education

Astral, 44, 60, 91, 94, 96, 99, 102, 106-110, 114, 117, 128-130, 132, 137, 152, 154-155, 167, 170, 202

Astrology, 92, 94, 114, 135, 144, 155, 164, 170, 178, 200, 218; Gnostic, 94

Astrosophy, 94, 184

Atlantean; see Atlantis, Culture-epoch(s), Epoch(s), Evolution, Race(s), Root-race(s)

Atlantis, 29, 89, **93**, 119, **132-134**, 136, **168**, 170, 184; Antediluvian World, the, 168; Atlantean epoch, 117, **133, 137;** Post-Atlantean epoch, **134, 136-137, 139;** Post-Atlantean culture-epoch, **136;** Oracles, 135; see also Root-race(s), Atlantean

Atoms, 44; astral, 44; etheric, 44; physical, 44

Attraction and Repulsion, 109

Augustine, St, 125, 149-150

Augustus, 200

Aura, cows, 96; human, **81, 89, 91;** First (lowest sheath), 89; Second (middle sheath) 89; Third (highest sheath), 89

Australia, 72, 74, 76, 82, 96, 190, 229

Austria, 16, **22-23, 25, 26,** 32, 33, 37, 65, 69, 76, 123

Austria-Hungary, 25, 37

Azuras, 137

Babylon, 114, 134, 144, 200

Bacon, Francis, 170

Bacon, Roger, 155

Bailey, Alice, 171, 223

'Balde, Felix', 28

'Bapak', 172

Barfield, Owen, 70, 99-100, 172

Bellah, Robert, **190-196,** 198, 199, 200, *239*

Bellow, Saul, 11, 71-72, 172

Bergson, Henri, 124, 125

Berlin, 16, 31, 34-36, 38, 43, 82, 131, 133-134

Besant, Annie, **42-46,** 59, 165-167, 169

Bible, 39, 80, 156, 232

Bio-dynamics (agriculture), 57, 67, 72, 74, 86, **95-96,** 101, 170, 183, 215, 223

Blake, William, 159, 165, 219, 252, 253, 256; Urizen, 159

Blavatsky, Madame, 20, 28-29, **41-44,** 52, 59, 69, 118, **119,** 133, 165, **166, 168-170,** 184, 205; *Isis Unveiled*, 165; *Secret Doctrine*, 44, 166; *Voice of the Silence, The*, 166

Boehme, Jacob, 158

Bohemia, 157, 158

'Book M', 29, 158

Book of Dyzan, 166

Botswana, 76

Brazil, 75

Breuer, Dr, 32

Bruno, Giordano, **154-155, 157,** 169, 170

Buddhi, 167

Buddhism, 18, 41-42, 94, 115, 145, 165-166, 171, 179, 185-186, 191-194, 197, 211, 218; Bodhisattva, 94; Buddha, the, 18, 100, 135, 145, 169, 179; Mahayana, 94, 165, 193; Nirvana, 191, 197; Theravada, 179, 191, 194, 197; Tibetan, 165

Burckhardt, Titus, 156, 175

Burning Desire, 109

Byzantium, 60, 150, 155

Cagliostro, 160

Caithness, Lady (Duchesse de Pomar), 164

Cameo, 152

Campanella, 154, 155, 170; see also Citta del Sole

Camphill, **76-80**, 83; children, 100; 'co-
    workers' (non-disabled adults), 77, 79;
    communities, 5, 57, 69, 72, **76-77**, 83,
    99, 100; rapid expansion, 69; 'curative
    education', 100; custom/ceremony, 78;
    and the Goetheanum, 79; members, 79-
    80, 100; movement, 57, 65, 69, 71, 73,
    76, 99; organisations, 71, 76; School
    of Spiritual Science, **57-58**; 'villagers'
    (disabled), 77; website, *230*
Canada, 71-72, 74, 214; see also North
    America
Cancer, 97, 125
Casaubon, Isaac, 151
Caste, 134, 166
Cathars, 203
Catholicism, 201-203, 209
Celtic esoteric stream; see Esoteric
    tradition, Celtic
'Celtic Twilight' movement, 164
Chains (Theosophical), 93, **167**, **169**
'Change of teeth', 102; see also Seven-
    year growth periods; etheric nature
Chardin, Teilhard de, **173-174**, 178, 179,
    194, 206
Charles, Emperor, 37
Charisma, 5, 16, 36, 38, 39, 48, 49, 50,
    51, 54, 71, 75, 76, 164; routinisation
    of, 38; Cherubim, 123, 124, 246
Chile, 75
China, 101, 146, 155, 191
Christ, 45, 62, 76, 80, 92, 94, 101, 112,
    114, 115, 118-119, 123, 130, 133-
    137, 142, 148, 151, 165, 169, 174,
    179, 184, 201, 220; see also Jesus
Christian Community, 5, 45, 65, 80, **81-
    83**, 97, 135
Christian Science, 41, 119, 179, 223
Christianity, 17, 19, 38, 58, 65, 139,
    142, 145-146, 149-151, 185, 189,
    204, 206, 210; Catholic 142, see also
    Catholicism; conventional, 139, 150,
    154, 222; esoteric, 133; esotericised, 35;
    medieval, 192; mystical, 165; orthodox,
    115, 149, 135, 196; Protestant, 142;
    sectarian, 189; traditional, 42
Christmas Foundation Conference, 1923-
    1924; see Foundation Event, 1924
Christmas Foundation Meeting, 48; see
    also Foundation Event, 1924
Christocentricity, 53

Christology, **135**, 148
Choleric; see Temperament
Citta del Sole, 170; see also Campanella
Class, Anthroposophical organisational
    structure, 26, **60-61**, **63-64**, 83, 87;
    school, 27, 68, 100, **103;** social, 18,
    31-32, 42, 73, 161, 191-193, 204; see
    also 'First Class'
Coleman, W.E., 166
Coleridge, S.T., 91, 120, 159
Collison, H., 46, 48, **54**
Columbia, 75
Comenius, 78, 158
Comte de Gabalis, Le, 170
Confessio Fraternitatis, 158
Contemplation, 17, 142, 150, 191, 197;
    Buddhist, 142; Hindu, 142
contemplative, **18**, 19, 22, 149, 185,
    186, 188-189, 196-197, 199, 202;
    authoritarian, 18; philosophical, 197;
    Upanishadic, 18, 199
Corpus Hermeticum, 151, 154, 203
Cosmogony, 111, 113, 145, 150, 163,
    167, **199-200**, 206, 207; Anthropo-
    sophical, 113; Christian, 111, 150;
    esoteric, 206; gnostic, 199; Mani-
    chean, 207; Schelling's, 163
Cosmology, 10, 11, 17, 169, 173, 176,
    191, 196, 199, 204; Anthroposophical,
    10-11, 16, 29, 35, 86, 89, **93-96**, 101,
    105-107, 123, 183; Christian, 192,
    205; gnostic, 162-163, 173-174, 176,
    202-203, 208; Hermetic, 151; Hindu,
    98; Indian, 113, 167; of 'modernity',
    174; orthodox, 142; Paracelsus', 156;
    Platonic-Pythagorean, 157; Ptolemaic,
    94; scientific, 163; spiritual, 159;
    Theosophical, 165-167, 169; Western
    esoteric, 179; Zoroastrian, 142
Counter-culture, 172, 208, 212, 218
Counter-Reformation, 154, 157-158
Crowley, Aleister, 141, 165, 208
Crystal Heaven, the, 118, 123-124
Cult, 17, 39, 45, 157, 163, 196, 205,
    210; esoteric, 223
Culture-epochs   (Anthroposophical),
    134-137, 169; *Ancient Indian*,
    134; *Eygypto-Chaldean*, 134; *Fifth
    culture-epoch*, 136; *Graeco-Latin*,
    135-136; *Persian*, 134; *Post-
    Atlantean*, 136; *Sixth culture-epoch*,

136; *Seventh culture-epoch*, 137
Darwin/Darwinian/Darwinism, 19, 30, 42, 118, 161, 162, 168, 171, 173-174, 177, 187, 204, 206, 210, 220
Death, 2, 17, 32, 36, 41-42, **47**, 49, 51-52, 54, 56, 58, 62, 65, 67, 81, 86, 89, 106, **108-109**, 130, 132, **136**, 143, 153, 155, **161-163**, 165, 178, 196, 215-216
Dee, John, 157, 159
Demiurge, 148-149
Demon(s) / demonic force(s), 152, 157; Anthroposophical, 21, 145; see also Ahriman, Lucifer
Denmark, 74
Depth-psychology, 162, 171-172, 175, 184, 194, 206-207, 212; see also Psychoanalysis
Deus ex machina, 162, 204
Deutschen Nationalliteratur, 30
Devil, 143; Anthroposophical, 135; see also Demon(s)/demonic force(s); Satan
Die Deutsche Wochenschrift, 32
Differentiation (Anthroposophical), 91, **112-114**, 116-117, 119, 124-129, **130-131**, **133-136**, 167, 173, 176, 208
Discrimination, **64**, 199-200; gender, 81, 221; lack of among Christian gnostics, 149; racial, **55**, 73, **221**; see also racism
Docetism, 201
Dominions, **124, 127**
Down's syndrome, 100
Drama, 44, 60, 72
Dualism, 12, 30, 143-145, 147, 151, 163, 176, 179, 190-193, 195-196, 210-211
Duration, 113, 122, 124-125
Durkheim, Emile, 187

Eabani, 21, 47
Earth, 6, 13, 22, 29, 34, 73, 89, 92-96, 101, 108, 110, 112-114, 119, 121, 122, 126-134, 136, 167, 169, 173, 206, 208, 210, 215, **220**; catastrophe, 132; forces, 97; life/lives, 6, 13, **34-35**, **108**, 113, 215, **220**; Mother, 22; occult meaning, 130
'Earth' (planetary embodiment), 6, **112-114**, **116-117**, 119, 121, **123-125**, 127, **129-133**, **137-139**, 167, 169

Eckstein, Friedrich, 31
Ecuador, 75
Eddy, Mary Baker, 41, 119
Edmunds, Francis, 71
Education, 9, 18-19, 26-27, 32, 36, 55, 57-58, 60, 62-63, 67-68, 71-72, 74-76, 98, 100-103, 109, 111, 127, 216-217, 223; Anthroposophical, 32, 60, 100, 102; adult, 20, 22, 26, 71-72, 74, 76-77, 101, 176, 214; curative, 32, 58, 98, 100; Waldorf, 9, 55, 58, 67-68, 71-72, 75-76, 83, 101-103, 223; see also Anthroposophical centres
Edward VII (King), 43, 46, 53, 120
Ego, 56; group, 130; see also Jung
Egypt, 13, 21, 41, 111, 118, 134, **143-147**, **150-152**, **154-155**, 160, 165, 167, 171, 173-174, 176, 182, 199, 201, 203-204, 207-208, 211
Egypto-Chaldean culture-epoch, 134
Einstein, Albert, 172, 206
Elemental beings/spirits, 90, **91**, **93**, **96**, 171; see also Gnomes, Goblins, Salamanders, Spiritual Beings, Sylphs, Undines
Elements, Four, **92**, 93 155; Fire, 92, 155; Earth, 92-93, 155
Elements, Seven (Theosophical), **167-168**
Eliot , T.S., 35, 165
Elizabeth (daughter of James I), 157
Elizabeth I, 157
Emerald Tablet, 156
Emerson, Ralph Waldo, 71, 174
Emerson College, 71, **101**; see also Anthroposophical centres, Education
Emmichoven, Dr Zeylmans van, 54, 57, 73
Encausse, Gerard (Papus), 164
England, 44, 48, 53, 59, 71, 76, 95, 154, 157-158, 162, 184; see also Great Britain
England, Church of, 184
English-speaking, 11, 41-43, 59, 65, 69, 73, 105, 119, 164, 193, 214
Enlightenment, the, **162**, **187-188**
Epoch(s), 29, 95, 112, 117, 119, 127-128, **130-134**, 136-139, 147, 169; Atlantis/Atlantean, 29, 117, 119, **132-133**; Hyperborian, 29, 130; Jupiter, 138; Lemurian, 29, 130-131; Polarian, 130; Post-Atlantean, **134**, 136-137, 139

Erzoberlenker, 81

'E.S.', see Esoteric Section , Theosophical

Eschatology, 112, 145, 150, 200, 210

Esoteric Section , Theosophical, 44, 165

Esoteric tradition, 203; 'Celtic', 39; 'Hibernian', 39; 'Nordic', 39; Rosicrucian, 39; Western, 6, 9, 11, **140**, 141, 161, 203, 220; esotericism(s), 42, 45-46, 53, 142, 158, 174, 185, 189, 205, 208; Anglo-Saxon, 42; Anthroposophical, 175; contemporary, 208; English-speaking, 43; German-speaking, 46; gnostic, 208; modern, 150; 19th Century, 206; Western. 29, 59, 83, 142, 159, 162, 175, 183

Etheric body, 91, **108-110**, 114, **127**, 129

Etheric nature, 80, 102, **106-107**

Ethic of individuality, 37

Ethical individualism, 47

Eunicke, Anna, **31**, **33-36**

Europe, 29, 37, 41, 42, 46, 49, 51, 55, 56, 57, 58, 64, 66, 73, 76, 82, 84, 103, 134, 136, 142, 146, 154, 158, 171, 193, 204, 212; middle, 37, 47

Eurythmy, 47, 57, 60, 63, 72, 75, 98-99, 103, 183, 214, 219; Jerusalem Academy, 75

Eve, 145, 176, 177, 199

Evolution, 12, 18, 21, 30, 38, 83, 88, 93-94, 115, 117-118, 122-127, 129, 132-133, 135-136, 138, 145, 150, 162, 167-169, 173-174, 177-178, 194, 216, 220-221; Atlantean, 133; Bellah's, 194; Darwinian, 173-174, 177, 220; spiritual, 129, 145, 150, 162, 168-169, 173, 177; Anthroposophical (Steiner's), 132, 135-136, 138, 167, 216; of consciousness, 174, 178; of the cosmos, 38; of the solar system, 133

'Fall' (from spirit into matter); Anthroposophical, **29-30**, 100, 111, 114, **112-118**, **129-130**; see also 'hardening'; Gnostic. **144-147**

Fama Fraternitatis, 158

Fancy/fantasy, 12, 38, 40, 91, 123, 159; see also Lucifer

Father, the, **147-148**, 201

Feet of Clay (Storr), 21

Festival of the Roofing of the Dome, 46

Ficino, Marsiglio, 150-151, 154, 156

Finland, 74, 101

First World War, **37**, 45-46, 52-53, 67, 84, 103, 134, 142, 162, 165, **171**, 175, **204-206**, 209, 212

First Class, **60-61**, 63-64, 83, 87; see also School of Spiritual Science

Flowing Susceptibility, 109

Fludd, Robert, 159, 170

Foundation Stone, laying of, 37, **48**, **51**, 53, 56, 211

Foundation event, 1924 (1923-1924 Christmas Foundation Conference), 38, 66

Fox, Kate and Margaret, 41

France, **82**, **101**, 103, **154**, 160, **162**, 164, 171

Frederick (Elector Palatine), 157-159

Frederick-William II, 160

Free will, 18, 101, 138, 153, 220

Freemasonry, **160**, 164; Gold-und-Rosenkreuz, 160, 164

Freud, Sigmund, **23**, 32, 50, 119, 174-175

Gandhi, 55

General Anthroposophical Society, 49, 51, 54, 56, 58, 60, 64, 66, 73, 83

Genesis, 113, 161-162, 199, 210

Geometry (including projective), 25, 93

Germany, 11, 35, **42-44**, 46, 48, 52, 53, 55-56, 67, 69, 74, **76**, **81-83**, 96, 101, 154, 160, 164, 222; Blavatsky, Madame in, 43; East, 82; post-Bismark, 35; post-war, 48, 53, 67; spread of esotericism in, 42; West, 53, 57, 64, **68**, 82, 99, 222; Wilhelminian, 37, **43**, 53; youth movement, 67

Glock, C. Y., **189**

Gnome(s), 90, **91**, 93, **96**, 171; see also Elemental beings

Gnosis, 6-7, 9, 13, **141-150**, **165**, 167, **171-174**, 176, 177, 182, 196, **199-204**, 208-209, 212; achieved via magic, 144; Anthroposophical, 231; availability of, 203; Christian, **145-146**, 150, 173, 196, 202; decline of, 212; dualism in, 143; Egyptian, 13; Manichean, 208; Modernity and, **161**, **163**, 172, **173**, **212**; missing in Theosophy, 165; return of interest in, 212; synthetic, 203; Syrian-Egyptian, 111, 118, **144-146**, 150, 152, 165, 167, 173-174, 176, **182**, 208; Valentinian, 172; in the West, 9, 140, 212; Western, **141-142**, 171-172, 177, 203, **212**

Gnosticism, 6, 11, 20, 41, 111-112, 114-115, **141-147**, 149-152, 159, 162-163, 170, 172-174, 176, 178, 180, **182-183**, 187-189, 195, 198, **201-204**, 206-**207-209**, 211-212; Alexandrian, 155; analogies with, 159, 172-173; ascetism in, 115; and Catholic orthodoxy, **198;** Christian, 77, 149; Christian suppression of, 201, 203; cosmogony, 199; cosmology, 162-163, 172-174, 176, 184, 203; dualism in, 147, 151; Hegelian philosophy and, 172; individual-gnosticism, **207-209**, 211; Jewish, 152; Jung's fascination with, 162, 174, 176; Manichean, 207; and modern scientific cosmology, 163; modern/modernity containing, 173, 179, 197-198, 201, **204**, 207; and mysticism, 188-189, **198**, **204, 208-209;** neo-gnosticism, **11**, 77, 202, 206; Pagan, 149; perceived potential dangers of, 172; Residual, 146; resemblances in Gurjieff, 171; resemblances in Wagner, **163**, 236, resemblances in Yeats, 164; revival of, **162-163**, 165, 179, 197-198; syntheses of, 141-143, **150, 152,** 154-155, 157, 162, 168, 171-172, **202-205;** revival, Renaissance, **150**, 152, 168, 202; revival, 19th century, 204; revival, Steiner's, 131; Syrian-Egyptian, 146-147, 152, 154, 171, 204; texts of, 202; thought systems/thinkers, 141, 143, 161, 182-183, 197, **199-200**, 202; transcendence of, 173; Valentinian, **114-115;** Western, 7, 11, 20, 112, 150, 163, 170, 177, 179, **195, 197-198, 204-205**, 212; see also Theosophy, Anthroposophy

Goblins, 93

Goethe, J. W. von, 11, 12, 25, 28, 30, **33-34**, 36, 67, **86**, 92, 99, 118, **122**, 136, 141, 159, 169, 210; *Fairy Tale*, 36, 159; *Faust*, 12, 67, 86, 131

Goetheanum(s), 5, **11-13**, 32, 37, 38,

40, 46, 48, 52, 54, 56, **57**, 58, **63-65**, **69**, 71, 79, **81-84**, 90, 94, 99, 101, 170; architecture/design, 32, 37, **84**, 99; connection with Camphill, 79; as factional focus, 54, 56-58, 64, 69; new, 32, 48, 84, 99; financing, 56; foundation stone, laying of, 37-38, 48; original, 32, 37, 40, **83**, 99; building of, 37, **46**, 84; burning of, 32, 37, 48, 52, 83; karma of, 48, 83; Rosicrucian antecedents, 170; serpent, 1, 18, 29, 79, 90, 94, 101, 105, 107, 112, 116, 130, **220;** ring at centre (symbolism of), **90, 94**; site of, 46, 52; fire, 37

Golden Dawn, see Hermetic Order of the Golden Dawn, The

Golgotha, 51, 135, 170; presence of Rosenkreuz, 170; see also Mythology, Steiner's, Rosenkreuz

Gospel(s), 39; St John, 98; St Luke, 135; St Matthew, 135

Grazie, Marie delle, 32

Great Britain, 41, 43, 46, 48, 55-56, 59, 64, **69-71**, 73-74, 76, 78-79, 81-82, 83, 74, 97, 103, 159, 160, 165, 186, 214, 218, 222; Anthroposophical Society in, 55, 57, 69, 79, 224; contemporary, 158; Edwardian, 43, 53

Greece, 45

Guaita, Stanislas de, 164

Gurdjieff, G. I., 20, 171-172, 207-208; 'Awakener of Conscience', 172

Haeckel, Ernst, 30, 34, 118, 131

Hartman, Edouard von, 34

Hartman, Franz, 44

Harwood, Cecil, 55, 57, 70

Hebrew, 17, 135, 145, 170, 199

Hegel, G.W.F., 44, 159, 163, 169, 172, 210

Hermes, 134, 141, 150-151, 156, 203

Hermetic Order of the Golden Dawn, the, 46, 54, **164-165**, 205

Hermeticism, 150, 154, 157, 159, 203

Hess, Rudolf, 56

Hesse, Hermann, 37, 68, 179; *Siddhartha*, 179

Hinduism, 17, 41-42, 113, 115, 118, 125-126, 165-167, 179, 191, 197, 199, 210; Atman, 177, 191, 197; Brahman, 18, 45, 177, 191; Kamaloca, 109

Hitler, Adolf, 53, 55, 172
Holland, 171
Hoyos-Sprinzenstein, Count von, 22
Huebbe-Schleiden, Dr, 42-44
Human Stage, 125, 127, 129, 139, 168
Hungary, 22, **26**, 75; see also Austria-
    Hungary
Huxley, Aldous, 171, 174, 179, **185**
Hyperborean epoch, 130

'I', the, **27**, 91, 102, **106-110**, **114-115**,
    117-118, 124, 130, 132, 134-138
Idealism, 102, 116, 243; German, 44,
    159, 169; philosophical, 18, 30, 179
Imagination (Anthroposophical), **89-92**,
    96, 101, 105, 107, 137, 197
Incarnation, 38, 66, 89, 90, 100, 108,
    109, 110, 154, 174, 183
India, 18, 42, 43, 59, **75**, 82, 143, 161,
    164-166, **179**, 180, 191
Individualism/individualist, 14, 18,
    30, 47, 56, 63, 88, 116, 136, 161,
    168, 200, 202, 204-205, **211;**
    contemporary, **204;** development of,
    30; egocentric, 18; epistemological,
    63, 202; 'esoteric', 204; ethical, 47,
    88; ideals, 161; and materialism,
    204, 220; of modernity, 168; growth/
    rise of, 116, 136; self-centred, 14;
    Steiner's opposition to, 30
Individuality, 100, 208; conscious,
    96, 138, 201; across repeated earth
    lives, 220; ethic of, 37; human, 102;
    multiplicity and, 153; spiritual, 86,
    101, 113, **116**, **118**, 146, 150, 168-169,
    183, 197, 204-205, 212; ascending,
    116, 138, 169, 204; development/
    evolution of/towards, 116, 118, 138,
    146, 150, 197, 201, 204; realisation
    of, 183; transcendent, 106
Individual-esotericism, 61
Individual-mysticism, 207, 210
Industrialisation, 41, 42
Inheritance, 54, 72
Inklings, 70, 99, 172
Inspiration (Anthroposophical), 89, **91-
    92**, 98, 101, 105, **107**, 120, 138, 197
'Institute for the Harmonious Develop-
    ment of Man', 171
Intellectual soul, 106-108, 135
Intuition, (Anthroposophical), 89, **91-**

92, 101, 105, **107**, 120, 183, 186,
    197
Intuition, 18-19, 30, 35, 38, 84, 88,
    91, 129, 162, 171; and dualism, 30;
    clear ideas from, 19; development
    of Steiner's, 18; inerrancy of, 38;
    sharing of Steiner's, 19; Steiner's
    expression of, 35; Steiner's insight
    into materialism, 30; Steiner as the
    sole achiever, 91
Intuitive, 16, 27, 52, 88, 123, 142, 144,
    146, 149, 153, 175, 184, 200, **205**
Iran, 142, 143, 144, 146, 200; see also
    Persians
Ireland (and Eire), 76, 164
Irenaeus, Bishop, 147, 149, 203
Iron Curtain, 57, 75
Isis, 142, 198
Islam, 17, 19, 111, 115, 185, 192, **195-
    197**, 210; Allah, 17; Mecca, 17;
    Muhammed, 17
Italy, **74**, 82, 152, 154

Jahweh, 17, 48
Jainism, 18; Mahāvira, 18
James, William, 124-125, 217
Japan, 75-76, 82
Jerusalem Eurythmy Academy, see
    Eurythmy, Jerusalem Academy
Jesus, 17, 22, **135**, 145, 148, 161,
    169; Besant's, 169; historical, 148;
    'Nathan', 135; 'Solomon', 135; see
    also Christ
Jesus People, 210
John the Baptist, 135, 220
Jonas, Hans, 143-144, 172, 182, 189, 197
Judaeo-Christian(-Islamic); Abrahamic,
    210; eschatology, 210; dualism, 210;
    orthodoxy, 143, 197; prophets, 196;
    tradition, 111
Judaism, 17, 19, 111, 115, 143, 152, 185,
    192, 196, 201, 210; Jews, 48, 152
Jung, C.G., 23, 162, 171, **173-178**;
    Actualised archetype, 177; Anima,
    176; Animus, 176; Ego, 175, 178,
    207; Synchronicity, **177**
Jupiter, 92, 130, 155

Kabbalah, 152-**154**, 163, 235-236, 256;
    integration with Christian doctrine,
    154; Jewish, 152; Lurianic, 153; pagan
    sources of, 154; 'practical', 154

Kabbalism, 18, 29, **150**, **152-155**, 157, 159, 164, **169-170**, 185-186, 196, 204, 208-209; basis of, 204; Christian, 154, 159; Hermetic-Kabbalism, **154-155**, 157; and alchemy, 155; Hermetic-Kabbalism-alchemy (see also 'Rosicrucianism'), 157-158, 160; Jewish, 152, 159, 185-186; Lurianic, 159, 164; popularised, 208-209; similarities to Anthroposophy, 169-170

Kafka, 172

Kali Yuga/Dark Age, 113, 134, 136

`Kama rupa`, 167

Kant, Immanuel, 16, 24, 27, 88, 113, **178**

Karma, 6, 12-13, 23, 29, 35, 38, 47-48, 77, 89, 94, 100, 105, 107-113, 115, 117-119, 121, 124, 132, 134-137, 165-166, 168169, 179, 184, 187, 189, 215; of Ahriman, 112, 115; in Anthroposophy, 29, 38, 47-48, 77, 94, 105, 108, 110; effects of the zodiac on, 94; Indian ideas of, 118, 168; and justice, 220; rebirth/reincarnation/repeated earth lives, 35, 47, 100, 108-109, 117-118, 136-137, 179, 215; Steiner's, 23, 35, 38, 47; in Theosophy, 165, 169

Katz, Steven, **186**

Kogutski, Felix, 28

Konig, Dr, 57, 76-78

Krishnamurti, Jiddu, 45, 53, 180; see also World Teacher

Latin, 144, 153, 170; Graeco-Latin culture-epoch, 135-136; see also Rome

Leadbeater, Revd Charles, **45**

Leader(s), 19, 22, 36, 38-39, 51-52, 71, 79; Anthroposophical, 46, 50; Charismatic, 16, 36, 39, 164; English, 54; European, 49; Larger than life, 50; prototypical, 50; Camphill, 57, 71, 77, 79; of cults, unscrupulous, 39; spiritual, 36, 39, 118, 164; Theosophy, German style, 36, 42, 44; Yarker Masonic Lodges, 44

Leadership; style (Steiner's), 50; Charismatic, **5**, 38, 39, **43**, 50-51, 54; Theosophy, German Section, 43; servant, 51; social psychological point of view on, 38-39, 50; theory, 38-39

Lebanon, 76, 101

Lectorium Rosicrucianum, 171

Lemuria, 29, 55, 119, 122, **130-133**, 168; 'continent', 130-133, 168; inhabitants, 55, 132; Lemurian epoch, **29**, 119, 122, 130-131; see also epochs

Lemures, 131; see also Lemuria, inhabitants

Lenkers, 81

Lessing, Gothold, 25, 29, 159

Levy, 10, 79, 172

Levy-Bruhl, 79

Levy, David, 10, 172

Lewis, C. S, 16, 70, 172

Liberalism, 37, 194, 198

Life-spirit, 91, 107, 117, 138

Lodges, Theosophical, 42-43, 45, 59; Masonic, 44, 164

Love, 31, 63, 68, 80, 88-89, 100, 124, 135-138, 154, **163**, **174**, 185; Christian ethic of, 154; Cosmos of, 135-137; Love (Anthroposophical), 124, 137-138; *personhood*, as identical with, 174; transforming power of (Christ Impulse), 80

Lower Sophia, **148-149**

Lucifer, 12, 21, 38, 40, 44, 91, 112, 115-116, 119, 123-124, 129-130, 132-133, **135-136**, 138, 218, 221; Anthroposophical macrocosmic demon/devil, 12, 21, **135-136**; conflict (with Ahriman), 112, 124; effects on Earth evolution, 116, 130, **132-133**, 138; and fourth epoch, 119; as 'Lesser Guardian of the Threshold', 91; intervention of, 119, 130; as karma of Ahriman, 112; as passion and fantasy, 12, 38, 40, 221; power of, **132**; power, heroin as, 218; rebellion of, 112, 115-116, 123, 129, 133; spirits in Moon phase, 116; Steiner's transcendence of, 91; see also Fancy/fantasy, Demon(s), Devil

Luria, Isaac, 152

Luther/Lutheran Church, 45, 74, 80, 156

'M', **28-29**, 158

Maccoby, M., **50**

Macrocosm, 6, 18, 21, 30, 90, 92, 94, 98, 102, 108, **110-118**, 122-123, 126-128, **131**, 138, **146-147**, 151-153,

155-157, 170, 173-174, **177**, 200, 202-203, 205-208, 221

Macrocosmic man, 30, **125-127**, 147, 152

Madagascar, 131

Magazin fur Literatur, 35

Magi(/magus), 150, 152, 154-155, 170; see also Magicians; Magic, practitioners of

Magic, 16, 38, 45, 52-53, 62, 95-96, 120, 144, **150-155**, 159, 164-165, 170, 173, 177 202; and alchemy, **155, 164**; Anthroposophical, 95-96, **170**; 'astral', 154-155, 170, 202; black, 52-53; in biodynamics, 95, 170; Christian, 155-157; Christian opposition to, 154; gnostic, 114, 144, 147, 150, 152, 155, 197, 202; kabbalistic views on, 153-154; natural, 95-96, **151**, 154; Rennaissance, **150-151, 203**; ritual, 95-96; for personal ends, 153; practitioners, 151, 154-155, 165, 170; in Shakespeare, 157; sympathetic, 151; sexual, **38, 45, 62**; Theosophical renunciation of, **164-165**, 170; white, 53

Magician(s), 16, 151, 155, 203; see also Magi; Magic, practitioners of

'Manas', 167

Manicheism, 20, **144-146**, 150

Manipulationism, **211**

Manu, 134

Manvantara, 113, 121, 128-129, 167

Marie Steiner, see Steiner, Marie; see also Sievers, Marie von

Mars, 92, 120, 130, 132, 155, 167; Oracle, 133

Martin, 10, 211

Marxism, 32, 36-37, **172-173**, 194, **210**, 218; in Anthroposophy converts, 218

'Masters', Tibetan, 28, 41, 44, 166, 171

Materialism, 12, 14, 18, **30**, 32, 34, 38, 57, 65, 72, 76, 87, 116, 118, 131, 159, 161-2, 175, 178, 193, 195, **203-204**, 206, 209-210, 212, 217, 220; embodied as Ahriman, 38, 40; see also Ahriman; atheistic, 41; Darwinian, 204; dichotomy with idealism, 116; experiential, 210; and individualism, 14, 18; modern, 28; 19th Century, 212; philosophical, 19, 35, 129, 131, 172, 204, 206; scientific, 27, 34, 42,

161-162, 206, 209, **212**

Mathematics, 27-28, 60, 92, 170, 212

Mathers, S.L. MacGregor, 164-165

Matter; as an offshoot of Spirit, 30; as fallen from spirit, 29; hardened, 112, 118; hardened from spirit, 18; over-hardened, 18, 115

Mayreder, Rosa, 32

Medicine, 22, 31-32, 57, 73, 75, 77, 119, 155-156, 159, 175

Medicis, 154-155

Medium (spirit), 41, 166, 216

Mendel, Gregor, 177, 241

Mephistopheles, 12, 131, 133

Mercury, 94, 155-156, 167; planet, 94, 155, 167; element 155-156

Mesmer, Anton, 162

Mesmerism, 162, 204

Mesopotamia, 145, 155, 199

Messiah, 152; of the Second Coming, 172; see also 'Awakener of Conscience', 'Bapak'

Mexico, 75

Michael Age, the, 170

Microcosm, 18, 21, 30, 40, 98, 101, 113-115, 146, 150-151, 153, 156, 167, 170, 173, 177, 203, 220

Mights, **93, 124**

Milton, John, 141, 165, 175

Mind (Anthroposophical), **147-148**

Mirandola, Pico della, 152-153

Mithras, 142

Mitteilungen, 46

Modernity, 6-7, 11, 35, **161-163**, 168, **172-174**, **178-180**, 187, 189-190, **193-195**, 201, 203-204, 207, 209-210, 212, 223

Moltke, General von, 46

Monads, 167-169

Mongols, 133

Moon, 6, 17, 32, 60, 79, 89, 94, 112-114, 116-117, 120, 123-124, 128-130, 132, 137-138, 155-156, 164-165, 167, 169, 184, 210; Angels' influence, 94; 'irreclaimable', 113, 138; literal lunar body, 112-113, 132, 137-138; magical/alchemical correspondence with, 155-156; 'moon-sphere', forces of, 89; phase(s) of, 79, 164; planting by, 79; planetary embodiment, 89, **112-114**, 116-7, 120, 123-124, **128-130**, 137-

8, 167, 169, 184; and psychoanalysis, 89; as spiritual water, 112
Moon, Rev'd, 17
Moonies, 210; see also Unification Church, Moon, Rev'd
Mormonism, 17
Moses, 135, 152
Muir, Edwin, 164, 169
Munich, 43, 44, 67
Music, 60, 77, 84, 98, 99, 100, 115; Anthroposophical hierarchy of the arts, 99; as crystallised spirit, 115; disturbed children, 77; in the 'First Class', 60; in gnosticism, 143; intervals and 'Spirit', 98; as 'Spirit', 77, 98; Pythagorean, 109; and romanticism, 163; of the spheres, 109; as therapy, 100
Mystery religions, 142, 198
Mysticism(s), 7, 65, 88, 96, 142, **174**, 180, 185-186, 188, 189, 198, 202, 204, **206-212**; Christian, **202**; cross-cultural, 186; distinction from gnosticism/esotericism, 142, **185**, 208; immanent, 212; Eastern, 180, 211; individual-, **207-211**; modern, 206, 209-210, 212; prevalence of, 209; Western, 212
Myth(s)/mythology, 21, 29, 49, 103, 105, 123, 125, 131, 188, **190**, 196, 198, 200, 204, 208, 220; Atlantis, 168; Climate of thought, 150; cosmogonic, 200, 208; Depth-psychology, 175; flying saucer, 178; Gnostic, 131-132, 151, 204; Manichean, 145; modern, 175, 178; Plato's myth of Er, 220; Roman, 131; Steiner's, 29, **170**; Rosenkreuz, **170**; Syrian-Egyptian, 147, 151; Valentinian, 147; world of, **190**
Mythical being(s), 190-191

Nachlass faction, 56, 58
Nag Hammadi, 142
Narcissism, 21, 50
Nature of man, 6, 32, 38, 108, 113, 168
Natures of Man, the, 107
Nazis, 53, 55, 56, 68, 70
Nazi(s)/Nazism, 11, 55, 56, 68, 70, 172, 173; Anthroposophist's admiration for, 55; conflict with Anthroposophy, 53; and Anthroposophical Education, 53; Anthroposophy tained/overshad-

owed by, 55; ideology, 53; prohibition of Waldorf Education, 68; Steiner, Rudolf, rejection of, 56
Neoplatonism, 7, 19, 149-150, 152, 198, 209
Netherlands, 46, 68, 82, 103; Anthroposophy, 73; conversion, 222; membership, current era, 74; Aquarius, 74; Camphill Communities, 77; priests in, 82; Netherlands Pedagogical Institute (N.P.I.), 73
New physics, the, 42, 172, 178, 206, 212
New religious movements, **210-211**
New Thought, **179**
New Year's Eve, 37, 48, 83; fire, original Goetheanum, 37, 48, 83; remembrance, old Goetheanum, 83
New York, **41**, **72**, 168, 171, **179**
New Zealand, 59, 72, 82, 101, 214
Newton, Isaac, 125, 159
Nicoll, Maurice, 171, 207; *Psychological Commentaries*, 171, 207; see also Ouspensky, P.D.
Nietzsche, Friedrich, **34**, 36, 43
Nigredo, 156, 176
North America, 17, 29, 42, 49, 56, 65, 75, 76, 82, 134, 171, 212; see also USA, Canada
Norway, 74, 77, 101
Nutrition, 97, 120, 125

Oberlenkers, 81
Occult chemistry; see Chemistry, Occult, Theosophy
Occultism, 11, 53, 159, 164, 172, 204, 205
Occultist, 19, 28, 117, 174; Blavatsky, Madame, 20; Gurdjieff, 20
One, the, 151-152
Oracles, 133, 135
Order of the Silver Star, 165
Order of the Star in the East, 45
Ordo Templi Orientis (O.T.O.), 44-45, 164; Steiner, Rudolph as leader, 164
Orthodoxy, 202, 209, 212; Christian, 20, 114, 149, 189; Catholic, 7, 81, 198, 201; Protestant, 204, 210; cosmological, 202-203, 212; Darwinian, 20; Judaeo-Christian, 143; Judaeo-Christian-Islamic, 197; scientific materialism, 209

Otto, Rudolf, 185, 202
Ouspensky, P. D., 171, 207, 218

Pacifism, 70, 221
Paganism, 56, 141, 149, **154**, 164, 208;
    esoteric, Himmler's, 56; gnostic,
    149, **154;** of Hermetic/Kabbalastic;
    magical sources, **154**, 164; of
    magical practitioners, 154; neo-pagan
    practises/Wicca, 208; recent revival
    of, 141; roots of 'Celtic Twilight'
    movement, 164; seen in Hermetic
    Kabbalistic fusion, 154; see also
    Neo-pagan, Wicca, Witchcraft
Pagel, Walter, 176
Painting (Anthroposophical), 60, 97, **99**
Palatinate, 157-159
Paracelsus, 117, 155-157, 159
Path of Knowledge, the, 6, **87**, 91, 101-
    2, **107**, 170
Péladin, Joséphin, 164, 171
Percept(s), 20, **87-8**, 185
Persians, **134**, 144; see also Iran
Personality, endowment of the Sun with,
    120, Human, survival after death, 41;
    schizotypal, 22
Philology, 99-100
Philosopher(s), 23, 185; professional, 185
Philosophy(/Philosophical), 13, **16**,
    18, 19, 24, 27, 35, **87**, 92, 131,
    172, 179, 197, 198, 204, 206;
    Anthroposophical, 60, **87**, 113;
    as Anthroposophical major, 217;
    contemplation/contemplatives, **197**;
    elements in Upanisadic Hinduism &
    Buddhism, 197; enactment of Orphic
    rite, 198; existential, 172; Hegel's,
    172; Huxley's, 174, 179, 185;
    Idealist, 18, 30, 179, 204; magical
    ('Christian'), 156; materialism, 19,
    35, 129, 131, 172, 204, 206; and
    subjectivism in, 206; occult, 154;
    professional, 60; Steiner's wrestling/
    interactions with, 13, 16, 19-20, 24,
    27, 87-88, 170; Utopian, 172
Physical world, 27, 32, 40, 106, 109,
    134, 135
Pimander (or Poimandres), 147, 151
Planetary embodiment(s), 6, **112**, **123**;
    Earth, **112-114**, **116-117**, 119, 121,
    123-125, 127, **129-130**, 131-134, **137-**

139, 169; Jupiter, 6, 112, 117, 120,
    123, 131, 132, 134, **137-138**; Saturn,
    112-114, 116-7, **122-128**, 130, **137-**
    138, 169, 184; Goetheanum, 130;
    Venus, 112, 117, 123, **138**; Vulcan,
    112, 117, 123, 136, **138-139**
Planets; Anthroposophical Spiritual Hier-
    archy, 93; influences on minerals,
    92; relation to vowels, 98; see also
    Eurythmy
Plants, Anthroposophical Spiritual Hier-
    archy, 93
Plato, 18, 33, 132, 141, 144, 161, 165,
    168, 220; Myth of Er, 220, *Republic*,
    52-53, 76, 170
Platonic Academy, 153
Pleroma, 118, 124, 132, 146-149, 174,
    177, 179, 201, 205; Gnostic, 118,
    124, 177, 179
Plotinus, 149, 151, 161
'Pneumatics' (Gnostic category), 149,
    153
Pomar, Duchesse de, see Caithness,
    Lady
Poimandres; see Pimander
Poland, 41, 75
Polarian epoch, 130; see also Epochs
Positivism, 113, 188
Post-Atlantean epoch, 134, 136-137,
    139
Post-war, 48, 49, 53, 57, 67, 71, 212
Powers, **93**, **124**
Pralaya, 113, 116, 121, 126-127, 129,
    137-138
Previous life, 47, 100
Priestley, J.B., 171
Primal Man, 145
Primal Semites, 133; see also Sub-
    race(s)
Primal Turanians, 133; see also Sub-
    race(s)
Primary realitites, 106
Principalities, **93-94**, 124, 127
Prokofieff, Sergei, **66**, 75
Proletariat/ proletarian, 16, 26
Prophecy/Prophet(s)/prophetic religion,
    17
Protestant/ism, 41, 54, 58, 97, 142, 151,
    154-155, 157-158, 161-162, 184,
    189-190, 192-195, **197**, 201, **203-**
    206, 209-210, 222

Pseudo-Dionysian/Pseudo-Dionysius, **124**, 154

Psyche, 148, 163, **175-178**, 218

Psychedelic drugs, 218

Psychic(s), 125, 149, 153, 216; Gnostic category, **149**, 153; Intra-psychic integration, 123; Pan-psychic, 125; undeveloped psychic state, cancer as, 97

Psychoanalysis, 31, 89, 162

Psychodynamic perspectives, 39

Psychological contract, 47, 50

Psychological theories/perspectives, 50, 123, 129, 169, 173, 175; Freudian, 23, 119; gnostic, 182; Jungian, 23, 52, 119, **175-178**, 207; see also Jung

Psychologism, 20, 88, 122

Pyrenees, 70, 146, 152, 203

Pythagoras, 98, 198

Quakers, 54, 70

Race(s), 55, 73, **168-169**; Atlantis/ Atlantean (fourth), 133, 168; current (fifth), 168; group souls, 221; see also Racism; Lemurian (third), devolution of, 55; negro, 55; see also Root-race; Sub-race(s)

Racism, **55-56**, 73, 190, **221**; see also Discrimination, racial

Radicals, 70

Raine, Kathleen, 159, 164

'Reading of the Hidden Script'; see Inspiration

Reality, **12**, 16, 20, 24, **27**, **33-34**, 47, 84, **87-88**, 90, 106, 116, 121, 122, 123, 135-136, 144, 162, 169, 175-176, **178-179**, **182-185**, 187, **191**, 194, 200, 206, 208, 210, 214; Anthroposophical, 183, 214; inner/outer, 24, 175; spiritual, 12, 136, **184**, 187

Rebirth, 62, 89, 102, **110-111**, 117, 132, **152-153**, 161, 168, 179, 184, **219-220**; spiritual (First Class Lessons as agents of), 62

Reformation, the, 7, 150, **154**, 157-158, **192**, 197, **201-202**; Counter-Reformation, 154, **157-158**

Reincarnation, 21, 23, 29, 54, 66, 109, 118, 134, 136, 164-166, 216, 219; Anthroposophical, 109, 118, 134, 136; Blavatsky on, 165-166;

Theosophists' reintepretation of, 165-166; and karma, 109, 118, 136; Steiner's views of, 21, **23**, 29, **47**, 54, **169-170**, 219; Steiner's views of, in specific individuals, 21, 23, 47, 54, 219; Steiner's views of, himself, 21, 23, 47; Steiner as Eabani, 21, 47; Ita Wegman as Gilgamesh, 47, 54; of Rosenkreuz, **169-170**; his ability to perceive, 29, 219; see also rebirth

Relativity, theory of, 87

Religion(s), 9, 11, **17**, **41-42**, 48, 65, 83, 154, 161, 192-193, 197-198, 205, 209, 212, 222; freedom of, 102; Anthroposophy, 102; comparative, 161; conventional, 209; decline of, 209; traditional/institutional, 41, 83; fundamentalist, 17; historic, 41, 65, 142, 144-145, 192-193; mystery, 142, 198; non-Christian, 42, 205; prophetic, 17, 197; quasi-, 212; spiritual, 9, 212; sociology, 9; wars of, 154

Renaissance, 7, 142, **149-157**, 160-161, 168, 170, 197, 201-203, 205, 209

Reuss, Theodor, 44

Reuter, Gabrielle, 34, 37

Revelation(s), 145, 198; Alice Bailey, 171; Anthroposophical (Steiner), 13, 16-18, 20-21, **38**, **44**, 48, 51, 65, 68, 76, **78**, 80-81, 87, 105-107, **111**, 118, 120, 122-123, **131**, 132, **139**, 144, 168, **182-184**, **206-208**, 211, **219-221**, 223; comparisons to modern science, 106-107, 113; difficulty in getting to know, 105; Konig's modification (Camphill), **78**; Rittelmeyer's version (Christian Community), 80-81; members' acceptance as absolute fact, 219; members' defense of, 93; members' desperate need for, 38; relationship to other belief systems, **111**; structural analysis of (lack of), 105, 111, 118; teaching (in Steiner Schools), **102**; divine, 162; gnostic, 146, 162, 202; Judeo-Christian-Islamic, 196; Lucius Apuleius (Isis), 199; Manicheist, 145; 'numinous', 16, 196; Psychological (Freudian, Jungian, etc.), 119; Theosophical (Blavatsky), 41-42, **166**, 171; see also Prophecy

Rhmoahls, 133; see also Sub-race(s)

Rig-Veda, 199

Rittelmeyer, Dr, 45, 80
Romanticism, 100, 163, 204; German, 42
Rome, 146, 149, 199
Root-race, 55, 132; fourth (Atlantean), 132-133; third (Lemurians), 55
'Rose Cross'; see *Fama Fraternitatis*; *Confessio Fraternitatis*; Rosenkreuz, Christian; 'Book M'
Rosenkreuz, Christian, 29, **158**, **164**, 166, 169-170, 205; Steiner's mythology of, **170**; repeated reincarnation of, **170**
Rosenroth, Knorr von, 163
Rosicrucian(s)/Rosicrucianism,   6, 29, 38, 45, 67, 70, **141**, **150**, **157-161**, **164**, **168-171**, **203-205**, 207; contemporary, 158; correspondences with/influence on Steiner's revelation, **29**, **38**, **67**, **164**, **168-170**; development from Hermeticism/ Gnosticism/Kabbalism/alchemy, **150**, **157-158**, 164, 203/204; followers' validity as, 67, 70; historical origins, **157-161**, 164, 168; influence on other esotericisms, 158-160, 164; membership statistics, 160, 164, 207; organisations within, 45, 67, 160, 171, 205, 207; see also Ancient Mystical Order Rosae Crucis (AMORC); Gold-und-Rosenkreuz Freemasonry; Lectorium Rosicrucianum; Rosicrucian Fellow-ship; Societas Rosicruciana in Anglia ('Soc. Ros.'); pagan roots, 164; ties with Ordo Templi Orientis (O.T.O.), 45, 164; see also Andreae, J.V.; Bulwer-Lytton; *Chemical Wedding* (Andreae); Dee, John; Freemasonry; Hermetic Order of the Golden Dawn; Hermeticism; Lévi; 'M'; *Rape of the Lock* (Pope), Rosenkreuz, Christian; Yarker, John; *Zanoni* (Bulwer-Lytton)
Rosy Cross, 67, **158**, **160**; see also *Fama Fraternitatis*; *Confessio Fraternitatis*
Royal Society (in the UK), 159
Rubedo, 156, 176
Rudolf Steiner children's home, 55
Rudolf Steiner College, 102
Rudolf Steiner House (London), **71**, 214, 220
Russia, 75

Sacraments   (Anthroposophical   / Christian Community), 81
Saint-Germain, Comte de, 160, 170
Sāka Gakkai, 211
Salamanders, 90, 93, 171; see also spiritual beings
Satan, 115, 148; see also Devil(s); Demon(s)/demonic force(s)
Saturn, 92, 112-114, 120, 122-128, 130, 131, 133, 134, 137, 138, 155, 169, 184; Anthroposophical creation myth, 112; Duration 124-125; evolution, 127; of the macrocosm, 6; influence on lead; see also planets; macrocosmic man, 127; men, 134; advanced, nature of, 128; new, 127; Oracle, 133; planetary embodiment, 112-114, 116-117, **123-128**, 137-138, 169, *245-246*; first, 112; Goetheanum, 113, 130; recapitulation of, 126, 128, 130; souls, 131; Spiritual Hierarchies (Principalities, Thrones), 124; warm bodies, 125; warmth, 120, 125; womb, 122
Schelling, Friedrich Wilhelm, 13, 44, 163
Schiller, J.C.F. von, 25, 34
Schisms, 5, 51, 53, 54, 64, 201
Schizotypal personality, 22; schizotypal personality disorder, 222
School of Spiritual Science, 5, 12, 49, 54, 57, 60-61, 64, 71, 79, 83, 86, 94, 96, 101, 183, 220
'Schools in Asia-Pacific', 75
Schroer, Karl, 28, 31, 33
Schuré, Edouard, 28, 31, 117, 174
Science of Knowledge (Fichte), 27
Science, Goethean, 33, 44, 84, **92**
Scientific materialism, 27, 34, 42, 161, 162, 209, 212; see also Ahriman, Materialism, Orthodoxy
Scientific method, 27, 92, 178
Scientology, 118, 207, 211, 218
Scotland, 76; see also Great Britain
Séances, 33; upper class, 41
Second (and Third) Class, 64
Second Coming, 35, 136, 165, 172
Second World War, **53-56**, 68, 70-72, 76, **134**, 205; see also Post-war
Second Coming, (Christian); Anthropo-sophical, 136; Messiah of the, 172; see also 'Awakener of Conscience', 'Bapak', Gurdjieff, Subud

Sects, 17, 54, 58, 74, 76, 97, 189, 205, 210, 215

Sefer-ha-Zohar, 152-153

Seer, 19, 36, 38, 43, 52, 62, 69, 123, 175

Semmering railway line, 23

Sense perception, 22, 34, 35, 110, 131

Sense world/Sense-world, 20, 23, 27, 35, 38, 91, 110

Seraphim, **123-124**, *246*; see also Cherubim, Spiritual Hierarchies

Serpent, 30, 111, 115, 118, 138, **220**; Anthroposophic, 13, **18**, **29-30**, 79, **90**, 94, **101, 105**, 107, 111-112, 115-116, 118, 138; Cosmological analogy, **18, 29-30**, 94, **101, 105**, 111-112, 115-116, 118, 130, 138; Goetheanum, 1, 13, **18**, 29, 79, **90**, **94**, 101, 105, 107, 112, 116, 130, **220**; in other spiritual interpretations, **13**, 29-30, 112, 118, 220; uroboric, 220

Seven-year growth periods, 20-**21**, 48, **102**

Sexual energy, 174

Shakespeare, William, **11**, 105, **141**, **157**, 214, **221**; *Tempest, The*, 157, 214

Sicily, 155

Sidney, Sir Philip, 157

Sievers, Marie von, **36- 38**, **44**, **47**, 49, **98**; cultural origins, 49; eurythmy, creation of, **47**; Speech Formation, creation of, **47**, 98

Sikhism, 17

Silence (Valentinian), **147-148**, 166

'Skin of the dragon'; see 'Slipping into the skin of the dragon'

Sleep, 87, **90**, 94, **108-109**, 125, **127**, **129**, 134

'Slipping into the skin of the dragon', 28, 30

Smart, Ninian, **41**, **185**

Smelser, N., **188**

Social embedding/embeddedness, 38, 49, 53

Societas Rosicruciana in Anglia ('Soc. Ros.'), **164**, 205, **208**

Solar system, 94, 101, **111-112**, **118**, **123-124**, 127, **133-136**, 138

Sophia (Wisdom – gnostic), 132, 147-149, 173, 176, 199, 201

Soul, 19, 28, 34, 63, 73, 87, **89-94**, 102,

106-110, 114, 120-121, 125, 136, 144, 147-148, 151, 153, 156-157, 175, 178, 184, 196; compared to butterfly, 102; duality/dualism, 136, 147; and eurythmy, 63; gestures, 63; reincarnation/rebirth, 28, 34; survival of, 196; see also Eurythmy, reincarnation/rebirth

South Africa, 72-73, 76, 221

Spain, 74, 82, 146, 152, 155

Specht Family, 31-32

Special care, children, adults, 76, 100; see also Camphill, villagers

Speech Formation, 47, **98-99**, 170, 214

Spinoza, Baruch, 125, 159

Spirit, 7, 10-11, **18**, 20, 23-25, **27-31**, **33-35**, 41, 44, 52, **61-63**, 65, 73-74, 77, 79, **86-88**, **91-92**, 94, **97-98**, 101, **105-117**, 122, 124, **126**, 130, **134-136**, 138, 141, **143-144**, **146-151**, 159, 165, 167, 169, 173, 175-176, 178, **182**, 184-185, 195, 200, 202, 205-207, 211-213, **219-220**; dualism, good/evil, 143-144; dualism, spirit/matter, **146-151**

Spiritual beings/'Spirit-beings', 27, 33, 90-91, 107, 110, 117, 127, 130, 138; see also 'Elemental beings'

Spiritual Hierarchies, 62, 89, 94, **116**, **123-125**, **127-130**, 132, 153, 167

'Spiritual science', 5, 12, 20, 24, 26, 39, 41, 47, 68, 81, **118-119**, 136, 178, 204; see also School of Spiritual Science

Spiritual soul, **106-107**, 132, 167

'Spiritual warmth', **112-113**; see also Planetary embodiments

'Spiritual water', **112**; see also Planetary embodiments

Spiritualism, **41**, **102**, 162, 166, 204

Spirit-world, 16, 23, 34, 52, 91, **109-110**, 116

Sri Lanka, 42, 131

Steffen, Albert, 47-48, 54-55, 118

Steiner, Marie, 39, 43, **56**, 58, **98**; death of, 56; restrictive use of copyrights, 56; see also Sievers, Marie von

Steiner, parents of Rudolf, **22-23**, 28, 31

Steiner, Rudolf (biography), 5, 11-12; actions taken, **19**, **21-22**, **24**, 26-30, 214; in the occult revival, 163; background, **16**, **22**, 65; intellectual,

25-28; intellectual, occult, 20, **28-30**; intellectual, initiation by 'M', 28-29; intellectual, in Theosophy, **28-29,** 32; intellectual, Rosicrucianism, 29; beliefs and perspective, **16**, 18-21, 23-25, **27-29**, 32; his karma and destiny, **23**; rejection of 'psychologism', **20-21, 23**; rejection of technology, 24, **30**; rejection of Theosophy, **29**; reincarnation of Eabani, 21; claims/assertions, 16, **19-21**, 24; claims of honesty of, 20; claims of inerrancy, 19, 38; perception of spirits (of the dead), **24**, **30**; perception of reincarnation, 29; perception of scientific materialism, relinquishing, **27**, 32**;** divergence from norm for culture, 19-20, 25-26; divergence from norm for era, 19, 24; divergence from norm for intellectuals, 19-21, 30-31; divergence from norm for prophets, 19-20; divergence from norm for religion, 26, 28; education and training, 16, 20, **25-27**; education at Technische Hochschule (Technical College), 28; education, influence of, 26; education: mathematics, **25**, **27**; philosophy, 27; science, **27-28**; education as isolating force, 26; emotional life, 19-20, 25-26; social bonds, **25-26**, 31-32; social bonds childhood to adults, 25-26; social bonds, rejection by children, **25-26**; social bonds, adolescent, 26, **28**, love, attraction to maternal figures, 31; see also Specht family, Eunicke, Anna; love, for his father, 24, 26; love, romantic, 31; need to share revelation, 16, **20-21, 30**; feeling of constraint, 16, **19-21, 24, 30, 32**; love, sense of disconnection/dislocation, **22-26**; experiences, sensory, 16, 19-20; experiences, lack of, **16**, 23, 31; experiences, omission of erotic, 21, **31**; experiences, spiritual, **16-17, 20, 23-25, 27-29, 32**; experiences, thinking as, 27; followers, attitude toward, 16, 21; Goetheanum, designer of, 12, 32, Goetheanum, sculpture, sculptor, 12; intellectual pursuits, **25-28, 30**; geometry/mathematics, **25, 27-28**; German, 28; literature,

25; philosophy, 27; science, 23, **27-28, 30**; life and times, 14, **16**; early, 21-26; lack of information on, 21-22; mannerisms and presentation, 16, **19-22, 25, 31-32**; physical appearance, **16, 19**; psychological interpretation of, **21-24, 26**, 32; residences, family home, 31; Kraljevec, Croatia, 22-23; Stationmaster's residences, 23; Pottschach, Austria, 23; Neudorfl, Hungary, 26; Inzersdorf, Vienna, Austria, 28; Vienna, 31; with Specht family, 31; Weimar, 25, 31; with Anna Eunicke, 31; Berlin, 31; Lodgings, 31; revelation of, 16; see Revelation; derivation of, 20; distancing from personal biography, 21; formation of, 32; teaching, choice as career, 26; as a resident tutor, 31-32; Specht family, 31; see also 'sleeping soul' as germ for Anthro. education; see Anthroposophical education

Steiner, Rudolf (life and works), 5, 67, 77, 84, 86, 219, 220, 223; born Austrian, 65; Camphill communities, 76; cautious silence of, 16, 19, 21, 35, 38; early experience, 30; need to communicate, 37; charismatic leadership, 43; childhood deprivation, 37; close associates of, 73; death of, 32, 41, 54, 67, 130, 165; death, schisms after, 49, 65; death, cause of, 39; death, copyright issues resulting from, 47, 58; death, movement's disempowerment by, 51; death, self-healing ethic, 52; death, work after, 86; defence of revelations, 93; early love interest, 31; female students of, 70; followers, 39, 220; followers, business institutions, 74; followers, dependence on, 39; followers, idealisation of, 38; followers, life styles, 220; followers, politics, 221; formative experiences, 21; impact of industrialisation on, 23; founding of the First Class, 61; friends of, 67; General Society Members, 64; Goethe, 122; honesty of, 20; illness, 39-40, 40; as a spiritual symptom, 52; imperfect translations, 54; in post-war Germany, 48; Inklings, 172; Kafka, 172; leaving Vienna for Weimar, 33;

lecture on Nietzsche, 43; life of, **11**, 14, 16, 37; see Chapter 1; mantra, 62; Marie von Sievers, 36, 39; meeting with, 36; marriage to, 39; mental health of, 21; nature of man, 106; the occult revival, 163; Ordo Templi Orientis, 164; parents of, 22; personal characteristics, 51; pre-existence of the soul, 23; personal life/private life, 38-39; as product of his times, 55; Projective Geometry, 93; prophetic experience, 17; as reincarnation of Eabani, 21; removal of Besant, Annie, 46; reverence for truth and knowledge, 75; school work, 27; 'supernatural inspiration', 38; sense of superiority, 39; sense perception, 35; sexual magic, association with practice of, 45; sexual magic; Anthroposophists' refutation of, 62; sexual magic, Absence of support for hypothesis, in Lessons, 62; sexual magic, leadership of esoteric society for, **38**; social life, 28; social awareness, 26; special reincarnation knowledge, 29; spiritual experience, 17; spiritual identity, 39; symbol of the Rosy Cross, 160; teachings on death, 62, 89, 106, 108, 109, 132, 136, 143, 153, 161, 196; Theosophy and German occultism, 53; as trans-human, 49; vegetarian tendencies, 51; Vienna years, 29; widow of, 38, 54; world-wide use of European seasons, 184; *Autobiography, An*, **13**, **16**, **21-24**, 26, 28-29, 33-34, 44, 131, 169; lack of references to Steiner's mother, 22; *Philosophy of Freedom, The*, 31, 87, 89-90, 131, 205; *Occult Science*, 44, 61, 94, 110, 115, 119, 122-123, 138, 147, 183

Rudolf Steiner movement, see Anthroposophy, Rudolf Steiner Movement
Sub-race(s), 133
Subud, 172
Sufism, 19, 171, 196
Sun, 9, 89, 94, **128-131**, 133, 134, 156; being of the (teachings of Hermes), 134; see also Osiris; 'chemical marriage' with Moon, 156; see also Alchemy; Oracle, Initiates of the, 133; Planetary embodiment, 6, **112-** **114**, 117, 120, **122-124**, **126-130**, **137-138**, 169, 184; Goetheanum, 130; 'Sun at midnight', title reference, 9; see also Lucius Apuleius; 'Sun-Being' as external appearance of Christ, 94, 134; see also Christ; the 'I', Post-Atlantean epoch

Sweden, 74, 101, 159, 218
Switzerland, 37, 46, 52, 64, 69, 74, 76, 82, 96, 222; Anthroposophical conversion, 222; Camphill Communities, 76; Christian community (Anthroposophical) priests in, 82; early bio-dynamic agriculture, 96
Sylphs, 90, 93, 171; see also spiritual beings
'Sympathy', 66, 109; see also 'Antipathy'
Syrian-Egyptian gnosis, 111, 118, 144-146, 150, 152, 165, 167, 173, 174, 182
Syzygy, 147-148

Tantric sex yoga; see Yoga, Tantric sex
Taoism, 177
Tarot, 160, 163-165
Teeth, change of; see 'Change of teeth'
Temperament, 97-98; see also Speech Formation; Zodiac
Templars, 146; Gnosticism of, 146
Temple, 48, 61, 67, 135, 170-171; Jerusalem, destruction of, 135; Jewish, 48; Rosicrucian, 67; AMORC, 171
Theosophical Society, 28, 41, **43-45**, 69, 75, 119, 133, **164-165**, 167; German Section, 43; General Secretary, 43; President, 44; headquarters, 43
Theosophical Esoteric Section, 44; see also E.S.; Yeats' expulsion, 165
Theosophists, 36, 38, 45, 59, 165, 166, 168; German, 36, 42
Theosophy, 20, 29, 36-38, 42, 44-48, 53, 55, 59, 75, 107, 113, 119, 126, 164-166, 168-171, 175, 179, 205-207, 212, 223; and Anthroposophy, 20; as an offshoot, 46; in Anthroposophy, 126; Berlin, 36; Blavatsky, Madame, 42; chemistry, occult, 44; Coleman, W.E., 166; decline in the 1920s, 53; Decline/rise of Anthroposophy, 53, 59, 165; England, Edwardian,

53; Gandhi, 55; Goetheanum, 29; German, 44; German-style, 44; Germany, 42; Wilhelminian, 53; Goetheanum, 47; and Golden Dawn, 46; India, 179; Indian cosmology, 113; International Congress, 44; Jung, 175; mid-20th Century, 53; as non-magical, 170; occult chemistry, 44; original Western influence, 165, 166, 169; pre-war, 205; relationship to Anthoposophy, 168-169; relationship to other movements, 171; Russia, 75; Steiner, Rudolf, 29, 37, 38, 107, 119; gulf between, 45; UK, 48; Viennese, 29; viewed as Eastern, 165

Thermodynamics, 113, 124

Thinking/thought, **20**, 21, 23, **27**, 28, **30**, 31-33, 35, 38, 40, 42-43, **47**, 62-63, **63**, 70-71, **76**, 83, 85, **87-92**, 93, 98-100, 102, 106,**109-110**, **113**, 114, **121**, 122,**131-132**, **134**, 135-136, 142, 144, 147, 150, 152-153, 155, 162, 173, 177, 179, 183, 187, **198**, **205-206**, 208-211; In Anthroposophy, **20**, **27**, **30**, **47**, 63, 70, 76, **87-89**, 91, 106, 113, **121**, 131-132; as absolute spiritual activity, **20, 89, 91, 106**; as direct experience of the spirit world, **27**, **30**, **87-89**, **136**; as reality, **20**, 27, **87**; as reflected in the aura, **89**; relation to spirit-world, **109-110**; 'sense-free thinking', 90; Eastern, 163, 167; Eastern influence on gnostic revival, 163; scientific, 190; Steiner's, 38; systems/structures/climate of, 13, 20; Aristotelian, 155; De Chardin's, 174; of the Christian Church, 201; Coleridge's, 159; gnostic/Western 'esoteric tradition', **141**. **149-150**, 152, 161, 200; mass marketing of, 159; Gurdjieff's, 171; Jung's 177; Neoplatonist, 151; Rosicrucian, 159; traditional legitimacies of, 161-162

Third Class; see Second (and Third) Class

Third World, 64, 76, 222; Anthroposophical conversion, 222

Thoth; Egyptian God of Wisdom, 150; identification with Trismegistus, Hermes, 150

Thought form(s), 119, 161-162, 182, 211; In Anthroposophy, 182;

Anthroposophy as independent from Theosophy, 119; Syrian-Egyptian (gnostic), 211;

Thought pictures, **90-91**; see also 'Initiation'

Thought-reading, 132; Lemurian communication by, 132

Thought world, Anthroposophical, 9, 231

Threefold Commonwealth, 6, 37, 47-48, 73, 103, 170, 221

Thrones, **123-124**; see also Spiritual Hierarchies

Tibet, 41; also see Buddhism, Tibetan, 'Masters', Tibetan

Tillich, Paul, 193

Tlavatli, 133; see also Sub-race(s)

Tolkien, J.R.R., 70, 172

Toltecs, 133; see also Sub-race(s)

Totalitarianism, 53

Transcendental Meditation, 180, 211

Transmigration, 147, 168; also see rebirth

Triados bank, 74

Trinity, the, 151, 154, 201; Anthroposophical, 94, 111, 116, 118, 123; 'Christian', 118

Trismegistus, Hermes, 150, 156; see also Thoth

Troeltsch, E., 189

UK; see Great Britain

Underhill, Evelyn, 165

Undines, 93; see also Elemental beings

Unification Church ('Moonies'), 17, 210

Urban VIII, Pope, 155

Uruguay, 75

USA, 41, 64, 71, 73-74, 76, 82, 206, 214, 222; see also North America

Utopia(n), 32, 37, 73, **170**, **172**, 210; Rosicrucian, 170

Valentinianism, 114-115, **146-147**, 149, 172, 199

Vaughan, Thomas, 13, 159

Vedanta (Advaita), **179-180**, 185, 212

Vedas, 134

Venus, planet, 94, 155; 'star', 151-152

Venus (stage/Planetary Embodiment), 6, 112, 117, 123, **138**, 155

Victoria, Queen, 41

Villagers, 26, 28, 77, 78, 79, 80, 197;

Austrian, 26, 28; Camphill, **77-80**; Hindu, 197
Vishnu Purana (tr. Wilson), 166
Vivekenanda, Swami, 179
Voegelin, Erich, 172, 210
Vorstand, the 56, **64**, 66
Vulcan (stage/Planetary Embodiment), 6, **112**, 117, 123, 136, **138-139**

Wachsmuth, Guenther, 55-56, 93; sympathy/admiration for National Socialism, 55
Wagner, Wilhelm Richard, 84, 119, **163**; *Ring, The*, 84, **119**, **163**
Waite, A.E., 160
Waldorf/Steiner schools/education, 9, 55, 58, **67-68**, **71-72**, **75-76**, 83, **101-103**; and Adult Education, 101; Anthroposophical studies/teaching in, 102; as an application/outreach of Anthroposophy, 76; attempts to ban, 101; aversion to positivistic intellectualism, 55; and curative education, 58; Christian Community priests teaching in, 83; class teacher in, 103; critics of, 102; fee reduction and teacher salary renunciation, 68; Free Waldorf School, Kassel, 68; growth of, 68-76; inseparability from Anthroposophy, 102; integration into local culture, **76**; intent of pedagogues in, 68; lawsuit against public schools re: adoption of, 102; school response to, 102; for mentally handicapped children, 68; origin of name, 67; Nazi prohibition of, 68; Nazi support of, 55; numbers of, 68; in Africa, 72, 73, 75; in Asia, 75, 76; in Australia, 76; in Europe, 68, 71, 75, 76; in North America, 71, 75, 76; in South America, 75; racial integration of, 72; public funding of, 9, 58, 101; avoidance of controversy over 9, 101; in the public schools, 102; teacher training in Anthroposophy, 102; teacher objections to occult spiritualism and pseudo-science instruction in, 102;

see also Education, Anthroposophical
Wales, 76; see also Great Britain
Wallis, **211**
Wars of religion, 154, 203; 16th Century, 154; French, 203
Wegman, Dr Ita, **38**, 47, **54**, 56, 73
Weimar, 25, 31, **33-35**, 46, 52-53, 134, 175; Republic, 52-53
Weimar Sophia edition, 33
Weleda, 55
White Mountain, Battle of the, 157-158
Wicca, 141, 208
Wilhelminian Germany. See Germany, Wilhelminian
Williams, Charles, 165
Wilson, Bryan, 10, 211
Wisdom, 110, 121, **135-138**, 148, 150, 170; archetype of, 110; Cosmos of, 135-137; inner, 137; Love, 137-138; Sophia, 148; Spirit World, Fifth region of, 110; 'Wisdom', 121
Witchcraft; recent revival, 141; Rosicrucian pamphlets as evidence of, 158
'Word', the, (of the universe) 98; see also Eurythmy
'Work', the, 171
Workers' Educational Association, 36
World-Soul, the, 151
World Teacher, 45, 53

Yates, Frances, 151, 154, 159
Yeats, W.B., 11, 24, 35, 42, 60, 141, 159, **164-165**, 175, 205
Yoga, 44, 62, 144, 165, 218; jnana, 144, 165; Raja, 44; Tantric sex, 62

Zanoni (Bulwer-Lytton), 164
Zarathustra, 134
Zeitgeist(s), 55, 93, 180, 211, 212; post-World War One, 212
Zodiac, 94, 98, 124-125, 170; effect on biography/karma, 94; relation to consonants; see eurythmy
Zoroaster/Zoroastrianism, 17, 115, 142, 143, 145, 210; derivation of Judaeo-Christian teachings from, 143; Mithras as an offshoot, 142; orthodox, 17; see also Zarathustra

Printed in the United Kingdom by
Lightning Source UK Ltd., Milton Keynes
139599UK00002B/21/P